Enrich Series on Chinese Currency Reform

Enrich Series on Chinese Currency Reform

With the continuous rise in the status and importance of China in regional and global economies, the influence of the Renminbi grows proportionately. Currency reform has become a crucial and inevitable policy choice for China. Based on recent theoretical frameworks and quantitaive analyzes, this series explores the relationship between China banking system reform, regionalization and internationalization of the Renminbi as well as the possible cooperation between the Renminbi, the Yen and other Asian currencies.

Vol. 1 Internationalization of the Renminbi: History, Theories and Policies

Vol. 2 Regionalization of the Renminbi

Vol. 3 Cooperation between the Renminbi and the Yen

Enrich Series on Chinese Currency Reform Vol.2

Regionalization of the Renminbi

Li Xiao and Ding Yibing et al.

Enrich Professional Publishing

Published by

Enrich Professional Publishing (S) Private Limited
16L, Enterprise Road,
Singapore 627660
Website: www.enrichprofessional.com
A Member of Enrich Culture Group Limited

Hong Kong Head Office:
1/F., Lemmi Center, 50 Hoi Yuen Road, Kwun Tong, Kowloon, Hong Kong, China

Beijing Office:
Rm 1108A, Culture Plaza, No. 59 Zhongguancun St., Haidian District, Beijing, China

Translated by Yang Mifen and Shao Qinghua

ISBN (Hardback)	978-981-4339-04-9
ISBN (ebook)	978-981-4339-07-0 (pdf)
	978-981-4339-89-6 (epub)

Enrich Professional Publishing is an independent globally minded publisher focusing on the economic and financial developments that have revolutionized new China. We aim to serve the needs of advanced degree students, researchers, and business professionals who are looking for authoritative, accurate and engaging information on China.

Printed in Hong Kong

Contents

Preface to the Series

Objectives of this study

As an emerging economic power in East Asia, China has a growing status and role in the regional and even the world economy; the status and role of the Renminbi (RMB) will change accordingly before gradually achieving RMB internationalization. However, in the current world monetary system, the US dollar as the main international currency possesses enormous advantages in the economies of scale and network effects. Different internationalization processes of the Yen and Deutschmark since the 1970s and the experience and lessons learned from these have demonstrated that, under the so-called "US dollar system", it is hard for some currencies to achieve internationalization at the global level. Improving the status and influence of a domestic currency through regionalization is a feasible choice for internationalizing a currency. Therefore the RMB has to take the road of regionalization before achieving its objective of internationalization.

The smooth advance of RMB regionalization will not only bring direct benefits such as increasing seigniorage income, and reducing transaction costs and risks, but more importantly the combination of RMB regionalization with the improvement of China's economic strength will effectively improve China's economic status and "soft strength" in the region, deepen China's economic and financial connections with other economic powers in East Asia, help to stabilize the economic and financial environment in East Asia, and push forward the constant development of the Chinese economy. Therefore, conducting in-depth and all-round discussion of RMB regionalization is of great significance that cannot be ignored.

The studies of RMB regionalization by Chinese and foreign academic circles started with RMB internationalization. After the outbreak of the Asian financial crisis, especially with the emergence of the eurozone and the exploration and progress of "dollarization" of Latin America, some scholars noticed the importance of RMB regionalization for internationalizing RMB and thus heated discussions began. However there are significant differences in the studies of many RMB regionalization-related questions. First of all, on the question of whether it is right to achieve RMB internationalization through RMB regionalization, Zhao Haikuan (2003) holds that efforts have to be made before developing the RMB into one of the future world currencies directly. Pan Liquan (2003), Li Chong (2002) and other scholars agree that RMB regionalization is a necessary stage or way of achieving RMB internationalization. Li Xiao et al. (2004) propose in a clear-cut term "RMB Asianization", and have made a preliminary analysis of its necessity, feasibility and choice of strategies. On the question of whether the RMB is ready to be regionalized, even internationalized, some scholars point out a number of China's disadvantages in the field of finance, including China's control of the capital account, incomplete financial markets, insufficient monitoring capacity, and the lack of global financial centers etc. All these have hindered the process of RMB regionalization and internationalization. Other scholars highlight the advantages of China in terms of real economy, thinking that the growing economic strength and its foreign economic relations will enable the RMB to become internationalized naturally. Some scholars point out that China, as the potential "market supplier" and "economic stabilizer" in East Asia, possesses the preliminary conditions for realizing RMB regionalization (Li Xiao et al., 2004). Thirdly, as for the path for RMB regionalization (or internationalization), the majority of scholars pay more attention to the circulation of the RMB in neighboring countries and its spontaneous marketization process (Li Chong, 2002; "RMB Internationalization" taskforce, 2006; Li Jing, 2004), focusing on studying the achievement of RMB regionalization through such a spontaneous process. Another viewpoint states that the circulation of the RMB in some neighboring countries and regions is non-institutionalized behavior rather than real regionalization, and that RMB regionalization has to be combined with institutionalized arrangements cooperated with related regions such as exchange rates and trade settlements and to be realized by the regions. As regards the process of institutional RMB regionalization, Yao Zhizhong (2004) holds that due to the asymmetric competition between China and other Asian countries, China can obtain the status of a leading currency without having to implement with other Asian countries an exchange rate coordination mechanism based on a common currency basket. Chen Yulu (2003) believes that in East Asia there is a competition relationship between the RMB and the Yen.

On the other hand, with the growing economic strength of China, foreign academics have shown much more interest in the RMB issue. Nakagawa (2004), Persaud and Spratt (2004), and others all believe that the RMB has the potential to become an international currency. Joseph and Schäfer (2004) hold the RMB will become an international currency in the next 20 years as China becomes more and more important in world trade and its capital account will become convertible. Yeh and Plasmans (2002) believe that money unification between Mainland China, Hong Kong and Taiwan will be the first step to RMB internationalization.

The issue of RMB regionalization has aroused great academic interest, yet the study of many related questions is still in its youth. Specific manifestations are as follows: firstly, (1) there is no clear understanding of the nature and characteristics of RMB regionalization itself, or explicit definition of currency internationalization, regionalization and convertibility, or any in-depth exploration of the mutual relationship among the three, or a strict and tidy theoretical analysis framework of the mechanism of currency regionalization. Secondly, there is no theoretical basis for the evolution path of currency regionalization and its reciprocal influence with the international monetary system. Thirdly, inspection and comparative analyses of the paths of the internationalization of different currencies are unavailable, making it hard to illustrate the necessity to realize RMB internationalization through RMB regionalization. Fourthly, the studies on RMB regionalization so far have focused too much on analyzing the spontaneous evolution paths of RMB regionalization under market forces, but have failed to combine them with the changes in the international financial structure and to put this within the institutional framework of regional monetary cooperation in East Asia for analysis, so they have failed to find necessary and feasible logic for "regional collective actions" and institutional arrangements for regionalizing RMB. It is precisely these deficiencies that make it hard for the current academic circles and government to put forward feasible ideas on the strategies for and paths of RMB regionalization.

This book aims at further exploring the rules of currency internationalization and regionalization, and the necessity, feasibility and path choice of RMB regionalization on the basis of related studies by many academics on RMB internationalization and regionalization.

The main contents and conclusions of this study book

This book sets out theories on currency internationalization and regionalization and looks back on the experience of the internationalization and regionalization of other currencies, and on the basis of observing the necessity of, advantageous and disadvantageous conditions for RMB regionalization under the current international monetary system, analyses the detailed path arrangement of RMB regionalization and studies the relationship between the RMB and the Yen, another major currency in East Asia, in the process of RMB regionalization.

Theories and related experience on currency internationalization and regionalization

The improvement of its economic strength and national power have greatly improved China's influence in the world economy, especially in East Asia, and made the global status of the RMB in the future an issue of much interest. Positive RMB participation in nationalization and regionalization not only conforms to the interests of China but also plays an active role in developing and stabilizing the economy in East Asia.

Experience has shown that the emergence of any country, especially a great power, promotes its money to go global before playing an important role in and greatly influencing the region or the world, while exploration of the paths of currency internationalization has to be guided by related monetary theories and in-depth theoretical thinking about the essence of monetary phenomena, especially currency internationalization. To start with, we borrow and extend the *Search Theories of International Money* by Kiyotaki and Wright (1989), proving that the functions of money as the medium of exchange and store of value are undergoing differentiation. For the sake of saving costs, fewer and fewer currencies display the function of a medium of exchange; for the sake of dispersing risks, currencies that serve as store of value are increasingly diversified. This means that the future international monetary system will not be led by a single currency, nor will it see many currencies competing in the field of international trade, but a few currencies will act as international money. Therefore the theoretical possibility of the RMB becoming an international currency is demonstrated.

Secondly, this book makes an overall review of the internationalization paths of the British pound sterling, the US dollar, the euro and the Yen on the basis of theoretical analysis. Throughout the history of international money in the past century, the domination and decay of the British pound sterling, the emergence of the US dollar, the birth of the euro and the bitter lesson of the path of "Yen internationalization" have all given valuable inspirations to the process of RMB internationalization and regionalization.

Despite the characteristics of the RMB, there are important elements that cannot be ignored in the process of internationalization and regionalization of any currency. Therefore successful experience has to be learned from the British pound sterling and the US dollar in order to strengthen the economic and trade power of the RMB, while US dollar regionalization and the birth of the euro have provided valuable paths for China to follow in order to achieve RMB regionalization. From the zigzagging "Yen internationalization" we can see that, apart from its own efforts, any country has to take into consideration "external factors" in the regionalization and internationalization of its currency and so it is a must to set foot on currency regionalization first before gradually realizing currency internationalization.

RMB regionalization - the only way to RMB internationalization

Since the 1980s, with financial globalization and the development of financial liberalization, both the scale and speed of private capital flow have been further accelerated. The monetary and financial crises which have thus arisen have had impacts on the current international monetary system and prompted many countries and regions to seek for a new pattern to stabilize and govern regional economy and finance. Consequently, changes have happened in the international financial pattern. The current process of currency internationalization in some countries and regions has been affected, which may be fully demonstrated by the birth of the euro and the progress of "dollarization" in some countries in Latin America.

In recent years, as the economic relations between China and the rest of East Asia have become increasingly closer and China's political and economic status in the world has been improved, residents in neighboring countries and regions of China have gradually recognized and accepted the RMB as the trading money and the clearing currency, and a large amount of RMB has begun to circulate outside the territory of China. In such circumstances the issue of RMB internationalization has attracted great attention from the Chinese monetary authority and Chinese and foreign theoretical field. As for the choice of the path of RMB internationalization, although some academics propose realization of RMB internationalization through other ways, most of them tend to favor the road of RMB regionalization first before RMB internationalization.

It is hard for any currency to challenge the existing currency hegemony on its own under the current international monetary system. The birth of the euro and the failure of the "Yen internationalization" tell people that currency regionalization is an important step towards currency internationalization. To take part in international competition a currency has to rely on the platform of regional economic cooperation and institution-based regional currency cooperation. One basic starting point for us to think about the strategies for RMB internationalization has to be based on the status of China as a regional power in Asia. Meanwhile, given the fact that the economic and financial foundations of China at the current stage are not strong enough to support direct RMB internationalization, and that the relationship between China's economic development and the East Asian economy is being constantly improved, and that countries in East Asia have reached the "East Asia's consensus" regarding regional monetary and financial cooperation, we believe that RMB regionalization is a road that must be taken to reach RMB internationalization. The issue of RMB regionalization must be taken into account and well planned within the overall structure of the East Asian monetary system.

The analysis of the costs and benefits of RMB regionalization has further provided a rational support for the choice of monetary strategies by China. The evolution of RMB regionalization may have some adverse impacts on the macro-economic policies and private economic sectors, but to an even greater extent it would bring enormous benefits for the development of China, including pushing forward economic and financial reform and development in China, increasing the wealth of the Chinese people, and improving the status of China in the region and even in the world etc. Fundamentally, RMB regionalization should be the result of spontaneous market forces, yet it needs the Chinese government to actively push it forward and provide corresponding policy supports so as to find the necessary and feasible logic and institutional arrangement of "regional collective actions" for RMB regionalization. If China can adopt necessary reform and policy strategies in the process of RMB regionalization, it can avoid disadvantages and fully enjoy the benefits brought about by RMB regionalization.

Analysis of the feasibility of RMB regionalization

At the current stage there are a series of favorable conditions for RMB regionalization but it is also faced with some barriers. According to general theories on currency internationalization, China is said to have a favorable position in terms of its economies of scale, economic relations with other economies in the region, economic status in the region, the role as a hub in regional division of work, and stable monetary policies. However, on the other hand, the RMB is significantly insufficient in terms of convertibility, the development and institutional construction of the foreign exchange market and Chinese financial market, the degree of being accepted in the region, and status in the international monetary system, indicating that it is hard to complete RMB regionalization overnight and that RMB regionalization has to be advanced step-by-step based on the reality.

In the long run, China has the potential to become the end-product market supplier in East Asia, which has become increasingly important with the steady growth of the Chinese economy and is a favorable factor for realizing RMB regionalization in more fields and at higher levels. However, on the other hand, China is yet to be able to be an end-product supplier, rather it plays the role of production aggregation and export platform. Becoming the regional end-product market supplier is far from being a task that can be accomplished within a day, so to increase current demand for using the RMB as the regional clearing currency it is also necessary to improve the ratio of export of final products from China to other economic powers in East Asia at a higher speed.

As regards the possibility of realizing RMB regionalization through regional monetary integration of some sort, the SVAR analysis results show that, on the whole, the weak correlations between China and the economic shock of other economic powers in the same region and especially that of real supply shocks would weaken the possibility of establishing a unified monetary area led by the RMB in East Asia in the fairly long term. But on the other hand, when a great power is in a long-term steady state, its weak correlation with the actual shock of other economies also demonstrates its capability of serving as the stabilizer of region economy and its currency may serve as the stabilizer of the monetary exchange rate in other regions. From this point of view the RMB, to some extent, still possesses the possibility of becoming the internal "anchor" of a region. The empirical analysis results of BBQ and MSAR show that, according to the traditional theories on and patterns of currency unification, realizing RMB regionalization through the Europe-style currency unification is faced with greater difficulties, yet China has the conditions for playing its role in East Asia using a different pattern or through different paths from those used in Europe and it may also influence East Asia in a way similar to the US dollar. Inspection of the OCA index shows that, on the one hand, the convergence effect of East Asia as a whole on America has been significantly reduced while the convergence of East Asia with China continues to be enhanced, yet on the other hand it shows that both China and Japan are not able to attract other economic powers in East Asia to join a currency area centered on themselves with absolute advantages. To advance regional currency cooperation at a higher level, China and Japan must cooperate closely.

In general, although RMB regionalization is faced with some barriers, there are a series of favorable conditions. It can be found through empirical analyses that some basic conditions for the RMB to become a regional key currency now exist and so RMB regionalization could be pushed forward step by step from now on.

Choice of the path of RMB regionalization

Entering the 21st century, the RMB has had a greater influence on neighboring countries and regions of China, which is especially true in its wide use in cross-border circulation and border trade. The outbreak of the global financial crisis in 2008 provided a chance for RMB regionalization to some extent. In this circumstance China adopted a series of measures, including the launch of trials of RMB settlement in foreign trade, the development of the RMB bond market and the expansion of currency swap arrangements with other economic powers in East Asia, meaning that RMB regionalization has been pushed forward steadily. Discussing how to effectively realize the objective of RMB regionalization on the existing basis is of great significance at the present stage.

We hold that, given the experience of and lessons from the internationalization of many currencies and the characteristics of the existing international monetary system that the RMB, as the currency of a great developing country, needs to be regionalized in a unique way in accordance with the demand of China for actual development and the new international environment.

In short, based on the current conditions, in order to be regionalized, RMB should be reformed from being peripheral to regionalized geographically; serve as the medium of exchange, the unit of account, and then storage of value in terms of monetary functions, and be advanced at two levels i.e. being non-institutionalized and institutionalized in terms of policies and measures. Advancing RMB regionalization through exchange rate cooperation should be pushed forward at the sub-regional level in a phased way based on the degree of closeness between China's and other East Asian economies and the influence of the exchange rate shock to trade and investment. Specifically, RMB regionalization may be pushed forward in the following several steps or at the following several levels:

Promoting the circulation of the RMB in neighboring countries in a steady way, creating the conditions for the RMB to serve as the clearing currency in some transactions between China and its neighboring countries and improving the degree of acceptance of the RMB by neighboring countries in their trade with China, while launching the construction of the RMB offshore financial market and RMB international bond market in a positive and steady way to enable the RMB to serve as the investment currency within a certain scope.

After the above has been accomplished, China and its neighboring countries, and even more East Asian economic powers, should sign an official settlement agreement to enable other economic powers in East Asia to generally adopt the RMB as the clearing currency in general trade, while making full use of currency swap agreements and other methods to enable the central banks in other East Asian economic powers to expand their official trade in the RMB with the People's Bank of China, making the RMB an official reserve currency in other East Asian economic powers, and gradually pushing forward RMB convertibility in official trade. On the other hand, the Chinese financial market must be gradually opened, the control of capital account loosened, and the mechanism of RMB reflux updated in order to enable the RMB to serve as an investment currency in a wider range and at a higher level. Meanwhile an RMB offshore center could be established in Hong Kong based on the progress and difficulty of capital account opening in order to give full play to the status and role of Hong Kong as a financial center and to limit the risks and pressure on overseas RMB circulation within a certain scope and to a certain degree.

Encouraging other East Asian economic powers to take the RMB as some kind of "anchor" currency spontaneously before making it the intervention currency in other foreign exchange markets in East Asia through internal economic reforms, restructuring and development, as well as the gradual transformation of the pattern of foreign trade in China.

Participating in and pushing forward currency cooperation in East Asia in a more positive and active way. On the one hand, regional financial arrangements may be used to make the RMB more attractive as a reserve and intervention currency; on the other hand, sub-regional exchange rate cooperation and arrangements may be advanced step by step before achieving the RMB's status as the "anchor" currency at the institutional level and finally making the RMB the key currency within the region.

The process of RMB regionalization has to be advanced at two levels i.e. the non-institutionalized and the institutionalized level, at the same time. Moreover the idea of unilateralism has to be avoided, emphasizing regional cooperation and coordination, especially having a good relationship with another major currency in the same region i.e. the Yen.

Currency regionalization cannot simply rely on spontaneous market forces, but needs the development of regional currency cooperation. As Eichengreen (1989) pointed out, even though a country owns an economic leading position this is not enough for its currency to naturally become an international currency or the leading currency in the region, as this calls for cooperation in varying degrees from other countries. Such cooperation includes the arrangements of not only market communications, but also institutions.

Pushing forward currency regionalization through regional cooperation requires effective coordination between the RMB and the Yen, because neither of them is strong enough to compete with or to replace the US dollar, and competition between the two would lead to limited benefits and enormous costs. Although Yao Zhizhong (2004) believes in the existence of asymmetric competition between China and other Asian countries, and that China can obtain its status as the leading currency without having to implement an exchange rate coordination mechanism based on a common currency basket, the experience of "Yen internationalization" shows that such asymmetric pressure is not enough to make the RMB the leading currency in the region but would make the RMB duplicate the failure of Yen internationalization. Besides, considering the real situation in Japan, without any coordination between the RMB and the Yen mutual competition would bring about losses to all parties. Therefore RMB regionalization must take the road of coordinating and cooperating with the Yen.

To achieve the objective of RMB regionalization, China has to conduct in-depth adjustments and reforms in the following aspects:

Firstly, it has to restructure its trade on the premise of maintaining a continued and sustained growth of the economy, gradually transforming the low-end value chain and processing trade into a trade pattern of exporting intermediary products and importing end products.

Secondly, it has to narrow the gap between urban and rural areas, regional gaps, and the income gap of residents while improving the income and consumption tendency of its residents and expanding domestic demand.

Thirdly, it has to improve the contribution rate of final consumption to GDP while rationally reducing the ratio of China's dependence on foreign trade, and then gradually transform the trade-pulled economic growth into a domestic demand-based economic growth, further push forward domestic reform of the financial system, and gradually loosen its control over capital accounts.

To sum up, the basic conclusion of this book is that RMB internationalization is of great significance to the sustained development of the Chinese economy and the improvement of China's economic status in the world, while RMB regionalization is the only way to RMB internationalization. Although RMB regionalization still faces a series of barriers, it may be found through empirical analyses that the basic conditions for the RMB to become a regional key currency already exist. Efforts have to be made at the non-institutionalized and institutionalized levels in order to push forward the process of RMB regionalization, during which coordinating the relationship between the RMB and the Yen is of great significance.

1

Chapter

Currency Internationalization and Regionalization

Entering the 21st century, China has become increasingly prominent in the world economy. According to the latest data released by the National Bureau of Statistics of China, the GDP of China in 2009 reached RMB33.54 trillion, up 8.7% year on year and ranking third in the world after the U.S. and Japan. With the improvement of China's economic strength and integrated national power, China's influence on the world economy, especially in East Asia, has been improved significantly. In this process the RMB, as the sovereign currency of China, has attracted more and more attention. Positive RMB participation in internationalization and regionalization not only conforms to the interests of China but also plays an active role in developing and stabilizing the economy in East Asia.

Experience has shown that the emergence of any country, especially a great power, will promote its currency to go global for playing an important role and greatly influencing the region or even the world, while on the other hand such a role or influence is much limited by the existing international monetary system and will have great impacts on the evolution of the international monetary system. Therefore exploration of the paths of currency internationalization has to be guided by related monetary theories and in-depth theoretical thinking about the essence of monetary phenomena, especially currency internationalization. The process of RMB internationalization has to be depicted based on summarizing the formation and development process of the global monetary system and the experience of all kinds of international currencies.

This chapter sets out theories on currency internationalization and regionalization and summarizes the historical experience in the formation and development of the British pound sterling, the U.S. dollar and the Yen, and thus may serve as a reference for RMB regionalization and internationalization.

Review of Theories on Currency Internationalization

Connotation of currency internationalization

Definition of currency internationalization

Different scholars have defined currency internationalization from different angles. Some scholars classify currency internationalization in the broad/narrow sense: when individuals and organizations of a country accept or use a currency of another country as the medium of exchange, unit of account and store of value, i.e. a currency performs these three functions outside its home country, this is currency internationalization in the broad sense; and currency internationalization in the narrow sense is limited to the use of a foreign currency (Zhou Lin and Wen Xiaozheng, 2001). From the perspective of morphological stages of internationalization, some scholars classify currency internationalization into three stages and levels. Specifically, the exchange rate relationship between one currency and other currencies is the primary state; opening up regular or capital account in proper ways is the medium state; and becoming the main form of capital storage by the world's other countries is the top state.[1] Other scholars classify currency substitution (the use of foreign currency in domestic trade) and currency internationalization, thinking that currency internationalization may be further classified into currency international usage including the currency-issuing country, and just the trade of another country (Cohen, 1998). Currency internationalization may also be understood from the dynamic/static angle. Seen from the static angle, it refers to one currency being used completely as a highly-convertible international reserve currency by other countries, being held by residents worldwide and being a medium of exchange in the international monetary system; while from the dynamic angle it refers to the subjective and objective economic process of one currency, based on the permission and policies of its issuing country, going out of its home country, being circulated, traded and converted around the world, becoming an international unit of account in trade settlement, international borrowing and lending and international reserves, and being widely accepted by the international market.

It is safe to say that currency internationalization is a dynamic process in which a national currency goes global and becomes a medium of exchange, instrument of payment and tool of international reserve over the world, as well as a relatively steady state formed from this process.[2]

Mundell (2003) believes that when currency circulation goes beyond the statutory area of circulation, or a fraction or multiple of the same currency is followed by other areas, the currency has been internationalized. There are also scholars who give the most direct and common definition: currency internationalization refers to one currency breaking through national limitation, and playing the function of medium of exchange, measure of value and means of storage in international trade and capital flow (Hartmann, 1998; Chen Yulu et al., 2005). It can be seen that currency internationalization is actually the internationalization of currency functions.

Internationalization of currency functions

A currency's international functions are the external extension of its domestic functions, which are as a vehicle currency, a reserve currency and an intervention currency (Trejos & Wright, 1996). Vehicle currency is the medium of exchange in inter-bank currency trade; reserve currency is a storage of value by the central banks of other countries and individuals and intervention currency is that foreign monetary authorities influence the prices and exchange rates of the currency by trading it. Functions in these three aspects may also be divided into those for the private sector and the official sector (See Table 1.1).

Table 1.1. Private and public functions of an international currency

Functions	Private Sector	Official Sector
Medium of exchange	Money instrument (Used for the settlement of international trade and the repayment of international financial debts)	Intervention Currency (Used as the intervention currency at the foreign exchange market and the financing currency in international settlement)
Unit of Account	Invoice Currency (Used as international financial tool and the invoice currency in foreign trade)	Pegging Currency (Used to express the exchange rate relationships and the anchor of other currencies)
Store of Value	Investment Currency (Used to evaluate deposits, loans and bonds)	Reserve Currency (Used as an international reserve by the currency authority)

Source: Set out by Hartmann (1998) according to Cohen (1971).

There are scholars who continue to analyze the above relationship, focusing on discussing the interrelationships among the abovementioned three functions. Bourguinat (1985) believes that the function as a vehicle currency of international trade precedes its function as storage of value, while the latter precedes its function as the unit of account i.e. there is this precedence relationship among the three. Pollard (2001) holds that the three functions are mutually promotional so that being used for the valuation of trade and financial assets would increase the possibility of a currency being used as a medium of exchange: in the official sector, if one country pegs its currency to the currency of another country, it is very likely to hold the pegged currency as its foreign reserve and use it to intervene the foreign trade market.

As can be seen, , there is an mutual-promotional mechanism among the three functions of an international currency. Any aspect which plays its role well will help the other two aspects to better play their roles while reducing the costs. If this is not the case it would influence its internationalization process. The

Deutschmark and the Yen are two typical examples. Due to the disadvantages of the Deutschmark in playing its role as a vehicle currency, its internationalization process developed very slowly,[3] while the internationalization of the Yen was more hindered by its disadvantages in playing its role as an invoice currency. A detailed analysis of this will be made below.

Quantization of currency internationalization

Some scholars have developed criteria or standards for the internationalization of a currency from different angles, mainly including:

Currency internationalization index

Li Yao (2003) believes that the internationalization of a currency can be specifically measured using "Currency Internationalization Index *I*" below:

$$I = \lambda_1 I_1 + \lambda_2 I_2 + \lambda_3 I_3 \quad (1\text{-}1)$$

Where λ_1, λ_2, λ_3 refer to the weight of respective indexes;

I_1 is the index of the sphere of overseas circulation of the currency,

$$I_1 = \sum A_i / A_0 \quad i = 1, 2, \ldots, n$$

Where I_1 is the index of the sphere of overseas circulation of the currency;

A_i refers to the *i*th country in which the currency circulates or that holds the currency;

A_0 refers to the number of countries that have trade with the country of the currency;

I_2 is the index of the currency outflow

$$I_2 = \sum Z_i / M_0 \quad i = 1, 2, \ldots, n$$

Where I_2 refers to the index of the currency outflow;

Z_i refers to the flow (or holdings) of the currency in the ith country;

M_0 refers to the total currency issued;

I_3 refers to the index of ratio of the currency reserves,

$$I_3 = \sum R_i / R_0 \quad i = 1, 2, \ldots, n$$

Where I_3 refers to the index of ratio of the currency reserves

R_i refers to the currency issued by the *i*th country as official foreign exchange reserves;

R_0 refers to the foreign exchange reserves of the currency's country.

The weights of I_1, I_2 and I_3 may be somewhat different, yet it is hard to judge the specific figures of the three. Under the premise of taking λ_1, λ_2 and λ_3 as 1, the author calculates the internationalization index of several currencies according to the data in 2000, of which the internationalization of the U.S. dollar is 10.25, that of Europe is 2.27, that of the Japanese Yen is 1.17. The internationalization index of the RMB is 0.19.

Ratio of currency internationalization in trade

Another index used to measure the degree of currency internationalization is the ratio of currency internationalization in trade. The so-called "ratio of currency internationalization in trade" refers to the share of a currency in world export as invoice currency to that of its foreign trade in the world trade. If the ratio is greater than 1 it indicates that the share of use of the currency is greater than that of its trade in the world, and the currency is of high internationalization, and vice versa. Seen from this angle, only the U.S. dollar and the Deutschmark are the most significant international currencies, the international ratio of which is much higher than that of other countries. They are followed by the British pound sterling and the French franc, and the Japanese Yen relatively lags behind.[4]

Conditions for currency internationalization

The key conditions for the internationalization of a currency have long been the key problem in the theoretical study of currency internationalization. In both Chinese and foreign theoretical studies, "factual approaches to the phenomenon" are mainly adopted.[5] That is, generalizing and summarizing through historical phenomena of an international currency and studying an international currency and the characteristics of its issuing country by analyzing its use of and the changes in the pattern of international currencies. After years of studies, a consensus has been reached i.e. the following several conditions are needed for currency internationalization: the economies of scale of the country issuing the currency; the significance of the country in the world trade; the scale, depth, liquidity and openness of the domestic financial market; currency convertibility; the historical inertia of the use of the international currency (Black, 1990; Bergsten, 1996, 1997; Mundell, 1998; Pollard, 2001; Hartmann and Issing, 2002; He Fan, 2004).

The economies of scale of the country issuing the currency

Econometrical studies on the economies of scale of the country issuing the currency and the potential use of the currency in the world market have shown that the economies of scale of a country is important to its internationalization because it is directly related to the significance of the country in world trade and the size of its financial market, which further determines the potential use of its currency in the world market. The study of Eichengreen and Frankel in 1996 showed that a 1% rise in the proportion of a country issuing a principal currency in the world's overall output value (calculated through purchasing power index) would drive the reserve of its currency in the central banks of each and all countries up by 1.33% correspondingly (C. Fred Bergsten, 2002). Eichengreen (1998) conducted a regression analysis of the share of the U.S. dollar, the Japanese Yen and the British pound sterling in foreign exchange reserves and the share of their respective GDP in the global GDP, only to find that each 1% rise in the ratio of a country's GDP in the world GDP would drive the share of its currency in global foreign exchange reserves up by 5%. A conclusion drawn from the regression analysis after taking into consideration lagged dependant variable and export share variable is that in the case of taking into consideration lagged dependent variable, the influence of the economies of scale of a country reduces significantly; after taking into consideration the export share variable, a more common pattern is obtained. It indicates that every 1% rise in the global share of a country's GDP would drive the ratio of its currency in foreign exchange reserves of other countries up by 0.8%.[6]

However the experience of Japan showed that the size of economy was not a sufficient condition to trigger currency internationalization. Seen from its economies of scale, Japan is the second greatest economic power in the world yet the international status of the Japanese Yen does not match it. This is the so-called "the Yen paradox." Another manifestation is that a low proportion of Japanese exports are in Japanese Yen, which is far lower than the corresponding level of that in other developed countries. This is worth consideration.

Position in foreign trade

The size of foreign trade plays an important role in currency internationalization, since the latter is to supply a currency outside of its home country which is inseparable from foreign trade. Generally speaking, the scale of international trade is positively correlated with currency internationalization. Historically, the development of currency in the early and late Middle Ages showed that an important characteristic of international currencies was that they were issued by economic powers that were active in international trade.[7] In their historical review of the development of international currencies before the Middle Ages and during the 13th century, and their analysis of international currency, common currency and monetary union after the 17th century, Gerald P. Dwyer Jr. and James R. Lothian (2003) draw the conclusion that the development of a country's foreign trade is of great significance to its currency internationalization.[8]

The position of a country in the world trade is obviously of great significance to its currency internationalization. Gerald Selgin (2000) believes that the wider area a currency covers, the more promising its internationalization process. In his "world currency theory," Rasul Shams (2002) starts from the angle of trade figures, thinking that the currency of the country with the largest share in the world trade volume has a better chance to function as an international currency. In addition, currency internationalization must be accompanied with currency outflow, from which it is safe to say that a trade deficit is more helpful for currency internationalization.

Maturity of the financial market

Differing from the above perspectives of analysis, it has been believed by some scholars in recent years that the maturity and efficiency of a country's financial market influence its currency internationalization. Philipp Hartmann and Otmar Issing (2002) believe that past discussions on currency internationalization tended to highlight the importance of product trade and the real economy, but recently more attention has been paid to the role of the financial market, international equity investment and international financing. The development degree of a country's financial market is reflected in its size and liquidity etc. A mature financial market is a potential guarantee and institutional backup for a currency to function. Generally speaking, the improvement of the quality and efficiency of the financial market can reduce market frictions and the transaction costs of currency and other financial assets, promote currency liquidity and stimulate the use of currency on a wider scope. Moreover a developed financial market can provide low-cost, safe and highly-liquid financial instruments, and thus is helpful for exporters and importers in managing foreign exchange risks in global trade activities (Huang Meibo, 2001).

It is safe to say that the greater the size, the higher the liquidity and the higher development level of a country's financial market, the more frequently is its currency being used in international financial trade. Empirically, the three major international currencies in the world in succession—Dutch guilders, British pounds sterling and the U.S. dollar—were all born in countries with mature financial markets (Cohen 1971, 1998), based on which Cohen makes relevant discussions from the perspectives of "exchange convenience" and "capital certainty." Gore S. Tavlas (1998) expresses similar opinions, pointing out that an international currency "issuer has to have a steady and uncontrolled financial market and its financial market has to have width (possessing a wide range of financial instruments) and depth (possessing developed secondary markets)"[9] Abdourahmane Sarr and Tonny Lybek (2002) generalize the characteristics of a mature financial market into five aspects: tightness, immediacy, depth, breadth, and resiliency.

Currency convertibility and credibility

Currency convertibility refers to the canceling of foreign exchange control over regular and capital accounts and realizing currency convertibility in regular and capital accounts. Currency internationalization is closely related to its convertibility, yet the two are by no means the same thing. As regards their relationship, Zhou Lin and Wen Xiaozheng (2001) believe that free convertibility is a stage of currency internationalization. So for a currency to become international it must be convertible, yet not necessarily be completely convertible at some specific stage.

Currency credibility comes from the stability of its value and public confidence in its future stability. Unstable currency value can lead to the loss of public confidence in the currency, which is not favorable for the internationalization process of a currency. Therefore price stability is an important prerequisite for developing the currency and maintaining its international status (Frankel and Goldstein, 1999; Maehara, 1993; Tavlas, 1990). Huang Meibo (2001) believes that for a currency with a stable value, people tend to have a basically certain acknowledgement in its value and will have enough confidence in it, so that using such a currency in international trade can save time and costs needed for people to obtain and deliver information. To play its role in each and all fields of its functions as an international currency and to gain an upper hand, it has to have a stable value. In addition, the expectation for continued appreciation of a currency will bring confidence in the future of the currency and is helpful for promoting and maintaining its international status.

Policy stability and continuity of a country supports the credibility of its make international cooperation more convenient and help promote macroeconomic coordination.[10] Barro (1986) believes that a government's reputation is a feasible way of solving the problem of time differences among policies. Once the government has set up a good reputation for strictly keeping its promises, maintaining its good reputation is an important motive for preventing the government from deceiving the public which will drive government policies to achieve the optimum effect.

Historical inertia

A currency also rises or falls due to "inertia." Inertia plays an important role in the process of currency internationalization, especially in maintaining the currency's international status. Eiji Ogawa and Yuri Nagataki Sasaki (1998) made an empirical analysis of the U.S. dollar only to find that, faced with medium-level depreciation, the international status of the U.S. dollar would not be lowered because of inertia.[11] As another example, in the early 20th century the U.S. had become the world's greatest economic power and its status was further consolidated during World War II. Even so it took the U.S. dollar 50 years to take the place of the British pound sterling, this being a typical example of inertia.

Transaction costs, economies of scale and the network effects interpret the causes for inertia, while the three factors are interconnected and integrated. In his early studies Swoboda (1968) stressed the role of transaction costs in the conversion of different currencies, pointing out that currencies used as medium of exchange should be those related to low transaction costs. Cohen (1998) holds that currency internationalization is borne out of economies of scale or reduced transaction costs, which is similar to barter, and that when different countries use different currencies the cost of searching information would be very high and it would be inefficient whereas when one or a few currencies are used in different countries, the transaction costs would be lowered accordingly. The greater the volume of trade using a single currency, the smaller the cost of information collection and conversion between two currencies will be. There are also scholars who hold that currency internationalization is a process of cooperation that promotes the reduction of transaction costs (Gerald P. Dwyer Jr. and James R. Lothian, 2003). This theoretical study also shows that currency internationalization will be affected by network externality — an extensive trade network formed under the influence of cross-border trading activities.[12] The holding of a currency by any person relies on other people's willingness to accept the currency and to use it in making payments. The higher the acceptance of a currency, the higher the value of using and maintaining the currency will be. To use an economic term, currency creates a positive network externality.[13]

Currency regionalization

Studies on the conditions for currency internationalization are of certain referential significance to the regionalization of the same currency.

Currency regionalization can be defined at two levels: firstly, a currency fully displays its functions as an international currency within a certain region, which is called "currency internationalization in a region"; secondly, regional monetary integration i.e. countries and regions of high economic correlations within a certain region carry out monetary and financial integration and cooperation before forming a unity and finally achieving a unified monetary system (Yu Qun'e, 2002). The first-level currency regionalization (internationalization) has been analyzed above. A necessary theoretical summary will be made regarding the second-level currency regionalization.

The Optimum Currency Areas theory

The Optimum Currency Areas (OCA) theory mainly studies the conditions for the formation of optimum currency areas and the standards of judgment. In *The New Palgrave Dictionary of Economics*, optimum currency area is defined as the "optimum" geographical domain having as a general means of payments either a single common currency or several infinitely convertible currencies whose exchange rates are pegged against each other and remain unchanged in regular exchange and capital trade; the exchange rate among countries within the region and those outside the region keeps floating.

In 1961 Robert Mundell was the first to put forward the "optimum currency areas" theory, followed by McKinnon (1963), Ingram (1969), Kenen (1969), Fleming (1971), Corden (1972). who interpreted attributes of optimum currency areas and others from the angles of economic openness, product varieties and financial integration.[14] The conditions for forming an optimum currency area may be summed up as follows.

Liquidity of the production factors

Put forward mainly by Mundell this may be interpreted as when the factors of production (capital and labor force) can flow freely, they may succeed in moving from the surplus country to the deficit country when there is imbalance of payments, enabling each economy within the region to make timely restructuring and economic cycles to gradually synchronize, which promotes the coordination and development of the economies in the region and eliminates imbalance instead of having to maintain a steady macro-economy through exchange rate floating. Areas up to this standard will become the optimum currency areas.

Economic openness

Put forward by McKinnon (1963), economic openness refers to the ratio of a country's traded goods to its non-traded goods in production and consumption.

Under the premise of the same stable external prices, open economic zones with close trading relations should form a common currency area before carrying out a fixed exchange rate in the area so as to stabilize prices, and a floating exchange rate outside the area with the purpose of changing the relative prices of traded goods and the actual salaries and wages.

Product varieties

Kenen (1969) holds that, in case of any change in foreign demands for imports, countries with a wider range of product varieties will be more flexible than those countries with a narrower range of product varieties in withstanding the influence of external shocks on the balance of international payments and employment. Therefore to adopt a fixed foreign exchange rate system among countries with a wider range of product varieties would be helpful in stabilizing domestic investments and adjusting to external shocks.

Financial integration

Ingram (1969) thinks that studies by Mundell, McKinnon and Kenan only take into consideration the balance of international payments for regular accounts but ignore the role of currency, while financial integration connected with the long-term free flow of capital should be the criterion for measuring an optimum currency area. Under the conditions of high financial integration any minor fluctuation in the interest rate may lead to sufficient transnational flow of capital, thus helping to avoid exchange rate fluctuations.

Inflation similarity

Fleming (1971) holds that commodity price stability is one of the main objectives of optimum currency areas, and that similar inflation rates are the prerequisite for implementing common currency policies. He changes his study perspective from micro to macro, thinking that high and low inflation rates within the same currency area will lead to different interests, and that countries with a high inflation rate may want to implement tight monetary policies while those with a low inflation rate may hope to maintain monetary policies. Different demands for monetary policies would incapacitate the ultra-national central banks. Therefore inflation rate similarity becomes an important prerequisite for constructing optimum currency areas.

Policy integration

Haberler (1970) et al. put forward the criterion of policy integration in the optimum currency area. To enable the normal operation of an optimum currency area, member states must coordinate their currencies, finance and other economic and social policies so as to seek a common ground. To this end, each member state must partially transfer their sovereignty while giving priority to the coordination of their monetary policies. Meanwhile they also put forward some other criteria such as similiarity of economic structure, fiscal integration and political factors etc.

Tavlas (1998) associates the influencing factors on the international use of currency with optimum currency areas, thinking that the criteria for optimum currency areas can be used to explain why international traders and investors would choose a specific international currency in transnational trade. Criteria for optimum currency areas such as inflation similarity, trade integration and a developed financial market can help explain why a currency will be used as an international unit of account, medium of exchange and storage of value. Other criteria also help explain the use of international currencies, as they can clearly illustrate some countries' vulnerability to external shocks which leads to fluctuations in their actual exchange rates. Compared to the currencies of countries more vulnerable to external shocks, the currencies of those countries less vulnerable to external shocks will go through fewer changes in the actual exchange rates.[15]

"One Market, One Currency" by Emerson and Gros

In the mid-1980s, with the acceleration of currency integration in Europe, theories on regional currency integration also made new progress. At the time, the direction of studies seemed to have turned from the past "establishing an 'optimum' geographical domain for a certain currency" to "designing an optimum currency for a certain geographical area." Therefore "EU economics" led by *One Market, One Currency* by M. Emerson and D. Gros (1992) emerged. Emerson and Gros hold that the choice of a currency had to be determined by market conditions, especially market demands; that specific currency room had to be divided by the network of actual currency trade; and that the room for each currency was the area being influenced by the currency's functional authority i.e. the response of a complete market at the currency-level "currency circle." Obviously it was the functional not the physical significance of the room that was highlighted. By then, as a medium of exchange and value, currency began to truly serve the market. No matter how big the market was, or how many countries were involved in it, as long as it was a unified big market a single currency would be the optimum choice. What Emerson and Gros did was to clear away ideological barriers to international currency integration. In the past currency had been tagged with the label of national sovereignty, and a unified currency became a key symbol of national unification, so sovereign countries were unwilling to abandon their control over their own currencies. Summoned by the idea of "one market, one currency" proposed by Emerson et al., more and more countries have realized that currency, in nature, serves the market, and in-depth international economic exchanges call for currency integration of some form. When a country fails to better play its currency functions and roles, if the transfer of control over currency is favorable for economic development and the improvement of national welfare, then the control over currency should be submitted to a higher ultra-national institution.[16]

The "GG–LL" model

The "GG–LL" model was put forward by Krugman. With the birth of the euro and the acceleration of dollarization in the Latin America, theories regarding whether each and all economic powers within a region should choose currency cooperation emerged at a proper time. The "GG-LL" model was one of these. The model further illustrates the OCA theory, pointing out that optimum currency areas are areas in which a number of countries are promoted to be closely related economically through the trade of commodity and service and the flow of factors of production. If the mobility between different countries are active, forming a currency area is beneficial for all member countries. Otherwise, it will be inappropriate. On the other hand, the "GG–LL" model interprets the issue of cost benefit by joining the group and becoming a member state of an optimum currency area. It starts with whether a single country joins the currency area to analyze the advantages and disadvantages and then determines whether it is good for a country to join the currency area. However it is overly simple and abstract, and it is hard in reality for people to describe the position of the cost-benefit curve, making it difficult to decide the threshold of joining the currency area.

In the theory of *Network Externalities and Switching Costs*, K. Dowd & D. Greenaway (1993)[17] proposed another perspective on carrying out cost-benefit analysis of regional currency integration. The theory points out that currency provides for its users a "network externality" and that the value of a specific currency depends on the number of users inside the "network." With the increase of users, the per capita benefit of people using the same currency will rise accordingly. However influenced by the historical environment and uncertain factors, especially the expensive "transfer costs" and some uncertainties in the process of transfer to the new currency, there is an "inertia" in terms of people's use of their national currency. Therefore to join the monetary union from the independent issue of currency is a major change, the driving force for which comes from the comparison of costs and benefits.[18]

Analyses from the above several aspects are all interrelated from the macroeconomic angle, in which the state is taken as the basic unit. Another side of the theories on currency internationalization is to make analyses taking manufacturers as the basic unit and to study the issue of micro-operational mechanism in currency internationalization.

A new methodology of monetary economics: The search theory

The search model in the early days was used to discuss unemployment and search for the lowest price. The core ideology of this analytical method was that the encounter between the seller and the buyer was not real-time due to different times and places of the trade. Individuals had to spend time and resources to search for the seller who sold the exact commodities they wanted to buy, and the seller was also willing to trade with the buyer using its commodities. In such circumstances, the birth of currency made trade easier.

The currency search model

Put forward by Kiyotaki and Wright, the currency search model is used to explain how currency appeared and gained value etc.[19] Due to the existence of differentiated products, barter trade became difficult and so the French franc appeared to solve the problem. The model thus established analyzed how some commodities became the medium of exchange or commodity money endogenously relying on their own attributes and external belief.[20] This currency model fails to interpret the issue of international currency.

Application of the currency search model in studies on international currencies

Matsuyama, Kiyotaki and Matsui (1993) took the first step forward in studying international currencies using the currency search model.[21] Matsuyama et al. constructed a two-country model of the world economy and studied some issued regarding international currencies. The model can be explained in this way: the existence of two countries each issuing its own currency; the growing population of each of the two countries, and the issue of currency by their respective governments through purchasing commodities from individuals i.e. currency creation brought about by seigniorage; the existence of one encounter or matching technique to describe the frequency (suppose the interaction between individuals and natives is more frequent than that between individuals and foreigners) of interaction between a certain person and other people (domestic or foreign) i.e. random matching by people for the purpose of trade and the encounter between people from the same country is more frequent than that of people from different countries; when two people encounter, one with currency and the other with the physical product to be sold, the two decide whether to make one-to-one trade of currency and product. Relevant parameter values such as expectation of other people's behavior jointly determine whether the trade will proceed and the circulation fields of each currency.

Three conclusions are drawn from the model: firstly, analyzed with the game theory, there are three equilibriums, namely circulation of a currency in its home country; transnational circulation of a currency; and circulation of each currency in other places than its home country; secondly, whether a currency can become an international currency depends on its economic scale and the level of international economic integration; thirdly, the internationalization of a currency may not always bring benefits for a country, that is to say, if the circulation of a currency is put under control in its home country, its circulation outside its home country can increase the welfare of the country issuing the currency; if the total money supply has been set, the circulation of the currency outside its home country will lead to a shortage of local currency and reduce welfare.[22]

The currency search model proposed by Matsuyama et al. provides an important prerequisite for setting up the micro-foundation of international monetary economics, and answers many questions that are impossible to ignore against the background of the models in the early days. For example, what attributes of a country enable its currency to become an international currency? When would local currency exist when the existence of international currencies is generally accepted? Do international currencies appear naturally along with economic integration? What are the costs and benefits of a currency when it serves as an international currency? The author finds two problems with the analytical methods of the model. Firstly, as with earlier search-based currency models, most exchange is set as one-to-one trade which makes price discussion and determination of the exchange rate impossible; secondly, different national governments and monetary authorities do not cooperate with each other, "which makes discussing policy issues impossible."

The two "problems" in the above model are solved in the studies made by Trejos and Wright (1996). To start with, given nominal price and endogenous exchange rate, Trejos and Wright adopt the bargaining approach that is introduced to the currency search model by Shi (1995), Trejos and Wright (1995).[23] Then they introduce the government into the model and assume that the government is faced with a great number of policy choices and the chance to collect seigniorage, while its behavior is affected by the actions of other countries. This extended model discusses a series of new problems, especially those related to different purchasing power.

Like the studies made by Matsuyama et al., Trejos and Wright list three different types of institutions (the equilibrium of different types): the circulation of two currencies in their respective home countries; the transnational circulation of a currency; and the transnational circulation of two currencies. Sometimes multiple equilibriums existed simultaneously. For the most common model, the author lists all equilibrium possibilities before proposing a set of simple assumptions with which to derive more strategic special cases and obtain the analytical results on the existence of different equilibriums at different times and their qualitative attributes.

The results are as follows: for currency being circulated in its home country, domestic prices of a country will improve along with currency expansion both at home and abroad; with other situations being the same, domestic prices will rise with the circulation of a foreign currency, and otherwise fall with the circulation of its home currency abroad. As far as a country is concerned, when its currency is circulating around the world while other currencies only circulate in their home countries, the former currency has a stronger purchasing power. The home country of the international currency will benefit from the use of its currency since it facilitates trade. But at the same time, prices expressed in local currency will rise due to the use of the international currency, which brings losses. However when a currency is used abroad, the seigniorage of its home country will increase. When a currency is used in the host country, the seigniorage in the host country will decrease.

By assuming that the government pays attention to maximizing its people's welfare or pursuing the maximization of the seigniorage, Trejos and Wright introduce government policies into the model endogenously. If the government chooses its policies independently, the results show that it is inefficient. For example, if at least one currency is circulating around the world and a government pursues seigniorage maximization, then cooperation between the two governments would bring more benefits for each of them. Trejos and Wright discover that, with other conditions being the same, if only one currency is circulating around the world the residents of the country issuing the currency will enjoy significantly better welfare than residents of other countries. The model also shows other characteristics: although the system of the two countries' currencies of circulating around the world would potentially help reach the highest level of welfare, it would produce the greatest non-cooperation incentive indicating that benefits from a unified currency also need a unified central bank.

The model shows the possible existence of multiple equilibriums and influences of the given monetary system, assuming that international currencies tend to be issued by countries with a relatively larger economic scale. Although the issue of inflation is ignored in the model it shows that a high tax rate on the currencies will reduce the possibility of their circulation abroad, which further increases the circulation of foreign currencies in the home country. This is consistent with the discussion on inflation and currency substitution.

The analysis method of the currency search model by Trejos and Wright is significantly different from earlier literature. As with the studies made by Matsuyama et al., the analysis objective of the model is endogenous trading media and their circulation domains, which is the difference between this analytical framework and previous studies on currency substitution.

Basically, the above model studies the function of currency as the medium of exchange. In fact there are still a great number of monetary economics-related methods of studying the search theory. For example, Noritaka Kudoh (2003) developed a search model to study the function of currency as storage of value.[24] Or work division, production structure, credit etc. are introduced into the model as endogenous variables before expansion studies are made to the currency search theory; or private information, government policies and financial intermediaries etc. are involved in theoretical studies of currency search. Peter Rupert, Martin Schindler, Andrei Shevchenko and Randall Wright (2000) make a list of related references for the purpose of integrating and sorting out the abovementioned studies.[25]

A brief comment on the currency search theory

The currency search model contributes methodological significance, and it is more technical than ideological.

From the angle of why economic entities need currency, the currency search theory studies the rationality and necessity of currency existence. It follows one main thread i.e. the origin of currency. Domestically or internationally, the objects of the currency search theory remain within the scope of classical political economics yet the study methods are more game theory, general equilibrium theory and welfare economics. As regards the study framework, it adheres to the method of inferring the overall situation from micro-behavior.[26]

In the aspect of studies on international currencies, the search theory model is good for studying currency endogeneity in international monetary economics.[27] It relaxes the excessive assumption premises in the traditional theoretical model and studies the emergence and equilibrium of international currencies endogenously. When answering the question of "which currency to circulate in which country," the traditional theory set in advance currencies and corresponding cash transaction models and utility equations, so at the beginning of the establishment of the model it had decided currencies and the corresponding countries where the currencies circulated. The search theory model solves the problem of "which currency to circulate in which country" endogenously.

The research idea regarding international currencies in the currency search theory provides a brand-new study perspective for RMB internationalization and regionalization. First of all, the possibility of multiple equilibriums should be taken into consideration i.e. it is not necessary to have a unified currency in East Asia nor a leading currency. The circulation of many currencies in many countries and regions is possible. Secondly, if regional single currencies appear in the future, the role of the RMB in the region will become increasingly greater (Lu Lei, 2003).

A trade development-based analysis: The invoice currency choice theory

The choice of the invoice currency in international trade has to be studied because the invoice currency and currency internationalization are closely related. Serving as the main invoice currency in international trade is an important symbol of a currency's economic status.[28] Studies on the choice of the invoice currency are made from the perspective of international currencies functioning as the unit of account. If the function and role of a currency as the invoice currency are given full play, making the currency important in international trade invoicing, it will promote the currency to better exercise its other functions as an international currency, contributing to its comprehensive internationalization. The invoice currency may be of the following several forms: producers currency pricing (PCP), local currency pricing (LCP), vehicle currency pricing (VCP), and the integrated use of the abovementioned three. There have been many conclusions drawn in the theoretical world regarding the choice of invoicing currency in international trade in the abovementioned four forms.

The Grassmann Rule

The Grassmann Rule was an early achievement in the choice of the invoice currency in international trade. When studying the use of the invoice currency in trade by Switzerland and Denmark, Sven Grassmann (1973) found that both countries tended to use the producer's currency as the invoice currency in trade. For industrial products, industrial countries tended to use their own currency as the invoice currency.[29] For example, when making an analysis with data in 1968, Grassmann found that 66% of the exports of Switzerland were denominated in Swedish krona while only 26% of imports were denominated in its home currency, and exports denominated in the U.S. dollar increased by 12%.[30] By 1995, 43.8% of the exports of Switzerland were denominated in Swedish krona and 18.4%[31] of imports were denominated in its home currency. His study shows that the trade in manufactured goods among industrial countries was mostly denominated in the currency of the exporting country, and the rest in the currency of the importing country. It was rare to use a third currency as the invoice currency. According to McKinnon, local currency is "the preferred currency habitat". This is the so-called Symmetry Theory and Grassmann Rule.[32]

Partial and general equilibrium analyses

Bacchetta and Wincoop (2002) use the monopoly model and the oligarch model to make a partial equilibrium over the choice of the invoice currency in trade by manufacturers. By comparing manufacturers' expected profits under different invoice currencies, they obtain the rational choice of the invoice currency in trade by manufacturers. When making the general equilibrium analysis, Bacchetta and Wincoop assume that changes in local and vehicle currency supply are uncertainties before expanding the partial equilibrium model into a two-country general equilibrium model. They then analyze the choice of the invoice currency by manufacturers in four situations i.e. rigid nominal wages, rigid actual wages, random actual wages and complete capital market, and find the conditions for choosing the invoice currency: 1) in the case of the vehicle currency being chosen as the invoice currency, LCP would not be used. As for which to choose, local currency or vehicle currency, the one that has smaller changes in exchange rate against the target currency should be chosen as the invoice currency; 2) the higher the difference among products, the greater the possibility of choosing PCP by manufacturers; 3) the greater the market share of the exporting country in the market of its trade partners, the greater the possibility of choosing PCP by the exporting country; 4) the larger the economic scale of the exporting country, the greater the possibility of choosing PCP by the exporting country; 5) the greater (smaller) the changes in money supply in the exporting country, the greater the possibility of choosing PCP (LCP) by manufacturers.

Devereux and Engel (2001) set up a dynamic general equilibrium model which covers different uncertainties between local money supply and foreign money supply to analyze different behaviors of choosing the invoice currency by different manufacturers in developed and developing countries. The analysis fails to compare the expected profits of PCP and LCP directly, but focuses on the conditions for one manufacturer to make the same choice as another manufacturer, while other manufacturers are assumed to make the same choice, either PCP or LCP. Conditions for choosing the invoice currency in the equilibrium situation that all manufacturers choose the same the invoice currency are further analyzed. It is found in the study that manufacturers,

Table 1.2. Conditions for choosing an invoice currency in export

Conditions	High/Large	Low/Small
(1) The ratio of the change rate of e to that of e^0	The other country's currency/vehicle currency	PCP
(2) Product differentiation	PCP	LCP
(3) Share of the exporting country in its trading partners' market	PCP	LCP
(4) Exporting country's economies of scale	PCP	LCP
(5) Ratio of the change rate of money supply in the exporting country to that in the importing country	LCP	PCP

Note: Condition (1) refers to the situation in which vehicle currency is available and LCP is not chosen, and even if the profit equation is the concave function of the exchange rate, LCP will not be chosen.

both local and foreign manufacturers, would all choose the currency of the country with smaller changes in money supply as the invoice currency. In other words, if changes in local money supply are small manufacturers would choose PCP and foreign manufacturers would choose LCP; otherwise, local manufacturers would choose LCP and foreign manufacturers PCP.[33] The policy significance of this conclusion lies in that the currency of a country with highly reliable monetary policies would be preferred and chosen as the invoice currency, while the transmission of exchange rate to the country's imports is lower and local prices are more stable. On the other hand, for countries with less reliable monetary policies, foreign export enterprises would choose PCP. The transmission of the exchange rate to local imports would then be greater, threatening local price stability.[34]

Fukuda and Ono (2004) use the monopoly competition model under open economic conditions to analyze the choice of the invoice currency by developing countries. The model further develops the partial equilibrium model put forward by Bacchetta and Wincoop (2002). The developed model has two significant features: firstly, it allows export manufacturers to use vehicle currency as the invoice currency. In developing countries there is competition among export manufacturers because of low product difference, so when their competitors adopt vehicle currency as the invoice currency, export manufacturers will naturally choose vehicle currency as the invoice currency also; and secondly, the model shows that cooperation failure would make vehicle currency as the equilibrium invoice currency.[35]

Industry characteristics and product structure

McKinnon (1979) points out the importance of industry characteristics in choosing the invoice currency, thinking that industries of homogeneous products or products to be traded in special markets tend to use a single low-transaction cost currency as the invoice currency.

Product structure of trade is very influential on choosing the invoice currency. Trade of primary products shows a strong single national currency model i.e. using a single national currency as the main invoice currency. Primary products such as crude oil, wheat and copper tend to use the U.S. dollar as the invoice currency. In terms of agricultural trade, Mukund Raj (2003) believes that trade in the agricultural sector would become a main indicator of currency dominance in the medium and long term. This is because the total value of a country's agricultural products would affect its exchange rate, while the exchange rate of its currency represents its international status. The logic shows that the agricultural sector would also play a role in promoting the "power" of the country's currency.[36] The common feature of primary and financial products is low product difference. In particular, they are always traded in very competitive markets. "In such markets, using the currency everyone is familiar with would reduce the costs of information and computerization. Using the same money instrument in the trade of similar products would connect competitive prices more efficiently, making the currency favored by both importers and exporters. Similarly, the greater the product difference, the lower the market competitive tension, and the lower the information quality of prices."[37]

Some relevant studies

Baron (1976) and Giovannini (1988) have also studied the invoice currency choice theory in international trade. Baron (1976) studies the determination of price and trade quantity at different prices. When monopoly manufacturers produce in one country before selling their products in another country, Baron assumes that prices have been set before the determination of the exchange rate and that when setting the prices, monopoly manufacturers could make a choice of using local currency or the currency of the importing country. He finds in his study that the expected price, profits and trade quantity relies on the choice of the invoice currency. For the linear equation where demand curve is price and marginal cost remains unchanged, taking the importers' currency as the invoice currency would help obtain the highest expected profits.[38] Giovannini (1988) extends Baron's (1976) analysis by adding the home market and taking into consideration general demand and cost equation. From the perspective of maximizing manufacturers' expected profits, Giovannini analyzes the choice of the invoice currency at the time monopoly manufacturers export their products with unchanged exchange rate, and obtains the conclusion that the choice of the invoice currency relies on the form of profit equation.[39]

Bilson (1983) develops a bilateral bargaining model for pricing and the choice of the invoice currency by the importer and the exporter, focusing on the incentives and driving force that the importer and the exporter seek before accepting the exporter's currency as the invoice currency. If the exchange rate-related domestic market price risk is greater than the exporter's cost risk, the importer would of course offset risk when accepting the export country's currency as the invoice currency.[40]

According to the study made by Hartmann (1996), two factors determine the choice of the invoice currency in trade i.e. transaction cost and acceptability. The lower the cost of some currency traded on the foreign exchange market, the greater the possibility of the currency being used as the invoice currency in trade. In addition, the higher the acceptance of a currency in other trades, the greater the possibility of it being used as the invoice currency in trade will be. Lower transaction cost and higher acceptability are mutually supportive. The higher a currency's acceptability the lower its transaction cost, and vice versa.[41]

By adopting the currency choice and negotiation theory, Saeed Samiee and

Patrik Anckar (1998) set up an analytical framework for currency choice in foreign trade at two levels i.e. manufacturers and the market, and obtained some conclusions on the choice of invoice currency at three levels. From the perspective of manufacturers they draw the following conclusions: 1) consumer-oriented exporters are more willing to choose LCP; 2) exporters capable of bargaining are more willing to choose PCP; 3) in case of a higher level of differences among exports, exporters are more willing to chose PCP; 4) price-setters are more willing than price-accepters to choose PCP; 5) in the case of small influence of importers on the overall volume of exports of the exporters, exporters are more willing to choose PCP; 6) LCP is preferred in long-term trade relations; 7) choosing LCP in exports is positively correlated with the size of manufacturers, the sales volume of exports and the value of transactions. From the perspective of the market, they draw the following conclusions: 1) in the case of a low competitiveness on the export market, exporters are more willing to choose PCP; 2) in the case that the exports are very important to the buyer, exporters are more willing to choose PCP; 3) compared with finished products exporters, exporters of daily necessities are more willing to choose the established trade currency on the market for daily necessities. Seen from the export performance: 1) the consumer-oriented exporters are doing better than other exporters; and 2) exporters that accept consumers' requirements on money of account are doing better than other exporters.[42]

Influences of currency internationalization: Benefits and costs of possessing an international currency

People pay attention to the issue of currency internationalization because countries possessing an international currency can gain exclusive benefits from it. Although possessing an international currency costs correspondingly, the benefits outweigh the costs comparatively.

Advantages of possessing an international currency

With its currency circulating around the world and being used by other countries, a country would benefit a lot from currency internationalization. Specifically the advantages include:

Making things more convenient for its citizens

With the country's currency becoming international, its exporters, importers, debtors and creditors would find using local currency more convenient than using foreign currencies because the risks of using local currency to trade or face changes in the exchange rate are reduced, and so are trading costs.

Creating more businesses for local banks and other local financial institutions

Bergsten (1996) and Tavalas (1998) hold that, with the expansion of the use of a currency worldwide, granting loans, making investments and purchasing commodities or services would have to be carried out through the financial institutions of the country issuing the currency, which would bring about more benefits to the financial sector.[43] Which currency is used in bank businesses has nothing to do with the bank's nationality. The depositors' and money borrowers' nationality does not have a fixed relationship with the nationality of the intermediary bank. However, it is clear that U.S. banks do have advantages when dealing with U.S. dollar business while British banks have comparative advantages when dealing with British pound sterling business, from which certain commissions are brought to the relevant banks.

Seigniorage

Generally speaking, seigniorage is the primary benefit a country obtains from its currency internationalization. In the Middle Ages seigniorage meant the tax collected by the rulers of each Western European country against the precious metals used to cast golden and silver coins. Seigniorage in the modern sense may be measured in two ways: in the narrow sense it is defined as "the profit that results from the difference in the cost of printing money and the face value of that money"; while in the broad sense it is defined as "the net output of home currency and its token financial assets due to local currency internationalization." Domestic collection of seigniorage is enforced through legislation, with all profits belonging to the state, and the central bank's benefits by issuing currency. Internationally, countries issuing international reserve currencies enjoy the same privileges in issuing international currencies and get profits from zero-cost issue of currency while the profits such countries obtain are the benefits of other countries' commodities, labor service and direct investments.

In a non-cash credit currency system, whether a country can get international seigniorage depends on whether its currency enjoys the status of an international reserve currency, so international seigniorage may be understood as the issuing profit of the international reserve currency. To obtain the currency of another country, a country must pay with actual products, services and its ownership over the actual capital stock. Such benefits may also be called "income advantage" i.e. countries possessing international currencies can use local currency to buy more foreign commodities and services, attract more investments, and provide more assistance to other countries.[44] International seigniorage income in the narrow sense is not very great, which is only a central bank's foreign exchange reserves in that currency equivalent to offering a low-interest rate loan to the country issuing that currency. International seigniorage income in the broad sense is an "excessive privilege" with which a country can borrow heavily from other countries. It is particularly true when higher foreign direct investment (FDI) and other foreign investment income can be obtained. The yield of overseas investments by the United States is higher than the interests on its debts, the annual difference of which is about 1.2%.[45]

Cohen (1971) believes that the size of international seigniorage income obtained by the country issuing an international currency depends on the nature of its international monopoly status. If the country has a complete monopoly status, its net seigniorage income is certain to be great. However in the face of competition from other internationally-acceptable monetary tools its net income would be reduced accordingly, because it has to pay interest on its debts so as to lure foreigners to keep maintaining its currency. Moreover the fiercer the competition from other currencies, the higher the interest paid to foreigners. As a result, in the circumstance of complete competition and with the capability of free flow of capital, countries issuing international currencies may be unlikely to get net seigniorage income. Cohen (1971) makes an empirical test on the net seigniorage income of British pound sterling during 1965–1969, only to find that the net seigniorage income of Britain from the international use of British pound sterling was zero.[46] According to statistics, U.S. dollar internationalization has brought to the U.S. an annual seigniorage income equivalent to 2% of its annual GDP.[47]

Flexibility

After a currency becomes an international currency, if foreign official institutions are willing to purchase assets denominated in that currency, it will help the country issuing the currency to finance its trade deficits, reducing the conflicts between domestic economic and overseas economic targets due to payment constraints. Once a currency becomes an international currency, the country issuing the currency may use the international advantage of its currency to intervene in its own economy and affect other economies so as to produce a spillover effect of its own monetary policy by changing its own monetary supply.

Reducing international reserves

With its great economic strength and special currency position, the country issuing the international currency, when faced with the gap of balance of payments, can not only issue more local currency to settle the gap but also raise other currencies more easily. Therefore it does not need excessive international reserves. Saving in international reserves enables the country that issues the international currency to invest as much capital as possible into production and operation, enlarge the size of its production, and reduce the loss of income due to the reduction of reserve currency and possible losses brought about by changes in the value of the reserve currency.

Promoting the development of the foreign trade, investments and finance of the country issuing the international currency

Zero exchange rate risk and the expectation of stable earnings would encourage enterprises in the country that issues the international currency to take more initiative in foreign trade and investments; and other countries' demand for international currency will enable such countries to open markets to the country that issues the international currency. All of these will promote the country that issues the international currency to expand its foreign trade and investment, boosting development of its domestic production and bringing it enormous profits.

Disadvantages of possessing an international currency

Besides bringing about earnings, possessing an international currency is very likely to bring losses. Chinn and Frankel (2005) hold that the adverse influences of possessing an international currency are mainly: firstly, greater fluctuations in currency demand. When a currency becomes an international currency, the demand for it will increase, making the demand for the currency more fluctuating. The fluctuation will also become greater along with capital flow. Central banks are sometimes concerned that currency internationalization will make controlling the money supply difficult. Of course, the same problem depends on whether central banks intervenes in the foreign exchange market; secondly, an increase in the average currency demand, which is another side of seigniorage. If foreign citizens can hold local currency, the inflow of capital will lead to local currency appreciation and the reduction of the competitiveness of exports on the international market; thirdly, the burden of responsibilities. When a currency becomes an international currency, the country possessing the international currency will have to consider the global influence of its actions, meaning that it cannot implement monetary policy simply from its national perspective.[48]

Tavalas (1998) also holds that the costs of currency internationalization are mainly composed of two parts. First, under the pegged foreign exchange rate system, the transfer of foreigners' preference will lead to a large capital flow, damage the monetary currency's capability of controlling the money base, and affect domestic economic activities. Second, under the floating exchange rate system, such a transfer will lead to great changes in the exchange rate, or limit the domestic policy capabilities of the monetary authority.[49]

In addition, domestic economic independence will also be affected. Against the background of economic globalization, the economic independence of each country will also be impacted to a certain degree. However, due to different levels of openness, countries issuing international currencies are in the center of the world economic system. With a very open financial system and a high economic openness, these countries have a great influence on other countries. Therefore, when developing their own policies, these countries tend to be affected by the flow of international means of production and other countries' economic policies. As a result, the implementation effect of their policies can be reduced greatly, or even fail, having negative impact on their domestic economy.

To sum up, we can safely draw several conclusions as set forth below by summarizing theories on currency internationalization.

First, currency internationalization is a process in which an international currency plays its role, and is mainly the internationalization of currency functions.

Second, a country's economic scale, international trade position, development of its domestic financial market, and currency credibility constitute necessary conditions, but not sufficient conditions, for its local currency to become an international currency. The historical inertia of international currencies has a great effect on currency internationalization.

Third, currency internationalization theory and currency regionalization theory are logically consistent. The latter is one analytical level of the former.

Fourth, currency internationalization is endogenous, as well as being the result of market choice in the world economic development process. International currencies emerge endogenously, since currency internationalization lowers search costs and overcomes the problem of "lack of dual-consistency of demand."

Fifth, becoming a main invoice currency in international trade is an important condition for currency internationalization. To choose which currency before taking it as invoice currency is a choice made by manufacturers for the purpose of maximizing their profits, which further proves the endogeneity and market choice features of currency internationalization.

Sixth, the welfare effects of currency internationalization are twofold. The internationalization of a currency will bring about not only profits, but also costs for the home country of the currency.

International Currency Experience

Based on the above summary and analysis we now, by combining the historical evolution of the international monetary system and especially the process of the internationalization of the British pound sterling, the U.S. dollar, the Deutschmark and the Japanese Yen, review their successful experience and the lessons from their failures to try to provide some reference for RMB internationalization and regionalization.

Changes in and characteristics of the international monetary system

The international monetary system (international monetary institution) is a whole set of international rules, arrangements, practices and institutions, showing the rules and order in international currency exchanges, capital flow, and settlement of creditor-debtor relations. Normally its core contents include: determination of international standard money and formation mechanism of international reserve currency; determination of the exchange rate system; and the regulating mechanism for disequilibrium of balance of payments.

From the point of view of time sequence, the international monetary system can be generally divided into three stages: the international gold standard system, the Bretton Woods System, and the existing Jamaica system.

The gold standard system

The so-called gold standard system uses gold of a certain weight and fineness as the standard currency, and establishes a currency system in which various currencies and the gold have a fixed conversion relationship in circulation. The gold standard system may be defined in a broad sense and a narrow sense. In the broad sense, it is a monetary system in which the standard unit of currency is gold of a fixed quantity and fineness, and it includes the gold coin standard system, the gold bullion standard system and the gold exchange standard system. In the narrow sense, it simply refers to the gold coin standard system. The international gold standard system is an international monetary system based on most countries' adoption of the gold standard system. It is the ultimate form of metal standard system.

The emergence of the international gold standard system was closely related to the development stages of the world economy. The industrial revolution in the last few decades of the 18th century not only contributed to the unprecedented improvement of the productivity of some developed countries, but also increased international economic connections. In particular, foreign trade became increasingly important in national economies, and international economic exchanges including trade, investment and credit grew, which all called for a stable and unified standard currency mechanism. At the time, Britain was the first country in the world to have completed industrialization. By the second half of the 19th century Britain had established, with its great economic strength, its hegemony in world trade and finance, and had taken the lead in transforming the gold and silver bimetallic standard system to the gold standard system, which was soon followed suit by some other countries. By the end of the 19th century most capitalist countries had implemented the gold standard system (See Table 1.3). Under the international gold standard system, gold fully displayed its functions as the international currency and the international monetary mechanism featuring the free circulation of gold (gold coin). The system actually had no uniform and standardized rules and laws, and countries participating in the international gold standard system all followed some basic rules of international gold standard operation.

The emergence of the international gold standard currency set a unified value standard for currencies, provided a stable price environment for international trade and investment, reduced fluctuations in foreign exchange and prices, and stimulated the development of international trade and investment. However, due to the limited growth of the world gold output, it was hard to meet various countries' demand for money supply in the rapid growth of international commodity production and sales for money supply, which objectively restrained gold from displaying its functions as the international currency. After the outbreak of WWI many countries issued fiat money and forbade the free outflow of gold in order to raise large amounts of war funds. It was then that international gold standard system was put to an end. The Genoa Conference held in Italy in 1922 decided to adopt the principle of "saving gold." Apart from the U.S. which implemented the gold standard system, and Britain and France which implemented the gold bullion standard system, other countries implemented the gold exchange standard system. Since the gold bullion and exchange standard systems did not have the features of the gold coin standard system, they were called an incomplete gold standard system. Shocked by the world economic depression during 1929–1933, the two systems were abandoned by all countries. After WWII, the U.S. dollar-centered

Table 1.3. Time table for different countries' adoption of the gold standard system

Country	Year	Country	Year
Britain	1816	Holland	1875
German	1871	Uruguay	1876
Denmark	1873	U.S.	1879
France and Austria-Hungary	1892	Belgium and Chile	1895
Switzerland and Japan	1897	Italy and Russia	1898
Greece	1874	Dominica	1901
Panama	1904	Mexico	1905

Source: Qian Fengyuan, Zhang Cuiwei and Zou Jianlun eds., *Great Circulation- International Currency Tale*, Beijing: The Economic Daily Press, August 2000.

international monetary system in fact became a gold exchange standard system, not a gold standard system in the typical sense.

The Bretton Woods System

After the gold standard system collapsed, the international monetary system became extremely chaotic and unstable, severely disturbing the normal international trade, monetary and financial relations. People were eager to reconstruct a unified international monetary system so as to achieve effective international economic cooperation and improve international monetary relations. In July 1944, 44 UN member states held the United Nations Monetary and Finance Conference, at which the *Agreement of the International Monetary Fund* was signed, and the Bretton Woods System was then set up. Under the Bretton Woods System, gold was still the monetary base; the U.S. dollar was set as the world's main reserve currency; and the "double-coupling" principle, namely the so-called U.S. dollar pegged to gold and the currencies of other International Monetary Fund (IMF) member states pegged to the U.S. dollar, was formed. The "double-coupling" system enabled the U.S. dollar to get the same status as gold, and it became the central currency and main international reserve currency in the international monetary system.

The establishment and operation of the Bretton Woods System and its exchange rate mechanism played an active role in world trade and economic development after WWII. The main reflections of this included: firstly, it set the "U.S. dollar with gold, and other currencies with U.S. dollar" double-hook principle, and put an end to the unstable disorderly state which had prevailed in the international monetary and financial field before WWII; secondly, while implementing the adjustable fixed exchange rate system, the currency exchange rate was relatively stable, contributing to the expansion of world trade and the development of international investment and credit; thirdly, the U.S. dollar became the primary international reserve currency, made up for the lack of international liquidity, and solved the problem of lack of international reserves caused by insufficient gold supply to a certain extent; fourthly, it enabled its member states to temporarily relieve their deficits on balance of payments; by offering various long, medium and short-term loans to its member states, the IMF temporarily relieved the deficits on balance of payments of its member states; fifthly, it promoted international trade cooperation and multilateral monetary cooperation. Under the system each member state was required to cancel foreign exchange controls, which objectively pushed forward the establishment and development of post-WWII international trade and monetary cooperation.

But the Bretton Woods System, established on the basis of the gold-U.S. dollar standard, had a fatal drawback i.e. the U.S. dollar being both a local currency and an international currency. As a local currency, its issue must be controlled by U.S. monetary policy and gold reserves; while as an international currency, the supply of the U.S. dollar must adapt to the demand for international trade and world economic growth. Since the gold output and gold reserves of the U.S. could not meet the needs of world economic development, the U.S. dollar was stuck in a dilemma under the "double-coupling" principle. That is, to meet the demand of world economic growth for the medium of international payments and reserve currency the supply of U.S., dollars had to increase constantly, while the constant increase in the supply of the U.S. dollar would make it hard to maintain the convertibility between the U.S., dollar and gold. Such a dilemma was first put forward by Robert Triffin, a professor from Yale University in the U.S. during the 1950s. Therefore it is also called the "Triffin Dilemma." It pointed out the internal instability of the Bretton Woods System and the inevitability of risks. But the fundamental drawback of the monetary system lay in the dual identity of the U.S. dollar and the "double-coupling" principle, leading to system crisis i.e. the U.S. dollar convertibility crisis, or people's confidence crisis in U.S. dollar convertibility.

In the early 1960s, because the gold output and gold reserves in the U.S. could not meet the needs of world economic and trade development the U.S.

dollar, as the only international currency at the time, had no other choice but to issue more money. U.S. dollar shortage became gradually replaced by the U.S. dollar surplus. Meanwhile, the trade balance of the U.S. dropped sharply; deficits in the balance of international payments emerged; and short-term foreign debts kept increasing. Consequently the credit of the U.S. dollar was doubted and it gradually lost its attraction as the international currency. Another major international currency—the British pound sterling—was also very unstable due to the decline in British national strength. All these long-fermented internal instabilities finally caused the British pound sterling crisis in 1962 and the gold crisis in 1968, during which the central banks of IMF member states used U.S. dollar positions to convert gold from the U.S., submerging the U.S. In fact with the amount of the U.S. dollar circulating in the world continually expanding the number of the U.S. dollars officially held by European countries had far exceeded the total value of gold reserves in the U.S., threatening the dominance of the U.S. In 1971 and 1973 respectively the U.S. dollar was depreciated twice. The then European Economic Community, Japan and Canada, among other countries, announced that their regional currency or local currency would float against the U.S. dollar. Finally, the Bretton Woods System collapsed.

The existing international monetary system

Before and after the collapse of the Bretton Woods System, the world financial situation was turbulent and the international community held long-term discussions and negotiations on establishing a new international monetary system. In the process of reforming the international monetary system and establishing a new system, there were all kinds of conflicts and struggles. Ultimately, all parties compromised a little and reached a consensus on some basic issues before signing an agreement, i.e. the Jamaica Agreement, in Kingston, the capital of Jamaica, in January 1976. In April the same year the IMF board passed the second revision of the IMF agreement, and the international monetary system then entered a new stage i.e. the Jamaica System stage.

The new international monetary system built on top of the *Jamaica Agreement* is not a total negation of the Bretton Woods System. On the one hand, the IMF organization set up under the Bretton Woods System is still playing an important role; on the other hand, although the status of the U.S. dollar has fallen greatly and the international status of the Deutschmark and the Japanese Yen has strengthened significantly, the U.S. dollar's position as an international currency has never wavered. From 1980 to 1993, of the foreign exchange reserves of different countries, the ratio of the U.S. dollar reduced from 68.8% to 61% while that of the German mark (renamed the Deutschmark after the unification of East and West Germany) rose from 14.9% to 16% and that of the Japanese Yen rose from 4.3% to 9%,[50] although the U.S. dollar still played an important role as the main international reserve currency.

Meanwhile, as a new international monetary system, the Jamaica System has distinctly different features from the Bretton Woods System. Being a relatively flexible institutional arrangement, it is highly applicable and conforms to the unstable, multilateral and unbalanced world economic development to some extent. First of all, under the Jamaica System, international economic exchanges keep developing rapidly; secondly, under the Jamaica System, the policy autonomy of all countries has been greatly strengthened and the stability of each country's open macro-economy has been further guaranteed; thirdly, the Jamaica System has withstood many shocks caused by different factors and it has showed a high degree of adaptability.

However there are imperfections in the Jamaica System, leading to many problems in its performance. First of all, the most crucial point is that it does not change the status and role of the U.S. dollar as the main international currency, so the potential "Triffin Dilemma" still exists. Moreover in the Jamaica System, the U.S. dollar still plays the function of an international currency yet does not need to undertake the responsibility for maintaining the stability of U.S. dollar, aggravating exchange rate fluctuations among the main currencies. Compared with changes in the exchange rate being limited within a relatively narrow scope under the Bretton Woods System, exchange rate adjustments under the Jamaica System are sometimes excessively volatile and in many circumstances may cause currency crises in some countries. Secondly, under the Jamaica System, the balance of payments of each country is not well regulated, which may be explained by the international debt crises in the early 1980s. Thirdly, the conflict of internal and external equilibrium still exists under the Jamaica System and becomes increasingly complicated due to large-scale international capital flows, making government regulation of the open macro-economy more difficult. In addition, with the changes in the international economic pattern and the constant emergence of new financial tools, the existing international monetary system is also faced with some new challenges. Such challenges come from many aspects, including the exchange rate system, international reserves, regulation of the balance of payments, emergence of new international currencies such as the euro etc., and have profound impacts on the reform of the existing international monetary system.

In general, the international monetary system at the present stage is mainly characterized by the following features:

The return of the "U.S. dollar system"

The so-called "U.S. dollar system" refers to the international monetary system under which the U.S. dollar that cannot be converted with gold plays key monetary functions, and the international financial system formed by U.S. dollar-centered short-, medium- and long-term working systems of international credits on the basis of this international monetary system (Okuda Hiroshi, 2002). With the collapse of the Bretton Woods System, the U.S. dollar lost its position as an international standard currency in the legal sense, and with the economic development in Europe and Japan and the acceleration of the monetary integration of Europe during the 1980s, the U.S. dollar became less attractive. However, until the early 1990s, the "U.S. dollar system" showed a significant reversion trend. Currently, the hegemony is still unshakable.

Three reasons contributed to the return of the "U.S. dollar system" during the 1990s. First of all the U.S., as a hegemony, enjoyed the priority in obtaining peace dividends from the ending of the "Cold War." The end of the "Cold War" enabled the U.S. government to change its U.S. dollar policy i.e. the U.S. tried under the new international political and economic situation to effectively achieve the reversed flow of international capital by recovering the position of the U.S. dollar as a powerful base currency and its developed financial markets with huge financial flows. Secondly, after its stock market crash in 1987, the U.S. saw the increasingly prominent phenomenon of investment institutionalization. All these institutional investors were of a very high level of expertise, capable of sensitively capturing investment chances around the world, and invested capital into emerging markets around the world making use of the opportunity afforded by some developing countries opening their financial markets under the "Washington Consensus"[51] and under the pressure of international organizations, forming a U.S. dollar-centered credit turnover or circulation system around the globe. Thirdly, after the building of the European monetary system, emerging market economies and especially East Asian countries and regions became the most important supports of the U.S. dollar credit turnover system and then of the recovery of the "U.S. dollar system." They obtained the U.S. dollars in the trade surplus of exports to the U.S. and used part of these dollars to import capital goods and another part to invest in national debts and other financial products of the U.S. government and store them as foreign exchange reserves in the U.S. In another sense, globalization and the opening of the U.S. market, the central country, are extremely important for the formation and maintenance of the U.S. dollar-centered global credit turnover system.

Financial globalization and the "incorporation" of emerging markets into the world financial market

Scientific and technological development, especially the progress of electronic and information technologies, has not only greatly reduced the transaction costs on the monetary market but has also pushed forward the liberalization of financial innovation and trade. Developed countries led by the U.S. have loosened or lifted monetary control, which has further promoted the integration of financial innovation into the monetary markets and expanded capital flows to an unprecedented scale since the heyday of the gold standard system. The financial market has basically achieved globalization. In the process, the convenience of using the U.S. dollar in transactions or the possession of in-depth and extensive monetary markets acts as a crucial basis for the U.S. dollar to still serve as the international currency.

On the other hand, in the same process, more and more developing countries have been engaged in the integration of monetary markets or the progress of globalization. According to statistics from the World Bank, the 12 countries[52] that are relatively highly incorporated into the world monetary market, including China, absorb about 80% of the capital flowing into developing countries. These 12 countries are mainly emerging markets, including China, South Korea, Malaysia, Thailand and Indonesia in East Asia. Therefore it is safe to say that emerging markets have become the leading and main force in integrating into the world monetary market. Although emerging markets can obtain benefits from the inflow of capital in their integration into the world monetary market, they are also faced with increased financial risks. In the case of large-scale flight of capital, monetary and financial crises are inevitable.

Development of regional monetary and financial cooperation and the lack of a global financial security network

Firstly, a major change in the international monetary system during the 1990s was the acceleration of the European monetary integration, which led to the European Monetary Union and the launch of the euro in 1999. In sharp contrast with Europe, although East Asia had witnessed rapid economic development since the 1970s and international division of work in the region and the ratio of capital and trade contacts had been improved greatly, institutional regional monetary and financial cooperation in East Asia failed to progress accordingly. After the outbreak of the Asian financial crisis in 1997, and especially since 2000, the situation has begun to change.[53]

Secondly, in the rapid development of financial globalization, a global financial security network to guard against the "U.S. dollar system" risk is missing. A common lesson could be learned from the two major financial crises which happened during the 1990s i.e. the financial crisis in Mexico and the financial crisis in Asia, with the increasing integration of the financial markets, it is very dangerous to not to build a global financial security network for a large-scale, market-oriented and rapid capital flow. In such circumstances, to make up for the unavailability of a global financial security network to some extent and to guard against financial risks from outside through regional monetary and financial cooperation becomes a feasible choice for a number of late developer countries.

It has to be noted that, since the further exposure of global economic imbalance and the global financial crises induced by the subprime crisis in the U.S. in 2008, it has been held by some people that the existing international monetary system characterized by the "U.S. dollar system" cannot be maintained any longer. But in fact, influenced by the following factors, the current "U.S. dollar system" may still continue for a long time.

Firstly, under the conditions of economic globalization, the sustainability of "financial hegemony" has been enhanced constantly. With the liberalization of capital flows after WWII, and in particular the development of financial liberalization, the means of international economic exchanges have undergone great changes. Under the current "U.S. dollar system" the results of international competition are usually "positive-sum," and mutual costs and benefits are highly interrelated. A prominent aspect of the global financial crises is that the main states and regions undertake the costs and losses of the crisis together. This indicates that, under economic globalization, the environment and conditions for hegemony replacement have been through great changes. Such changes may be more conducive to the continuation of the hegemony, especially the "financial hegemony," of the U.S. in the fairly long term.[54]

Secondly, the global financial crises which have happened since the 1970s showed that during these crises and in a period after them the U.S. dollar was still a powerful currency, reflecting the market confidence in the functions of the U.S. dollar as a key global currency.

Since the 1960s, after the outbreak of a financial crisis, regardless of the causes of the crisis or the places in which the crisis took place, the U.S. dollar has always been the "straw to clutch at" by other governments or investors in their efforts to ensure their asset security and avoid risks. The position of the U.S. dollar has not fallen but has risen.[55] It remains the same even after the birth of the euro. In fact the heavy economic losses suffered by the euro zone during this global financial crisis were even greater than those suffered by the U.S. The rapid appreciation of the U.S. dollar during these crises demonstrates that the current international monetary system is still led by the U.S. dollar, and that the euro is incapable of taking the place of the U.S. dollar and becoming a dominant international currency.

Thirdly, given the current political, economic, military and cultural strengths of the U.S., it is impossible for any power in the so-called international relations pattern featured by "one superpower and several major powers" to take the place of the U.S. and become a hegemony in the short term.

In the world today, the U.S. is a typical "financial state" that controls financial hegemony. Comparatively speaking, developed and developing countries including Japan and China are all "trading nations" (Li Xiao, Ding Yibing, 2006). The U.S. has become a great power around the world not by relying on starting wars or setting up, controlling or plundering colonies but by relying on a free market system with an extremely high efficiency in terms of resource allocation, with which it mobilizes or allocates world resources and makes other countries heavily dependent on its economy and finance. Today, with a developed, open, in-depth and profound financial market, the U.S. can not only indulge in making monetary policy focusing on its domestic economic objectives but can also seek more seigniorage income in the form of inflation or U.S. dollar depreciation by misusing the monopoly position of the U.S. dollar as the main medium of exchange in international trade. Meanwhile, because the U.S. provides markets for the world to maintain the reversed flow of U.S. capital, it not only enhances other countries' trade dependence on the U.S. and its position in negotiations on the world economy, but also helps the U.S. to take world resources, commodities and wealth by maintaining an unbalanced economic system and to make other countries maintain the existence of the U.S. dollar as a competitive currency (Hua Min, 2006).

Fourthly, for a fairly long time in the future, it will be hard for all the economies in East Asia to get rid of their dependence on the U.S. market. The status of the U.S. as the end-product market supplier in East Asia will not change significantly in the short run.

Although regional trade in East Asia has been developing rapidly since the 1990s, the goods exchanged are mainly semi-finished products, parts and capital goods produced in the process of separated production, and the end products market still depends on the U.S. and other countries and regions outside East Asia. The ratio of the U.S. in the export of end products by the East Asian economic community has shown a descending trend, yet it remains the largest supplier on the end-product market in the region. Given the long and tortuous course of economic restructuring, it is impossible that a new end-product market supplier will appear and take the place of the U.S. in East Asia in the short run. Neither Japan nor China can play a similar function or role.

It is worth noting that the outbreak of the global financial crisis has strengthened the desire and motive of all East Asian economies to stimulate economic growth by maintaining the pattern of export surplus. Experience shows that export growth has always been the best path for East Asian economies to recover or promote economic growth. Despite changes of all sorts in the domestic savings rates or ways of consumption in the U.S. in or after the crisis, the U.S. market remains their most important export target.

In sum, after this crisis, the U.S. dollar-centered global credit turnover system will still operate vigorously. It is difficult for all the East Asian economies to escape their dependence on the U.S. end-product market, so they will keep supporting the system, and the "U.S. dollar system" will see no fundamental changes for a fairly long time in the future. This is the most important realistic background for thinking about the issue of currency internationalization at the present stage.

The empirical model of currency internationalization

Seen from the development history of international currencies, there are mainly two paths for a local currency to grow into an international currency: firstly, by relying on the overall advantages of its home country and using its great national power as the backup before realizing internationalization in the form of "individual combat," which usually succeeds with hegemony replacement; secondly, the home country abandons its sovereignty over its currency, takes an active part in regional currency cooperation, and realizes currency internationalization through regional currency integration by relying on the power of "collective action." It is safe to say that the above two development paths have also formed the two typical development models of currency internationalization.

Early international currencies

The role models for single national currencies developing into international currencies and then achieving local currency internationalization are the British pound sterling and the U.S. dollar. When analyzing British pound sterling and U.S. dollar internationalization, it is necessary to start even earlier. From the development history of early international currencies we can see that there is a long-lasting tradition of the development pattern of currency internationalization, or of a national currency growing into an international currency. In most development periods of the international currency, one currency has always led in the overall situation of international currencies while a few other currencies also played important international roles, and most of the other currencies could be ignored (Philipp Hartmann and Otmar Issing, 2002).[56]

Most international currencies before the British pound sterling were metal coins. Since all of them were made of precious medal, they were convertible as long as their home countries lifted control over them. However different currencies had different international positions (degrees of currency internationalization) due to their different economic and political backgrounds. The British pound sterling in the Edwardian era and its fabrications were widely used in areas that were not under the British rule as good money. The gold ducaten and silver grosso in Venice, the gold florentine, the Maria Theresa thaler and the sovereign were all once used in international transactions as full coins that attracted great attention and had priority before circulating extensively.[57] In addition, currency internationalization during the period of coins was usually the result of imperial conquests and expansion. From the Carolingian system to the coinage system in Britain, the essence of international currencies as precious metal did not change but the standards of the currency system were changing. Charlemagne promoted silver bullion coins under the Carolingian system to most parts of Western Europe by conquest.[58]

There was a convenience for currency internationalization during the coinage period i.e. foreign countries could imitate what they saw as advanced good money. Such currency internationalization should be named currency unification among different countries, being similar to dollarization in these days. However the key difference lies in the fact that currency issuers in the coinage era were different countries and that due to the nature of coins as precious metal, some strong good money could be imitated by other countries and regions leading to pro forma internationalization of the strong good money. Strictly speaking, whether it can be termed currency internationalization is doubtful.

With the development of banks and the issue of notes, paper money issuing systems emerged and different countries set up their own central banks to issue their own paper money. Early paper money still took precious metals such as gold and silver as reserves. Driven by trade and credit, the issue of paper money gradually broke through the constraint of precious metals and paper money issue taking other currencies as reserves appeared. Entering the era of paper money, national factors in the concept of money were promoted, and currency and sovereignty were closely linked. The geographical scopes of paper money were like islands that were separated yet interactive, and "currency islands" were both separate and interconnected. In the period of fiduciary currency, international currencies became international symbols under sovereignty states and currency internationalization in the real sense appeared.

British pound sterling internationalization under the gold standard system

Being the center of the international monetary system during the 19th century before declining since the 20th century, the British pound sterling is a good example for studying the gold standard system under currency internationalization. British pound sterling internationalization was achieved under the circumstance of extremely unbalanced global economic development and developed with the backing of the economic hegemony of Britain. In particular, it was closely related to the status of Britain as a world trade hegemony and world factory. It is safe to say that British pound sterling internationalization was the highest reflection of British economy, trade and financial hegemony. Specifically, the realization path can be divided into three stages with each stage being integrated, showing the following dynamic development features of currency internationalization: firstly, establishment of a British pound sterling system with a stable currency value and maintaining the free convertibility of the British pound sterling; secondly, creation of a network of free trade with other countries; thirdly; setting up unilateral preferential tariff zones in the British Empire. Corresponding measures taken at each stage were all aimed at making full use of the Britain's advantaged position in global trade to push forward the adoption of the British pound sterling in international trade and investment and to allow the British pound sterling to fully play its role as an international currency.

The great development of British trade begun in the 17th century. The industrial revolution promoted the rapid acceleration of British trade. Apart from cotton textiles and iron, the British exports increased by 50% respectively during 1779–1783 and 1789–1793; and by 1/3 during 1799–1803.[59] Entering the 19th century, trade by Britain continued to develop vigorously (See Table 1.4). In the middle of the 19th century a great change happened in the field of trade i.e. development in the direction of free trade. In the waves of free trade, foreign trade by Britain experienced rapid development with the value of exports increasing by 40% during the 1940s, 90% during the 1950s, 47% during the 1960s, and 12% during the 1970s.59 Before and after the 1960s, Britain held an unapproachable leading position in the modern industries, producing about half of the world's iron and coal and consuming nearly half of the world's raw cotton output.[61] This fully reflected the dominance of Britain over the concurrent international trade. During 1860–1870 Britain's foreign trade accounted for 1/4 of the world trade volume, double that of France which was then the second largest trading nation in the world. As the industrial revolution spread in Europe and to other places around the world, the ratio of Britain's foreign trade fell gradually to 16% during 1900–1913. However it was still greater than that of Germany, France and the U.S.[62] It was safe to say that trade had an unprecedented influence on Britain. Even the U.S. today is only at half of the level of Britain 30 years ago in terms of its ratio of imports and exports to its GDP. At present and in the future, it is very likely that the U.S. economy will never be as dependant on export trade as Britain was during the Victorian times.[63] Meanwhile the status of Britain as the international investment leader also contributed to British pound sterling internationalization. Throughout the 19th century Britain was the most active country in the world in terms of making foreign investments, and the total amount of its foreign investments was always in a leading position. As early as in 1825, the size of foreign investments made by Britain had reached USD500 million and by 1870 the amount had grown by ten times to USD4.9 billion. During the same period only France had a certain scale of foreign investments, but its total amount of foreign investments accounted for only half of that of Britain. During 1870–1913 foreign investment by Britain kept growing at a high speed, with the annual growth rate reaching 7%; in 1913 the amount of foreign investments made by Britain hit USD19.5 billion , being larger than the sum of foreign investments made by France, Germany and the U.S. (See Table 1.5).

The trade, foreign investments and industrial development of Britain laid a solid foundation for British pound sterling internationalization. There were many reasons why the whole world chose the British pound sterling as the international medium of payments. It was partly because of the status of Britain as the largest trading nation in the world, a main transporter and the sole largest source of foreign capital in world trade, and partly because of the stable value of the British pound sterling during 1821–1914 for its adherence to the gold standard system. However what is equally important is that accepting banks and insurance agencies in Britain were highly creditable, and any bank notes endorsed by them could be discounted on the London discount market at the world's most preferential discount rate. All these factors enabled London to become the world financial center, and the British pound sterling the commonly accepted currency.[64]

Table 1.4. Annual growth rate of overseas trade of Britain (%)

Year	Import	Export	Year	Import	Export
1840–1860	4.5	5.3	1890–1900	2.6	0.7
1860–1870	4.4	4.4	1900–1913	1.5	3.3
1870–1890	2.9	2.1			

Source: Werner Schlote, British Overseas Trade, Oxford (1952).

Table 1.5. Foreign investments made by major countries, 1825–1913

Unit: USD 1 million

Countries	1825	1840	1855	1870	1885	1900	1913
Britain	500	750	2,300	4,900	7,800	12,100	19,500
France	100	300	1,000	2,500	3,300	5,200	8,600
Germany	—	—	—	—	1,900	4,800	6,700
The U.S.	N	N	N	N	N	500	2,500

Note: " — "means estimated figures unavailable; "N" means negligible.

Source: Charles Kindleberger, *Financial History of Western Europe*, Chinese version, Beijing: China Financial Publishing House, 1991, 308.

British pound sterling internationalization reached its development peak against the background of the world gold standard system. At the close of the 18th century, long after silver had stopped circulating in Britain, Britain had adopted the de facto gold standard system. By 1821 Britain achieved a complete legal gold standard system. The gold standard system ensured the stability of the value and enhanced the international credibility of the British pound sterling. Foreign financial institutions and businessmen had confidence in the convertibility of the British pound sterling into gold. The British pound sterling was extremely stable and the possibility of depreciation was never a concern. Compared with gold the British pound sterling was even better in some aspects, for it was more convenient. That was why British importers and exporters who dominated world trade were willing to use it in receipt and making payments. By the end of the 19th century, the transformation to the gold standard system in all countries around the world had been completed. Although the gold standard system existed for a fairly short term as an international monetary system, less than 20 years (or no more than 40 years) from 1897 (or 1880 in some people's opinion) to 1914,[65] the international gold standard system did create important conditions for improving the international status of the British pound sterling. Between 1870 and WWI Britain dominated the world financial system, making the system provide capital for transactions paid in British pound sterling. Britain was leading world trade in a more liberalized direction.[66] When the British pound sterling was widely recognized in the world economy, gold played a subordinate role in settling international debts. Most payments were made either by transferring British pound sterling bills payable, or by trading foreign exchange bills payable, or by transferring credits on bank accounts, although the number of payments made in the latter two ways was not large before 1914. Therefore sterling bills were used to raise money for import and export not only for Britain but also most of the other regions in the world.[67] It made the international gold standard system before WWI a British pound sterling-centered system, under which the British pound sterling and the gold were united as one. Considering the special characteristic of the British pound sterling, the international monetary system during this period may be called the "British pound sterling standard."

The status of London as the world financial center interacted with, before promoting the development of, British pound sterling internationalization. Organized markets for a number of commodities were set up in London as Britain became increasingly important in the world trade. Such markets achieved enormous development thanks to the continuous growth of re-export trade in Britain in the early days, but kept developing under the promotion of free trade. They also stimulated the development of the British shipping industry and enabled insurance businesses, including the risk of carriage, to keep growing. As a result the significance of London as the international commercial and financial center increased rapidly. For example, discount banks, commercial banks, insurance companies and other institutions, and other professional financial agencies that later provided important services for the fast expanding international economy, grew in number. That is why since the early 19th century London surpassed Amsterdam, Hamburg and Paris in terms of its status as the financial center of both Europe and the world.[68] London was the main gold, monetary and financial market in the world during 1870–1913, where foreigners stored a considerable amount of liquid assets (that were convertible into gold), delivering long-term assets to the world. During this period the British pound sterling and short-term credit financing accounted for about 60% of world trade.[69]

Because of the status of Britain as the international trade and payment hub,

London became the center of international liquidation. The trade deficits of Britain with Europe and North America, and its trade surplus with dominions and colonies, facilitated the rise of settlement in British pound sterling, the pattern of which was effectively implemented through the banking system in London. The fat that London became a main insurance, transportation and commodities market was also partly thanks to its central position in the international trade of the British Empire, which not only brought about growing invisible benefits but also promoted the status of the British pound sterling as an important invoice currency and money instrument.[70] Meanwhile Britain issued foreign bonds evaluated in local currency. Such bonds were sold in British pound sterling in London, and since London banks earned commissions by serving as the intermediaries between French debtors and creditors, most of the bonds were bought by French investors. For the French it was a valuable lesson, after which investors and railway borrowers used the French franc directly in trade (Pratt, 1984).

Two conclusions may be drawn from an overall review of British pound sterling internationalization in the 19th century:

First, setting up a monetary system with stable currency value and a developed financial market was the institutional foundation of British pound sterling internationalization. Britain was the first to establish the gold standard system with stable currency value, and relying on the superior status of the Bank of England adopted the rediscount rate policy to regulate short-term capital flows, influence the balance of payments, and achieve sustained convertibility of the British pound sterling. Meanwhile making full use of financial innovation, expanding the capacity and improving the vitality of the domestic financial market made London the world's most developed international financial center in the 19th century. The stable monetary system and developed financial market allowed the British pound sterling to become more flexible in dealing with financial shocks, greatly enhancing the confidence of other trading nations in holding the British pound sterling for the long term and providing an institutional guarantee for the establishment of the British pound sterling-centered international gold standard system.

Second, the industrial and trade advantages of Britain and the Britain-centered network of free trade were the guarantee and the most important driving force for British pound sterling internationalization. The realization of international primacy of the British pound sterling relied mainly on the establishment of the Britain-centered international production system and the Britain-centered network of free trade gradually formed based on this. With a series of major technical breakthroughs in iron and steel, textiles and other industries, Britain gradually forged the spearhead of global industrial production and set up a Britain-centered international production system. The system thus established played a role that cannot be ignored in the process of British pound sterling internationalization. On the one hand, Britain controlled the European market for industrial goods with advanced technologies, and forced other European countries to join the Britain-and France-centered network of free trade after these countries realized industrialization before finally enabling Britain to enter its heyday in 1870; on the other hand, with a gigantic colonial system, Britain governed a number of colonial countries represented by Canada, Australia and New Zealand, and used the opportunity to promote the British pound sterling to a wider region. Meanwhile its consolidated colonial system made each of its colonial countries to side with Britain at times of economic downturn in Britain, and formed unilateral preferential tariff zones in the dominion, ensuring the continued stability of the international status of the British pound sterling. Therefore the formation of the Britain-centered free trade network was crucial for British pound sterling internationalization. It is safe to say that realization of British pound sterling internationalization was actually the reflection of British trade hegemony in the financial field.

Obviously, the British pound sterling pattern is an excellent example for achieving currency internationalization through trade hegemony. However there have been enormous changes in the modern international economic environment. It is difficult for a currency to become a world leading currency by simply relying on its trade advantages. In this regard, Japan was a typical example of failure.

U.S. dollar internationalization that gradually shed reliance on precious metals

As regards the currency internationalization development pattern of national currencies developing into international currencies, the U.S. dollar was more typical than the British pound sterling, and more representative. Even today the U.S. dollar is still the primary and the most widely adopted currency in the world, being widely used in international economic, trade and financial activities. The process of U.S. dollar internationalization may be divided into three stages: the preparation before the Bretton Woods System; the U.S. dollar internationalization during the Bretton Woods System; and the U.S. dollar internationalization after the collapse of the Bretton Woods System.

The preparation before the Bretton Woods System

Prior to the 18th century the U.S. was a British colony. After the American War of Independence it established a federal republic; and after the American Civil War the capitalist industries in the U.S. achieved comprehensive development. The rapid industrialization in the second half of the 19th century helped the U.S. to become the world's largest industrialized country and the No. 1 industrial power in one leap. In such aspects as main industrial indicators and the development of industries of strategic significance over the national economy, the U.S. was far ahead of other developed capitalist countries. The ratio of the U.S. in world industrial production improved rapidly. According to the estimation of German economic historian Jurgen Kuczynsk, the ratio of American industrial production to world industrial production was only 17% in 1860, but was as high as 36% by 1913; the same ratio of Britain over the same period fell from 36% to 14%. The rapid development of modern industries laid a solid foundation for the development of foreign trade by the U.S. From 1860 to 1910, the value of U.S. exports increased from USD333.58 million to USD1,744.98 million. Over the same period, the value of imports by the U.S. increased from USD362.17 million to USD1,556.95 million. In the meantime, the position of the U.S. in world trade improved significantly. In 1870 the U.S. share in world trade was 8% but by 1913 it had increased to 11%, making it the third largest trading nation in the world, second only to Britain and Germany. Against such a background, the U.S. changed the de facto gold standard system into the official gold standard system and eliminated the status of silver as standard currency in 1899, making it part of the gold standard system-based international monetary system. The U.S. dollar as an international currency began to take prominence.[71]

Although during 1860–1913 the U.S. had become the world's greatest industrial power in terms of the most fundamental economic strengths, it lagged behind Britain, France and Germany in developing such strengths and giving play to their role. It was between the two world wars that it managed to transform from the world's greatest industrial power to the world's greatest economic power. During this period it not only further enhanced its leading position in the field of industrial production, but also caught up with or even exceeded Britain and Germany in international trade and the world's financial field, and the U.S. dollar became the most popular currency in international economic exchanges. WWI had immeasurable impact on the U.S. economy, greatly stimulated the demand of domestic and foreign markets for U.S. products, and enabled the U.S. to use its industrial and agricultural capabilities to the utmost. In 1912 the then American President William H. Taft officially proposed "dollar diplomacy" in his State of the Union address i.e. the policy to substitute dollars for bullets, which was a frank wish to expand American businesses. The U.S. government did everything possible to support all legal and efficient enterprises set up by overseas Americans. "Dollar diplomacy" was the U.S. government's effort to pave the way for the U.S. dollar, provide a strong backup for U.S. monopoly organizations to enter Latin America and control the economic development of Latin American countries, and lay a solid foundation for the U.S. to compete for economic and financial supremacy so as to make full preparation for challenging the status of the British pound sterling as the international currency. Meanwhile the outbreak of WWI exposed the political instability in Europe. A great number of holders of idle assets lost confidence in the local economy and shifted their attention to the U.S. instead of injecting capital into their local economy even if the local economy was faced with the urgent need for reconstruction. In this way, badly needed capital and technologies flew into the U.S. and its economy achieved rapid development.

During 1914–1918, U.S. economic strength expanded rapidly. Calculated at current prices, the GNP increased from USD38.6 billion in 1914 to USD84 billion in 1918, more than double. Another influence of WWI on the U.S. economy was that it greatly weakened its potential competitors. Germany was defeated, Austria-Hungary collapsed, and the economic strength of Britain was seriously weakened, leading to major shifts in the world economic powers. Between the two World Wars the U.S. quickly rose up as a great power in international trade. In 1913 the total volume of imports and exports of the U.S. was USD4.28 billion, which soared to USD13.51 billion by 1920. The foreign trade turnover then kept falling to USD9.64 billion in 1929 and USD5.46 billion in 1939 due to the economic crisis in 1921 and the Great Depression during 1929–1933. Despite the fluctuations in foreign trade turnover, the status of the U.S. in world trade increased somewhat. According to the estimation by Rostow, in 1913 the U.S. foreign trade accounted for 12% of world trade, British foreign trade 16%, and German foreign trade 12%; by 1929, the percentage of the U.S. had risen to 14%, that of Britain had fallen to 14%, and that of Germany had fallen to 9%. The U.S. had taken the place of Britain and became the real greatest power in international trade.

The Second World War was a tragic catastrophe for many European and Asian countries, and greatly weakened the national power of these countries. The only victor of the war was the U.S. During WWII it became even stronger and richer, obtained dominance in world politics and economy, and gradually established its status as the world hegemonist. In 1947 the industrial production of the U.S. accounted for 42% of the world total and it contributed 55% of the world's steel and base metals production, 70% of the world's petrol production, and 70% of the world's gold reserves. Its ratio in the world export turnover soared from 14.2% in 1937 to 32.5%. In the capitalist world, the hegemonist was the U.S.[72] The two World Wars not only contributed to the economic hegemony of the U.S. but also laid a solid foundation for U.S. dollar internationalization. In the WWII the U.S. stayed away from the European battlefield and thus was not economically affected by the war. On the contrary, it made a fortune by selling munitions valuing more than USD47 billion to Britain, France and other allies, and took the opportunity to occupy the vast markets of Western European countries and their dependencies. For half a century the U.S. had been showing its heels to European countries economically, while setting up its political and military hegemony, creating a special historical background for the establishment of the Bretton Woods System.

The U.S. dollar internationalization during the Bretton Woods System

By learning from the experience and lessons of the economic chaos during the 1930s, the U.S. realized that to build a new world financial, trade and investment system under its control it must establish the dominance of the U.S. dollar in international economic exchanges and set up a U.S. dollar-led international monetary currency. It would shock the established interests of the British pound sterling. In the struggle for interests between the U.S. dollar and the British pound sterling, the U.S. took the upper hand and the Bretton Woods System was born. In July 1943, the U.S. put forward the "White Plan" on the basis of eliminating foreign exchange control and each country's restrictions over the transfer of international capital. With the purpose of setting up international financial institutions, stabilizing the exchange rate, expanding international trade, and promoting global economic development, it tentatively proposed to link the U.S. dollar with gold through the fund currency unit "Unita" (USD10 equals 1 "Unita" which then equals 137 grains of gold). On 1 July 1944, in the Bretton Woods in New Hampshire in the U.S., delegates from 44 countries attended the United Nations Monetary and Financial Conference (referred to as the Bretton Woods Conference). As mentioned above, the *Agreement of the International Monetary Fund* and the *Agreement of the International Bank for Reconstruction and Development,* jointly known as the *Bretton Woods Agreement,* were executed at the conference, establishing a U.S. dollar-centered international monetary system i.e. the Bretton Woods System.

During 1947–1953, the average annual growth rate of the U.S. GNP was 3.94%, and reached 8.4% during 1950–1951; and the annual growth rate of industrial production was 6.5%, which reached 12.51% during 1950–1951. During this period, in order to reconstruct and recover their respective economies, European countries needed to import enormous amounts of capital goods and raw materials from the U.S.; while the vast number of developing countries, just getting rid of colonialist rule, also needed to import capital goods in order to develop their national economies. Due to the great demand for imports and the increasingly great demand for the U.S. dollar around the world, a "U.S. dollar shortage" appeared around the globe. However with the rapid economic growth of all countries after economic recovery, their exports to the U.S. gradually increased leading to constant deficits of the U.S. in the balance of payments. The balance of the U.S. dollars held by each country increased greatly, changing the "U.S. dollar shortage" in the early days after WWII into a "U.S. dollar glut." According to IMF statistics, during the 1960s, the increase in officially held U.S. dollar reserves grew faster than the total volume of world currency reserves as did the increase in the actual volume of trade. That is, foreign governments were holding excessive the U.S. dollars. The U.S. dollar reserves in the reserves of world countries during 1949–1971 increased by 16 times, while gold reserves increased only a little (See Table 1.6).

In some sense the Bretton Woods System actually recovered the gold-based classical gold standard system, under which the U.S. dollar took the place of the British pound sterling and elbowed the British pound sterling out of the international monetary system in the form of a formal institutional framework. It was a significant difference between U.S. dollar internationalization and British pound sterling internationalization. However the fatal drawback of the Bretton Woods System i.e. the Triffin Dilemma could not be overcome. Under the frequent shocks of the dollar crises during the 1960s, the U.S. stopped its obligation to convert the U.S. dollar into gold in 1971. After that the currencies of other Western countries de-linked from the U.S. dollar, and the Bretton Woods System collapsed.

The U.S. dollar internationalization after the collapse of the Bretton Woods System

Another important difference between U.S. dollar internationalization and British pound sterling internationalization is the emergence of the real U.S. dollar standard after the collapse of the Bretton Woods System. At the time, the international monetary system was in chaos in terms of both the exchange rate system and the standard currency. To solve the problem, the Jamaica System was established. Under the Jamaica System, the floating exchange rate system

Table 1.6. Composition of world currency reserves

Unit: USD1 million

Currency Composition	1949	1969	1970	1971
Gold	33.5	39.1	37.2	39.2
SDRs	—	—	3.1	6.4
Reserves in IMF	1.7	6.7	7.7	6.9
Foreign Exchange Reserves	10.4	32.4	44.5	77.6
U.S. Dollar	3.2	16.0	23.9	50.7
British Pound Sterling	6.9	9.0	6.6	7.9
European Dollar	0.3	7.4	14.0	19.1

Source: IMF, *International Financial Statistics* (1950–1972).

became legal and diversified exchange rate systems were allowed. The exchange rate of the U.S. dollar vis-à-vis other major currencies showed different trends (See Table 1.7).

Although the Bretton Woods System was finally replaced by the Jamaica System featuring floating exchange rates, the inertia effect of the U.S. dollar as the international currency ensured its unshakable status. The U.S. dollar remained the main invoice currency and the medium of exchange, as well as an important means of value storage in the international trade and financial market (See Table 1.8), and maintained its strong international position. As mentioned above, neither the European integration process nor the establishment of Japan as a main economic and financial force put an end to the dominance of the U.S. dollar as an international currency, and the U.S. dollar-led international standard currency pattern—U.S. dollar standard—has been able to continue. So far, in the early 21st century, the U.S. dollar is still the primary reserve currency favored by foreign central banks and governments. The share of the U.S. dollar held by other governments as reserves has risen instead of fallen. The U.S., treasury bonds market is still the most liquid financial market in the world, making holding foreign exchange reserves in U.S. dollar more attractive to the central banks of other countries. The U.S. dollar is still the invoice currency and money instrument leading international trade. Petroleum and other commodities are still priced in the U.S. dollar.[73]

Meanwhile, entering the second half of the 1990s, the U.S. economy gave a very eye-catching performance, achieving low inflation, high growth rate, high employment, rapid rise of labor productivity, and a substantial improvement of its fiscal balance, quickly regaining other countries' dependence on the U.S. dollar. Within the three years 1996–1998 the U.S. economy maintained a supernatural growth momentum, with its physical GDP growth rate exceeding 2.4%, unemployment rate being under 5.5%, the publicly recognized level of unemployment, and the inflation rate falling somewhat.[74]

All in all, during this period the U.S. dollar was no different from other international currencies in nature but through relying on the powerful historical inertia of being an international currency and its powerful economic strength it maintained a relatively high level of internationalization after getting rid of the restraint of precious metals. Therefore the characteristics of the pattern of U.S. dollar internationalization can be generalized as: great economic hegemony laying a solid foundation and the international monetary system providing a consolidated institutional backup for U.S. dollar internationalization; and the historical inertia of international currency enabling the long-term maintenance of U.S. dollar internationalization.

On the whole, U.S. dollar internationalization is a more mature form developed on top of the British pound sterling, as well as a new pattern of currency internationalization after further changes have happened in the international economic and financial environment. By studying the path and influencing factors of U.S. dollar internationalization, we can learn the following.

Firstly, grasping major historical chances is the key to the success of U.S. dollar internationalization. The two World Wars greatly weakened the British Empire and the European power blocs, and helped the U.S. to become the world's most powerful industrialized country in one leap. The prolonged wars greatly shocked the trade and financial foundation within which the British pound sterling system maintained its stability, and created the conditions for the rise of the U.S. dollar. The Bretton Woods System led by the U.S. was a total transformation of the British pound sterling system. Seen from the world economic situation at the time, the U.S. was incapable of maintaining the long-term stability of the Bretton Woods System and so it is safe to draw the conclusion that launching the Bretton Woods System was aimed at breaking the monopoly of the British pound sterling and making the necessary preparations for the new era of the U.S. dollar. In the 1970s the main competitor of the U.S. i.e. the Soviet Bloc collapsed gradually, providing a new chance for the U.S. to break the "Cold War" situation, set up a new U.S.-centered international economic order in an overall manner, and consolidate the status of the U.S. dollar as international trading currency, invoice currency and reserve currency. It is safe

Table 1.7. Exchange rate of the U.S. Dollar to major currencies

Year	Swiss francs	Deutsche Mark	French francs	British pound sterling	Japanese Yen
1973	3.224	2.703	4.708	0.4304	280.0
1974	2.540	2.410	4.445	0.4258	301.0
1975	2.620	2.622	4.486	0.4942	305.2
1976	2.450	2.362	4.970	0.5874	292.8
1977	2.000	2.105	4.705	0.5247	240.0
1978	1.620	1.828	4.180	0.4915	194.6
1979	1.580	1.732	4.020	0.4389	239.7
1980	1.761	1.959	4.516	0.4193	203.0
1981	1.792	2.255	5.748	0.5241	219.9

Source: Zhou Lin and Wen Xiaozheng: *Currency Internationalization*, Shanghai: Shanghai University of Finance and Economics Press, Jan 2001, p. 64.

Table 1.8. Comparison of the status of the U.S. Dollar, the Euro and the Japanese Yen in the international monetary system as of the end of 2001

	U.S. dollar	Euro	Yen
Shares of National Foreign Exchange Reserves (%)			
All Countries	68.3	13.0	4.9
Industrial Countries	74.5	9.7	5.5
Developing Countries	64.1	15.3	4.5
International Monetary Market (USD1 billion)			
Commercial Bills	102.70	80.5	13.50
Other Instruments	59.8	43.6	32.60
Currency Issued	162.50	124.10	46.20
International Bonds Market (USD1 billion)			
Floating-Interest Rate Bonds	906.70	666.50	97.90
Fixed-Interest Rate Bonds	2563.4	1523.80	300.90

Source: IMF Annual Report 2002, BIS *Quarterly Review* (March 2003).

to say that accurately grasping a number of opportunities was crucial for the final establishment of the U.S.-centered brand-new world monetary system that took over from the British pound sterling system.

Secondly, consolidating the U.S.-centered network of free trade through opening the market was an important guarantee for U.S. dollar internationalization. With its technological advantages and the stimulation of the demands of war, the U.S. had become the most powerful industrial producer in one leap at the end of WWII. To promote its core status and consolidate the foundations of the need for U.S. dollar primacy, it actively pushed forward the building of a free trade system after WWII in a comprehensive manner. After the Bretton Woods System collapsed, it vigorously pushed forward U.S.-China economic and trade cooperation, expanded its influence in Asia, and enhanced the role of the U.S. dollar in international trade settlement. The building of the U.S.-centered free trade network after WWII consolidated the advantages of the U.S. in international trade and became an important guarantee for U.S. dollar internationalization.

Thirdly, constructing a U.S.-centered developed international financial market and realizing the financial hegemony of the U.S. is a distinct characteristic of U.S. dollar internationalization. Compared with the British pound sterling, the greatest differene with U.S. dollar internationalization is that it built a U.S.-centered developed international financial market. Based on its trade hegemony, the U.S. gradually built the world's most open and extensive financial market through a series of financial innovations and perfected infrastructures. With the developed financial market, and foreign financial and holding investments, the U.S. obtained the right to form and develop operating rules on the international financial and capital market step by step, built a U.S.-centered developed international monetary market, and finally achieved the upgrade of the U.S. dollar from trade hegemony to financial hegemony.

As can be seen from the major differences between U.S. dollar internationalization and British pound sterling internationalization, at the present stage when the financial sector sees a substantial improvement of its economic status, gaining dominance on the international capital market and markets for various financial products is equivalent to maintaining the U.S. centered international trade system, both being the most important factors for keeping the U.S. dollar hegemony status. It means that it is not easy for other currencies to fight for global hegemony against the U.S. dollar in a short term, and that financial development to a certain extent is an important prerequisite for currency internationalization at the present stage. For RMB internationalization, this is of self-evident significance.

Evolution of "Yen internationalization"

It has been nearly 30 years since Japan proposed "Yen internationalization". But on the whole the results have been unsuccessful since the Japanese Yen has failed to become the real international currency and still exists as a "vassal" to the U.S. dollar. The main reason for the dilemma of "Yen internationalization" is that, under the current "U.S. dollar standard" international monetary system, Japan overlooked the regional economic foundation for a local currency to become an international currency and tried to take a separate road to make its currency directly into an international currency. After the Asian financial crisis, Japan put forward the new "Asianization of the Yen" strategy on the basis of a positive reflection on its "Yen internationalization" strategy, which was undoubtedly a positive factor for economic cooperation, and especially the launch of currency cooperation in East Asia. As a great economic power in East Asia, the implementation of the "Asianization of the Yen" strategy by Japan will have great influence on the construction of a currency system in East Asia and on local economic growth in the future. On the whole, "Yen internationalization" was a "passive" process. In particular, for a fairly long term before the Asian financial crisis, the Japanese government and most Japanese enterprises had a negative attitude toward it. Each measure or progress of "Yen internationalization" was "forced" to a great extent. According to the changes in the attitude of the Japanese government or the Japanese people toward "Yen internationalization," we may divide "Yen internationalization" into three consecutive stages, namely the negative stage, the neutral stage and the positive stage.

The negative stage of "Yen internationalization" — During the late 1960s and the 1970s

"Yen internationalization" was put on the agenda in 1984. Since the Japanese economy entered its "takeoff" stage, especially after Japan became the second greatest economic power in the capitalist world at the turn of the 1960s and the 1970s, its economic strength was increasingly enhanced, and the market demand for the Japanese Yen as an international currency had been growing. It was extremely significant in the collapse of the Bretton Woods System and the outbreak of the oil crisis (after the oil dollar came into being and began to promote European capital market expansion), allowing Japan to establish its solid status in the world economy as a promising developed country, and the Japanese Yen became an international hard currency. At this point, Japan had to pay attention to the international status of the Japanese Yen.

As early as in July 1960, Japan had created the non-resident Yen deposits free settlement system and introduced the so-called Yen foreign exchange system. It was mainly because of the influence of Western European countries' recovery of currency convertibility in December 1958 that the Yen held by non-resident and residents became convertible. According to research done by Japanese scholars, the earliest document that put "Yen internationalization" on the agenda was the report of the "Committee on the International Status of the Yen" put forward by the Japan Economic Research Center, a research organization in the Japanese financial community. The report read, "It is unrealistic for the Yen to be widely used as a reserve currency, like the U.S. dollar and British pound sterling, in other countries, but it enjoys a broad prospect for being extensively used as a settlement currency in trade and capital transactions. So it is necessary to prepare and create an environment for that." (Toru Iwami and Masahiro Kawai, 1990) Influenced by "the Nixon Shock" and the collapse of the Bretton Woods System, Japan was unable to maintain the "1 U.S. dollar to 360 Yen" fixed exchange rate system, and faced waves of market frenzy of selling the U.S. dollar to buy Japanese Yen. On 14 February 1973, Japan began to adopt a complete floating exchange rate system. During the process, measures for Japanese financial market internationalization developed rapidly. In November 1970, Japan allowed the issue of foreign debts priced in Japanese Yen. In September 1972, issuing bonds priced at foreign currencies by non-residents in Japan was also permitted. The former acted as a countermeasure for "Yen internationalization", while the latter mainly aimed at activating U.S. dollar-centered foreign currency trade on the market in Tokyo. In April in the same year, the Tokyo dollar call market was set up. In July 1973, the Japan Economic Research Center proposed in a report entitled *New International Monetary Order and the Yen* to make efforts to promote the internationalization of the Tokyo market and expand the overseas use of Yen. But on the whole, as of the end of the 1970s, within Japanese banks and the Japanese Finance Ministry the opinion that "'Yen internationalization' would disturb the domestic financial policy" was the mainstream voice and so the mainstream attitude toward "Yen internationalization" was obviously negative. In the annual report of the International Finance Bureau of the Japanese Ministry of Finance in 1978, it was pointed out: "In the circumstance of too many Yen bonds being issued in Europe, the foreign exchange market will be negatively influenced, which will further have unpredictable influences on the Japanese economy."

On the other hand, although the financial deregulation measures taken by Japan after the oil crisis were helpful for the use and utilization of Yen by non-residents, real deregulation of foreign exchange management was not realized under U.S. dollar dominance. To promote faster development of the already-launched trade and capital liberalization, financial trade liberalization was essential, making it necessary for Japan to revise its *Foreign Exchange and Foreign Trade Control Law*. In December 1979 Japan reformed its *Foreign Exchange and Foreign Trade Control Law* before beginning to formally implement it in the following December. The new *Foreign Exchange and Foreign Trade Control Law* followed the principle of "liberalization in principle, control on occasions",[75] but in fact financial administration with distinct features of administrative control still played a forceful role in controlling specific applications. "Yen internationalization" during this period had another important feature i.e. the function of the Yen as a settlement currency was strictly separated from its function as a reserve currency. People began to discuss or advocate Yen internationalization as a settlement currency, but avoiding or prohibiting Yen internationalization as a reserve currency. This was related to the instability of Japan's economic status at the time, and reflected the fact that the Japanese policy developers paid greater attention to the negative influences of local currency internationalization on domestic financial policies and the stability of its foreign exchange market. In addition, discussions on "Yen internationalization" in Japan at the time were also aimed at uplifting the national strength and prestige of Japan (Masuda, 1998).

The neutral stage of "Yen internationalization" — From the 1980s to the end of the 1990s

In 1980 the revised *Foreign Exchange and Foreign Trade Control Law* came into effect, liberalizing the foreign exchange trade among financial institutions before increasing the opportunities and possibilities of using the Yen in foreign trade and leading to a substantial rise in the number of transactions priced in Yen in Japanese foreign trade (Kikuchi, 2000). In February 1981 the Japan Economic Research Center released a report entitled *The International Status of the Yen during the 1980s*, proposing policy suggestions on "Yen internationalization." The suggestions principally included: 1) carrying out international coordination of the overall demand and intervention policies of countries possessing reserve currencies; 2) making institutional improvements and adjustments, and working for diversification of assets denominated in Special Drawing Rights (SDR) to promote the role of SDR; 3) developing a short-term government securities market and striving to achieve perfect BA markets denominated in Yen and other domestic financial and capital markets. It indicated that Japan had already realized that underdeveloped BA markets denominated in Yen and other Yen short-term markets were the main barrier for "Yen internationalization." However, although Japan had created conditions for the "Yen internationalization" at institutional levels, "Yen internationalization" in Japan failed to make any practical progress.

Entering the 1970s, trade conflicts between Japan and the U.S. became increasingly intensified as the U.S. government kept requiring Japan to open its market and put more items of Japanese industrial products exported to the U.S. under control. By the early 1980s, the fields of U.S.-Japan conflict or the American requirements on Japan's opening its market extended to the financial and capital trade fields. In November 1983, the U.S.-Japan summit meeting decided to set up a dedicated Yen-U.S. Dollar Committee to resolve the problem. It was, without doubt, an intention of the then U.S. President Ronald Reagan to launch a political offensive for his winning the presidential campaign in the following year and serving another term, but more importantly it was because of the sluggish financial liberalization in Japan and the expansion of the Japan-U.S. trade imbalance. In the U.S. the financial world backed a high value of the U.S. dollar under the conditions of a floating exchange rate, but since the 1980s export enterprises had been opposing the policy to connive at uncontrolled U.S. dollar appreciation. Although the U.S. government required Japan to open its market to solve the problem of the Japan-U.S. trade imbalance during the process, no specific actions regarding the exchange rate were taken. When it came to the summer of 1983, the weakening of U.S. enterprises' competitiveness by the high value of the U.S. dollar began to draw the attention of the U.S. government and the U.S. Congress, making them start thinking about correcting the problem of the foreign exchange rate featuring a high-value U.S. dollar and a low-value Yen. Therefore, after October in the same year, the U.S. government changed its usual practice of allowing the foreign exchange rate to develop in an uncontrolled way and required explicitly that Japan correct and adjust the foreign exchange rate. Faced with the pressure, the Japanese government took integrated economic countermeasures aiming at promoting the international trade in Yen and preparing and creating financial and capital markets at the end of October in the same year. Subsequently Takeshita Noboru, the then Japanese Minister of Finance, and Donald Thomas Regan, the then U.S. Secretary of the Treasury, issued a joint statement, in which it was proposed to set up a Yen-U.S. Dollar Committee in the following year. Until then the Japanese Ministry of Finance had held a "positive, phased, prudent and independent" attitude toward "Yen internationalization" but in fact had been opposing rapid "Yen internationalization" (Kamikawa and Imamatsu, 1997).

In May 1984, both sides released the *Yen–U.S. Dollar Committee Report*, and the Japanese Ministry of Finance released the *Financial Liberalization and "Yen Internationalization" Present and Future*. In March 1985, in response to the above two reports, the private advisory body of the Japanese Financial Minister, the Foreign Exchange etc. Review Conference released the *Reply to* "Yen internationalization" (Reply 1 in short). As shown in Table 1.9, the *Yen-U.S. Dollar Committee Report* covered three main aspects: 1) expansion of the Euro-Yen market; 2) liberalization of the financial and capital markets; 3) entry of foreign financial institutions into the Japanese market. *Financial Liberalization and "Yen Internationalization" Present and Future* put forward some specific measures for financial liberalization, and proposed to shift the focus of "Yen internationalization" from regular trade to capital trade. Specifically, these were about setting up a relatively flexible foreign debts issuing system denominated in Yen, pushing forward the liberalization of Euro-Yen debit and credit, relaxing the control over the issue of non-resident bonds, establishing a Tokyo offshore financial market etc. On the whole, they reflected the will of the U.S. While Reply 1 was composed of three parts: "Fundamental Ideas on the 'Yen internationalization'"; "Liberalization of Euro-Yen Bonds"; "Liberalization of Medium-and Long-term Euro-Yen Loans". In general Reply 1 adopted a more positive attitude toward "Yen internationalization". It clearly defined "Yen internationalization" as intended "to improve the utilization rate and value of the Yen in international trade," and explained the significance of "Yen internationalization". As for strategic steps, it proposed to avoid the adverse influences of "Yen internationalization" on the Japanese financial market, advance the development of the Euro-Yen market which was disconnected with its domestic market, and advocated the gradualism road of "separating the foreign and domestic markets". The Japan Offshore Market (JOM) created in December 1986 was no more than a measure for "separating the foreign market and domestic market" adopted by Japan to keep its domestic financial and capital market from being disturbed and influenced under the pressure of the U.S.

The Yen-U.S. Dollar Committee held six conferences in succession and another four after being renamed the "Japan-America Financial Market Working Team". Subsequently, both sides shifted their attention to the development of and changes in the international financial market based on financial market liberalization. After reaching a series of agreements, bilateral negations were suspended for a while before being resumed in 1993 to discuss market entry and other issues. On the whole, the establishment of the Yen-U.S. Dollar Committee and the agreements reached under it promoted financial and capital market liberalization in Japan and helped to make some achievements on mutual

Table 1.9. Content summary and implementation status in the *Yen-U.S. Dollar Committee Report*

Content Summary	Time of Implementation
A. Expansion of the Euro-Yen market	
1. Issue of non-resident Euro-Yen bonds	
(1) Acknowledgement of foreign private enterprises	December 1984
(2) Relaxation of standards on issuing bonds	April 1985
2. Relaxation of standards on resident Euro-Yen bonds	April 1984
3. Opening of Euro-Yen bonds underwriting business by foreign financial institutions	December 1984
4. Tax collection on the sources of interests on resident Euro-Yen bonds held by non-residents	April 1985 Discontinued
5. Acknowledgement of the issue of Euro-Yen CD	December 1984
6. Euro-Yen loans receivable	June 1983
(3) Non-resident short-term loans receivable-oriented liberalization	June 1984
(4) Resident short-term loans receivable-oriented liberalization	Non-resident-oriented / April 1985
(5) Medium- and long-term loans receivable liberalization	Resident-oriented / July 1989
B. Liberalization of the financial and capital market	
1. Abolition of the upper limit on term deposits	
(1) Down-regulation of CD issuing unit (300 million Yen to 100 million Yen)	
(2) Shortening of the Issue Term of CD (3 months at least to 1 month)	The above three were terminated in April 1985
(3) Acknowledgement of new-type large-sum market interest rate-linked deposits	
(4) Relaxation and abolition of the control over large-sum deposits interests	After October 1984, foreign-funded banks were recognized
(5) Review of the liberalization of the interest on small-sum deposits	
2. Launch of treasury business in foreign-funded banks	June 1985
3. Creation of BA market denominated in Yen	June 1984
4. Abolition of the control over foreign currencies' convertibility into Yen	July 1984
5. More flexible rules on the issue and operation of foreign debts denominated in Yen	April 1984
6. Abolition of the control over foreign loans receivable denominated in Yen	
C. Foreign financial institutions' participation in the Japanese market	
1. Participation in the trust business	Realized in 1985 (participation of 9 institutions had been recognized by June 1985)
2. Opening of Tokyo Stock Exchange membership	Institutional reform-inclusive review (opened to 6 foreign securities companies in December 1985)

Source: Takao Kamikawa and Imamatsu Eietsu, *Political Economy of the Japanese Yen — Asian and the World System*, School of Combined Learning, 1997, Japanese version, p. 192.

market entry. However, as stated above, "Yen internationalization" failed to make real progress. (See Table 1.10 and Table 1.11 for details). During the 1990s barely any progress was made in Yen internationalization, and its utilization in foreign trade decreased.

"Yen internationalization" during this period proceeded under U.S. pressure. Japan took a relatively positive stand comparing with that in the previous period. But on the whole Japan was neutral, as seen from the results — no significant progress was made in "Yen internationalization." Characteristics of the "Yen internationalization" strategy of the Japanese government over this period may be reduced to the following two aspects:

Firstly, the pursuit of pro forma "Yen internationalization." For a long time "Yen internationalization" had been developing under two pressures: the pressure from the U.S. government requiring Japan to open its market; and market pressure i.e. the pressure of Yen appreciation. Under the combined influence of these two pressures, the promotion of "Yen internationalization" by the Japanese financial authority was a typical passive process, making it only exist in form. Faced with too much pressure from the U.S. the Japanese financial authority paid too much attention to protecting its domestic financial and capital market from external influences and did everything on the premise of not damaging or affecting its domestic financial and taxation order. The attitude and intention of the U.S. also influenced it considerably. Although the U.S. required "Yen internationalization," it was aimed at forcing Japan to open the Tokyo financial market and enhancing the participation of American financial institutions there. Thus the U.S. needed Japan to "negatively" push forward the process of "Yen internationalization." In this regard, both sides held surprisingly consistent viewpoints (Kikuchi, 2000). Meanwhile, faced with the pressure of Yen appreciation, the Japanese government had been adopting such means as expanding imports and increasing domestic demand, but failed to make efforts to reform its financial system. For example, in early 1995, the exchange rate of the Yen rose rapidly to USD1 to 80 Yen. In April the Japanese Cabinet meeting on economic policies issued the *Emergent Economic Countermeasures for Yen Appreciation*, focusing on improving the participation of Chinese enterprises and other foreign enterprises in the construction of its international airports, expanding economic development, attracting more investments in Japan, dealing with non-performing loans of financial institutions etc. Although it mentioned the slogan of "Yen internationalization" it stayed at pushing forward trade denominated in Yen and enhancing its liaison with the monetary authorities in European countries.

Secondly, the development of "Yen internationalization" starting with the liberalization of Euro-Yen trade led to the separation of "Yen internationalization" domestically and internationally. The Japanese financial authority did this with two purposes: 1) preventing "Yen internationalization" from influencing its domestic financial system; 2) becoming active instead of passive so as to control the development of the Euro-Yen bonds market in Japan. However, correspondingly, it led to two consequences: 1) reform or liberalization of the domestic financial market was slowed down artificially, and

Table 1.10. Currency categories in Japan's foreign trade (%)

	1987	1990	1995	The 1st half of 2001
Export				
U.S. dollar	55.2	48.8	51.5	53.0
Japanese Yen	33.4	37.5	37.6	34.2
Others	11.4	13.7	10.9	12.8
Import				
U.S. dollar	81.7	75.5	68.9	70.4
Japanese Yen	10.6	14.6	24.3	23.2
Others	7.6	9.9	6.8	6.4

Source: Bank of Japan. Quoted from Okuda Kitamura, The U.S. Dollar System and Euro and Japanese Yen, Japanese Economic Review Agency, 2002, 324.

Table 1.11. Euro-Yen loans, Euro-Yen debts and Foreign debts denominated in Yen

	1987	1990	1995	1997
Euro-Yen Loans [1]				
Non-residents	32,530	31,210	22,250	24,340
Residents	51,800	228,640	345,800	336,290
Euro-Yen Debts [2]	1,405	1,819	3,713	7,351
U.S. dollar	581	700	1,444	3,617
Yen	226	293	645	284
Mark	150	164	727	1,302
Foreign Debts Denominated in Yen ①	4,975	5,750	9,765	7,202

Notes: 1. Unit: 100 million Yen; 2. Unit: USD100 million

Source: Bank of Japan. Quoted from Okuda Kitamura, "The U.S. Dollar System and Euro and Japanese Yen", *Japanese Economic Review*, 2002, p.324.

opening the market failed to induce reforms; and 2) the Euro-Yen bonds market failed to expand smoothly to improve "Yen internationalization."

The positive stage of "Yen internationalization"— Since the 1990s

After the outbreak of the Asian financial crisis, especially after the emergence of the euro, the strategy of "Yen internationalization" adopted by Japan changed greatly. This is mainly reflected in: 1) "Yen internationalization" has become a regional instead of a functional strategy. The strategy of "Yen internationalization" and relevant measures used to start with "Japan to the world" and was aimed at making the Yen an international currency so as to denominate transactions and capital trade in Yen and making the Yen the reserve currency by foreign central banks. Now "Yen internationalization" is a regional instead of a functional strategy i.e. "Yen internationalization" focuses on the use of the Yen and the expansion of the functions of the Yen as an international currency in Asia (Guan Zhixiong, 2003). 2) Specific measures of "Yen internationalization" pay more attention to perfecting the domestic financial and capital markets, and making up or correcting financial reform which had been inconsistent domestically and internationally.

The strategy of "Yen internationalization" becoming regional more than functional marks the formation of the strategy of "Yen Asianization". That is, the past experience of "Yen internationalization" and the practices of European countries indicated that it was extremely difficult or infeasible for the Yen to become an international currency separately and directly under the current "U.S. dollar system," making the process of developing the Yen into a region-based international currency i.e. realizing Yen internationalization through Yen Asianization, a feasible method. In other words, to become an international currency the Yen must shed its dependence on the U.S. dollar. Substantial fluctuations in the exchange rate of the Yen are unavoidable it fails to develop independently, to achieve which the road of Yen regionalization must be taken and Japan must first get the agreement of Asian countries on the status of the Yen as a "region-based international currency" (Kikuchi, 2000). As regards "Yen Asianization," relevant Japanese government departments and scholars have put forward many plans and ideas which may be divided into two categories: 1) promoting the status of the Yen through the common-pegged currency basket system; 2) enhancing the role of the Yen by constructing a regional currency system.

However, on the whole, no desired effects have been made in this "positive stage." According to the studies done by domestic and foreign scholars the causes include:

Firstly, the development of economic and trade relations in East Asia since the 1990s has failed to support the conclusion that "expansion of trade between Japan and East Asia will lead to an increase in the regional trade denominated in Yen" (Kamikawa and Imamatsu, 1997), and the deepening of the economic dependence between Japan and East Asia has failed to contribute to the progress of "Yen internationalization."

Secondly, the establishment of the Tokyo Financial Center has failed to contribute to Yen internationalization, but has served as a medium of exchange denominated in the U.S. dollar, playing the part of supplementing and supporting the status of the U.S. dollar.

Thirdly, the current international monetary system still adopts the "U.S. dollar standard". Due to the failure to "internationalize the Yen", the basic international monetary pattern has been transformed from the "flying-geese model" featured by a leading U.S. dollar escorted by the Deutschmark and Yen in the mid-1980s to that featured by the two poles of the U.S. dollar and the euro (Deutschmark) and the subordination of the Yen to the U.S. dollar since the mid-1990s. Even in East Asia where the status and role of the Yen have made some "progress," the level and degree of "internationalization" of the Yen are very low. East Asia is still a "U.S. dollar zone," where the Yen partially plays the role as a reserve currency among the functions of the U.S. dollar.

Fourthly, under the conditions of the current "U.S. dollar system" or "U.S. dollar hegemony," "trading nations" will inevitably face, in their emergence and development, the pressure of exchange rate appreciation and the exchange rate will of course be adjusted along with the pressure. During this process "trading nations" have to take measures to protect the autonomy of their national monetary policies and should never let their own monetary policies become subordinate to the policy objectives or exchange rate policies of "financial nations." Therefore, while positively relaxing capital control and launching domestic financial reforms, it is a rational choice to reduce the shock and influence of speculative capital through regional monetary cooperation i.e. achieving the functional objectives of currency internationalization through a region-based currency internationalization strategy.

Regional-based currency internationalization

The second mode of currency internationalization may be called currency regionalization featuring the replacement of a national currency by a regional currency, currency regionalization through currency cooperation, and currency internationalization through currency regionalization. There are principally two paths of currency regionalization: monetary union and currency substitution, which can be simplified as "euroization" and "dollarization." "Euroization" refers to the process whereby regional member states, after long-term exchange rate stability and coordination, abandon their respective monetary sovereignty through assimilation of economic indicators and policies before jointly creating and using a new currency and taking the euro in reality as a symbol. It is a development pattern of equal and agreement-like monetary union. "Dollarization" refers to the process whereby the general public in some Latin American countries choose to use the U.S. dollar instead of local currencies in economic trade, or when such countries cancel local currencies by legislation before using the U.S. dollar directly in trade due to the bad reputation of their own currencies or the government's failure to maintain the value of the local currency. It is a pattern of involuntary "monetary unification".[76] As far as dollarization is concerned, although it brings about benefits, it also brings high costs. Therefore some economists believe that dollarization should never be taken as a regular method in resisting monetary and financial crises.[77] Dollarization has to be the last measure to take in emergencies. So far only Panama, Ecuador and other small countries are implementing dollarization. Therefore, in terms of the patterns of currency regionalization, dollarization is not highly representative while euroization is of more typical significance.

For a long time European finance spearheaded world finance and served as a standard paradigm for world finance. In the millennium-long evolution of the financial system, from money changers to modern commercial banks, from the first stock exchange to modern capital markets, from merchant adventurers' marine insurance to the modern insurance system, from public banks, the Bank of England to modern central banks, from Florence, Amsterdam to London and New York, from currency war to monetary union, Europe spearheaded the world in most cases and guided other countries' financial direction. The European financial system is still the paradigm of the world financial system.[78] The launch of the euro at the end of the 1990s was a great innovation in international currencies, changing the long history of a single currency issued by a single country serving as the international currency, and starting the unification of international currency regionalization.[79] In some sense the euro pattern is the leading paradigm of today's currency internationalization provided by European finance to world finance.

Regional economic integration within the European Union is the result of intentional government policy promotion. The birth of the euro is the result of coordination and cooperation among all EU members. After about half a century it has now formed a unique pattern of currency internationalization. Internationalization of the euro has gone through four main stages.[80]

The first stage was about foreshadowing and putting forward suggestions. On 1 September 1950, 16 European countries set up the European Payments Union for mutual currency settlement and free currency convertibility. As the European economy became more and more integrated, they became more and more eager for a common exchange rate mechanism and currency integration. At the Hague European Summit held in December 1969 it was proposed the European Monetary Union be set up i.e. the *Warner Plan*, so as to achieve monetary unification in three stages starting with stabilizing the exchange rate. Due to the oil crisis and the serious economic crisis which broke out during the 1970s the Warner monetary union plan failed, but it laid a theoretical foundation for the subsequent establishment of the European monetary system.

The second stage was about making legal and institutional preparations. After the economic crisis, the plan to set up the European Monetary Union was put on the agenda for the second time. At the Hague European Summit held in April 1978, the French and German prime ministers proposed to set up an European Monetary System. An agreement was reached by the European Community at Brussels in December in the same year and it was decided to formally build the European Monetary System with 17 member states including the Federal Republic of Germany, France, Italy, the Netherlands, Belgium, Luxembourg, Denmark and Ireland (Britain, Spain and Portugal joined the European Monetary System later). After its establishment, the European Monetary System stabilized the exchange rate within the European Community to some extent, and enabled all member states to reduce the shocks to their financial systems due to the U.S. dollar crisis induced by the macroeconomic disorder in the U.S..

The third stage was the primary stage of euro integration. In June 1988, the then Chairman of the EC Commission Delors submitted to the ministers of finance of the 12 EC member states a report entitled *EC Economic and Monetary Union*, proposing such important concepts as free currency convertibility, free capital flow, financial integration and fixed member state exchange rate etc. In 1991, the 12 EC member states reached an agreement on setting up the European economic and monetary union i.e. the *Maastricht Treaty*, providing that the European Central Bank would be established no later than January 1997 and that euro would be formally launched on 1 January 1999. In June 1997 the 15 European Union member states passed the *Treaty of Amsterdam*, deciding to officially launch the agenda arrangements on the euro in a phased way. The European Monetary Union was also launched on time.

The fourth stage involves the substantial progress made towards euro internationalization. On 1 January 2002 the euro became a tangible currency and quickly took the place of the 12 currencies in circulation before becoming the sole legal currency in this region. With a legal identity, euro then became an international currency.

The emergence of the euro was an event of great historical significance in international finance in the 20th century. The euro, the product of regional monetary integration based on European economic and trade integration, has succeeded in integrating national currencies into a single currency. Since a single currency solves the problem of monetary differences in all euro countries, the problem of currency internationalization has disappeared in the euro countries. However, around the globe, the euro is still a secondary international currency weaker than the U.S. dollar and it cannot match the U.S. dollar in terms of playing a role as an international currency. The euro still has a long way to go to catch up with and surpass the U.S. dollar and to move from currency regionalization to the high-level road of monetary internationalization.

Seen from the status quo of euro internationalization, on the one hand the status of the euro as a reserve currency has improved step by step. By 2006 the share of the euro in international official foreign exchange reserves had reached 25.8%, far higher than that of the British pound sterling (4.4%) and the Yen (3.2%). As the euro appreciates gradually, many central banks have begun to replace U.S. dollar reserves with the euro, contributing to the rise of the status of the euro as a reserve currency. However it has to be noted that the main emerging economies hold an enormous amount of foreign exchange reserves in the U.S. dollar and have bought enormous amounts of U.S. treasury bonds in order to maintain the relative stability of the value of the U.S. dollar. Therefore it is very unlikely that the status of the euro as a reserve currency will improve substantially, or surpass the U.S. dollar.

Moreover the role of the euro as a trading currency is very limited. Seen from the conclusion of business on the foreign exchange market in recent several years, the euro has maintained its position as the second largest trading currency but yet has maintained its trade share at about 37%, registering a great gap with the U.S. dollar. Although showing a slowly declining trend, the U.S. dollar has maintained its absolute primacy. In 2007 the share of the U.S. dollar in trade on the foreign exchange market still hit 86.3%. Seen from the monetary objects in foreign exchange trade, the main trading partner of the euro remains the U.S. dollar. In 2007, the total volume of trade between the U.S. dollar and the euro reached USD840 billion, accounting for 74% of the total volume of trade in the euro, while that of trade between the euro and the British pound sterling and the Yen was USD70 billion and USD64 billion respectively, accounting for only 18% of the total volume of trade between the U.S. dollar and the British pound sterling and the Yen. In addition, in the trade with other non-major currencies, the U.S. dollar held an absolute primacy. Therefore, from the angle of serving as a trading currency, the euro has limited internationalization and is greatly dependent on the U.S. dollar.

In spite of the slow progress of euro internationalization, and many controversies over the development prospects of the euro and currency regionalization, it has to be admitted that the euro pattern provides a new choice of path for currency internationalization. Countries in the euro zone share the fruits of currency internationalization thanks to monetary unification. In particular, some of them used to have low levels of currency internationalization but now possess a higher-level, region-based international currency and have achieved local currency internationalization smoothly, although they lost their independent national currencies. Those of them which had seen some development of local currency internationalization have been able to increase their monetary strength and achieve higher-level currency internationalization. Of course, this pattern of achieving and expanding currency internationalization through regional currency integration needs to be tested by practice and time.

Summary

Theories are abstract and popular, while history is referential. Discussions from these two aspects will provide complete ideas on RMB regionalization and internationalization.

Theoretically, internationalization of a country's currency is a process that synthesizes all elements and factors, such as the country's economic scale, trade status and pattern, product mix and regional structure, financial market maturity and openness, currency convertibility and credibility, and the costs of trade, historical inertia, even its political influence. All these will greatly influence its currency internationalization or regionalization. On the other hand, not all of the above-mentioned factors are necessary conditions for currency internationalization, making it necessary to seek theoretical support for RMB internationalization and regionalization from a multiple of angles. Based on the reality of China, RMB regionalization has to be accompanied by closer trade connections with neighboring countries, reducing the costs of RMB payments or trade, ensuring the stable and rapid development of the Chinese economy, and cultivating a greater sense of political responsibility before making efforts accordingly.

From historical experience, the internationalization paths of the U.S. dollar,

Yen and euro, and their inspiration for RMB internationalization, may be reduced to the following several points.

The path of U.S. dollar internationalization may be generalized as: becoming the sole international invoice currency and the equivalent international reserve currency as gold through global institutional arrangements on the monetary exchange rate; having a dominant position in the world credit monetary system relying on the preset advantage of U.S. dollar stock after de-linking with gold and losing its institutional foundation; and consolidating and developing such an advantage with the powerful global political and economic strength of the U.S. to keep the U.S. dollar serving as the "bellwether" of international currencies. The pattern of U.S. dollar internationalization is special due to specific historical conditions. It was the transitional link from the world metal standard system to the modern credit currency system. History chose the U.S. dollar before endowing it with a boom period that lasted for nearly 30 years as well as with many "inherent" advantages, keeping all other currencies too far behind to catch up. The two World Wars in the first half of the 20th century helped the U.S. realize its dream of surpassing Britain, while also laying political and economic foundations for U.S. dollar internationalization. Today it is hardly possible for other currencies to achieve internationalization through international institutional arrangements. Even so, the U.S. dollar internationalization has given us some inspiration i.e. a constant increase in economic strength is a very important factor for a currency to develop into an international currency.

The experience and lesson of "Yen internationalization" tells us that currency internationalization is closely related to a country's economic strength, and its capital account liberalization, but what is more important is the perfection of its financial system and the efforts made by more than one country. Due to the fact that the Japanese financial system was far from able to meet the requirements of local currency internationalization and adopted the impractical "Yen internationalization" principle, Japan introduced financial bubble inflation and economic recession.

In addition, there are two reasons for the failure of "Yen internationalization." Firstly, the Japanese financial system was by nature a "U.S. dollar dependence" system. That is, due to U.S. dollar primacy and the dependence of Japan on the American commodities market, Japan had to accumulate enormous amounts of foreign exchange reserves in the U.S. dollar. Although it became a main creditor nation, its capital exports had to be settled mainly in the U.S. dollar. More importantly, a specific capital cycle came into being between Japan and the U.S. as did a "passive and active" relationship between the Yen and the

U.S. dollar. To some extent the Yen became a tool to help the U.S. carry out its international economic or financial policies, being dominated or influenced by the U.S. dollar and losing its independence. Secondly, in such circumstances, the Japanese government made two mistakes over "Yen internationalization": 1) the strategy of "Yen internationalization" was carried out "internationally" instead of "domestically." That is, Japan paid attention to the development and construction of the Euro-Yen market and the Tokyo Offshore Financial Market, but ignored or failed to fully reform its domestic financial and capital markets due to interference by domestic vested interest groups; 2) it overlooked the regional economic and financial environment that could promote Yen stability, and advanced Yen internationalization while paying little attention to or being unable to conduct regional monetary cooperation (Tetsuji Murase, 2000).

The failure of "Yen internationalization" shows that, under the current international monetary system featuring the "U.S. dollar system," achieving currency internationalization does not totally depend on the efforts of one country. Attention must be paid to the regional economic foundation for a currency to become an international currency, and it must be based on regional economic development and cooperation before gradually achieving currency internationalization through currency regionalization.

The birth of the euro has provided not only empirical support for the OCA theory but also an empirical pattern for the internationalization of a non-hegemony currency, namely that in the current international monetary system led by U.S. dollar hegemony "the logic of collective action" is a rational choice for a local currency to become an international currency. It was difficult for a single currency in European countries to shake off the global hegemony of the U.S. dollar, but as a whole and through regional cooperation it could greatly reduce the cost of challenging the hegemonic currency and becoming an international currency. Therefore EU members took the initiative to transfer their currency sovereignty and abandon independent currencies before making a certain political compromise to form a regional union and demonstrate the OCA theory. Countries in the euro zone share the fruits of currency internationalization thanks to monetary unification. In particular, some of them used to have low levels of currency internationalization but now possess a higher-level, region-based international currency and have achieved local currency internationalization smoothly, even though they have lost their independent national currencies. Those of them which had seen some development of local currency internationalization were able to increase their monetary strength and achieve higher-level currency internationalization.

The emergence of the euro zone benefited from the similar historical and cultural backgrounds and more or less the same level of economic development of European countries, to a great extent enabling such countries to think beyond the national concept on currency sovereignty. Given the enormous economic differences and political barriers among countries and regions in East Asia, currency cooperation in East Asia cannot completely follow the path of euro internationalization, but it can at least get some helpful inspiration from it. The birth of the euro was based on currency regionalization, not promoted by the direct currency internationalization of any country. It was with the in-depth development of regional economic cooperation that European countries achieved regional monetary integration before realizing currency internationalization.

Meanwhile it is worth mentioning that achieving currency internationalization in Europe among its member states through regional monetary integration was conditional. Establishment of the euro zone was based on common political and economic interests, and bonded with similar cultural backgrounds. Comparatively speaking, each and all member states were very close to the construction conditions of the OCA theory, and there was a core currency among regional currencies to play a leading role. Considering the enormous economic differences and political barriers in East Asian countries, monetary cooperation and RMB internationalization in East Asia cannot totally copy the path of euro internationalization.

On the whole, if we make a general survey of the rise and fall of countries with economic hegemony in global economic history, it is easy to see that the replacement of the old hegemony by the new one was achieved not by the new one fighting against the old one but by the new one cooperating with the old one.[81] Therefore in current international financial affairs, in the internationalization process of emerging national currencies, it is very difficult and costly to challenge or dispel the dominant hegemonic currency. In other words, an attempt by a country to challenge the international hegemonic currency through "direct internationalization" instead of regional monetary and financial cooperation is very unlikely to succeed. The birth of the euro and the failure of Yen internationalization are two typical examples in this regard.

On the other hand, in the current international monetary system, regional factors have become important conditions that restrain a local currency from becoming an international currency, and currency regionalization is an important step towards currency internationalization. Although the RMB has its own characteristics, some important factors cannot be ignored in the process of any currency internationalization or regionalization. Therefore successful experience has to be learned from the British pound sterling and the U.S. dollar in the process of RMB internationalization so as to enhance the economic and trade strength of the RMB, and U.S. dollar regionalization and the birth of the euro have provided a valuable reference for RMB regionalization. From the zigzag of "Yen internationalization" we can also see that apart from the country's own efforts in its currency internationalization and regionalization, "external factors" should not be ignored. Therefore it is essential to firstly rely on currency regionalization before gradually achieving currency internationalization.

2

Chapter

The Regionalization of the RMB

The analysis of experience in currency internationalization made in Chapter 1 shows that currency regionalization is an important step towards currency internationalization under certain conditions, or that currency regionalization is a practical choice for currency internationalization under certain circumstances. In this chapter we will further analyze, on the basis of the domestic conditions and external environment faced by China, the necessity of RMB regionalization, and demonstrate that RMB regionalization is the only way to RMB internationalization.

Launch of the Issue of RMB Internationalization

Since the 1980s, with financial globalization and the development of global liberalization, the flow of private capital has accelerated in both scale and speed. The monetary and financial crises that have thus arisen have continued to shock the existing international monetary system, forcing many countries and regions to try to find a new pattern to stabilize and control regional economy and finance. On the one hand, it has led to changes in the international financial architecture; on the other, it has influenced the current process of currency internationalization of some countries and regions. The birth of the euro and the "dollarization" in some Latin American countries serve as the best demonstrations.

Over this period, Chinese scholars began to study RMB internationalization[1] (Zeng Xianjiu et al., 1989). Early studies on RMB internationalization were basically about how to achieve free convertibility of the RMB (Zhang Yiwei, 1994). Before the Asian financial crisis, preliminary progress had been made in studies on RMB internationalization. Theorists began to discuss the necessity and possibility of RMB internationalization based on the conditions and rules of currency internationalization and then analyzed the economic effects of RMB internationalization i.e. the benefits and costs of RMB internationalization, while briefly putting forward the development stages of and strategic ideas on RMB internationalization (Jiang Boke, 1994; Zheng Muqing, 1995a, 1995b; Hu Dinghe, Cheng Haiyong, 1996; Ke Meishui, 1996; Wang Zhengbao, 1996). The outbreak of the Asian financial crisis attracted people's attention to the issue of exchange rate arrangements in East Asia. The birth of the euro made people consider international monetary cooperation and regional monetary integration. In particular, in the circumstance of Japan's reconsideration of its "Yen internationalization" strategy and the RMB winning a good international reputation in the financial crisis, the issue of RMB internationalization became more of a focus of study among Chinese and foreign scholars. Entering the 21st century, due to the expansion of circulation of the RMB in neighboring countries and regions, the progress of China's accession to the WTO and the launch of the China-ASEAN Free Trade Area, theorists have paid great attention to RMB internationalization and have actively explored the feasibility and path of RMB internationalization. Generally, Chinese scholars' studies on RMB internationalization since the Asian financial crisis may be summed up in the following several aspects.

RMB capital account convertibility and its relationship with RMB internationalization

Many Chinese scholars and economists believe that capital account convertibility is the foundation of and an indispensable condition for currency internationalization (Dong Mu, 2001; Jing Xuecheng, 2002; Wang Yubao, 2003). For example, Jing Xuecheng holds that "RMB internationalization is a long process, which has to be discussed after achieving capital account opening." Cao Yong (2005) points out that although technically speaking free currency convertibility and internationalization have different connotations and denotations, a RMB that is not completely convertible will only be an international currency with incomplete functions and the scope of RMB circulation will also be greatly limited.

But there are scholars who hold opposite opinions. Zhao Haikuan (2003) holds that although a mature international currency is convertible, complete currency convertibility may not be necessary in the initial stage of currency internationalization. Ding Jianping et al. (2006) point out that when studying the functions of the RMB as a regional international settlement currency, there is no need to take full convertibility as a prerequisite for the initial step of RMB internationalization and that the factor of the increasingly expanding Chinese market is greater than the restraint of insufficient convertibility.

There are also scholars who point out that RMB internationalization is an important condition for achieving capital account convertibility. By studying the differences between non-international currency convertibility process and international currency convertibility process, Li Yao (2003) disproves that RMB internationalization is an important restraining condition that affects RMB capital account convertibility. Zhao Qingming (2005) believes that there is no successive relationship between capital account convertibility and currency internationalization, but there is a mutually-influential relationship. He treats and studies RMB internationalization as a condition for smoothly realizing capital account convertibility.

On the necessity, status quo and feasibility of RMB internationalization

The necessity of RMB internationalization

As early as in 1994, Jiang Boke estimated the enormous potential benefits of RMB internationalization based on the barter for physical resources with the RMB. Subsequently, scholars explained the necessity of RMB internationalization from the angle of the benefits of currency internationalization (Zheng Muqing, 1995a, 1995b; Jiang Ling, 1997). Chen Yulu et al. (2005) make a rough estimation of the possible economic benefits of RMB internationalization, and stress that the benefits of RMB internationalization are enormous and unstoppable. Liu Aiwen (2005) analyzes the necessity of RMB internationalization from five aspects, namely that RMB internationalization is helpful for improving China's international influence and discourse power over currency; RMB internationalization is helpful for avoiding the risks of currency and maturity mismatches; RMB internationalization is helpful for increasing seigniorage; RMB internationalization is helpful for deepening the financial system reform in China; and RMB internationalization is helpful for enhancing China's autonomy in currency policies.

Meanwhile, many scholars have analyzed the necessity of RMB internationalization from the angle of the existing international environment and China's development strategy in the future. Liu Qun (2006) holds that, as China's overall economic strength is increasingly enhanced and the RMB becomes more and more active in international political activities, then it is inevitable that the RMB will become an international currency. He also points out that the RMB's serving as a world currency is an allocation of resources around the world which is beneficial to China. Li Xiao and Ding Yibing (2006) point out that, under the current "U.S. dollar system," China is faced with the same dilemma of any "trading nation". Moreover the Chinese economy is becoming more and more internationalized and is growing far ahead of its currency, being currently a non-international currency. Therefore China needs to go further to achieve its currency internationalization through RMB Asianization. Zhang Qunfa (2008) believes that, based on U.S. dollar hegemony and the challenges of the EU and Japan to U.S. dollar hegemony, RMB internationalization is an inevitable choice if China wants to maintain its economic security and especially to resolve the "conflicted virtue"[2] in its rapid development.

The status quo of RMB internationalization

Some Chinese scholars hold a very positive attitude toward the status quo of RMB internationalization. Lin Xingguang (2002) concludes that, from the PPP-backed RMB appreciation pressure, the RMB has become a strong currency and even a quasi-international reserve currency in Asia. Sun Jie holds that the RMB is yet to be internationalized, but there are signs of such a trend, and that the strong position of the RMB becoming an international currency has already presented. More scholars believe that neighboring countries and regions have had a certain degree of international acceptability which objectively creates a favorable condition for RMB internationalization, but it is still a long way to go to finally achieve RMB internationalization. Li Huamin (2003) points out that the overseas circulation of the RMB indicates that RMB internationalization is still in the initial stage. Kan Jingyang (2006) holds that the RMB has been widely accepted by neighboring countries, and has become a regional hard currency, yet given China's capital control and other factors it is not yet the time for RMB internationalization; and that currently China has to set its monetary strategy as achieving the status of the RMB as a region-based international currency. Li Xiao and Ding Yibing (2006) hold that the circulation of the RMB in neighboring countries and regions of China is a spontaneous market phenomenon, not the result of institutional regional monetary and financial cooperation, so it is not yet the time to say that RMB Asianization has been achieved. Zhong Wei (2008) points out that the extensive circulation of the RMB in Southeast Asia is the primary stage of RMB internationalization, which will provide convenience for neighboring economies in using the RMB in trade, valuation, settlement and storage of reserves, and lay a foundation for RMB internationalization in the future.

On the basis of comprehensive judgments of the status quo of RMB internationalization, relevant scholars have studied and estimated the overseas circulation of RMB. Wang Yafan (2002) analyzes the status quo, causes and management methods of the use and circulation of the RMB in China's neighboring countries and regions. Ma Ronghua and Rao Xiaohui (2007) have estimated the annual overseas demand for RMB during 1997–2005 to find that it increased from about RMB1.9 billion in 1997 to about RMB31.1 billion in 2005. Dong Jihua (2008) updates the research method of Ma Ronghua and Rao Xiaohui before estimating the quarterly amount of RMB held abroad during 1999-2005 to find that since 1999, more and more RMB had been held abroad, increasing from over RMB8 billion to over RMB25 billion in 2005 and even reaching RMB106 billion in 2003. Zhong Wei (2008) systematically has analyzed the amount of RMB in circulation and that in storage in neighboring countries, thinking that the steady appreciation of the RMB against the U.S. dollar is a strategic opportunity for advancing RMB internationalization and that measures to making the utilization of the RMB more convenient in neighboring countries have to be launched to steadily promote the expansion of overseas RMB storage.

The feasibility of RMB internationalization

It is generally believed in Chinese academic circles that China possesses some basic conditions for achieving RMB internationalization. Zhao Haikuan (2004) points out that the RMB has now become competent to serve as an international currency and that it has to be pushed forward before developing into one of the international currencies, or at least into being capable of playing part of the role of an international currency. By comparing the reality of China today and that of Germany and Japan during the 1980s, Zha Yonggui (2005) points out that China possesses the initial conditions for RMB internationalization but that there exist great gaps compared with the conditions in Germany and Japan at that time. After analyzing China's economic strength, foreign exchange reserves, macroeconomic conditions, financial and foreign exchange reforms and exchange rate stability, Hu Zaiyong (2004) holds that China possesses certain conditions for RMB internationalization. Liu Aiwen (2005) analyzes the practical possibility of RMB internationalization from such aspects as currency value stability, economic strength, regular account convertibility and the development of the financial market. Wang Sicheng (2008) believes that, with the constant economic development and increasingly growing international status of China, the stable advance of RMB internationalization has become a sure trend and analyzes the driving forces for RMB internationalization from three aspects i.e. the increasing economic strength of China, the rapid increase of the amount of RMB in circulation in neighboring countries and regions of China, and China's adjustment of its foreign economic development strategy.

Meanwhile scholars think that even though RMB internationalization is the general trend it cannot be rushed, and that the conditions for RMB internationalization have to be created by advancing RMB reform, enhancing monetary integration and circulation, and participating in regional monetary cooperation among other measures.

Whether a local currency can become an international currency does not depend on the subjective wishes of the home country but is determined by the country's economic strength and its influence in international trade, investment and finance (Pan Liquan, 2000). Cheng Enfu et al. (2003) point out that the reform and opening up in China has laid a solid practical foundation for RMB internationalization, and that the necessary conditions for advancing RMB internationalization must be created with such measures as consolidating the microeconomic foundation and establishing non-symmetry interest rate marketization and an open financial monitoring system. Cai Yiping (2005) makes some policy suggestions on RMB internationalization in a targeted way on the basis of the three major conditions for currency internationalization i.e. the "currency value stability" standard, the "reasonable exchange rate system" standard and the "complete convertibility" standard. He Juan (2005) analyzes the conditions for RMB internationalization from three aspects: politics, economy and government attitude. Liu Qun (2006) points out that to develop the RMB into a world currency, China needs to cultivate internationalized financial institutions and entities, exploring various international financial businesses and making efforts in the direction of achieving an internationalized financial institution and financial business environment.

In terms of monetary integration, Chen Yanyan et al. (2005) focus on the strategies for RMB internationalization before analyzing the feasibility of achieving monetary integration within the countries' sovereignty rights, thinking that, in the strategic process of RMB internationalization the RMB, Hong Kong dollar and Macau pataca must be firstly integrated to achieve sub-regional monetary integration. Li Jing (2006) proposes to take Hong Kong as the trial of RMB internationalization. Taiwan could refer to the pattern of Hong Kong launching RMB businesses in the future. Development of economic and trade relations between Mainland China, Hong Kong and Taiwan is helpful for accelerating market integration and the progress of monetary and financial cooperation in a bilateral sense. There are also a group of scholars proposing to use the RMB actively in foreign economic exchanges and enhance the circulation of the RMB abroad (Liu Qun, 2006). Tao Shigui (2003) believes that constructing a circle of RMB convertibility in countries and regions neighbouring China is conducive to laying a foundation for the RMB to go global. Currently China is featuring steady economic development, sufficient foreign exchange reserves and stable RMB value, indicating that it is the right time to set up the circle of RMB convertibility. The RMB Internationalization Research Taskforce (2006) thinks that the utilization of the RMB in investment and bilateral trade settlement between China and its neighboring countries and regions has to be further expanded and that achieving RMB internationalization in its neighboring countries and regions and in Southeast Asian areas much populated by the Chinese should be made the near and medium-term phased goal; the close economic and trade relations between Hong Kong, Macau and Mainland

China should be made full use of to advance RMB internationalization.

It is suggested by some scholars that regional monetary cooperation in East Asia can create conditions for the realization of RMB Asianization[3] and internationalization. Li Xiao, Li Junjiu and Ding Yibin (2004) point out that although the conditions for achieving complete RMB internationalization are not yet in place, seen from the situation in China and East Asia the prerequisites for RMB regionalization are partly possessed including that China has become an important force for stabilizing economic growth in East Asia along with the expansion of its economic aggregate, that the status of China as "market supplier" in East Asia has been increasingly enhanced, that China is becoming increasingly open to the outside world, and that the RMB has gained a certain degree of international acceptability in the China's neighboring countries and regions. Therefore it is proposed to develop the RMB into an international currency through institutional regional monetary cooperation in East Asia. Li Yang and Cao Honghui (2005) point out that China's active participation in the promotion of the development of the Asian bonds market is helpful for promoting the circulation of the RMB in the neighboring areas of China before advancing RMB Asianization and internationalization and creating an appropriate financial environment for the Chinese economy to become incorporated into Asia and to go global. In their study, Han Minchun and Yuan Xiulin (2006) think that, from the perspective of trade, the influences of China's foreign trade development on the trade volume, structure and market shift of other Asian countries have created the necessary conditions for RMB regionalization. In the future China will enhance its economic, political and cultural cooperation with other Asian countries and regions, and the trend will be constantly strengthened.

Development strategy of RMB internationalization

Through comparative analyses, some Chinese scholars advocate learning from the currency internationalization of developed countries so as to provide a reference for the path of RMB internationalization. The group of scholars led by Chen Hong (2004), Li Xiao (2005) and Xu Mingqi (2005) make careful analyses of the progress of "Yen internationalization" and summarize the experience and lessons in an in-depth way. Li Xiao (2005) points out that, as an emerging "trading nation," China must summarize and absorb experience and lessons from "Yen internationalization". In his opinion, the main reason that led "Yen internationalization" into a dilemma was that in the current international monetary system featuring the "U.S. dollar standard," Japan ignored the regional economic foundation for a local currency to become an international currency and tried to take a direct and functional currency internationalization road. Xu Mingqi (2005) analyzes the issue of RMB internationalization and regionalization from the experience and lessons of "Yen internationalization", holding that the RMB has to first become a settlement currency for regular account trade in East Asia before becoming a medium of international financial activities and assets. Li Jianjun and Tian Guangning (2003) point out that, of the three major world currencies today, U.S. dollar internationalization relies on global exchange rate collaborative arrangements; euro internationalization relies on the regional institutional arrangements of federal monetary sovereignty; and Yen internationalization relies on the development of the real economy and financial deepening policies. In the increasingly competitive international economic environment, RMB internationalization can only be achieved gradually by relying on the improvement of China's comprehensive national strength and the promotion of its international status. With the completion of the great cause of national unification, Mainland China, Hong Kong, Macau and Taiwan will form a powerful economic entity and the four local currencies can be integrated into a single one and achieve currency internationalization. By observing the paths of U.S. dollar, euro and Yen internationalization, Sun Jian, Wei Xiuhua and Tan Aipeng (2005) point out that RMB internationalization should firstly be achieved within the region. There are two possible choices to realize RMB internationalization i.e. implementing the "euro pattern" within Mainland China, Hong Kong, Macau and Taiwan, or launching the "Yen model" in Southeast Asia, East Asia and on a greater scope. In their opinion, for China, the two paths are compatible.

But in general there are some divergences regarding the path of RMB internationalization. The Chinese academic circles hold two views: 1) RMB internationalization should take the road of independent internationalization like the British pound sterling and the U.S. dollar; 2) RMB internationalization should be achieved through RMB regionalization. Currently, the latter one is the mainstream view.

Independent or direct RMB internationalization

Given the various barriers that exist in regional financial cooperation which hinder the coordination of a regional currency and exchange rate mechanism and may possibly slow down the evolution of RMB internationalization, some scholars hold that RMB internationalization should be achieved directly and independently by skipping the stage of RMB regionalization. Zhao Haikuan

(2003) thinks that, due to the different situations and objectives of regional currencies and international currencies, the contradictions to be resolved are also different and they do not form a ladder relationship i.e. it is not necessary for a local currency to develop into a regional currency before becoming an international currency. On the contrary, it is much easier and simpler for the RMB to become a world currency instead of a regional currency. Therefore we must never reject the possibility of the RMB developing into a world currency just because it is not yet a currency with unified circulation in Asia. It will cost a lot to establish a unified currency in Asia; the level of political and economic integration among Asian countries is too low; and the political and economic differences among the countries cause wars in some areas within the region, therefore Liu Qun (2006) believes that the possibility of establishing a unified currency in Asia even in the fairly long term is almost nil because Asia is far from being able to meet the requirements of the OCA theory in terms of the integration of the market for means of production and the capital market, or the coordination of fiscal and monetary policies. It determines that to carry out currency integration in Asia is quite impossible in the fairly long term. Compared with the possible development of the RMB into an Asian currency, the possibility of the development of the RMB into a world currency is more objective and practical. As long as it is powerful enough, the RMB will become a world currency without the need to firstly become an Asian currency.

RMB regionalization propels RMB internationalization

After the outbreak of the Asian financial crisis, especially with the emergence of the euro and the discussions and progress on "dollarization" in Latin America, many scholars have noted the importance of RMB regionalization to the realization of RMB internationalization. In their opinion, RMB regionalization may gradually expand RMB influence before finally pushing forward the evolution of RMB internationalization (Pan Liquan, 2000; Li Chong, 2002). Ba Shusong (2003) points out that, prior to full RMB convertibility, practical strategies have to be taken in order to push forward RMB internationalization, that it should start with the border trade-driven RMB regionalization strategy, and that the convenience of using the RMB as the settlement currency in international trade must be gradually promoted in a purposeful way to improve RMB utilization. Li Xiao, Li Junjiu and Ding Yibin (2004) point out that under the current international monetary system, a local currency must achieve internationalization through the "collective actions" of regional institutional cooperation. Direct RMB internationalization may bring enormous risks and losses to the economic development of China, and China has to combine the development of economic policies with the objective of regional monetary and financial cooperation and push forward RMB Asianization with multi-dimensional and multi-layered efforts to try to lay an economic foundation for RMB internationalization. The opinion that stresses "direct" RMB internationalization in a one-legged manner or equals the spontaneous RMB circulation in the neighboring countries and regions of China to "RMB regionalization" is incorrect. Cao Honghui (2006) thinks that China has to take RMB regionalization as the core of RMB internationalization before finally forming, with practical steps of RMB regionalization, an optimum currency area with RMB as its key currency in Asia so as to enhance financial stability in Asia, break the deadlock of the global monetary system reform, and open new paths of currency internationalization apart from the U.S. dollar and euro. Qin Yanning (2003), He Jia, Mai Fu (2005) and Zhang Ying (2006) think that with the execution of the *China-ASEAN Free Trade Framework Agreement*, the economic and trade cooperation between China and ASEAN (Association of Southeast Asian Nations) members and the deepening of their economic development will surely call for enhanced communication and cooperation in the financial field while the China-ASEAN Free Trade Area will construct a better platform for RMB regionalization, and RMB regionalization will become an inevitable choice in real economic development.

Although scholars have reached a consensus over the basic strategy of achieving RMB internationalization through RMB Asianization, they have three different opinions on how to achieve RMB Asianization: 1) the "regional cooperation assent" that insists on achieving RMB Asianization through regional cooperation; 2) the "regional cooperation negation" that exists in contrast to "regional cooperation assent" and insists on independent RMB Asianization; 3) the neutral "phased regional cooperation" theory.

Regional Cooperation Assent Theory

Scholars holding this point of view think that, at the current stage, China has to achieve RMB Asianization by participating in monetary cooperation in East Asia, namely enabling RMB regionalization to a certain extent in the form of institutional cooperation. As regards the pattern of regional monetary cooperation in East Asia, domestic scholars generally hold two opinions:

The first opinion believes that East Asian countries and regions have to directly carry out cooperation within the entire region. Wan Zhihong and Dai Jinping (2003) point out, upon an empirical analysis, that the relationship between the overall integration and the macroscopic symmetry of East Asia backs up the current efforts made to push forward exchange rate cooperation in East Asia, and that monetary and trade integration in East Asia has to be developed throughout the entire region. McKinnon (2003) points out that East Asia should be pegged to the U.S. dollar only, believing that an exchange rate system pegged to the U.S. dollar will be helpful for the East Asian dollar bloc as a whole. However most Chinese scholars are not in favor of this, thinking that East Asia should gradually "de-dollarize," and so they have proposed two different paths to advance RMB Asianization on the basis of cross-region cooperation:

Firstly, they propose to advance RMB Asianization by pegging to the Asian Monetary Unit (AMU).[4] Xie Luoqi and Huang Minghua (2006) believe that the launch of the Asian Currency Unit (ACU) is an important chance for China, which could not only enhance the discourse right of the RMB among Asian currencies but also avoid risks induced by major world currencies in the ACU on the international financial market, making it a driving force for advancing RMB Asianization and internationalization. There are also scholars pointing out that, through the ACU, China may close the RMB exchange rate to the equilibrium exchange rate with the help of the international financial market (Zhang Bin, 2004).

Secondly, they advocate the dominance of a number of currencies and giving play to the role of the RMB and Yen as the common "monetary anchor" in East Asia. Li Ping and Liu Peizhi (2003) propose the setting up of an exchange rate coordination mechanism that takes the RMB and Yen as the joint currency anchor. The joint currency anchor has a similar status to the U.S. dollar in the Bretton Woods System. That is, the currencies of all East Asian economies are connected through the currency anchor to the U.S. dollar and other international currencies and by coordinating the exchange rate and other macroeconomic policies of East Asian economies, the exchange rate is maintained at a rational level over a certain period that is good for the stable development of East Asian economies and regional economic integration. Future monetary cooperation in East Asia needs to be transformed from this low-level and scattered monetary cooperation mechanism to a higher stage in a progressive way. Some scholars also point out that, seen from the occurrence of financial crises and the status quo of the U.S. economy, taking the U.S. dollar as the anchor currency in Asia will bring adverse impacts on the economic development in East Asia, but currently neither the Yen nor the RMB is qualified to become the anchor currency in East Asia (Shen Guobing, 2004). Therefore efforts have to be made to realize "competition with cooperation" between China and Japan and seek sincere cooperation between both currencies in terms of exchange rate arrangements, liquidity and the future common currency (Chen Yulu, 2003; Luo Junchong, Zhou Yu'e, 2008). In so doing, the RMB and Yen exchange rates against the U.S. dollar may be kept stable at the present stage, while a special dual-system framework could be constructed taking the RMB and Yen as the common currency anchor before a joint RMB–JPY floating exchange rate system is formed in East Asia (Zheng Haiqing, 2003).

The second opinion holds that regional monetary cooperation should be carried out firstly at the sub-regional level, then the regional level. Scholars holding this opinion have put forward the following corresponding paths for advancing the RMB Asianization strategy:

Firstly, some scholars propose to push forward RMB Asianization through monetary integration. Zhu Fang (2003) points out that two sub-regional currency areas have to be established firstly in East Asia i.e. the ASEAN currency area and the RMB currency area, to facilitate local monetary cooperation. Comparatively speaking, conditions for setting up the RMB currency area are more mature. Sun Jian, Wei Xiuhua and Tang Aipeng (2005) point out that there are two paths to achieve RMB Asianization, namely constructing a "euro pattern" within Mainland China, Hong Kong, Macau and Taiwan; and constructing a "Yen pattern" in Southeast Asia, East Asia and a larger region. Other scholars think that RMB Asianization has to be initiated from a "greater China economic circle" (Liu Zhenlin, 2006), integrating the RMB, Hong Kong dollar and Macau pataca first before achieving currency integration in the sub-region (Zheng Hangbin, 2003, Chen Yanyan et al. 2005). However it will be hard to involve Taiwan in the initial integration (Cao Yong, 2005). Based on this, China could strengthen its cooperation with ASEAN, gradually set up the China-ASEAN Economic and Monetary Union, try regional currency integration in East Asia (Liu Zhenlin, 2006), and finally reduce the RMB peg-centered sub-regional currency area to a Japan–Korea economic platform, achieve the symmetric cooperation of the RMB and Yen, and realize RMB Asianization (Li Xiao, Li Junjiu and Ding Yibin, 2004).

Secondly, many scholars in Chinese economic circles pay great attention to the common currency basket system. For example, Ding Yibin (2006) thinks that East Asian countries should use a pegged currency basket composed of currencies in East Asia, such as the ACU, while the ACU maintains a weighted exchange rate stability to major currencies outside East Asia. It is actually a "dual" currency basket system. Liu Lizhen (2006) holds that East Asia should use a currency basket pegged to a "mixed anchor" i.e. pegging the currency basket to currencies both in and outside East Asia. Although scholars have quite different opinions on constructing a currency basket, most of them hold that with China's great influence in the economic development of Asia, the process of pushing forward exchange rate cooperation is the process through which the RMB will gradually evolve into one of the core currencies in Asia; and divide the specific steps on the currency basket peg into three stages: the first stage is constructing a currency basket system on the basis of local economic development; the second stage is building a sub-regional common currency basket peg before determining a central exchange rate system in areas with similar levels of economic development and structures, and relatively close economic exchanges; and the third stage is setting up a common currency basket system and forming a unified exchange rate mechanism in the whole East Asia region (Li Xiao and Ding Yibin, 2003).

Regional Cooperation Negation Theory

Some Chinese scholars hold that RMB regionalization can be achieved by relying on the RMB's competitive edge and strategies, and that it is unnecessary to participate in currency cooperation in East Asia. Specifically, there are two viewpoints:

Firstly, it is believed that China now has got an upper hand in the competition among East Asian countries, so it is unnecessary for it to participate in regional monetary cooperation. Yao Zhizhong (2004) points out that, due to the asymmetric pressures of competition between China and other Asian countries, the requirement of other Asian countries for a stable RMB exchange rate is much higher than that of China for a stable exchange rate of these countries, allowing China to have a very favorable position in Asian exchange rate coordination. China thus does not need to implement the common currency basket-based exchange rate coordination mechanism as other Asian countries do. He further points out that maintaining a stable RMB exchange rate is the most important strategic point for the RMB to become a key currency in Asia.

Secondly, it is thought that it is not yet the time to launch a common Asian currency in East Asia and it is advocated to accelerate RMB Asianization by advancing the overseas issue of government and corporate bonds denominated in RMB. Li Daokui has pointed out that the Chinese government had to calm down and deal with the AMU proposed by the Japanese scholar Eiji Ogawa et al. and ACU proposed by Asian Development Bank, and that both the AMU and ACU would bring adverse influences to China when the RMB was yet to become an international currency and there were no international assets denominated in RMB. When the RMB became the main means of trade in East

Asia or even in the world, discussions on the AMU or ACU will be conducive to China. Li Daokui (2008) further points out that China has to take dual-track steps to push forward RMB internationalization, give full play to the role of the domestic and foreign markets, and implement capital account convertibility in a phased and progressive way, gradually improve the operating efficiency of the financial markets, make full use of the advantages of Hong Kong, and try as much as possible to expand the size of the RMB securities market to create mature conditions for RMB internationalization.

Phased Regional Cooperation

There are two differences between "phased regional cooperation" and "regional cooperation assent," namely 1) whether RMB internationalization in the neighboring countries and regions of China is taken as the starting point of RMB Asianization and internationalization; and 2) whether the construction of the institutional regional currency cooperation is divided into stages. "Phased regional cooperation" is different from "regional cooperation negation" in that it advocates realizing, after the realization of RMB internationalization in the neighboring countries and regions of China, RMB Asianization through participation in regional monetary and financial cooperation. On the whole, "phased regional cooperation" highlights the improvement of RMB acceptance through spontaneous RMB flow and market role at the present stage before achieving RMB internationalization in China's neighboring countries and regions, and pushing forward RMB regionalization through phased cooperation arrangements.

When discussing the specific development stages of RMB internationalization in the neighboring countries and regions of China, some scholars hold that, after advancing RMB internationalization in the neighboring countries and regions of China or achieving internationalization of some of the functions of the RMB, an institutional cooperation mechanism could be established and capital accounts be opened directly to advance RMB regionalization. He Huigang (2007) proposes that RMB internationalization must keep in tune with the opening of RMB capital accounts and the flexibility of the exchange rate system, and that RMB internationalization has to take the progressive road of "RMB internationalization in the neighboring countries and regions of China-RMB Asianization-RMB internationalization." Specifically, the first stage is to push forward RMB internationalization in China's neighboring countries and regions, namely to expand international trade and increase the circulation of the RMB in all the neighboring countries and regions of China through market orientation or through market orientation and government policies; the second stage is RMB Asianization, which is the process during which the RMB becomes a key currency in East Asia, and during which the construction of the free trade zone and regional monetary union are two important channels to promote policy implementation; and the third stage is achieving RMB internationalization.

Meanwhile there are also scholars proposing that, upon the realization of RMB internationalization in the neighboring countries and regions of China, efforts should be made to firstly increase the general trade denominated in RMB and construct an RMB offshore market in East Asia in order to improve RMB acceptance in East Asia (referring mainly to countries and regions other than Japan), then to advance RMB Asianization and internationalization through an institutionalized cooperation mechanism. Cao Honghui and Hu Zhihao (2007) point out when explaining the strategic ideas on RMB internationalization and regionalization that whether the RMB can be regionalized or internationalized mainly depends on the results of market choice, economic fundamentals, and the economic closeness between China and the world, especially Asia. Given the fact that China is gradually taking the place of the U.S. to become a main supplier on the export market in East Asia, it should be encouraged to use the RMB as an invoice and settlement currency in regional trade, expand the use of the RMB in consumption and travel in neighboring countries and regions, develop the regional RMB securities market, and lay a foundation for the RMB to realize its functions as an international reserve currency in neighboring countries and regions. Then institutionalized means such as promoting the building of an exchange rate coordination mechanism may be adopted to advance RMB Asianization. In her study, Jia Huiyan (2005) points out that RMB internationalization should be a dynamic process, and a phased strategy should be taken and corresponding policies should be developed. All such strategic steps cannot be fulfilled without the offshore financial market. She divides RMB internationalization into four stages: the first stage is RMB circulation in neighboring countries and regions of China driven by border trade and travel consumption; in the second stage, the RMB gradually becomes overseas loan assets, which is also the initial stage of the formation of the RMB offshore market; in the third stage, the RMB will be able to become investment assets in Asia with the increase in the amount of RMB held by other Asian countries, indicating the official establishment of the RMB offshore market; and the fourth stage is the mature stage of RMB internationalization, when the RMB becomes the main reserve assets for other Asian countries and a regional currency. Most scholars holding such an opinion suggest that the specific steps to RMB Asianization may not be achieved through capital account liberalization but that China, as the largest "market supplier" in Asia, has to give play to the functions of the RMB as a regional settlement currency to achieve RMB Asianization. They advocate setting up an RMB offshore market in Hong Kong. After RMB flows out of Mainland China and is converted, it would be hard to distinguish and control regular account expenditure and capital account expenditure, which in fact means the basic opening of the RMB capital account through the construction of the RMB offshore market. Through such a path choice, the RMB will be able to overcome the shortcomings of non-liberalization of capital account and enjoy the benefits brought about by the realization of RMB Asianization.

All in all, in the current conditions, advancing RMB regionalization in stages instead of directly launching institutionalized cooperation is a rational choice. However there are still problems in the above-mentioned relevant discussions: 1) stage division is vague and without clear definition, which needs to be further corrected; 2) how to advance RMB regionalization by stages is not clearly described; 3) what is worth noting is that, even if institutionalized cooperation arrangements are unavailable in the process of advancing RMB internationalization in neighboring countries and regions of China, the necessity of carrying out coordinated cooperation in some form to some extent must never be ignored.

When summarizing the abovementioned studies by Chinese and foreign scholars on RMB internationalization we can see that early studies on RMB internationalization mainly focused on the cost, benefits and necessity analysis of RMB internationalization, while later studies shifted the focus to exploration of the paths of RMB internationalization. Currently a consensus on the cost, benefits and necessity of RMB internationalization has been reached in the academic circles. But in the analysis of the paths of RMB internationalization, most scholars tend to agree with RMB regionalization first. Of course, there are objections that advocate achieving RMB internationalization through other ways. It is worth pointing out that current literature on RMB regionalization focuses too much on analyzing the spontaneous evolution paths of RMB regionalization under market forces, but fails to combine it with the changes in the international financial structure in an organic way or to put it within the institutional framework of regional monetary cooperation in East Asia, so it fails to find a necessary and feasible logic of "regional collective actions" and institutional arrangements for RMB regionalization.

RMB Regionalization — The Only Way to RMB internationalization

The term "RMB regionalization" refers to the process in which RMB strives to become the regional key currency by participating in institutionalized monetary and financial cooperation in East Asia. It is an indispensable key step to RMB internationalization. The current domestic and foreign economic and financial environment of China determines that RMB regionalization is necessary. Is it true that currency internationalization, regardless of the currency, has to experience currency regionalization? The answer is negative. Prior to U.S. dollar internationalization there was no process of promoting the U.S. dollar in the region before advancing it to the world. On the contrary, U.S. dollar regionalization did not begin until after the realization of U.S. dollar internationalization, when the U.S. set up a "U.S. dollar currency area" in South America. However, given the characteristics of the current international monetary system, changes in the international financial pattern, the lesson of "Yen internationalization" and the progress made in monetary cooperation in East Asia, and according to the conditions of China, the path of RMB internationalization is not like that of U.S. dollar internationalization nor that of euro internationalization, but has to actively seek for coordination and cooperation with other currencies in East Asia so as to achieve the objective of RMB internationalization within the overall framework of regional monetary cooperation in East Asia.

The necessity of RMB internationalization

Seen from the economic development history of developed countries, when an economy develops to a certain stage its currency internationalization will be an inevitable subject. As China's economic strength keeps increasing and the Chinese economy becomes increasingly involved with the world economy, RMB internationalization will surely become a trend and objective of the growing Chinese economy.

First of all, RMB internationalization will become a powerful driving force for economic growth and reform in China, promoting the Chinese economy to develop faster and better, greatly reduce such adverse factors as fluctuations in the exchange rate and costs of foreign trade and investment, and push forward the development of China's foreign economic relations. RMB internationalization will also promote the development of the financial industry in China, accelerate financial system reform to further meet the need of RMB internationalization with a perfected financial system, speed up realization of free RMB circulation, and push forward the development of stocks, bonds, foreign exchange and offshore financial markets in China. RMB internationalization will progressively improve China's status in the international financial field, reduce the pressures and adverse impacts on China's economic development due to the powerful financial hegemony of the U.S., and actively influence economic stability and safe production in China.

Secondly, RMB internationalization will create favorable conditions for China to develop its economic policies and take economic regulation measures. It will enhance China's monetary policy autonomy, and help China get rid of the "Meada Conflict" that is harassing developing countries, namely to that to maintain an external equilibrium developing countries must sacrifice their internal equilibrium and cannot focus on domestic economic goals without worrying about their balance of payments and level of exchange rate. RMB internationalization will provide the necessary conditions for China to develop economic policies to serve its domestic economy and obtain significant economic policy effects.

Thirdly, RMB internationalization will make China more influential and give China more discourse right in global economic activities. Since China would have the right to issue an international currency it could affect, to some extent, the financial economy of countries and regions that use the RMB when developing monetary policies, and improve its international status. It will also promote the international monetary system to be more multilayered, change the passive position of China, and reduce the adverse influences of the international monetary system on China's economic development. RMB internationalization will give China more discourse right when participating in regulation development in global affairs to bring China more economic and political benefits, and improve China's international status in global economic affairs.

All in all, to enable China's economy to develop more stably and faster, RMB internationalization is essential. As far as the currency conditions and situation are concerned, conditions for direct RMB internationalization are yet to be fully available and thus RMB internationalization must be achieved through RMB regionalization.

Direct internationalization of a single currency under the current "U.S. dollar system" is difficult to achieve

The current international monetary system is a "U.S. dollar system" in nature. If the Bretton Woods System backed up by the great economic strength of the U.S. is a "strong U.S. dollar system," the current international monetary system can be called a "weak U.S. dollar system." Although the U.S.-centered fixed exchange rate system set up under the Bretton Woods System has collapsed, and there is a trend of diversification of reserve currencies in the international monetary system, the de-linkage of the U.S. dollar from gold has not really weakened the status of the U.S. dollar. The world hegemony of the U.S. dollar set up under the Bretton Woods System has not ended. The U.S. dollar has changed from being a substitute for world's currency in the past to become an actual key currency, and the Bretton Woods System has become a hidden "U.S. dollar system." Under the current international monetary system, the U.S. dollar still holds the dominance.

Under the "U.S. dollar system," the U.S. is a typical "financial nation" that enjoys financial hegemony. Comparatively speaking, other subsequently developed countries and most developing countries are "trading nations." Under the "U.S. dollar system" featuring the powerful financial hegemony of the U.S., direct internationalization of any currency of any "trading nation" is very difficult to achieve.

Generally speaking, under the "U.S. dollar system," the main reflections of the American financial hegemony may be summed up in four aspects, which all determine the difficulty of direct internationalization of a currency under the "U.S. dollar system."

Severely unbalanced rights, responsibilities and obligations brought about by the open and developed financial market of the U.S.

The U.S. has the world's most developed and open financial market, which forms the foundation that supports its "financial hegemony." The open and developed infrastructure and the extensive scale of the American financial market have not only endowed the U.S. with the right to develop rules on the current international financial and capital market, but also provided the most extensive, safest and the most convenient investment venue and opportunities. On this basis the U.S. can simply ignore its trade balance deficits within an affordable limit and provide large amounts of the U.S. dollar to the world through trade deficits. The result is that many "trading nations" have greater and greater U.S. dollar trade surpluses, but they have to channel a great part of the trade surpluses back into the development financial market of the U.S. in the form of investing in U.S. treasury bonds to support the economic operation of the U.S.[7] Because of the need to make up for long-term regulation account deficits with the inflow of overseas assets or loans, the U.S. naturally becomes the world's largest debtor nation. At the end of 2006 the foreign debts of the U.S. reached USD1.08 trillion, of which short-term foreign debts accounted for 41.5%, and the ratio of foreign debts to its current GDP reached 81%.[8] In sharp contrast, it has never been seen in history that most of the overseas assets held by the world's largest creditor nation[9] are denominated in the currency of the world's greatest debtor nation (Guan Zhixiong, 2003). It is a typical reflection of the U.S. financial hegemony under the "U.S. dollar system" which also reflects the severity of the dilemma faced by "trading nations." It can be imagined how difficult direct currency internationalization of a "trading nation" would be faced with the dilemma that the U.S. has severely unbalanced rights and obligations.

The U.S. can focus on its domestic economic objectives without having to worry about its balance of payments and exchange rate.

Since the U.S. holds the core position in the international monetary system, and has been developing its currency policies independently without having to take into account the official intervention in the foreign exchange market by other countries; and the domestic commodity prices in the U.S. are not influenced by fluctuations in the exchange rate, the U.S. Federal Reserve Board can just ignore the inflation in or monetary policies of other countries when setting the price level in the U.S. (McKinnon and Kenichi Ohno, 1999). So other countries have to undertake all consequences of the U.S. economic policies. Even if they have excessive deficits in the balance of payments or non-equilibrium exchange rate, they are unable to make timely and corresponding adjustments according to their own economic conditions but have to undertake most of the pressures for economic adjustments. Often the U.S. may take measures to force its trading partners to carry out economic adjustments,[10] meaning that "trading nations" are unable to maintain their own monetary sovereignty. Under the pressure of regulating their own economies and the pressures that should have been undertaken by the U.S., it is very difficult for "trading nations" to adopt direct currency internationalization.

The monopoly of the U.S. that takes the U.S. dollar as the main medium of exchange in international trade

Compared with its main trade partners, the U.S. can maintain a high domestic inflation rate while promoting the continual depreciation of the U.S. dollar against the currencies of its main trade partners so as to get more seigniorage income. Taking Japan as an example, although the currency of a "trading nation" like Japan is forced to constantly appreciate it cannot benefit from this. Domestic enterprises in Japan and Japanese residents get no benefits from Yen appreciation. Since the Japanese financial market is not open and lacks vitality it is hard to be efficient, making Japanese enterprises explore the establishment of a system capable of "dealing with both Yen appreciation and Yen depreciation" in isolation. Although in the long run Yen appreciation could promote the growth of production and enhance competitiveness, few Japanese financial leaders agree that Yen appreciation is good for the Japanese economy because Japan has failed to get rid of the export-oriented dependence system and can only improve its export competitiveness through Yen depreciation (Kikuchi, 2000).

The "U.S. dollar system" makes "trading nations" dependent on the U.S. dollar.

Under the "U.S. dollar system" almost all US foreign trade is settled in the U.S. dollar, giving birth to a significantly asymmetric dependence of other "trading nations" on the U.S., the "financial nation," and leading to the formation of a "U.S. dollar dependence system" in "trading nations." To a great extent, "trading nations" are thus unable to ensure their own currency sovereignty. Taking Japan as an example, most of its foreign trade is settled in foreign currencies (of which the U.S. dollar accounts for a large part), leading to a greater real-time transmission effect on the exchange rate in Japan than in the United States. The asymmetry of such a transmission effect leads to significantly different monetary policies on dealing with changes in exchange rate in Japan and the U.S. As a result, although Japan adopts the floating exchange rate system, the U.S. can still influence Japan's exchange rate, its domestic price level and its monetary policies (mainly interest rate policies). It is difficult for "trading nations" to escape the "dependence on" the U.S. dollar formed under the international monetary system featuring the "U.S. dollar system."

Therefore, under the current U.S. dollar hegemony-led "U.S. dollar system," without the "collective action" of regional monetary cooperation, it will be impossible for a country to succeed in its efforts to achieve currency internationalization. Meanwhile, as a modern "financial nation," the U.S. enjoys and tries hard to maintain all the benefits brought about by the central position of the U.S. dollar in the international monetary system, making it the last country willing to push forward reform of the international monetary system. Any currency that tries direct internationalization, since it challenges the hegemony of the U.S. dollar, will be resolutely opposed and suppressed by the U.S., making the internationalization process more difficult.

RMB internationalization at the current stage cannot be accomplished in one step

A weak financial foundation — A weak domestic financial system and imperfect domestic financial market

Seen from the experience of British and U.S. currency internationalization, a developed domestic financial system is an essential guarantee for enhancing the credibility of a currency and gradually improving a country's international status. Without a developed and perfected domestic financial market, currency internationalization will be out of the question. Currently the financial market in China is not mature enough to meet the development requirements of RMB internationalization. The imperfections of the Chinese financial system at the current stage mainly include:

The monopoly of state-owned commercial banks has led to a very vulnerable financial system.

China's financial system is less developed and is still centered on commercial banks. In particular, state-owned commercial banks hold an absolutely dominant position. Seen from the condition of assets of financial institutions in the Chinese banking industry in 2006, the assets of state-owned commercial banks accounted for 55% of all and those of policy banks and various commercial banks accounted for 83%, having a complete monopoly on China's credit market. The share of foreign-funded banks and that of non-bank financial institutions was 2.11% and 2.41%, respectively, being in the earliest stage of their development.[11] The commercial bank system with a complete monopoly makes the Chinese financial system to very fragile and unable to face the complicated financial situation, significantly preventing the Chinese financial market from opening up to the outside world. For RMB internationalization, an open and perfect financial market is essential.

The stock market is less developed, featuring poor financing capability

Since the 1990s the Chinese capital market has been developing fast. In particular the size of the stock market has kept expanding before reaching its peak in 2000, when the total market value of stocks reached RMB4.8 trillion and accounted for 53.8% of the current GDP. However in the early days of the Chinese stock market there were negotiable shares and legal person shares, of which negotiable shares accounted for about 30% of the total shares. The phenomenon of the same share having different rights severely restricted the Chinese stock market marketization from developing further. After 2000 the Chinese stock market shrunk continually. By 2005 the total stock value was only RMB3.2 trillion, a decrease of 1/3; and the ratio of negotiable stock value to current GDP was only 5.8%.[12]

By comparing the domestic equity financing and the increase in bank loans in China, we can see that funds for the development of Chinese enterprises mainly come from bank loans. In the early 1990s the amount of equity financing accounted for less than 2% of bank loans, before developing somewhat. In 2000 the ratio hit 11.55%. But after that the financing capability of the Chinese stock market reduced rapidly to the level of the early 1990s. The less developed Chinese stock market cannot take the place of commercial banks before becoming an important financial channel for national economic development.

In addition, by comparing the amount of equity financing and the investment in fixed assets, we can see a great gap between the two. The contribution of equity financing to the Chinese economy was less than 1% in the early 1990s, and not more than 5% in 2000.[13]

As the "stock market reform" was launched smoothly, the Chinese stock market gradually realized free circulation of legal person shares on the book, removing a major chronic problem from the Chinese stock system. But only with constant perfection of a series of matching systems can the stock market play its role in financing and play a greater part in pushing forward RMB internationalization.

The Chinese bond market is less developed

Seen from the issue of securities in China, national debts and policy bank bonds have been dominant, of which policy bank bonds have grown more vigorously. By 2006 the scale of policy bank bonds issued had exceeded national debts issued, reaching RMB898 billion. Comparatively, securities markets in other forms were less developed and it was not until 2004 that other financial bonds were issued. Although the corporate bonds market has long existed, it is relatively small in size.

Seen from the trusteeship on the Chinese bond market in 2008, government bonds, central bank bills and policy bank bonds accounted for 32.27%, 31.85% and 24.3% of the market share respectively.[14] Together they dominated the Chinese bond market. The truly marketized commercial bank bonds, enterprise bonds and short-term financing bonds developed slowly, showing the low development level of the Chinese bond market.

Thus the Chinese financial market is relatively isolated and undeveloped, so it is unable to provide better support for RMB internationalization. Realization of RMB internationalization in one step is impossible.

Less developed economic fundamentals — The lack of core competitive advantages in China's economic growth

It has been demonstrated that having a strong real economy plays an important role in a country's currency internationalization. In the early days of British pound sterling and U.S. dollar internationalization it was essential to establish their core competitive advantages. Britain became the world's first industrialized country in one leap with leading technologies in the textile and steel industries, while the U.S. became the most powerful industrialized country after Britain, relying on the extensive applications of new technologies in the steel, auto and chemical industries as well as a series of developments and breakthroughs in the field of electronic technologies. Although China has made breakthroughs in terms of its economic aggregate and has become the most active emerging economy in the world, its economy is yet to be developed and it has not established its core competitiveness. It thus has no significant technical advantages in some fields.

The value added ratio of China's hi-tech industry is low

Of the value added ratios of the hi-tech industry of different countries, those of the U.S., of Japan and of Germany have significant technology leadership, reaching 41.2%, 38.7% and 40.5% respectively, far higher than that of China (23.9%).[15] It indicates that there is still a great gap between China and developed countries in terms of advanced productivity, which leads to the lack of core competitive advantages of China and keeps China at the low end of the industrial chain in the international division of work.

The added values of main industries in China are low

As shown in Table 2.1, compared with major developed countries the annual per capita increment of the Chinese manufacturing industry was only USD14,000, accounting for 18% of that of the U.S. and 13% of that of Japan, registering enormous gaps. More importantly, the difference between the per capita added value of China's hi-tech industry and that of the Chinese manufacturing industry as a whole is small, increasing by only 18%, while the difference between the two indicators in developed countries is very significant. There the per capita added value of the hi-tech industry is 31% higher than that of manufacturing industry as a whole, indicating the low technical content of the hi-tech industry in China.

The level of R&D in China is low

Seen from the overall R&D expenditure of different countries in the world (see Figure 2.1), the U.S. ranks the first, followed closely by Japan. The R&D expenditure of China is more or less equivalent to those of France and Britain. However, seen from the ratio of R&D expenditure to GDP, that of China is 1.49%, showing an obvious gap. Japan has the highest ratio at 3.39%, more than double that of China, fully demonstrating the fact that China is less developed in the field of technical investment. Seen from industrial R&D intensity, that of

Table 2.1 Per capita added value by country's industry

Unit: USD 1,000

	China (2006)	U.S. (2006)	Japan (2003)	Germany (2005)	France (2005)
Manufacturing industry	14.3	109.3	78.9	76.1	75.3
Hi-tech industry	16.9	143.4	100	98.1	97.2

Source: The Ministry of Science and Technology of the People's Republic of China http://www.most.gov.cn.

China is obviously low. In particular, the R&D intensity in its hi-tech industry is 5.7, being only 1/5 of that of developed countries (Table 2.2). Such a low level of investment in technical R&D will surely lead to a growing gap between the industrial development in China and the technologies in the world's advanced countries. To improve its competitiveness, China has no other choice but to keep introducing external technologies.

Obviously, China has to make vigorous efforts to improve its backward financial and economic foundations. China is still adopting the traditional financial system centered on state-owned commercial banks without the intervention of other financial intermediaries, leading to the lack of competitive vitality of its financial market. Meanwhile the Chinese stock market has poor financing capabilities and a low level of financial openness. The necessary financial fundamentals for RMB internationalization are unavailable; on the

Fig. 2.1. Total R&D expenditure of selected countries and their ratios to GDP

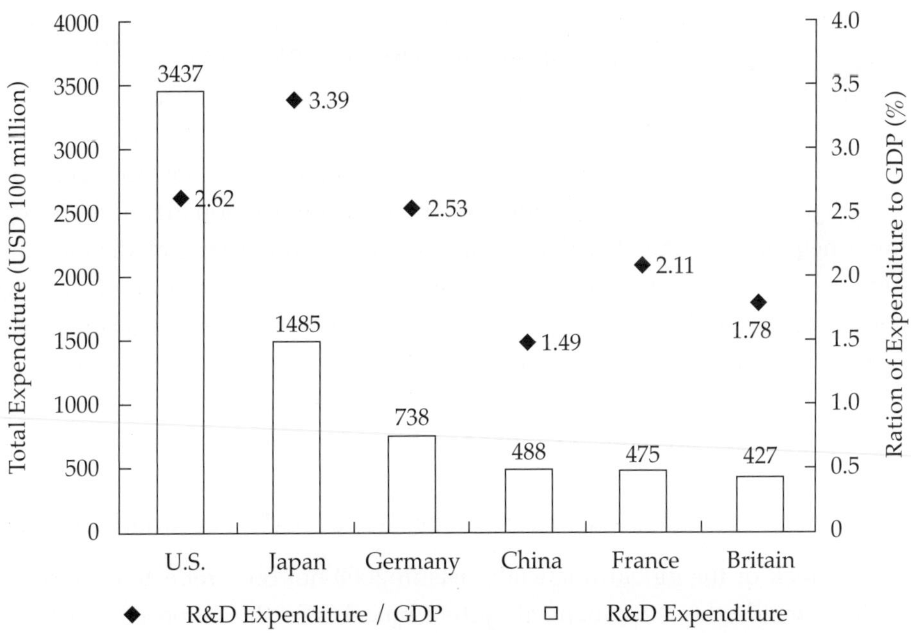

Note: Data on China are for 2007 and those on other countries are for 2006.
Source: The Ministry of Science and Technology of the People's Republic of China. http://www.most.gov.cn.

Table 2.2. Comparison of R&D intensity of industries in selected countries

Industry	China (2006)	U.S. (2003)	Japan (2003)	Germany (2005)	France (2002)	Britain (2003)
Manufacturing Industry	3.4	8.5	10.1	7.6	8.9	7.2
Hi-tech Industry	5.7	29	25.7	20.9	31.6	27.6

Note: R&D intensity is calculated according to the percentage of R&D expenditure in industrial added value.
Source: The Ministry of Science and Technology of the People's Republic of China http://www.most.gov.cn.

other hand, as a developing country, China lags far behind developed countries in terms of industrial technologies and its industrial structure is led by labor-intensive industries, making it lack core competitive advantages and keeping it at the low end of the global industrial chain. The unfavorable competitive status of China will restrain the expansion of the international influence of the RMB. The above-mentioned two factors are principally caused by institutional shortcomings and sluggish economic development. Fundamental changes to them are nearly impossible in a short term. However the two factors are indispensable necessary conditions for achieving RMB internationalization. Therefore RMB internationalization will be a long and arduous process.

In addition, since RMB has not been connected with the international community for long, even though RMB internationalization has now been put on the agenda the "direct" or independent RMB internationalization strategy cannot help achieve the objective of participating in financial globalization and rationalizing the allocation of financial resources given the failure of the "Yen internationalization" strategy. On the contrary, it may bring enormous risks and losses to the economic development of China. Therefore RMB regionalization should be the first step, which aims at cultivating a regional economic foundation and constructing a strategic platform for RMB internationalization.

The global financial crisis and the necessity of RMB regionalization

The outbreak of the global financial crisis in 2008 not only reflected a series of problems inside the U.S. financial system but also further exposed a series of inherent shortcomings of the U.S. dollar-centered international financial system such as reserve currency simplification, the lack of a trans-national monitoring system etc., and promoted thinking on reforming the international monetary system around the world. The reform of the international monetary system will undoubtedly provide a new chance for RMB internationalization. Accordingly, in the current conditions, what the reform of the international monetary system will be like or what the direction the reform of the international monetary system will take will also determine the choice of the RMB internationalization strategy and promotion path.

"U.S. dollar system" sustainability and the direction of reform of the international monetary system

It has to be admitted that the inherent shortcomings of the "U.S. dollar system" are one of the reasons for the global financial crisis. An opinion has thus been formed that the fundamental cause of this global financial crisis lies in the excessive and unrestrained supply of the U.S. dollar, which makes it difficult for the current "U.S. dollar system" to continue. Accordingly, China's strategic countermeasure should be making use of the historical opportunities provided by this financial crisis, pushing forward the adjustment and reform of the international monetary system, and trying to have a greater voice in reforming the international monetary system and reconstructing the world economic order (Xia Bin, 2009). It has firstly to be noted that neither excessive U.S. dollar supply nor global economic imbalance that is closely related to excessive U.S. dollar supply is the direct reason for this financial crisis. Secondly, the current global economic imbalance or excessive U.S. dollar supply is actually the recurrence of the old problems of the international monetary system in the new era. Any global or regional financial crisis will deepen the general understanding of the shortcomings of the current international monetary system, but such deepening of understanding will never be the main reason for any crisis. The current global economic imbalance is a structural problem in nature, which is the basis for the existence and operation of the "U.S. dollar system." The process of solving the problem will be long-lasting and complicated. It is hard to fundamentally solve this structural problem simply by adjusting the order of the international monetary system.

Another key problem that deserves further consideration is: what kind of reforms of the current defective international monetary system can be carried out and in what ways. Or put it another way, should we reform the entire international monetary system, or reform or adjust its shortcomings or disadvantages? If it is reform or adjustment of its shortcomings, this means that we think the system is sustainable in the fairly long term. All we need to do then is to make all efforts, including carrying out feasible adjustments of the current international monetary and financial management system and pushing forward regional monetary and financial cooperation, to prevent and reduce possible risks of the current international monetary and financial management system. If it is comprehensive reform of the current international monetary system, the following four questions must be taken into consideration: 1) Is there a perfect international monetary system? 2) Is the U.S. dollar really falling? 3) History shows that international monetary system reform or adjustment is usually accompanied with hegemony replacement (or major reforms of the international pattern), or the latter can be said the prerequisite for the former, then how should we understand the decline of U.S. hegemony or the possibility of U.S. hegemony being replaced at the current stage? 4) The more crucial problem is that, after this financial crisis, can the economies in East Asia as important supports for the "U.S. dollar system" quickly shed their dependence on the "U.S. dollar system"?

As regards the above questions, it has to be firstly pointed out that there is no perfect international monetary system. Neither the past gold standard system nor the current "U.S. dollar system" is perfect. The same is true of all international economic systems that have ever existed in human history, for they all had conflicts and problems. However, problems do not equal unsustainability. As has been analyzed above, due to the improved sustainability of the "financial hegemony" under the conditions of economic globalization, market confidence in the U.S. dollar's serving as a global key currency still exists; the current international economic and political pattern of "one superpower and several major powers" will continue; it will still be hard for economies in East Asia to get rid of their dependence on the U.S. market and such economies will continue acting as supports of the "U.S. dollar system"; and the current "U.S. dollar system"-centered international monetary system is still highly sustainable.

Although the global financial crisis exposed many disadvantages and problems of the current international monetary system i.e. the so-called "U.S. dollar system", such disadvantages and problems have long existed and thus are not the root causes for this crisis. Fundamental reform of the international monetary system is, to a great extent, the result of major adjustments of the international political and economic situation. After this crisis the U.S. dollar-centered global credit turnover system will continue showing a strong operational capability; it will be hard for economies in East Asia to escape their dependence on the end-product market of the U.S. in the short term, making such economies continue their support for the system; and no fundamental changes will happen to the "U.S. dollar system" for a fairly long term in the future.

In this case, it is safe to say that, over a fairly long period, it will be hard to fundamentally reform the current international monetary system. However the shortcomings of the system indicate the necessity to adjust it. Therefore reforms can only be carried out on the basis of maintaining the basic structure of the current international monetary system. On the one hand, feasible and specific adjustments of the current international monetary and financial management system may be carried out globally; on the other hand, regional monetary and financial cooperation may be carried out in different regions, while efforts can be made to improve the international status and role of currencies other than the U.S. dollar, launch the trial of non-sovereign reserve currency, progressively ameliorate the international monetary system with such regional improvements, and approach the objective of pushing forward international monetary system diversification. Such reform direction and forms will surely have great influence that cannot be ignored on the choice of paths of RMB internationalization.

Reform of the international monetary system and RMB regionalization

The reform of the international monetary system will act as a new chance for RMB internationalization. As a great power with a continually improving international economic status and which takes active part in economic globalization, China not only has to participate actively in the exploration of proper ways of international monetary reform so as to ensure a relatively stable external monetary and financial environment, but also needs to make full use of the process of international monetary reform, develop financial strategies accordingly to push forward RMB internationalization, improve the international status and role of the RMB, and reduce potential risks of external financial turmoil. In the process the specific strategies and paths of RMB internationalization will inevitably be restricted by the direction and possibilities of the international monetary system reform. In turn, it will also affect the process of international monetary system reform.

After the outbreak of the global financial crisis, the Chinese monetary authority was faced with a dilemma in making strategic choices. On the one hand, it actively proposed to reduce its dependence on the U.S. dollar through RMB internationalization and the reform of the international monetary system, while on the other hand, it slowed down RMB appreciation out of its concern for the decline in exports and restored the relatively stable state with U.S. dollar exchange rate over a period. The phenomenon reflected that, on the one hand, China had realized the adverse position of the RMB in the current international monetary system and the disadvantages thus produced, and hoped to change the situation; on the other hand, since adjustments of the economic growth model and economic restructuring in China was hard to complete within a short term, traditional methods had to be adopted in order to maintain economic growth and promote employment. So for a fairly long time to come China would not be able to change the current system, and would even rely on such a system to some extent.

In this context, the Chinese monetary authority has been seen to adopt measures at three levels i.e. RMB internationalization, the strengthening of regional monetary cooperation, and reform of the international monetary system, as its choice of international financial strategy since the end of 2008. The problem now is that, according to the abovementioned possibility of reforming the international monetary system and the real conditions of China, what is the relationship or logic between the three levels of measures?

Firstly, it is safe to say that the former two are "subsequent confirmation" of some of the facts and partly the result of market choice. However reforming the international monetary system is more of a strategic objective. On the one hand, it expresses China's concern about possible U.S. dollar depreciation due to quantitative easing, a policy adopted by the Federal Reserve on the other hand, China wants to get an upper hand in the future reform of the international monetary system by putting foward the demand. However in the current conditions China is not able, nor is qualified, to take the initiative in challenging the financial hegemony of the U.S. independently. China is one of the greatest beneficiaries of the system and still needs to survive and develop relying on the system over a certain period. What it needs to do now is to try, as much as possible, to reduce the losses or risks of relying on the system instead of overturning or challenging it. It is by no means right to deem means as objectives. Therefore, as regards the reform of the international monetary system, China has to pay attention to: 1) not challenging the status of the U.S. dollar separately and proactively, or becoming the challenger of the current U.S. dollar-centered international monetary system and its rules; 2) not proposing the so-called "democratic reform" in the IMF, the World Bank and similar international agencies, or their transformation into WTO-like institutions, even though they are irrational in many aspects such as the rules of procedure, voting rights, governance structure etc. This does not conform to the interests of the world or to those of China. In other words, China should not aim to fundamentally change the international monetary system now but to improve it partially so as to better safeguard its own interests. In this regard, regional monetary and financial cooperation may improve the financial stability and anti-risk capabilities at the regional level, while the progressive advance of RMB internationalization can promote the diversification of the international monetary system and reduce the uncertainty brought about by excessive dependence on the U.S. dollar. These not only conform to the strategic objective of reforming the international monetary system but also function as effective supplements and improvements to the current international monetary system, and thus are feasible measures for reforming the current international monetary system.

Secondly, as far as the relationship between RMB internationalization and the strengthening of regional monetary and financial cooperation are concerned, it has to be noted that the rapid development of the Chinese economy in recent years is, in a way, the result of making full use of the reform and opening up and the globalization process. This "economic rise under the conditions of an open economy" has closely connected the Chinese economy with the world economy, especially the economy in East Asia, and formed an unprecedented mutual dependence. It not only requires China to take into consideration possible external pressures that will be brought about by the implementation or adjustments of its foreign economic strategies, including the strategy of RMB internationalization, the fact that the China's economy and that of East Asia are closely connected, and the restriction of such mutual dependence on RMB internationalization strategic choice, but also enables China to make use of its close economic relations with East Asia before actively participating in regional monetary and financial cooperation so as to, on the one hand, avoid barriers to RMB internationalization due to its own shortcomings in economic and financial fundamentals, while on the other hand offset international pressures through the collective action of regional monetary cooperation and reduce the cost of RMB internationalization. In turn, RMB regionalization will further enable East Asia to gradually reduce its excessive dependence on the "U.S. dollar system" before developing to an even higher level under certain conditions. Seen from this sense, RMB internationalization and regional monetary and financial cooperation are mutually supportive and promotional.

Specifically, the relationship between the current RMB internationalization strategy, the reform of the international monetary system, and regional monetary and financial cooperation can be reduced to the following several points:

Firstly, achieving the objective of RMB internationalization at the present stage will be restricted by the current international monetary system featuring the "U.S. dollar system." The international status of the U.S. dollar and the dependence on the U.S. and other external markets of the East Asian production network in which China acts as the processing and assembly hub not only make it more difficult to achieve the objective of RMB internationalization, but also limit the freedom of China when choosing RMB internationalization paths. On the one hand, it indicates that direct global RMB internationalization at the present stage is faced with difficulties, making it better that RMB internationalization begin with RMB regionalization; on the other hand, it means that the RMB can escape its excessive dependence on the "U.S. dollar system" through RMB regionalization, in some way, in the future. That is to say, to take the road of RMB regionalization is not dictated by realistic conditions but also able to complete the task of gradually changing the current international monetary pattern to some extent.

Secondly, at the present stage, it is hard to create a global institutional environment for RMB internationalization by making fundamental adjustments of the institutional arrangements of the international monetary system. To achieve RMB internationalization at the global level purely through the spontaneous choice by market forces faces a sea of troubles when the Chinese financial departments still have many deficiencies and China lacks enough discourse right in international trade due to its less developed economic technologies. Therefore, offering some convenient conditions and a convenient institutional environment for other countries to accept the RMB as an international currency through some kind of institutional arrangements will have a multiplier effect. But the problem is, as pointed out above, that to carry out a fundamental reform of the international monetary system is unrealistic for the time being, making it harder to create a global context for RMB internationalization through such reforms.

Thirdly, internationalization of RMB at the present stage has better conditions at the regional level.

At the institutional level although it is very difficult to create an international currency identity for the RMB through institutional arrangements at the global level, it is not infeasible to create the conditions for RMB regionalization through some kind of formal or informal institutional arrangements on the basis of monetary and financial cooperation in East Asia. The development of monetary and financial cooperation in East Asia will make other East Asian economies more willing to accept the RMB as the settlement and reserve currency in trade, and make it easier for the RMB to be recognized and used by other economies in the region.

At the market level, the real economies in East Asia are closely associated and becoming increasingly integrated. The Chinese economy is playing an increasingly important role. In particular, with the execution and implementation of the *China-ASEAN Free Trade Agreement*, China's status as the largest "market supplier" in East Asia is on the rise. Meanwhile, the multilateral CMI arrangements under promotion indicate possible further breakthroughs in regional monetary and financial cooperation. In this context, the RMB has an unparalleled market appeal in East Asia.

Fourthly, to integrate the factor of regional cooperation into the strategic arrangements of the RMB before promoting RMB regionalization through regional monetary and financial cooperation can effectively advance the process of RMB internationalization. It has to be admitted that, thanks to the rising economic status of China in East Asia, even adopting the "unilateral" RMB internationalization strategy may make progress at the regional level. But it must be noted that, firstly, in East Asia, the appeal of the RMB as the invoice, settlement and reserve currency at the present stage is not great enough to allow it to take the place of the U.S. dollar and other international currencies, and that China's economic status and improved economic strength may not necessarily lead other countries to have the need to accept the RMB;

secondly, since China and other East Asian economies are so closely connected economically, to ignore regional cooperation and coordination in advancing currency internationalization will bring great risks to China and other East Asian economies, and reduce the appeal of the RMB in the region; thirdly, not to take into consideration the factor of regional cooperation will also prevent China from achieving the objective of providing an end-product and financial market for other economies in East Asia, and weaken the market foundation for the RMB to become a regional key currency.

All in all, the idea of not taking into consideration the factor of regional cooperation but adopting "unilateralism" in the process of RMB internationalization will not only cause great problems for RMB regionalization but also have adverse impacts on RMB regionalization. Conversely, to integrate the factor of regional cooperation into the strategy of RMB internationalization will promote the process of RMB regionalization and help achieve the objective of RMB internationalization. Firstly, to actively combine RMB internationalization and regional monetary and financial cooperation will reduce institutional barriers to RMB regionalization and speed up the process of the RMB's development into a regional settlement and reserve currency. Secondly, through the arrangements of regional monetary and financial cooperation, RMB regionalization will not rely only on the financial resources of China but can also make full use of regional resources, reducing the risks faced by China in the opening of its financial market and RMB capital account convertibility, and helping achieve the objective of RMB regionalization under the condition of incomplete RMB convertibility. Thirdly, it is helpful for the stable economic growth and progressive economic restructuring in China and the further strengthening of the economic connection between China and other East Asian economies, and will further improve the economic status and role of China in East Asia, laying a more solid foundation for RMB regionalization.

Therefore, for the sake of RMB internationalization, China has to fully refer to the current foundation and future development of regional monetary and financial cooperation, take into consideration the common interests of East Asia, view regional monetary cooperation and exchange rate coordination at a deeper level as an important background factor that must be considered in order to achieve RMB internationalization, get rid of the excessive dependence of the RMB on the U.S. dollar using the platform of regional monetary cooperation, and achieve the objective of RMB regionalization.

Fifthly, RMB regionalization is also a real path to reforming the international monetary system. As mentioned above, not only does RMB internationalization need to be achieved through regional monetary and financial cooperation, but also RMB regionalization and regional monetary and financial cooperation in the future will decide the future of the international monetary system to a great extent. Therefore the strategy of RMB internationalization determines the future of the international monetary system to a large extent while enhancing the monetary and financial cooperation in East Asia so as to advance RMB regionalization is an important link to push forward the diversification of the international monetary system and gradually reform the international monetary system.

To sum up, no fundamental changes to the current international economic pattern and the basic architecture of the corresponding monetary and financial system will happen in the short term. The current international monetary system is sustainable. In such a situation, on the one hand it is hard to reform the current monetary system fundamentally in the short term, so it is necessary to progressively push forward the diversification of the international monetary system at the local and regional level; on the other hand, direct RMB internationalization at the global level is difficult to achieve. To improve the RMB's status and influence through RMB regionalization is a feasible choice of path. In this sense, the current international financial strategy in China has to be pushed forward at three levels simultaneously i.e. RMB internationalization, regional monetary and financial cooperation, and the reform of the international monetary and financial system, the three of which can promote one another. In line with the current international economic pattern and situation as well as the basic characteristics and real situation of China's economic development, China has to organically combine the reform of the international monetary system and the strategy of RMB internationalization to advance RMB internationalization within a feasible scope, and play a positive role in diversifying the international monetary system through effective development of RMB internationalization. Such a basic principle determines that, at the present stage, RMB regionalization has to be adopted in order to push forward RMB internationalization.

The "East Asia Consensus" helps advance the process of "RMB regionalization"

Since the outbreak of the Asian financial crisis in 1997 the countries and regions in East Asia have initially reached an "East Asia Consensus" on carrying out regional monetary and financial cooperation, and have launched a series of "collective actions." The formation and development of the "East Asia Consensus" vigorously promotes the process of "RMB regionalization" and makes it an inevitable choice for China to participate in East Asian monetary and financial cooperation.

Formation of the East Asia Consensus

As different economies in East Asia gradually recovered from the financial crisis in 1999, their governments and respective academic circles held discussions on the root causes of the financial crisis at a deeper level and realized more and more clearly that two main lessons could be learned from the crisis: 1) in a situation of large-scale and fast flow of international capital and fierce fluctuations in the U.S. dollar and the Yen exchange rate, the exchange rate system pegged to the U.S. dollar is problematic; 2) in East Asia, an area where real economies are highly associated, underdevelopment, imperfections and other inherent shortcomings of the regional monetary cooperation system have had serious adverse influences on regional financial stability and economic development; efforts made by individual countries and regions to deal with large-scale flow of international capital would help little to prevent the recurrence of monetary and financial crises; and to set up the relevant regional macroeconomic indicators and monetary and financial indicators monitoring systems, crisis relief mechanisms and regional monetary system would be more important than relying on help from the IMF and other international institutions. Based on such an "East Asia Consensus," the policy authorities of all countries and regions in East Asia began to explore and actively try various original forms of regional monetary cooperation.

Regional monetary cooperation driven by the "East Asia Consensus"

In October 1998, Japan proposed the "New Miyazawa Initiative" in the name of its Finance Minister Kiichi Miyazawa, intending to set up an Asia Fund with a total of USD30 billion. Of this, USD15 billion would be used to meet the demand of countries suffering from the financial crisis for medium- and long-term capital. On 18 October 1999, Malaysian Prime Minister Mahathir put forward the initiative to set up the "East Asia Monetary Fund" at the East Asia Economic Summit, proposing to try to reach multilateral agreements firstly in East Asia and then in other Asian countries or regions. The scale of the "East Asia Monetary Fund" he proposed to set up was smaller than the IMF and would be a fund that totally belonged to East Asia. In November 1999 an informal summit attended by ASEAN, China, Japan and South Korea was held in Manila, the capital of the Philippines, at which a joint statement was issued to point out the possibility of creating a common market and a single currency in East Asia. In May 2000 the 10 ASEAN member states and the Chinese, Japanese and South Korean finance ministers held a meeting in Chiang Mai, Thailand, at which they held out extensive discussions and reached a consensus on the monetary and financial cooperation in East Asia before signing the *Chiang Mai Initiative* (CMI). The CMI aimed at setting up a larger Asian Reserve Fund in the future so that Asian currencies could support one another when under shock to avoid speculative attacks. In implementation, the original *Asian Swap Arrangement* (ASA) was expanded and *Network of Bilateral Swap and Repurchase Agreements* (BSA) was set up.

After the CMI was put forward in May 2000, a series of breakthroughs in East Asia regional monetary cooperation have been made. These mainly include:

CMI Multilization

Since the execution of the CMI, a series of bilateral or unilateral BSA were signed one after another among major East Asian countries and began to develop in the direction of a multilateral swap framework. As of the end of April 2008, under the CMI, the 10 ASEAN member states plus China, Japan and South Korea had signed 16 bilateral swaps agreements valued at a total of USD84 billion. After the ASEAN 10+3 Finance Ministers' Meeting in Istanbul in 2005, Hyderabad in 2006, the 10th ASEAN Plus Three Finance Ministers' Meeting was held in Tokyo, Japan on 5 May 2007, at which it was announced consent to set up an East Asia Foreign Exchange Reserve which was available for any of its member states in times of currency crisis. The launch of the East Asia Foreign Exchange Reserve enabled local monetary cooperation in East Asia to make a great step forward on the basis of the CMI (see Table 2.3). The East Asia Foreign Exchange Reserve, in nature, was to change the BSA into multilateral agreements under the CMI. At the ASEAN 10+3 Finance Ministers' Meeting held in Puji Island, Thailand on 22 February 2009, the regional foreign exchange reserve set up under the CMI was expanded from the original USD80 billion to USD120 billion, and a consensus was reached on the primary elements of the reserve in May 2009. Of which it remained unchanged that ASEAN would contribute to 20%, and China, Japan and South Korea 80% of the reserve.[17] Eventually, on 29 December 2009, the finance ministers and governors of the central banks of the ASEAN 10+3 and the president of the Hong Kong Monetary Authority formally signed the *Chiang Mai Initiative Multilateral* (CMIM). Although the RMB failed to be selected as one of the reserve currencies directly, and currency swaps among CMI parties would be still carried out between their own currencies and the U.S. dollar, it was a great breakthrough in regional monetary cooperation. After the completion of an independent oversight body, the regional reserve may become a new platform for financial cooperation in East Asia.

Information communication and the common test mechanism

East Asian countries and regions are now holding preliminary discussions and conducting studies on the construction of a regional monetary and financial monitoring system. ASEAN, China, Japan and South Korea have studied such problems as the monitoring of capital flow, an early pre-warning system etc., and set up a regional cooperation seminar in November 2001 with the main purpose of providing a dialogue mechanism for the relevant government staff of all East Asian countries regarding the establishment of a regional monitoring system. The ASEAN Plus Three Finance Ministers' Meeting held in Puji Island, Thailand deliberated and released the *Action Plan to Restore Economic and Financial Stability of the Asian Region,* reflecting several consensuses reached among ASEAN member states, China, Japan and South Korea on strengthening regional financial and monetary cooperation, dealing with crises together etc., taking the establishment of an independent regional economic monitoring mechanism and the strengthening of regional economic monitoring capability as important content, and making vigorous efforts to push them forward.

Development of the regional bond market

Even though East Asia has the highest savings ratio and enormous amounts of foreign exchange reserves, a great amount of capital flows into developed financial markets led by that of the U.S. under the current "U.S. dollar system," leading to the result that East Asia has to depend on the inflow of short-term capital from outside to develop its own economy. The dual currency mismatches thus caused become the main root for financial market turmoil and even financial crises. After the outbreak of the Asian financial crisis, East Asian countries and regions realized that underdevelopment of the regional capital market would especially jeopardize the development of the bond market, and developing a regional bond market thus became an important agenda item in regional monetary and financial cooperation. Therefore at the meeting held in Tokyo on 28 February 2003, ASEAN member states, China, Japan and South Korea formally launched the ABMI, planning to involve the governments of and private enterprises in East Asian countries in the issue of the Asian Basket Currency (ABC), which would be traded, managed, with its interest rate set, guaranteed and recognized by East Asian financial institutions. On 2 June in the same year, the 11 central banks and monetary authorities of the Executives' Meeting of East Asia and Pacific Central Banks (EMEAP) issued a proclamation announcing the formal launch of the Asian Bond Fund (ABF, Phase 1) with an initial size of USD1 billion. The ABF, a common fund set up by EMEAP economies with their official reserves,

Table 2.3. Suggestions on CMI reform and development reached at past ASEAN Plus Three Finance Ministers' Meetings

Time	Meeting no.	Main contents of CMI reform and development
May 2001	Fourth	To assess the main principles within the CMI framework in the subsequent three years
May 2004	Seventh	To further assess CMI (the so-called "2nd-stage CMI assessment"), and try to find ways to improve CMI efficiency.
May 2005	Eighth	To take all measures to improve CMI efficiency: 1) improve ASEAN 10+3 economic surveillance before integrating it into the CMI framework; 2) clearly define the process of launching Bilateral Swap Agreements, introduce the collective decision-making mechanism, and take it as the first step to make CMI multilateral; 3) double the size of some bilateral swap agreements so as to significantly improve the overall size of the current bilateral swap agreements; 4) improve the mechanism to draw capital, and raise the amount of capital readily available for use without the need of IMF loan assistance from 10% to 20%.
May 2006	Ninth	To require ASEAN Plus Three Deputy Finance Ministers' Meeting to organize a new taskforce to further study all possible paths of improving regional mobility aid mechanism so as to diversify CMI or enter the post-CMI period.
May 2007	Tenth	Agreed, in principle, to set up a self-managed foreign exchange reserve constrained by a single agreement, and take it as the form of CMI multilateral, required ASEAN Plus Three Deputy Finance Ministers' Meeting to make in-depth studies of key problems in CMI multilateral, such as the monitoring process, the definition of eligible reserves, shares of member states and rules on drawing capital etc.
May 2008	Eleventh	ASEAN Plus Three announced the setting up of a common foreign exchange reserve fund valuing USD80 billion. The move would develop CMI into a regional monetary fund in Asia. The common foreign exchange reserve fund provided proper foreign exchange reserve management for each East Asian country in the form of earmarking. Since the share of contribution would determine the right to vote, according to the current way of contribution, China, Japan and South Korea who jointly contribute 80% to the reserve would become the "locomotive" of the trigger mechanism of the common foreign exchange reserve fund.

(Cont'd)

Time	Meeting no.	Main contents of CMI reform and development
February 2009	Special Finance Ministers' Meeting	ASEAN Plus Three Special Finance Ministers' Meeting released the *Action Plan to Restore Economic and Financial Stability of the Asian Region*, according to which CMIM expanded the common reserve fund to USD120 billion , and it was proposed to set up an independent regional monitoring entity. The *Action Plan to Restore Economic and Financial Stability of the Asian Region* prepared for the institutional construction of the CMI multilateral mechanism, while acting as a platform for policy coordination and monetary cooperation at a higher level.

Source: Joint Ministerial Statement of ASEAN 10+3 Finance Ministers' Meetings, May 2000–May 2007.www.aseansec.org.; Gao Haihong, ASEAN, China, Japan and South Korea Common Foreign Exchange Reserve Fund: *An Important Measure to Establish the Asian Monetary Fund*, Policy Brief No. 08030, www.rcif.org.cn; Gao Haihong: *CMI New Measure: To Guarantee Asian Financial Stability with Multilateral Institutional Cooperation*, Policy Brief No. 09091, www.rcif.org.cn. http: / / www.most.gov.cn.

would invest in the package sovereign and quasi-sovereign U.S. dollar bonds issued by EMEAP members (apart from Japan, Australia and New Zealand) so as to improve the liquidity of such bonds and enable other investors to enter the Asian bond market. After the establishment of ABF1, to open a regional Asian bond market denominated in Asian currencies and issued on Asian markets was put on the agenda. On 16 December 2004, EMEAP announced that ABF2 with a total amount of USD2 billion set up by EMEAP members would be officially launched at the beginning of 2005. On 12 May 2005, ABF2 officially entered the implementation stage. Currently the launch of ABF3 is under preparation.

Regional exchange rate cooperation and the ACU

The outbreak of the Asian Financial Crisis fully exposed the disadvantages of the original exchange rate arrangements in East Asia in the following three aspects: 1) they led to exogenous monetary policies and were not up to the requirements of the economic development cycle of East Asia; 2) they were contradictory to the trade pattern of the East Asian economic community, and regular exchange rate fluctuations between the Yen and U.S. dollar caused fierce fluctuations in the regular accounts of all the East Asian economies; 3) the exchange rate system pegged to the U.S. dollar instead of an exchange rate coordinative mechanism produced a crisis infection and multiplier effect. Therefore after the completion of the discussions on policy development and mechanism construction, and implementation of crisis assistance, the issue of regional exchange rate coordination and cooperation was put on the agenda. At the ASEAN 10+3 Finance Ministers' Meeting held in Istanbul in May 2005, the policy administrations of all East Asian countries and regions pointed out in a joint statement the necessity for enhancing dialogue and coordination on economic policies (including exchange rate policies). Subsequently the Executives' Meeting of the China, Japan and South Korea Central Banks decided to renew the BSA while pointing out that maintaining exchange rate stability and strengthening policy coordination were the common need of the three parties. In such context, the ADB proposed to start to develop and release the ACU, the weighted average of Asian currencies.

Although the ADB does not reveal the specific form of the ACU, it may be similar to the AMU discussed by Japanese scholars (Ogawa and Shimizu, 2005). The latter is a currency basket composed of the 13 currencies of the ASEAN member states, China, Japan and South Korea. The weight of each currency depends on the weighted average ratio of its home country's real GDP to regional real GDP and its home country's volume of foreign trade to the regional total volume of foreign trade. The ACU in itself is a weighted average exchange rate index for reference, and has three aims: 1) to enable all East Asian policy authorities to understand the changes in the exchange rate of East Asian currencies as a whole against the major external currencies of the U.S. and Europe; 2) to enable all policy authorities in East Asia to understand the changes in their own currency exchange rate against the regional weighted average exchange rate, help reflect the relative stability among all currencies in East Asia, and provide a basis for policy dialogues on adjustments of the relative prices among regional currencies; 3) to prepare for issuing ACU-denominated bonds, and the private sector may set the spot and forward prices of the ACU for each currency in East Asia and other major currencies in the world. But the ACU is also an effort at regional policy cooperation and establishment of a monitoring system. It is not binding on the policies of East Asian countries, nor possesses the functions as a unit of account, let alone acting as reserve assets or the means of payment. Currently the ACU has a limited substantive influence on regional exchange rate cooperation, but it is undeniable that it has the potential to play a greater role.

It needs to be especially pointed out that, after the Democratic Party of Japan took office in September 2009, the Japanese Prime Minister Yukio Hatoyama mentioned the construction of an "East Asian Community" many times when meeting with Chinese and South Korean leaders, which met a positive response from the latter. The idea of an East Asian Community soon took root. At the China, Japan and South Korea Foreign Ministers' Meeting held in Shanghai on 28 September 2009, Chinese Foreign Minister Yang Jiechi indicated that China would actively participate in the integration of East Asia cooperation; the Japanese officials also said for the first time that the dream was expected to come true within the next 10–15 years. On 12 December 2009, Chinese Vice Chairman Xi Jinping said in an interview with reporters from mainstream Japanese and South Korean media that the East Asian Community was a common objective of China and Japan, that the proposal of the Japanese Prime Minister Yukio Hatoyama to set up an East Asian Community demonstrated the positive attitude held by the Japanese government toward East Asian cooperation, and that the idea was consistent with the process of Asian integration was an objective East Asian countries, including China and Japan, were pursuing. The above discussions on the East Asian Community demonstrate that the East Asian Consensus is deepening. The further promotion of future monetary and financial cooperation in East Asia is a positive sign.

Active participation of China driven by the East Asian Consensus

With the East Asia Consensus, China has become increasingly active in regional monetary cooperation in recent years. Since 2001, the bilateral currency swaps between China and other countries in East Asia have been developing very fast and this is becoming an important force for promoting financial stability in East Asia. As of the end of April 2008, within the framework of CMI, ASEAN member states and China, Japan and South Korea had signed 16 bilateral swap agreements of which six bilateral swap agreements were signed by and between China, Japan, South Korea, Thailand, Malaysia, Indonesia and the Philippines, with the total amount reaching USD23.5 billion (of which China promised to contribute USD16.5 billion).[19] Thailand was the first country to sign a bilateral swap agreement with China, followed by South Korea, Japan, Malaysia and Indonesia in turn (see Table 2.4). As early as in October 2003, the Chinese Premier Wen Jiabao put forward the initiative to "advance the CMIM" for the first time at the ASEAN 10+3 Summit, proposing to integrate the relatively unstructured bilateral swap mechanism into a multilateral capital assistance mechanism, which promoted the construction of a multilateral regional foreign exchange reserve.

The "collective actions" taken under the East Asian Consensus created a hard-won opportunity for pushing forward RMB regionalization and enhanced the influence of the RMB in East Asia, creating conditions for achieving RMB regionalization. For example, prior to 2008, the bilateral swap agreements signed between China and other East Asian countries were denominated in U.S. dollars, reflecting the profound influence of the U.S. dollar in East Asia.

However with the constant strengthening of the economic strength of China, corresponding adjustments of the invoice currency chosen were made in the bilateral swap agreements signed by China with other East Asian countries after 2008. The bilateral swap agreement of RMB180 billion signed by and between China and South Korea in February 2008 was denominated in both RMB and South Korean won. Moreover China and South Korea are studying the possibility of converting swaps into reserve currencies. The bilateral swap agreement of RMB80 billion signed by and between China and Malaysia in February 2009 was also denominated in both RMB and ringgit. In January 2009, China signed a bilateral swap agreement of RMB200 billion/227 billion Hong Kong dollars with the Hong Kong government, which further reflected the determination of the Chinese government to maintain economic and financial stability in Hong Kong with the RMB.

To sum up, to improve the international competitiveness of its currency

Table 2.4. Bilateral swap agreements signed between China and other East Asian economies

Swap Sides	Currencies	Specific Arrangements
China–Thailand	RMB–Thai Baht	Both sides signed a bilateral swap agreement worth at most USD2 billion in December 2001.
China–South Korea	RMB–South Korea Won	Both sides signed a bilateral swap agreement worth at most USD2 billion in June 2002, and another bilateral swap agreement worth RMB180 billion/38 trillion won in December 2008.
China–Malaysia	U.S. dollar–Ringgit RMB–Ringgit	Both sides signed a bilateral swap agreement of USD1.5 billion in October 2002; and another bilateral swap agreement of RMB80 billion/40 billion Ringgit in February 2009.
China–Indonesia	U.S. dollar–Indonesian Rupiah	Both sides singed a bilateral swap agreement of USD1 billion in December 2003 before increasing the amount of bilateral swap to USD2 billion in October 2005, and then USD4 billion in October 2006.
China–Japan	RMB–Yen	Both sides signed a bilateral swap agreement of USD3 billion in March 2002 before renewing it in September 2007.
Mainland China–Hong Kong,	China RMB–Hong Kong dollar	Both sides signed a bilateral swap agreement of RMB200 billion /227 billion Hong Kong dollars in January 2009.

Source: The People's Bank of China.

and to realize currency internationalization at the present stage, a country must make use of the regional economic cooperation platform and rely on the overall framework of institutional regional monetary cooperation. Therefore the opinion that stresses "direct" RMB internationalization in a one-legged manner or equalizes the spontaneous circulation of RMB in the neighboring countries and regions of China to "RMB regionalization" is incorrect. China must realize RMB internationalization through progressive "RMB Asianization."

The Costs and Benefits of RMB Regionalization

Currency regionalization is a double-edged sword, bringing both benefits and costs. The analysis of the costs and benefits of RMB regionalization will become an important reference for pushing forward RMB regionalization.

Analysis of the benefits of RMB regionalization

Conducive to increasing the real national wealth of China

Obtaining seigniorage income

As has been demonstrated in Chapter 1, under the non-convertible credit currency system, whether a country can obtain seigniorage or not depends on whether its currency enjoys the status of an international reserve currency. Therefore international seigniorage may be understood as the profit from issuing a reserve currency. Although the channels for RMB inflow and outflow at the present stage are complicated, and there are monitoring and statistical difficulties, so accurate data on the net outflow of RMB are unavailable, many scholars have analyzed in various ways the possible seigniorage from RMB regionalization. According to the estimate of Zhong Wei (2002), the seigniorage income brought about by RMB regionalization will be USD15.28 billion by 2010, about USD22.46 billion by 2015, and about USD30.02 billion by 2020. He thus draws the conclusion that RMB regionalization will bring to China an annual stable seigniorage income of about USD2.5 billion. By analyzing the benefits of U.S. dollar internationalization Cheng Yulu et al. (2005) calculate that, if achieved in 2010, RMB regionalization will bring in RMB750 billion from currency internationalization. With the help of the formula "seigniorage income = trade balance of RMB settlement + consumption of domestic residents (in RMB) in Hong Kong - consumption of Hong Kong residents (in RMB) in Mainland China – interest paid by People's Bank of China Shenzhen Central

Sub–branch to the Hong Kong's Banks for the latter's RMB deposits," Liu Lizhen and Xu Qiyuan (2006) estimate that seigniorage income of RMB in China's economic exchanges with Hong Kong from March 2004 to the end of 2005 was RMB12.41 billion. Of course, as regards the relations between currency regionalization and seigniorage income, pushing forward currency regionalization should happen before assessing seigniorage income. Paying too much attention to the acquisition of seigniorage may very likely bring an enormous reversal risk of currency internationalization to China.

Reducing the risks of foreign exchange reserves and the loss of national wealth

The national foreign exchange reserves of China begun to increase rapidly after 2004. As of the end of February 2006, its foreign exchange reserves had exceeded those of Japan, making it the world's No. 1 in terms of foreign exchange reserves. The foreign exchange reserves of China exceeded USD1 trillion for the first time in October 2006, USD1.5 trillion as of the end of 2007, about USD1.95 trillion as of the end of 2008,[20] and USD2.4 trillion in early 2010. The current foreign exchange reserves in China are far more than needed. Excessive foreign exchange reserves will, on the one hand, increase the RMB counterpart of foreign exchange reserves and make it difficult for the People's Bank of China to regulate the economy using monetary policies; on the other hand shrink the foreign exchange reserves dramatically due to the constant appreciation of RMB against the U.S. dollar. More importantly, the trend of U.S. dollar deprecation presents a serious risk of shrinkage to the China's enormous foreign exchange reserves. Since the "subprime crisis" in the U.S. induced global financial crises in September 2008, the U.S. government has invested trillions of the U.S. dollars to save bankrupt financial institutions or those on the verge of bankruptcy. In a situation when it remains hard to contain the crisis and economic recession, the U.S. government will surely handle it with more fiscal expenditures. To make up the growing fiscal deficits, the U.S. can only take three measures: 1) to increase taxes; 2) to ask foreign countries, especially those with enormous amounts of foreign exchange reserves such as China and Japan, to purchase more of its treasury bonds; 3) to have the deficits bought by the Federal Reserve. Currently it is unlikely that the U.S. will increase taxes to deal with severe crises. In fact the Chinese government has to keep buying U.S. treasury bonds in spite of the great risk of U.S. dollar depreciation so as to maintain the value of the stock of its foreign exchange reserves.[21] The enormous foreign exchange reserves have become the "hostage" of the U.S. On 18 March 2009 the Federal Reserve announced at the latest policy meeting its decision to buy U.S. treasury bonds valuing USD300 billion within the following six months. Meanwhile, to offer greater support to the housing market, the Federal Reserve announced purchase of another USD750 billion of real estate mortgage bonds secured by Fannie Mae (Federal National Mortgage Association) and Freddie Mac (Federal Home Mortgage Association), making the amount of relevant bonds bought that year amount to USD1.25 trillion; meanwhile, the Federal Reserve will buy another USD100 billion of bonds issued by Fannie Mae and Freddie Mac, making the amount of relevant agency bonds mount to USD200 billion. The amount of mortgage bonds purchased by the Federal Reserve will increase USD850 billion before reaching USD1.45 trillion. It is the second time in nearly 40 years that the Federal Reserve has announced purchase of U.S. treasury bonds on such a large scale, which is also a formal declaration that the U.S. has entered the era of a quantitative easing policy.[22] Obviously its move to directly buy U.S. treasury bonds and agency debts will undoubtedly increase banknote printing, and inevitably lead to U.S. dollar depreciation. It will lead to great shrinkage of the U.S. dollar reserves.

Faced with such a serious situation, the Chinese monetary authority has to take measures to adjust the composition of its foreign exchange reserves in the near future. At the same time it must accelerate RMB regionalization in the long run to, on the one hand, reduce U.S. dollar reserves, and on the other hand to deal with the risk of U.S. dollar depreciation through regional monetary and financial cooperation. After realizing RMB regionalization it will be unnecessary to stock foreign exchange reserves on a large scale or hold a large amount of U.S. dollar reserves, which will reduce risks and losses brought about by large amounts of foreign exchange reserves before reducing the loss of national wealth caused by foreign exchange reserves. Meanwhile China can directly import various resources from other regions of East Asia and increase its real national wealth by exporting RMB through RMB regionalization. The trade deficit brought about by RMB regionalization will enable China to surpass its real national income and expand its real national absorption (e.g. buying foreign commodities, services and assets with RMB) to some extent, before multiplying its national income through the multiplier effect[23] and stimulating the increase in national income and wealth.

Conducive to promoting the development of China's real economy

RMB regionalization allows the RMB to be extensively used in inter-regional denomination, payment and settlement. Most cross-currency payment, such as international trade settlement, capital lending and borrowing, and the repayment of the principal and interest on the international financial market can all be done in RMB, which of course is conducive to the expansion of foreign economic exchanges of China and promotes the development of the real economy. Specific benefits mainly include:

Promoting the development of foreign trade

RMB regionalization will reduce the risk of exchange rate fluctuations faced by China in regional foreign trade. For importers and exporters, the exchange rate risk is one of the main risks they face. The best way to avoid it is to use their home currency in trade denomination and settlement. In this way, RMB regionalization will be a great convenience for Chinese importers, exporters, investors and consumers, enabling them to use more of their home currency in international economic transactions in East Asia so as to reduce or avoid the problem of exchange rate risk.

The reduction of the risk of exchange rate fluctuations will promote the development of China in East Asia. RMB regionalization will not only exempt exporters from the cost outlay in hedging foreign exchange receipts and disbursements, but also make it easy to provide export credit for foreign importers in RMB so as to further improve export competitiveness. Meanwhile it will create favorable conditions for China to provide a wider export market for other countries in East Asia, expand foreign trade, and make its economic relations with these countries closer. Currently, in East Asia, China has obtained an important position in terms of the scale of its foreign trade. In 2007 the total volume of exports of China to East Asia contributed to 38% of the total volume of its exports, and that of imports to China from East Asia accounted for 48% of that its total imports.[24] Meanwhile the ratio of foreign trade volume of China to the total volume of foreign trade of the 13 main countries and regions in East Asia has been rising gradually since 1996, from 14.16% in 1996 to 35.30% in 2007.[25] Therefore RMB regionalization will advance the further development of China's foreign trade, enhance China's competitiveness in the import and export trade in the region, and improve China's trade association with other countries.

Advancing the development of foreign investment

To Chinese residents and enterprises, the RMB being widely accepted in the region means reduction of the cost of currency trade, reduces investment risks caused by fluctuations in the exchange rate, and further ensures investment benefits. RMB regionalization will create very favorable conditions for China to make direct investment in the region.

Currently, seen from the balance of international investment projects, the foreign investments of China are at a low level. In 2007 the total assets of international investments made by China reached USD753.2 billion and the total debts reached USD1.266 trillion, registering a great investment surplus. It can be seen after analyzing international investment projects that the greatest investment surplus came from direct investments. The size of foreign direct investments to China reached USD742.4 billion, 7 times greater than the foreign direct investment made by China,[26] indicating a very limited influence by China on foreign direct investments. Seen from the regions with its foreign direct investments, China has had a limited influence on foreign direct investment in Asia and East Asia. Of the foreign investments made by China to East Asian economies in 2006, 39.3% was made to Hong Kong, followed by that to Singapore which only accounted for 0.75%.[27] Apart from Hong Kong, China, China's investments in other East Asian economies and the share of its investments in all are low. RMB regionalization can neatly solve the problem of the supply of foreign exchange that has become a barrier to foreign investments. Chinese investors can use RMB directly to make foreign investments, which will greatly improve their foreign investment capacity.

RMB regionalization will not only contribute to the expansion of China's foreign direct investments, but also promote the level of internationalization of Chinese enterprises to enable them to participate in international competition and enhance their international competitiveness. RMB regionalization means a more open Chinese market and more effective allocation of resources. Enterprises will have to treat economic restructuring seriously and positively in order to adapt to market demands; their innovation mechanism will be further enhanced and facilitate industrial and economic restructuring, as well as the development of the real economy.

Conducive to the coordination and balance of domestic and foreign economic policies

Compared with a common local currency, an international currency has an inborn deficit financing capacity. Upon the realization of RMB regionalization, the trade surplus of other Asian countries and regions with China will be settled by accepting RMB liquidity, which will reduce the demand for the U.S. dollar of its Asian trade partners. For China, it will bring about RMB supply from abroad i.e. RMB repatriation.[28] It will strengthen China's capacity for financing its international balance of payments.

Generally speaking when local currency regionalization or internationalization fails, tighter economic policies are needed in order to improve the balance of payments, which will cause a rapid economic decline. To ameliorate the situation expansive economic policies are needed to stimulate the economy which will further deteriorate the balance of payments i.e. leading to a further expansion of the amount of deficits. However when the RMB becomes a regional currency, the People's Bank of China will be able to finance and deal with deficits in the balance of payments by issuing more RMB to some extent. With the capability of making up the deficits of the balance of payments using RMB i.e. with "trade deficit financing" capability, China will no longer have to tighten its economy, which is costly, in order to adjust the deficits of short-term balance of payments and sacrifice its domestic economic benefits to maintain an external equilibrium. On the contrary, its capability of trade deficit capability will be enhanced, which helps resolve the contradictions of domestic and foreign balanced policies.

RMB regionalization will effectively avoid the contradiction between internal and external equilibriums in terms of policy choice, which can improve the independence of monetary, fiscal and trade policies to some extent, reduce the shock of external financial crises and economic fluctuations to the Chinese economy, improve the Chinese economy's own capability of fending off financial and economic shocks, and help maintain the stable development of the Chinese economy.

Conducive to pushing forward the reform and development of the Chinese financial market

Promoting reform of the Chinese banking industry and the financial mechanism

The Chinese financial system is underdeveloped and is dominated by commercial banks, especially state-owned commercial banks. As mentioned above, having a complete, stable and open financial system is a necessary condition for a country's currency internationalization. To achieve RMB regionalization, China must carry out the necessary reforms and open up its financial system. Along with RMB regionalization, more foreign-funded banks and foreign financial agencies will keep entering the Chinese financial market, placing higher requirements on the operational mechanism and level of the Chinese banking industry. China needs to keep perfecting its banking and financial service industries, improve the operational efficiency of its banks and the quality and level of its financial industry, set up a highly-efficient banking system that is up to international requirements, and accelerate the reform of the financial system in terms of capital, business scope, service and risk management so as to adapt to the requirement that the Chinese financial market has to go global.

Promoting the opening up of the capital account in China

Of the 43 capital transactions classified by the IMF, as early as in 2004 nearly half of the capital account transactions were basically unrestricted or less restrictive, over 40% of the capital transactions had been subject to greater restrictions, and only slightly more than 10%29 were under strict restrictions. In recent years, the process of opening up the capital account has been proceeding.

The process of RMB regionalization is a process in which the RMB achieves convertibility in the region. Opening the capital account has to keep pace with RMB regionalization, the rate of which has to be coordinated with the dilution of the risk of RMB liberalization. Therefore the opening up of RMB capital accounts has to be combined organically with the process of RMB regionalization according to the new features of the Chinese economy and the changes in China's external economic environment so as to promote the stability and development of Chinese finance.

Enhancing China's financing capability in the region and promoting the development of the China's capital market

As has already noted the Chinese capital market is still underdeveloped, featuring a low financing capability. Not only is the Chinese stock market underdeveloped, but also the Chinese bond market needs to be further developed. National debts and policy bank bonds have been taking the dominant position, while the development of real marketized commercial bank bonds, corporate bonds and short-term financing bonds has been slow. In its international indirect investment position in 2007 there was a significant deficit in China's foreign investment in securities. Its foreign investment in securities reached USD239.5 billion, while its investment in Chinese securities was only USD142.6 billion.30 It can be seen that the Chinese securities market is more backward and its capital market features a poor financing capability.

Along with RMB regionalization, international capital liquidity will improve gradually as will China's financing capability in the domestic and foreign financial markets. Meanwhile the development of the Chinese capital market will speed up, and the demand for a sound and perfect capital market is increasingly great, thus RMB regionalization will promote the fast development of the Chinese capital market.

Improving the status of the RMB in foreign exchange transactions and promoting the development of the Chinese foreign exchange market

Seen from the transactions on the foreign exchange market, the main currencies in the transactions since 2000 are the U.S. dollar, euro, British pound sterling and Yen, of which the U.S. dollar dominates. The share of RMB in foreign exchange transactions has been slim, only 0.5% in 2007, being extremely mismatched to the share of the Chinese economic aggregate in the world. Seen from the distribution of currencies in foreign exchange transactions, strong currencies such as the U.S. dollar, euro and British pound sterling are mainly involved in swaps i.e. the share of spot foreign exchange transactions is 30%; while the RMB is mainly engaged in spot foreign exchange transactions and in only 7% of swaps, indicating that the Chinese foreign exchange market is yet to become mature and has limited currencies in trading.31 It may help reduce the exchange rate risk brought about by speculation on the foreign exchange market in the short run, but is not conducive to the improvement of the international influence of the RMB.

RMB regionalization will expand RMB influence and improve the share of the RMB in foreign exchange transactions, which will further improve the international influence of the RMB, increase RMB transactions, and promote the development and expansion of the Chinese foreign exchange market.

Promoting the establishment and development of the offshore financial market

Considering that RMB convertibility and complete capital account liberalization are yet to be realized, it is essential to set up an offshore financial market in the process of realizing RMB regionalization. The State Council of China has now decided to launch a trial of RMB Cross-border Settlement Center in Hong Kong. Given the financial status of Hong Kong in Southeast Asia and the world, to establish an RMB offshore financial market in Hong Kong will become the general trend.

The RMB offshore financial market will greatly promote the development of international finance and trade in China since it will speed up international capital flow, reduce the cost of international loan capital, make the international market more competitive, and facilitate the business activities of transnational companies.

Cost income from offshore financial businesses can improve foreign exchange income, provide job opportunities for residents by providing services, and improve the technical level and overall quality of practitioners in its financial industry. The inflow of loan capital may increase the surplus of capital account in its balance of payments. The inflow of foreign banks may stimulate transnational companies to invest in China, accelerate China's economic development, and improve the reputation and status of the Chinese financial market in the world financial market. RMB regionalization can promote the establishment and development of the RMB offshore financial market, and thus will make a great contribution to the development of the Chinese financial market.

Conducive to the improvement of China's international status

Helping improve China's international status in finance, trade and investment

RMB regionalization will speed up domestic financial reforms in China, drive the Chinese financial industry to go global, and enhance the international competitiveness of the Chinese financial industry. Meanwhile the RMB will serve as a means of international trade settlement and denomination in a wider scope, contributing to the further development and expansion of China's foreign trade and investment. RMB regionalization will improve China's international status in finance, trade and investment.

Promoting regional monetary cooperation and expanding China's influence in the region

The realization of RMB regionalization will greatly improve the status of the RMB in the region, endow the RMB with more and more international monetary functions, and help solve the difficulty faced by emerging economies in East Asia in choosing their exchange rate system. It will further promote regional monetary cooperation, promote the establishment of a regional economic and financial monitoring agency, improve regional economic and financial monitoring capability, increase the anti-crisis capability of East Asia, and maintain regional economic and financial security and stability.

With the realization of RMB regionalization China can influence to some extent the finance and economy of countries that take RMB as their foreign exchange reserves when developing its monetary policies, which will greatly improve the regional influence of the RMB and win China the right to participate in developing regulations on international affairs in East Asia.

Improving the position of the RMB in the international monetary system

RMB regionalization will enhance the position of the Chinese economy in East Asia and make the regional market more integrated. With the support of the regional market, the RMB will greatly improve the current unequal international monetary system, improve its status in the future monetary system, promote the diversification of international currencies, improve the international monetary pattern, and perfect the international monetary system.

Improving China's political status in the world

With RMB regionalization the international influence of the RMB will keep increasing, which will make China more and more important in world politics and give China an increasingly greater right of discourse. It indicates that China can gain more economic and political benefits in developing or revising regulations on international affairs before achieving its development goals and realizing its long-term interests.

Cost analysis of RMB regionalization

RMB regionalization will have corresponding costs while bringing benefits to China. Here it is proposed to analyze the cost of RMB regionalization from two perspectives i.e. the policy cost and the economic cost. The influence of RMB regionalization on Chinese government policies will be discussed first, and then an analysis given of some possible shocks that may be suffered by the Chinese economic and financial sector in the process of RMB regionalization.

Influence of RMB regionalization on China's macroeconomic policies

When developing its macroeconomic policies, a government intentionally uses certain policy instruments to regulate the macroeconomic operation in a planned manner so as to achieve the four basic policy objectives i.e. full employment, stable commodity prices, economic growth and the balance of payments. Generally speaking, there are mainly three macroeconomic policy tools i.e. fiscal policy, monetary policy and exchange rate policy. In an open economy it is difficult for a country's macroeconomic policies to play their role fully and separately without being affected by the external environment. Correspondingly, in pushing forward RMB Asianization within the framework of regional monetary cooperation in East Asian, the coordination and cooperation between China and other East Asian countries in monetary, fiscal and exchange rate policies will be a problem that must be faced and one which will certainly disturb the effect of China's policies.

Affecting the independence and effectiveness of the monetary policy of China

According to the "Mundell-Fleming" model, implementing a fixed exchange rate system by a country in the context of free capital flow will cost the independence of its monetary policy, because its central bank will be kept busy stabilizing the exchange rate. Only when a floating exchange rate is implemented can the monetary policy be independent. Krugman further puts forward the so-called "Impossible Trinity" i.e. the trilemma in international economics that suggests it is impossible to have all three of the following at the same time: a fixed exchange rate, free capital movement, and an independent monetary policy. No more than two of these can be realized at the same time.

When the RMB becomes a regional key currency this indicates, to some extent, that the objective of free capital flow has been achieved, that the independence of Chinese monetary policy will be greatly affected, and that stabilizing the exchange rate will have to rely on the means of interest rate to very great extent, bringing national economic development under the control of the external environment to an even greater extent. Moreover, in the current situation where the RMB is circulated in several neighboring countries and regions of China, it is circulating in cash which exists along with personnel and commodity mobility. Therefore it is very unlikely that the RMB will either be gathered abroad or show repatriation on a large scale. However, if RMB regionalization is achieved and the main means of circulation are various financial instruments, it will definitely have an impact on the monetary policy in China and inevitably lead to the problem of "exposure to monetary policy", namely a tighter monetary policy may partly be "diluted" due to acquisitive repatriation of monetary capital, and a more relaxed monetary policy will, driven by the interest margin, contribute to monetary capital outflow. It will weaken the control of domestic RMB by the People's Bank of China before interfering with the effects of the macroeconomic regulation of China.

Meanwhile, after the realization of RMB regionalization, the connection between the Chinese financial market and the world financial market will become increasingly close. The spillover effect on China's domestic policies will partly or greatly weaken the influence of China's monetary policy on China's economic variables, while the foreign feedback effect will enable foreign monetary policy to affect domestic monetary policy. Both effects may lead to currency substitution, capital flight and the inflow of a great deal of capital, which means that China's monetary policy will deviate from the expected objectives and partly lose its effectiveness.

Affecting the independence and effectiveness of China's exchange rate policy

Under open economic conditions, when a country adopts a macroeconomic policy, the policy will often be offset by an opposite policy adopted by other countries. Therefore to avoid the emergence of "beggar-thy-neighbor policy" and stabilize the exchange rate, it is necessary to strengthen the coordination and cooperation of the policies of different countries. Higher-level regional monetary cooperation in East Asia would be carrying out regional exchange rate coordination. It sets new requirements on the development of national exchange rate policies in East Asia, and to some extent affects their independence. Since China is a great power in East Asia, if RMB regionalization is achieved and the RMB becomes a key currency in East Asia, the RMB will of course play the role as the currency anchor and China will need to sacrifice some independence in exchange rate policy while stabilizing the exchange rate.

Since China began to reform the RMB exchange rate formation mechanism in 2005, the international community has been expecting RMB appreciation. How to anchor such expectation and cultivate the credibility of the Chinese monetary authority becomes important for improving the efficacy of the exchange rate reform (Li Jing, 2006). However pushing forward RMB regionalization will inevitably increase the amount of RMB in circulation outside China, and weaken the stability of the Chinese foreign exchange market. When the monetary authority hopes to control the exchange rate fluctuations within a specific scope with exchange rate policy, the enormous amount of overseas RMB will pose a potential threat to the effectiveness of the policy. In particular, when speculators hope to gain profits by disrupting the exchange quotation in China, it will be harder for China to implement its foreign exchange rate policy.

On the other hand, once the RMB becomes a foreign exchange reserve currency in East Asia, excessive supply or demand of RMB in East Asia will directly affect the balance of its demand and supply in the entire world market, leading to the consequence of RMB being sold out or panic buying of RMB. Eventually the RMB exchange rate will depreciate or appreciate, which will pose a great challenge to the development and implementation of the RMB exchange rate policy.

Having to take its regional responsibilities into consideration when developing the macroeconomic policies of China

To improve its international influence, China needs to not only develop its overall economic, financial, military and technical strengths but also have a great sense of responsibility. In pushing forward RMB regionalization, China needs to take into consideration the importance of balanced domestic and foreign economic policies. All monetary and financial policies developed by China in the future will not be purely national economic policies but also a kind of "regional policies" (Wei En, 2002).

China is committed to the stability and development of East Asia. When the Asian financial crisis broke out in 1997, the Chinese government resolved "not to devalue the RMB," reducing the economic stresses of those countries whose currencies had been devalued and maintaining the stability of the economic order in East Asia on the one hand, and setting China's image of being a responsible great power and promoting China's international status and influence. Due to the great political divergences, economic gaps and cultural differences among East Asian countries, it is problematic to implement regional policy coordination. As a great power in East Asia, China must undertake more responsibilities and risks, requiring China to base its macroeconomic policies on East Asia, have close policy coordination and cooperation with other East Asian countries (especially Japan), and maintain the stable relations and common development among East Asian countries while promoting its own economic development and stability.

It is also worth noting that, if the RMB does become a key currency in East Asia in the future, other currencies in the region may choose to peg to the RMB at which point the RMB will have to play the role as the regional stabilizer. RMB exchange rate stability depends to a great extent on the U.S. dollar. It becomes a currency anchor in East Asia by pegging to the U.S. dollar. Therefore RMB regionalization is a process of "de-dollarization" in some sense. Only in so doing can macroeconomic losses in East Asia be prevented due to exchange rate fluctuations between the RMB and the U.S. dollar. China needs to keep pushing forward reform of the RMB exchange rate system, perfect the RMB exchange rate formation mechanism, and avoid big fluctuations of the RMB exchange rate by implementing the relevant monetary and exchange rate policies while carrying out necessary international cooperation to push forward the process of "de-dollarization" in East Asia before achieving exchange rate stability in the region.

Influences of RMB regionalization on the Chinese economic and financial sectors

The Chinese real economy may be more vulnerable to external shocks.

RMB regionalization has to be achieved through institutional regional monetary cooperation besides the market role, which will make the economic linkage among East Asian countries closer and may even lead to periodic economic fluctuations. In such circumstances, economic turmoil or inflation in any country in East Asia will affect China through the monetary transmission mechanism and make the real economy in China suffer. Before the complete realization of RMB regionalization, due to the fact that the capital account in China has not been fully opened or to other factors, the influence of economic fluctuations in other East Asian countries is controllable. But once the RMB is ready to circulate in East Asia, the real economy of China will be more vulnerable to external shocks.

In addition, if the RMB becomes the settlement or reserve currency in East Asia, overseas demand for it will increase greatly and China will have to face the great pressure of undertaking the enormous trade deficits with other East Asian countries. The trade development pattern will be constrained or challenged. Currently China implements an export-oriented trade strategy and pulls its economic growth through investment and trade, which is very unfavorable for RMB regionalization. In the future China will have to play the role of end-product market supplier in East Asia, transform its economic and trade development pattern, and turn the trade-driven economic growth pattern into a domestic demand-driven economic growth pattern.[32]

The potential instability of the Chinese financial sector will increase.

The world market, especially the world financial market, has been fluctuating in recent years. Both the Asian financial crisis in 1997 and the global financial storm caused by the "subprime crisis" in the U.S. have greatly affected the world economy. However compared with other countries, China suffered little in these financial crises. This was without doubt mainly because of the better economic situation in China and its sufficient foreign exchange reserves, but the RMB capital account having not been totally opened and the RMB not being used around the world on a large scale is also one of the most important reasons.

When RMB regionalization is achieved, the Chinese economy will be closely linked to the economies of other East Asian countries which also means that its connects with the world economy will be closer. In such circumstances, due to the removal of monetary control, any slight change in the international financial market will directly affect China, making its financial sector potentially unstable. In particular the most instable factor on the international financial market i.e. large-scale international hot money has been extraordinarily sensitive to minor changes in a country's macro-economy. It can manipulate the market by taking every opportunity, get profits by rapidly changing the direction of capital flow and speculation, while producing a gigantic "herd effect", extending one country's financial crisis into a regional or global financial crisis.

Seen from historical experience, to shock the Chinese financial market international speculators must first of all hold a necessary amount of RMB capital, which is impossible in the short term when the RMB has not become fully convertible or extensively and heavily used around the world. However once the RMB becomes a regional currency, the neighboring countries and regions of China will hold more and more RMB. When the RMB held by them reaches a certain amount, international speculators may take measures to control part of the RMB in circulation in the world market and launch attacks at times of economic difficulties or using loopholes in China, such as suddenly selling a great amount of RMB to convert it into other currencies.[33] If China is not capable enough or readily prepared, such behavior may greatly shock the financial sector of China. Moreover if RMB regionalization has been achieved but the RMB has not become an international currency, China may face the shock of speculation in the world and regional markets. More importantly, speculative capital flow will lead to great deviation in the RMB exchange rate. The inflow of great amounts of capital will increase money supply in China and force China to face the pressure of RMB appreciation; on the contrary, RMB outflow on a large scale may lead to RMB supply shortage and bring about the pressure of currency depreciation.

In addition, RMB regionalization may also induce the risk of capital flight[34] Generally speaking, capital control may prevent capital flight. Under the condition of RMB inconvertibility, the level of capital flow is low and the cost is high, which limits the potential for capital flight. If RMB regionalization is achieved it will mean that the RMB can circulate freely at least within the region, which will lead to the outflow of capital that tends to transfer inside China and greatly increase the possibility of capital flight.

Apart from the costs analyzed above, the expansion of RMB circulation outside China may also make it more difficult to control and supervise cash RMB. After RMB regionalization, the People's Bank of China will find it more difficult to supervise cash RMB due to the difficulty in monitoring overseas demand for RMB and overseas RMB circulation. It may lead to an increase in abnormal cross-border flow of RMB in illegal activities, especially an increase in the amount of counterfeit RMB, which will on the one hand bring economic losses to China and damage the reputation of the RMB and on the other hand make it more difficult to crack down upon money laundering and counterfeit RMB.

A conclusion may be drawn from the above analysis, which is that a regionalized RMB costs while bringing about benefits. In general, RMB regionalization is more beneficial than costly for China. It is impossible to get profits from RMB regionalization under non-RMB regionalization conditions, and the risks of RMB regionalization can be controlled by taking corresponding measures. For example, the influence of RMB regionalization on China's macroeconomic policies may be solved by more effective policy portfolios and strengthened through the monitoring of cross-border RMB flow; the possible adverse impacts of RMB regionalization on the Chinese economy and finance may be reduced by perfecting the Chinese financial sector, strengthening the construction of enterprises, and positively reforming the exchange rate formation mechanism. China has to avoid possible disadvantages while going after profits, and combine RMB regionalization with the necessary domestic reforms, before being able to enjoy the profits brought about by RMB regionalization.

Summary

In recent years, as the economic relationship between China and the rest of East Asia has become increasingly closer and China's political and economic status in the world has been improved, residents in neighboring countries and regions of China have gradually recognized and accepted the RMB as the trading money and the clearing currency, and large amounts of RMB have begun to circulate outside the territory of China. In such circumstances the issue of RMB internationalization is attracting great attention from the Chinese monetary authority and from Chinese and foreign theoretical field. As for the choice of the path of RMB internationalization, although some academics propose to realize RMB internationalization through other ways, most academics tend to take the road of RMB regionalization first before realizing RMB internationalization.

It is difficult for any currency to challenge the existing currency hegemony on its own under the current international monetary system. The birth of the euro and the failure of "Yen internationalization" tell us that currency regionalization is an important step towards currency internationalization. To take part in international competition, a currency has to rely on the platform of regional economic cooperation and institution-based regional currency cooperation. One basic starting point for us to think about the strategies for RMB internationalization has to be based on the status of China as a regional power in Asia. Meanwhile, given the fact that the economic and financial foundations of China at the current stage are not strong enough to support direct RMB internationalization, the relationship between Chinese economic development and the East Asian economy is being constantly improved, and countries in East Asia have reached the "East Asia Consensus" regarding regional monetary and financial cooperation, we believe that RMB regionalization is a road that must be taken to reach RMB internationalization. The issue of RMB regionalization must be thought about and planned for within the overall structure of the East Asian monetary system.

The analysis of the costs and benefits of RMB regionalization has further provided a rational support for China to choose its monetary strategies. The evolution of RMB regionalization may bring about some adverse impacts on the macro-economic policies and private economic departments of China, but to an even greater extent it would bring enormous benefits to the development of China, including pushing forward the reform and development of economic finance in China, increasing the wealth of the Chinese people, and improving the status of China in East Asia and even in the world etc. Fundamentally, RMB regionalization should be the results of spontaneous market forces, yet it needs the Chinese government to actively push it forward and provide corresponding policy support so as to find the necessary and feasible logistical and system arrangements of "regional collective actions" for RMB regionalization. If China can implement certain reform and policy strategies in the process of RMB regionalization, it can avoid the disadvantages while going after profits, before fully enjoying the benefits brought about by RMB regionalization.

3

Chapter

Feasibility Analysis of RMB Regionalization

There is a long-running debate in theoretical circles over the conditions for a currency to become an international currency. It is generally believed that a currency with three functions, namely standard of value for international trade, medium of international payment, and store of value is an international currency from the perspective of the private sector; from the perspective of the public sector, an international currency has three functions including a benchmark for other economies to set their exchange rate, an intervention instrument for the foreign exchange market and an official foreign exchange reserve. The currency with all the above-mentioned six functions is a completely internationalized currency, such as the British pound before 1920 and the U.S. dollar after 1945. The currency that plays only part of these functions is not a completely internationalized currency, such as the Japanese Yen.[1]

To date, almost all studies about the economic and financial conditions for the internationalization of a currency have been carried out for a completely internationalized currency.[2] This is insufficient given what is happening. The internationalization of a currency features not only phases of evolution over time but also special expansion. Against the backdrop of the changing international monetary and financial structure, it is quite necessary to provide a ladder for a currency to finally become internationalized (become a completely internationalized currency) with the help of "regional collective actions." Therefore it is more realistic and relevant to emphasize researches on the conditions for a currency to become a regional key currency (regionalization). We believe that, against the background of regional monetary integration and regional monetary cooperation, a currency must at least have the following five preconditions to become a regional key currency.

First, the currency–issuing country's economic scale, stability of economic growth and capability to provide an export market for neighboring regions. For a country, a larger economic scale means more stable economic growth, a more attractive environment for foreign investment, a higher degree of industrial and trade ties with other members of the region, and more possibility of becoming a "market provider" for the region. As such, the demand of residents and non-residents for the currency of the country will increase and the possibility of monetary cooperation with relevant economies within the region will also increase.

Second, the openness of the currency–issuing country's economy. Under the conditions that financial liberalization and international capital flow keep growing, the traditional single indicator for the openness of a country's economy to the outside world is outdated and a comprehensive indicator should be adopted to examine the degree of integration of a country into the world economy. It should include trade openness and investment openness as well as financial openness (Dai Jinping and Xiong Xingmei, 2001). The higher the three indicators are, the higher the degree of the country's economic integration into the world economy will be and the greater the possibility of its currency becoming a regional key currency will be.

Third, the acceptance degree of a currency within the region, that is the degree and scope of a currency being used in international transactions. The more extensive the scope of a currency being used in the region means a larger scale of circulation, more possibilities of the emergence of the "network effect" and "scale effect", more profits from using the currency, and more possibilities of realizing regionalization through some institutional cooperation.

Fourth, the international credibility of a government in monetary and financial policy and its capacity in policy coordination with other members of the region. If the monetary and financial policy implemented by a government has more "spillover effects" on other members of the region and the consistency and continuity of the monetary and financial policy promised by the government is stronger, then the government will obtain stronger credibility, enhance its capability in multi-lateral policy coordination within the region, promote regional monetary and financial cooperation, and improve the status and role of the currency during this process.

Fifth, the institutional environment faced by a currency both at home and abroad. A more improved internal institutional arrangement and money convertibility in particular means a more sound market mechanism, a more favorable external institutional environment, and more possibility for the currency to realize regionalization.

East Asian countries and regions affected by the Asian financial crisis have increasingly recognized the role of a regional key currency in the wake of the outbreak of the crisis. The international community has started to value the influence of the RMB internationally as a result of the failure of "Japanese Yen internationalization," the performance of China in making vigorous efforts to turn the situation with its own economic strength and resolute policy implementation amid the financial turmoil, China's fast economic growth since entering into the 21st century and its improving status in the economic development of East Asia. This chapter takes the conditions for the formation of a regional key currency as the master line to share insights on the feasibility of RMB regionalization in line with the China's current economic situation.

The Status Quo of RMB Regionalization

Basic situation of the RMB

On 1 December 1948, the People's Bank of China (PBOC) was founded and issued the first set of RMB banknotes. The issue of RMB solely by the PBOC was one of the key measures adopted to celebrate the liberation of the entire nation and it eliminated all kinds of currencies issued by the Kuomintang (KMT), put an end to the decades-long inflation under the rule of the KMT and the nearly 100-year-long history of the circulation of foreign currencies and gold as well as silver coins in the Chinese market, promoted the victory of the people's liberation war across the board, and played a pivotal role in economic recovery in the early stage of the foundation of the New China. After the founding of the New China in 1949, the RMB went through several stages of reform to meet the needs of constantly adjusted economic development, which has played an important role in economic recovery and development. China has now accomplished a series of preliminary reforms of the RMB and achieved great results in RMB convertibility and the establishment of a foreign exchange market with the reform and opening up, and especially the rise in China's position in the global economy.

The state of RMB convertibility

RMB convertibility is a key measure of financial reform that is necessary but takes a long period of time. RMB convertibility is expected to boost China's integration into the global economy, better implement the reform and opening up program, and create more social wealth. In general, the process of RMB convertibility over the past 30 years since the reform and opening is a progressive, transparent and slow process that adopted relevant supporting policy measures. In the 1980s, China gradually stepped up its efforts to move forward towards RMB convertibility after it formally launched the reform and opening up program, but it was basically a progressive process in exploration. In the 1980s China was just breaking through the old system and creating a new market, so the RMB did not see much progress in convertibility. By the 1990s China had stepped up efforts in the reform of the market in foreign exchange resource allocation. On the basis that foreign exchange was retained and business foreign exchange entered into the forex swap market, China officially implemented the regulations on domestic residents' foreign exchange swap in 1991 and the foreign exchange of domestic residents could be used in the swap. In July 1992 the meeting of directors of the State Administration for Foreign Exchange branches made it clear that conditions must be created for the realization of RMB convertibility due to the improving strength of Chinese economy and the needs of foreign trade development. In 1993, the market mechanism was introduced into the field of handing in foreign exchange to the central bank and the PBOC was responsible for the purchase. As such, about 80% of foreign exchange resources could be bought and sold according to market prices.[3] The Third Plenary Session of the Fourteenth Central Committee clearly set the target of making the RMB convertible. On 1 January 1994 the system of foreign exchange purchase and sale was implemented, allowing conditional convertibility of RMB current accounts and opening the prelude of RMB convertibility. By the end of December 1996, China realized full convertibility of the RMB current account four years ahead of schedule.

China has never stopped making efforts to realize capital account convertibility of the RMB. After 1996 the Chinese government took a relatively relaxed attitude towards capital attraction while improving the financial system and supervision system, and only imposed more restrictions on capital outflow. After 2002 the Chinese government started to slowly relax restrictions on capital flow. For instance, the quota of securities investment for foreign institutional investors increased from RMB10 billion to RMB30 billion and restrictions on RMB-related business were also relaxed for foreign banks. Over the past more than ten years, RMB capital account convertibility has seen great progress. By 2007, according to the standard for capital transaction classified by the IMF (43 capital accounts altogether), 8 are now convertible in China, 11 are less restricted, 18 are more restricted and 6 are seriously restricted.[4] It is clear that the RMB has in effect realized partial convertibility in terms of capital account.

Developed countries (regions) such as Europe and Japan realized currency convertibility in current accounts in 1961 and 1964 respectively, but Britain, France and Japan did not give up foreign exchange control until around 1980. Emerging markets such as South Korea and Thailand started currency convertibility in current accounts in 1986 and 1990, and realized this in 1996 and 1994 respectively. Economies with sound performance in economic transformation, such as India, started to transform in 1991 and only realized rupee capital account convertibility by 2002. In comparison, the process of capital account convertibility of the RMB still follows the traditional path and seeks to make RMB capital account freely convertible when the macro-economy and micro-economy become more mature in all aspects.

The development landscape of the RMB foreign exchange market

The establishment of the RMB foreign exchange market in China has witnessed huge progress after the "7.21" foreign exchange reform in 2005. In early 2006, the RMB foreign exchange market introduced the market maker system that provides bilateral offers for purchasing and selling and increases market liquidity. In the same year, the "over-the-counter" system was put in place in the spot foreign exchange market and the RMB forward market also practiced the "over-the-counter" trading method, which saved trading costs and expanded trading scale. As of August 2005, non-bank financial institutions and non-financial businesses can apply to be members of the inter-bank market and have added to trading products in forex. On 15 August 2005, the inter-bank market formally rolled out RMB forward forex trading business and the RMB and forex swap business on 24 April 2006; in December 2007, RMB foreign exchange swap trading was officially carried out in the inter-bank market which increased currencies traded in the spot foreign exchange market at the same time. From the perspective of the trading system, in April 2007, the China Foreign Exchange Center implemented the new system that supports the spot, forward and swap trading of RMB and the new generation of foreign exchange trading system that has two markets, namely the exchange market of RMB to foreign currencies and the exchange market of foreign currencies to RMB on the one hand, and two

Table 3.1. The turnover of the foreign exchange markets distributed according to currencies (%)

Currencies	2001	2004	2007	Currencies	2001	2004	2007
U.S. Dollar	90.30	88.70	86.30	Ruble	0.40	0.70	0.80
Euro	37.60	36.90	37.00	Indian Rupee	0.20	0.30	0.70
British Pound Sterling	13.20	16.90	15.00	RMB	0.00	0.10	0.50
Japanese Yen	22.70	20.20	16.50	New Taiwan Dollar	0.30	0.40	0.40
Hong Kong Dollar	2.30	1.90	2.80	Brazilian Real	0.40	0.20	0.40
Singapore Dollar	1.10	1.00	1.20	Currencies of Emerging Markets	16.90	15.40	19.80
Korean Won	0.70	1.20	1.10				

Note: The total turnover share is 200% as two currencies are involved in each transaction.
Source: Bank for International Settlement (BIS).

trading models namely tendering and enquiry on the other. Compared with the situation prior to the foreign exchange reform, the Chinese foreign exchange market has seen great progress (refer to Table 3.1).

If we look at the distribution of transactional varieties in the foreign exchange market (Table 3.2), we can see that strong currencies such as the U.S. dollar, euro and British pound are typical swap trading, that is the share of over-the-counter trading is about 30 percent. But the foreign exchange trading of the RMB is mainly over-the-counter trading while swap trading only accounts for 7 percent, showing that the Chinese foreign exchange trading market has yet to mature and the methods of trading are simple. This might help reduce exchange rate risks triggered by speculations on forex in the short run, but will not help improve the RMB's international influence in the long run.

Table 3.2. The turnover of foreign exchange market distributed by transaction varieties in 2007 (%)

	Over-the-Counter Transaction	Forward Transaction	Swap Transaction		Over-the-Counter Transaction	Forward Transaction	Swap Transaction
U.S. Dollar	29.70	10.9	59.40	Indian Rupee	42.60	27.50	29.80
Euro	36.90	12.10	51.10	Chinese RMB	61.40	31.30	7.40
British Pound Sterling	32.50	10.0	57.40	New Taiwan Dollar	47.10	40.60	12.30
Japanese Yen	40.40	12.10	47.50	Brazilian Real	50.20	47.30	2.50
Hong Kong Dollar	18.40	7.00	74.60	Thai Baht	18.90	13.30	67.80
Singapore Dollar	22.50	7.90	69.60	Philippine Peso	36.90	32.50	30.50
Korean Won	44.70	29.40	25.90	Indonesia Rupiah	43.70	39.30	17.00
Ruble	70.70	5.00	24.30	Average	32.60	11.70	55.60

Source: Bank for International Settlement (BIS).

When we analyze the scale of transactions of the Chinese foreign exchange market, according to the statistics of the BIS, the average daily turnover of the Chinese mainland in 2007 accounted for 0.2% of the international foreign exchange market in terms of the traditional forex market and 0% in terms of the derivative market; the proportion of the Hong Kong Special Administrative Region was 4.4% and 0.9% in these two markets respectively; and the proportion of Chinese Taiwan was 0.4% and 0.1%. Among all currencies in trading, the proportion of the RMB was only 0.5%, the Hong Kong dollar 2.8% and the Taiwan dollar 0.4%. We can see from Table 3.3 that, in the inter-bank forex market in 2007, the total turnover surpassed USD2 trillion, up by nearly 90% year-on-year, the total volume of foreign exchange swap transactions reached USD0.3 trillion and the total volume of foreign exchange forward transactions was only USD0.02 trillion. Compared with the average daily trading volume of the international forex market of USD3.2 trillion, the trading scale of the Chinese forex market was quite limited.

Table 3.3. Trading volume of the inter-bank foreign exchange market

Trading Category and Trading Time	Yearly No. of Trading	Yearly Trading Turnover (USD100 Million)	Daily Trading Volume (USD100 Million)
Forward Trading			
2006	1,476	140.61	0.5786
2007	2,945	22.82	0.920
Foreign Exchange Swap Transaction			
2006	2,732	508.56	2.990
2007	15,896	3,146.41	13
Currency Swap Transaction			
2007	4	0.8	
Total Trading Volume			
2006		Over 10,000	
2007		20,000	

Source: BIS, *Investigation Report of the Central Bank on Foreign Exchange and Derivative Market Activities*, November 2007. Quote from: Yang Rong and Chen Jie, "Development of the Chinese Foreign Exchange Market since the Exchange Rate Reform", *The Banker*, Issue 11, 2008.

Status of the RMB in the international monetary system

In recent years, China's economic status keeps rising internationally but not in international foreign exchange transactions. Table 3.4 shows the proportion of different currencies in the trading volume on the international foreign exchange market between 1995 and 2007. We can see from the table that the top five currencies remain the U.S. Dollar, the Euro (or Deutsch Mark), the Japanese Yen, the British Pound and the Swiss Franc, accounting for 160%, and the currency pairs are mainly the U.S. Dollar and the above-mentioned currencies, taking up more than 55%. Just taking 2007 as an example, the leading currencies for transaction in the traditional foreign exchange market included: U.S. Dollar (86.3%), Euro (37%), Japanese Yen (16.5%), Pound (15%) Swiss Franc (6.8%), Australian Dollar (6.7%), Canadian Dollar (4.2%), Swedish Krona (2.8%), Hong Kong Dollar (2.8%), Norwegian Krone (2.2%). Among the transaction currency pairs, U.S. dollar pairs account for 86%, Euro 10% and other currencies pairs are only 4%. U.S. dollar pairs mainly include: USD/EUR (27%), JPY/USD (13%) and USD/GBP (12%). The Euro pairs mainly include: JPY/EUR (2%), EUR/GBP (2%) and EUR/CHF (2%).

Table 3.4. The share of different currencies in the trading volume in the international foreign exchange market (%)

Currencies	1995	1998	2001	2004	2007
Proportion of Each Currency					
U.S. Dollar (USD)	83.3	87.3	90.3	88.7	86.3
Euro (EUR)			37.6	37.2	37
Yen (JPY)	24.1	20.2	22.7	20.3	16.5
Deutsche Mark (DEM)	36.1	30.1			
British Pound Sterling (GBP)	9.4	11	13.2	16.9	15
Swiss franc (CHF)	7.3	7.1	6.1	6.1	6.8
Total	160.2	155.7	169.9	169.2	161.6
Proportion of Currency to U.S. Dollar					
USD/EUR			30	28	27
USD/DEM	22	20			
USD/JPY	21	18	20	17	13
USD/GBP	7	8	11	14	12
USD/CHF	5	5	5	4	5
Total	55	51	66	63	57

Source: BIS, *Investigation Report of the Central Bank on Foreign Exchange and Derivative Market Activities*, Issue 11, 2007. Quote from: Yang Rong and Chen Jie, "Development of the Chinese Foreign Exchange Market since the Exchange Rate Reform", *The Banker*, Issue 11, 2008.

From the perspective of the development of the international foreign exchange market in the recent dozen years, the top five remain basically unchanged. A currency's status in the international market is closely linked to the economic condition of the country. In this sense it will take a long time for the RMB to realize internationalization.

The status quo of RMB circulation in neighboring regions

Thanks to decades of development, the number of China's trade partners keeps increasing and neighboring countries have become China's key trade partners over time, which has led to great development of the RMB as a means of exchange in border trade. As previously mentioned, the swap between the RMB and other currencies has developed rapidly at the same time under the promotion of the CMI. All this has boosted the circulation of the RMB in neighboring countries and regions.

The RMB's overseas circulation landscape

chinese scholars have conducted much research on the circulation landscape of the RMB in neighboring countries. It was after the outbreak of the Asian Financial Crisis in 1997 that the RMB started to flow beyond the border on a large scale. The currencies of neighboring countries and regions have depreciated substantially in succession while the RMB exchange rate remains stable, which has shored up the confidence of residents and non-residents of neighboring countries in holding RMB.[5] It is estimated that Hong Kong is now holding most overseas RMB and the steady stock of RMB has reached RMB25 billion or so. Zheng Xiaozhou (2007) noted that the volume of RMB in transactions has skyrocketed after the UnionPay Card could be used in Hong Kong. During the three years between 2004 and 2006, the amount of RMB in transaction with UnionPay Card increased from RMB2.845 billion to RMB12.36 billion in the Hong Kong Special Administrative Region and thus the RMB has turned out to be a major medium of exchange for mainland tourists in Hong Kong.[6] Vietnam ranks the second in terms of holding the most overseas RMB as its flow remains at RMB5–6 billion each year. It is widely acceptable for mainland Chinese to use RMB for payment and settlement in Vietnam and the accumulated stock of RMB there has reached RMB3.8 billion. Mongolia and Singapore also have about RMB1 billion in stock. In line with the circulation landscape of the RMB in Southeast Asian countries, Zhong Wei (2008) concluded after research that the yearly circulation of RMB via tourism stands at RMB400 million in Indonesia. The cross-border circulation volume of the RMB is RMB5 billion in Singapore through multiple channels. In the border trade between China and Vietnam, the yearly circulation volume of RMB is about RMB5–6 billion . Hong Kong records a yearly RMB circulation volume of RMB18.8 billion through tourism and backflow channels.[7] In the north of Laos, east of the Shan State of Burma and north of Chiang Mai in Thailand, the RMB has been widely circulated and used.

It is obvious that the transnational circulation of RMB is still quite limited at the moment, but it has a strong influence in Vietnam, Laos, Burma and Thailand. In addition, Hong Kong has a large stock of RMB, which has created a sound precondition for the establishment of the RMB offshore market (refer to Table 3.5).

Table 3.5. Circulation and usage of the RMB in neighboring countries and regions

Countries and Regions	Circulation and Usage
Hong Kong	Since Unionpay Card can be used in Chinese Hong Kong, RMB transactions have surged, During the three years between 2004 and 2006, the transaction amount paid by Unionpay Card in Hong Kong jumped from RMB2.845 billion to RMB12.36 billion (Zheng Xiaozhou, 2007). The tourism and backflow channels have resulted in a yearly RMB circulation volume of RMB18.8 billion in Hong Kong and the stock of RMB in Hong Kong has now stabilized at about RMB25 billion (Zhong Wei, 2008).
Mongolia	50% of currency circulated within the border of Mongolia is RMB and this proportion has reached 80–90% in the northwest five provinces of Mongolia bordering China. The RMB is widely used for transactions and settlement among residents and for valuation of commodities (Wang Yafan et al., 2002). According to our surveys, the cash outflow of RMB from China to Mongolia recorded 2.206 billion RMB and the inflow posted RMB1.203 billion in 2004, thus the retention of RMB in Mongolia was about RMB1 billion (Zhao Zhihua, 2006).
Russia	The RMB generally cannot be used in Russia and its circulation is mainly concentrated in Chinese people engaging in economic and trade activities in Russia, Russian border traders, and speculators in foreign currency. The circulation scope of the Ruble is rather bigger and it can be used for trade settlement, thus the stock of Rubles in China is 3–4 times more than the stock of RMB in Russia and the net stock of Rubles in China is around 6–8 billion (Guan Jian, 2006).

(Cont'd)

Vietnam	95% of the frontier trade and the extension of frontier trade, such as tourism and investment, in the border region with China are settled with RMB. In the early stage, use of the RMB was mostly concentrated in ports and border trade points. In recent years the RMB has been extended to the hinterland of Vietnam, such as Hanoi and even Ho Chi Minh City, and has been widely accepted for payment and settlement in Vietnam (Fang Guozhi, 2008). The stock of overseas RMB in Vietnam stabilizes at about RMB3 billion through trade channels and RMB800 million via tourism channels, thus the accumulated stock of overseas RMB stands at RMB3.8 billion. The cross-border flow of RMB is about RMB5–6 billion each year (Zhong Wei, 2008).
Singapore	The stock of RMB in Singapore is kept at RMB1 billion through travel intermediaries, money exchange points and remittance centers, and the transnational flow through multi-channels stand at RMB5 billion (Zhong Wei, 2008).
Indonesia	RMB flowing in Indonesia is about RMB400 million through tourism and the stock is RMB100 million or so (Zhong Wei, 2008).
Burma, Laos and Thailand	RMB has been widely circulated and used in three provinces in the north of Laos: Luang Namtha, Phongsaly and Oudomxay, Burma's Shan State Special Zone 4, Kengtung, Thachilek, and the north region of Chiang Mai of Thailand. In Burma's Shan State Special Zone the RMB has replaced the Kyat to become the key currency in circulation, the financial budget of the government of the special zone is calculated in RMB, all fiscal revenues are RMB and banks in the special zone provide services for deposit and withdrawal of RMB in cash and RMB transfer business. Laos does not have controls over RMB circulation but does not provide services for RMB-related business. In June 2007, the stock of RMB in the four provinces of Laos in the north and Burma's Shan State Special Zone (4) was about RMB600 million (Lu Hao, 2007). Part of the stock of RMB in Thailand was about RMB500 million (Zhong Wei, 2008).

Source: Zheng Xiaozhou, Renminbi: "From 'Unpopular' to 'Full Circulation', *Shanghai Securities News*, June 29, 2007; Zhong Wei, "The Status Quo, Problems and Countermeasures of Renminbi Circulation in Neighboring *Countries"; Management World*, Issue 1, 2008; Zhao Zhihua, "Investigation Report on the Circulation Situation of Renminbi in Border Trading Ports between China and Mongolia", *Huabei Finance,* Issue 2, 2006; Wang Yafan, Guan Tao and Wen Jiandong, *Moving Towards Renminbi Convertibility: Practices of Incrementalism in China*, The Publishing House Of Economic Science, 2002; Guan Jian, "Comparisons between the Renminbi and the Ruble in Border Areas between China and Russia", *Heilongjiang Finance*, Issue 12, 2006; Fang Guozhi, "The Status Quo and Strategy of Renminbi Circulation in ASEAN", *South China Finance*, Issue 5, 2008; Lu Hao, "Surveys and Thinking on the Situation of Renminbi Circulation in Border Areas between China and Burma and between China and Laos", *Times Finance*, Issue 9, 2007.

When it comes to the overall size of RMB outflow, Xu Qiyuan and Liu Lizhen adopted a gap estimation method to estimate the stock of RMB in Hong Kong between 2000 and 2005 with M1 as the statistic caliber and concluded: between 2000 and early 2001, the stock was HKD20 billion; between 2001 and early 2003, the figure jumped from HKD30 billion to HKD60 billion; between early 2003 and late 2003, it dropped to HKD47.7 billion due to the impact of the SARS epidemic; between late 2003 and early 2004, it again hit a historical high to HKD97.8 billion, or more than RMB100 billion ; between early 2004 and late 2005 it dropped to some extent but still stood at HKD60 billion or so. Ma Ronghua and Rao Xiaohui (2007) and Dong Jihua (2008) made estimates of the economic data of the years between 1999 and 2005 using the econometric model. We can see from Table 3.6 that the results concluded by the two articles are basically the same. The circulating amount of overseas RMB started to drop gradually after it peaked in 2003 and this might be the results of the Chinese monetary authority strengthening the management of overseas RMB circulation and promoting the backflow of overseas RMB. From the perspective of the overall trend, the amount of overseas RMB will keep mounting with the rising influence of the Chinese economy.

The RMB as an international account unit

From the perspective of money function, the function of an international currency as a unit of account is mainly manifested by its functions as the quote currency and exchange rate anchor. At present, the function of the RMB as an international unit of account is rather limited and it is typically reflected in the settlement of border trade.

Table 3.6. The amount of overseas RMB between 1999 and 2005
(RMB100 Million)

Year	Dong's Calculated Results	Ma and Rao's Calculated Results	Year	Year, Dong's Calculated Results	Ma and Rao's Calculated Results
1999	80	360	2003	1061	635
2000	356	375	2004	931	309
2001	251	394	2005	258	311
2002	983	512			

Source: Ma Ronghua and Rao Xiaohui (2007), and Dong Jihua (2008).

Fang Zhiguo (2008) believed after he inspected the border trade between China and Vietnam that 95% of border trade and the extension of border trade such as tourism and investment between the two countries are settled by RMB. In the early days RMB was mainly used in ports and frontier trade points, but the use of RMB has extended to the hinterland of Vietnam including Hanoi and even Ho Chi Minh City in recent years. The RMB is been widely accepted by people for payment and settlement in Vietnam. Lu Hao (2007) noted after investigation that the RMB has replaced the Kyat to become a major circulating currency in Burma's Shan State Special Zone (4), the government of the Special Zone uses RMB to calculate the financial budget, all fiscal income and expenses are conducted in RMB and banks in the Zone can provide services for RMB cash deposit and withdrawal as well as transfer business. Apart from ASEAN countries, 50% of currencies in circulation are RMB in Mongolia and the proportion has reached as high as 80% – 90% in five provinces of Mongolia in the Northwest bordering China. The RMB has been widely accepted by residents for trading settlement and commodity valuation.[8]

Currency swap between China and other countries

In the wake of the Asian Financial Crisis, many East Asian countries recognized that no country or region cannot prevent the deepening and spreading of crisis just by itself and that strengthening regional financial cooperation is an effective way to maintain financial market stability and guard against the recurrence of financial crisis. Since then, under the CMI framework, China has actively strengthened monetary coordination with its East Asian counterparts. As is shown by Table 2.4 of the previous chapter, China has inked a series of Bilateral Currency Swap Agreements with East Asian nations in order to enhance the regional influence of the RMB and its capability to withstand risks.

China's Position and Role in the Development of the East Asian Economy

China's economic ties with other East Asian economies

After World War II the whole of East Asia shaped increasingly close ties in industry and trade under the lead of the economic take-offs of developed countries such as Japan and with the global industrial transformation. Since the reform and opening up, especially since the 1990s, China has taken the opportunity of its economic take-off and development to rapidly integrate itself into the East Asian economy and has started to play an increasingly important role.

The openness of East Asian economies to the outside world

we can see from the horizontal comparison of the openness of China, the Eurozone and other East Asian economies in 2001 (see Table 3.7) that China has been close to or surpassed some countries in the Eurozone (such as Italy and Greece) in foreign trade ratio, foreign finance ratio, foreign investment ratio and comprehensive openness. Within the East Asia region, the degree of comprehensive openness of China and Japan is lower than other members, but the comparison between the two is more significant considering their actual and potential economic scale. Japan as the largest creditor country in the world has a higher foreign finance ratio (40.60%) than that of China (34.12%, but China surpassed Japan in foreign trade ratio, foreign investment ratio and comprehensive openness to the outside world. This reflects the fact that the Chinese market is open while the Japanese market is relatively closed. The openness of the Chinese economy keeps increasing, which will create the necessary objective conditions for the Asianization of the RMB.

When we look at each of the countries, China's foreign trade dependence is now as high as 70%, representing the world highest (it is only 30% for Japan and the U.S.). This demonstrates to some extent that Chinese economic growth relies heavily on the contribution of trade (refer to Table 3.8). The excessive dependence reflects that domestic resources are excessively consumed by its trade partners, which is not favorable for China's economic growth in the long term and China to become the market provider for end products of East Asia. We can further see from Table 3.9 that China's ultimate consumer spending and its net export contribute little to the GDP growth. In this sense, China should adjust its trade structure, increase the contribution rate of domestic demand to GDP and gradually restructure its economy by switching from a trade-driven economy to a domestic demand-oriented economy while reducing its dependence on foreign trade.

The impact of China's foreign trade on other East Asian economies

Over the past more than two decades, China's export growth rate has considerably surpassed the average growth rate of world trade and its share in major export markets like the U.S., Europe and Japan keeps rising rapidly. Beyond that, China's export structure has changed dramatically, which can be reflected by the fact that the export of energy and raw materials that was essential in the 1980s is no longer significant, the share of agricultural products in export has dropped substantially, but the share of manufacturing produces

Table 3.7. Comparison of openness between East Asian economies and the Eurozone in 2001

Unit: USD1 billion / %

Country / Region	(1) GDP	(2) Total Foreign Trade Volume	(3) Foreign Financial Assets and Total Liabilities	(4) Total Foreign and Inward Investment	Foreign Trade Ratio (2)/(1)	Foreign Finance Ratio (3)/(1)	Foreign Investment Ratio (4)/(1)	Comprehensive Degree of Openness (%)
The Eurozone	6,096.16	1,830.63	4,938.21	366.70	30.03	81.01	6.02	39.02
France	1,306.88	592.41	917.45	135.69	45.33	70.20	10.38	41.97
Germany	1,849.29	1,054.50	1,319.20	74.28	57.02	71.34	4.02	44.13
Italy	1,086.34	479.24	277.84	36.63	44.12	25.58	3.37	24.36
The Netherlands	383.21	409.76	485.57	100.41	106.93	126.71	26.20	86.61
Belgium	226.79	367.88	322.42	-	162.21	142.17	-	-
Luxembourg	19.20	0.02	376.23	-	0.10	1,959.53	-	-
Spain	582.14	268.18	282.58	49.24	46.07	48.54	8.46	34.36
Portugal	109.87	61.69	98.46	13.82	56.15	89.61	12.58	52.78
Austria	189.20	136.71	152.96	8.94	72.26	80.85	4.73	52.61
Finland	121.24	74.65	72.37	12.20	61.57	59.69	10.06	43.77
Ireland	102.21	133.89	286.88	15.27	131.00	280.68	14.94	142.21
Greece	116.88	39.41	33.23	2.20	33.72	28.43	1.88	21.34
Average of East Asia	-	-	-	-	-	-	-	80.66
Japan	4,141.40	752.18	1,681.56	44.69	18.16	40.60	1.08	19.95
Chinese Mainland	1,191.46	509.65	406.51	51.13	42.78	34.12	4.29	27.06
Hong Kong	164.00	390.97	780.29	31.81	238.40	475.79	19.40	244.53
South Korea	427.24	291.54	165.65	5.95	68.24	38.77	1.39	36.13
Singapore	85.65	237.61	202.90	18.83	277.42	236.89	21.98	178.76
Malaysia	88.05	161.87	43.99	0.82	183.84	49.96	0.93	78.24
The Philippines	71.38	64.01	40.16	1.95	89.67	56.26	2.73	49.55
Thailand	114.80	127.16	70.41	3.98	110.77	61.33	3.47	58.52
Indonesia	145.31	83.13	58.50	3.28	57.21	40.26	2.26	33.24

Note: Comprehensive Openness Degree = (Foreign Trade Ratio + Foreign Finance Ratio + Foreign Investment Ratio)/3.

Source: Calculated based on *IMF* International Financial Statistics, relevant data of May 2003.

has risen by a large margin (see Table 3.10). In particular, the export of office and communication equipment, mechanical and transportation equipment and other finished products has grown substantially in recent years. During the same period, the economic growth of China's major export markets—the U.S. and other developed countries—has been much slower than that of China, their

Table 3.8. Comparison of foreign trade dependence of China, Japan and the U.S. (%)

Year	China	Japan	U.S.	Year	China	Japan	U.S.
1990	35	20	21	2003	57	22	24
1995	44	17	23	2006	72	30	28
2000	44	21	26	-	-	-	-

Note: Foreign Trade Dependence = Total Import and Export/GDP

Source: Prepared based on relevant data of Key Development Data & Statistics of the World Bank.

Table 3.9. The contribution rate and the pull of China's three major types of demand to GDP between 1990 and 2006

	Final Consumption Expenditure		Gross Capital Formation		Net Export of Goods and Services	
Year	Contribution Rate (%)	Pull (Percentage Point)	Contribution Rate (%)	Pull (Percentage Point)	Contribution Rate (%)	Pull (Percentage Point)
1990	47.8	1.8	1.8	0.1	50.4	1.9
1995	44.7	4.9	55.0	6.0	0.3	0.0
2000	65.1	5.5	22.4	1.9	12.5	1.0
2003	35.3	3.5	63.7	6.4	1.0	0.1
2006	39.2	4.3	41.3	4.6	19.5	2.2

Note: 1. This table is calculated based on comparable prices; 2. The three major types of demand refer to the three items of GDP including total volume of ultimate consumption, gross capital formation and total net export of goods and services ; 3. Contribution rate refers to the ratio of the increments of the three major types of demand to that of GDP; 4. The pull refers to the product of GDP growth rate and the contribution rate of the three major types of demand.

Source: *China Statistical Yearbook* (2007).

economic structure and demand structure have not changed obviously, and the structure of their export region has changed little. Among those countries with the same export market and similar comparative advantages with China, the East Asian economies have been the first affected by export markets like the U.S. Between 1980 and 200 the proportion of U.S. imports from East Asia rose from 22% to 24% and has even stagnated and slowed down since the 1990s. But between 1980 and 2003, China's share in the import market of the U.S. surged from 0.5% to 11.3% and it has replaced the other East Asian economies to some extent.

According to above analyses, we can assume that China will maintain its existing advantages in trade and expand to replace other East Asian economies over time in the medium and long-term.

On the one hand, the leading factors for China's export scale and major structural changes include its low labor costs, huge productivity and rather integrated industrial system. In this regard and on economic scale, other East Asian economies are a far cry from China and and the gap cannot be bridged even in quite a long period of time. The competitiveness of Chinese products will keep strengthening in developed markets for some time to come.

On the other hand, from the perspective of export mix, China is now replacing other East Asian countries in the export of middle and low-tech finished products but not yet in high-tech finished products (see Table 3.11). But as China's export product mix becomes more advanced, there is a big potential for Chinese finished products to replace those from other East Asian economies, especially in the U.S. and European markets, and China is expected to become a leading exporter in East Asia.

Change of China's status in industrial division labor of East Asia

For a long time the industrial connections and trade development of East Asia have featured an obvious openness. That means that East Asian economies bring in capital, technologies or parts and components and capital goods from developed countries like Japan to process and assemble them, and then export them to developed nations led by the U.S. Since the 1990s this special "triangle tradel" mode in East Asia has changed a lot due to the rapid rise of the Chinese economy and a new "triangle trade" model with China at the core has started to take shape. Correspondingly, the industrial connections of East Asia are also undergoing changes.

We use the "intra-industry trade index" of East Asia to measure the relative role of intra-industry trade and inter-industry trade in driving the development

Table 3.10. Changes in China's import and export structure (%)

Year	Agricultural Products	Energy and Raw Materials	Chemical Products	Primary Products	Mechanical and Transportation Equipment	Other End Products
SITC2	0,1,4	2,3	5	6	7	8
			Export			
1985	14.9	35.6	5.0	16.5	2.8	12.8
1990	11.4	14.1	6.0	20.6	17.5	28.2
2000	4.9	4.9	4.8	17.4	33.1	34.3
2005	3.1	3.3	4.7	17.0	46.3	25.5
2007	2.7	2.4	5.0	18.1	47.5	24.4
			Import			
1985	4.4	8.0	10.5	28.0	39.0	4.5
1990	8.6	10.1	12.5	21.7	40.3	6.2
2000	2.5	18.0	13.2	18.9	40.8	5.7
2005	2.1	20.4	11.8	12.3	44.1	9.3
2007	2.1	23.4	11.3	10.8	43.3	9.2

Source: UN, Comtrade Database.

Table 3.11. The share of all kinds of manufactured products exported by East Asian economies in the world market (%)

Economies	Resource-intensive Products	Low-tech Products	Middle-tech Products	High-tech Products	All Manufacturing Industries
Mainland China					
1990	1.3	4.9	1.2	0.7	1.9
2000	2.5	12	2.7	4.1	4.7
South Korea					
1990	0.8	4.9	1.8	2.8	2.1
2000	2.3	3.3	3.2	4.5	3.4
Taiwan					
1990	0.8	5.2	1.6	3.4	1.6
2000	0.7	4	2.1	4.9	3.0
Singapore					
1990	2.6	0.9	1.1	4	1.9
2000	1.3	1	0.9	5.9	2.7

(Cont'd)

Economies	Resource-intensive Products	Low-tech Products	Middle-tech Products	High-tech Products	All Manufacturing Industries
Hong Kong					
1990	0.2	3	0.5	1.2	0.6
2000	0.1	1.5	0.1	0.4	0.5
Malaysia					
1990	1.3	0.6	0.4	1.6	0.8
2000	0.3	1	0.9	3.7	1.8
Thailand					
1990	0.8	1.4	0.2	0.7	0.7
2000	1.3	1.5	0.8	1.5	1.2
Indonesia					
1990	1.2	0.8	0.1	0	0.5
2000	1.7	1.6	0.4	0.2	0.7

Source: Lall and Albaladejo, 2004, table 5.

of trade. Intra-industry trade is also known as "two way trade," and means that a country imports some kind of products while exporting the same kind of products. It is different from inter-industry trade, which is also called "one way trade". The degree of intra-industry trade is closely related to the definition of industry. The international practice is to regard trade in products that have the same three leading figure in their Standard International Trade Classication (STIC) number as two way trade. There are many indicators for measuring intra-industry trade (such as the Grubel-Lloyd Index or G-L Index for short, the modified G-L Index, the Aquino Index etc.) This text adopts the G-L Index and the calculation formula is as follows:

$$\prod T = 1 - \frac{|X_i - M_i|}{(X_i + M_i)} = 1 - 2_{\max} \frac{(X_i , M_i)}{(X_i + M_i)} \qquad (3\text{–}1)$$

Where X_i refers to the total exports of the i industry of a country; M_i refers to the total imports of the i industry of a country. The formula of the total intra-industry trade index of all industries of a country is as follows:

$$\prod T = 1 - \frac{\sum |X_i - M_i|}{\sum (X_i + M_i)} \qquad (3\text{–}2)$$

$0 \leq \prod T \leq 1$, the closer $\prod T$ is to 1, the higher degree of intra-industry trade between the two countries; the closer it is to 0 indicates a higher degree of inter-industry trade between the two countries.

We calculated 10 categories of products (one digit of the SITC) and the (total) G-L Index of 9 East Asian economies over the past two decades and selected data of the years of 1984, 1990, 1996 and 2003 (see Table 3.12). Generally speaking, between 1984 and 2003, the G-L Index of Chinese Hong Kong, South Korea, the Philippines, Thailand and Malaysia kept growing. The G-L Index of Japan, Singapore, Indonesia and the Chinese Mainland kept rising between 1984 and 1996, but it dropped a little between 1996 and 2003 (typically for primary products). Industrial finished products mainly had a higher G-L Index in Japan and Singapore, those with a higher G-L Index in ASEAN countries are primary products, but the G-L Index of 6 categories of products in the entire East Asia region is rather higher.

The intra-industry trade, especially the intra-industry trade of the manufacturing industry, of the nine East Asian countries is on the rise. This reflects that the decentralization of the production process in East Asia has developed obviously as the original "triangle trade" model is replaced within the context that developed nations such as the U.S. are still the leading markets for the export of the ultimate products of East Asian countries. The decentralization of production procedures is demonstrated by the rapid expansion of trade in parts and components and intermediate products within the region, but the trade outside of the region has not shown corresponding changes. For example, between 1985 and 1996, the proportion of parts and components from East Asia imported by Europe only rose from 16.6% to 17%, remaining basically stable, while the import by the U.S. dropped from 36.2% to 22.3%, but the share within the East Asia region increased from 43.5% to 58.5% over the same period (Ng and Yeats, 1999). Another trend that merits our attention is that, apart from Japan, other East Asian economies have increasingly become providers of parts and components within the region. Also during the years between 1985 and 1996, Japan's imports of parts and components from East Asia decreased a little from 28.7% to 25.6% while the proportion of the imports by other East Asian economies surged from 14.2% to 32%. This indicates that it is different from the traditional "triangle trade" model in which Japan exported parts and components as well as intermediate products to other East Asian economies and then the latter exported the processed products to markets such as the U.S. At the moment, more and more East Asian economies are starting to provide capital goods such as parts and components as well as intermediate

Table 3.12. The G-L Index of each category of products of nine East Asian economies in 1984, 1990, 1996 and 2003 and the total G-L Index

Country/Region	Year	Total	0	1	2	3	4	5	6	7	8	9
Japan	1984	0.627	0.157	0.304	0.132	0.017	0.570	0.957	0.548	0.167	0.640	0.659
	1990	0.772	0.097	0.094	0.124	0.047	0.396	0.989	0.944	0.301	0.922	0.857
	1996	0.799	0.065	0.165	0.175	0.070	0.143	0.892	0.919	0.459	0.789	0.762
	2003	0.792	0.094	0.142	0.303	0.046	0.198	0.869	0.826	0.501	0.826	0.488
Hong Kong	1984	0.849	0.425	0.711	0.866	0.155	0.374	0.666	0.707	0.996	0.551	0.823
	1990	0.914	0.558	0.917	0.871	0.421	0.681	0.829	0.839	0.958	0.761	0.453
	1996	0.937	0.566	0.943	0.832	0.618	0.691	0.881	0.863	0.884	0.842	0.519
	2003	0.949	0.446	0.793	0.925	0.212	0.445	0.893	0.896	0.968	0.851	0.454
South Korea	1984	0.726	0.831	0.306	0.153	0.204	0.047	0.477	0.678	0.968	0.243	0.431
	1990	0.789	0.767	0.791	0.208	0.118	0.012	0.507	0.846	0.968	0.357	0.571
	1996	0.837	0.545	0.477	0.258	0.275	0.115	0.822	0.877	0.895	0.996	0.947
	2003	0.849	0.413	0.873	0.331	0.304	0.113	0.982	0.852	0.682	0.852	0.759
Singapore	1984	0.873	0.821	0.626	0.848	0.875	0.965	0.886	0.621	0.930	0.896	0.371
	1990	0.941	0.776	0.987	0.897	0.996	0.999	0.832	0.643	0.984	0.894	0.942
	1996	0.966	0.764	0.953	0.975	0.986	0.997	0.953	0.711	0.960	0.806	0.914
	2003	0.919	0.696	0.956	0.923	0.828	0.982	0.666	0.767	0.922	0.952	0.512
Indonesia	1984	0.513	0.661	0.801	0.664	0.289	0.457	0.147	0.905	0.085	0.992	0.751
	1990	0.657	0.542	0.569	0.976	0.297	0.115	0.311	0.759	0.075	0.408	0.449
	1996	0.776	0.979	0.980	0.808	0.454	0.121	0.453	0.760	0.442	0.247	0.861
	2003	0.751	0.920	0.859	0.655	0.664	0.033	0.790	0.542	0.937	0.181	0.233

(Cont'd)

Country/Region	Year	Total	0	1	2	3	4	5	6	7	8	9
The Philippines	1984	0.650	0.652	0.970	0.436	0.097	0.111	0.266	0.749	0.399	0.640	0.937
	1990	0.754	0.940	0.782	0.957	0.170	0.132	0.300	0.567	0.483	0.569	0.891
	1996	0.787	0.708	0.646	0.523	0.213	0.194	0.212	0.420	0.231	0.373	0.403
	2003	0.858	0.795	0.594	0.630	0.248	0.223	0.226	0.492	0.123	0.304	0.766
Thailand	1984	0.556	0.197	0.998	0.853	0.040	0.561	0.104	0.835	0.292	0.579	0.383
	1990	0.709	0.358	0.589	0.779	0.116	0.363	0.240	0.623	0.540	0.374	0.424
	1996	0.797	0.375	0.860	0.990	0.251	0.350	0.436	0.697	0.764	0.595	0.522
	2003	0.850	0.420	0.918	0.848	0.381	0.742	0.778	0.839	0.967	0.607	0.816
Malaysia	1984	0.611	0.629	0.234	0.250	0.447	0.040	0.279	0.669	0.372	0.822	0.438
	1990	0.740	0.859	0.491	0.366	0.434	0.074	0.326	0.680	0.364	0.724	0.153
	1996	0.862	0.684	0.926	0.636	0.501	0.045	0.639	0.823	0.371	0.706	0.376
	2003	0.913	0.799	0.863	0.840	0.610	0.106	0.960	0.949	0.489	0.701	0.704
Chinese Mainland	1984	0.762	0.825	0.950	0.974	0.045	0.722	0.490	0.817	0.335	0.406	0.841
	1990	0.880	0.678	0.629	0.925	0.391	0.281	0.720	0.950	0.670	0.318	0.391
	1996	0.908	0.713	0.541	0.556	0.923	0.364	0.659	0.956	0.783	0.255	0.442
	2003	0.886	0.507	0.649	0.255	0.549	0.074	0.573	0.957	0.986	0.419	0.858

Source: Li Xiao, Ding Yibing and Qin Tingting, "The Improvement of China's Status in the East Asian Economy: Investigations Based on Trade Orientation", *Forum of World Economy and Politics*, Issue 5, 2005.

products and to decentralize the production process to other economies within the region. During this process it is more difficult for a single provider to have a defining influence on the development of the division of labor system of the entire region due to the more decentralized providers of capital goods. But when we look at this from another perspective, we will see that China as the largest real and potential demander for capital goods in the region has started to play a more and more important role in the regional industry division of labor system.

Looking at the scatter diagram of trade intensity of the East Asian economies, China and the U.S. (see Fig. 3.1.), we can find that East Asian economies are entirely in the Chinese area. This demonstrates that China has a closer trade ties with other East Asian economies compared with the U.S. We can see from the scatter diagram that the economies of East Asia can be generally divided into three groups: the first group includes Japan, Malaysia, Thailand, Indonesia and Singapore. These countries are distributed in the area of China, but they are closer to the area of the U.S., indicating relatively closer trade ties with it; the second group includes South Korea, Chinese Taiwan, the Philippines and Macao SAR that have closer trade ties with China and represent China's key trade partners compared with those of the first group; the third group includes Chinese Hong Kong that has weak ties with the U.S. in trade and relies heavily relies on the Chinese Mainland in trade. In addition, Hong Kong as a Special Administrative Region of China is the first region for the RMB to extend its international influence.

But if we look at the scatter diagram of trade intensity of the East Asian economies, China and Japan (see Fig. 3.1) we can see that the distribution of East Asian economies is more scattered and they are generally divided into three groups: the first group includes Indonesia and Thailand that are fully in the area of Japan. They have stronger trade ties with Japan but relatively weaker trade ties with China; the second group includes the Hong Kong SAR and Macao SAR which have the closest trade ties with the mainland due to their special relationship; the third group includes South Korea, Singapore, Taiwan, Malaysia and the Philippines whose trade intensity is equivalent with both Mainland China and Japan and they are located in the border of the two regions. As the third group includes the leading economies of East Asia, this means that neither China nor Japan can control the region of East Asia alone. China needs to first strengthen the comprehensive cooperation between the Chinese RMB and the Japanese yen if it seeks to enhance the international influence of the RMB and cooperation with East Asian currencies, as this is an important link for RMB internationalization. Only by doing so can China's regional economic foundation be fully secured.

Development of direct investment within East Asia

Mainland China's status has not only become increasingly important in trade of capital goods within the region but has also maintained a strong momentum in FDI attraction, which rose from USD5 billion in early 1990s to USD60 billion in 2004, up 12-times. China has become the most important FDI attractor within

Fig. 3.1. Scatter diagram of East Asian economies' currency and trade intensity of Mainland China, the U.S. and Japan

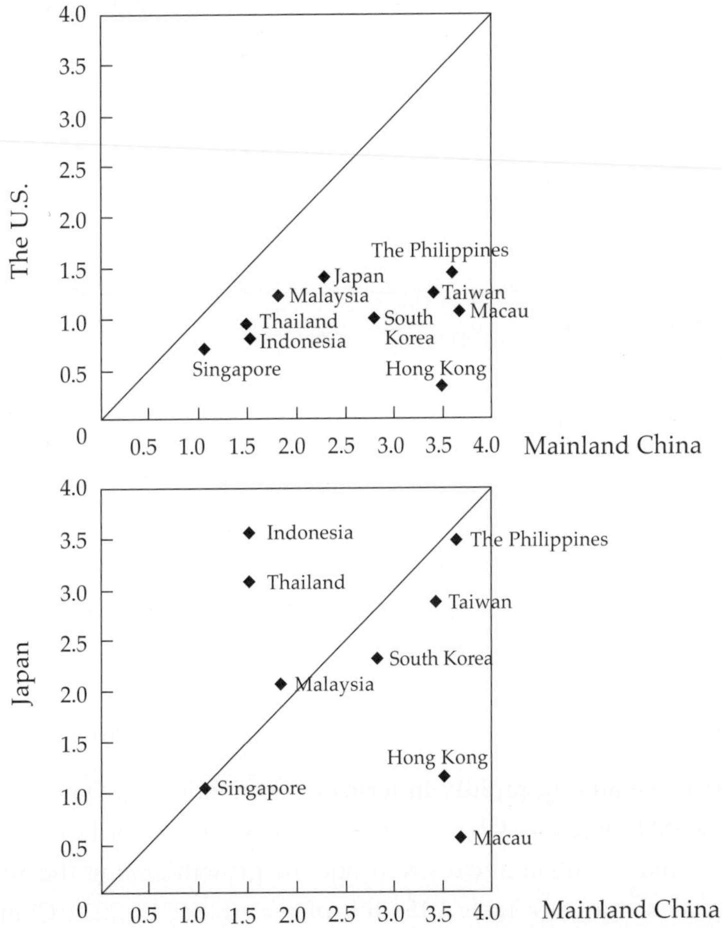

the region (see Table 3.13). Following Hong Kong and Japan, Singapore's direct investment in Chinese mainland grew significantly between 1990 and 2000, especially in the manufacturing industry that witnessed a rise from 48.1% in 1990 to 68.3% in 2000, up by 20% during the 10 years. Direct investment in China has become another key channel for production decentralization in East Asia apart from the export of capital goods. In the field of FDI, China is also playing a greater role in regional industrial division of labor in an opposite way to that of Japan.

China has obviously stepped up its efforts to make direct investment in Asia in recent years. Between 2005 and 2007 the proportion of its direct investment rose from 37% to 63% (Table 3.14), which has increasingly shown its focus on Asia. In comparison, China's FDI in Latin America contracted from 53% to 18 percent during the same period. As a whole, China's FDI is mainly concentrated on emerging countries (regions) and it remains unchanged in other African and European regions.

Table 3.13. Direct investment of other East Asian economies in the Mainland China in 2002

	Japan	Hong Kong	Taiwan	South Korea	ASEAN
FDI Amount of Exports (USD100 Million)	41.90	178.61	37.91	27.21	32.56
Proportion in FDI Net Amount of Exports (%)	13.31	100.94	81.27	101.75	57.20

Source: www.chinafdi.gov.cn

The influence of Chinese economic development on the East Asian economy

China has become the stabilizer for the economic development of East Asia

China is expanding rapidly in terms of economic aggregate and has become an essential force for stabilizing the economic growth of East Asia. As of 1993, only China has maintained fast economic growth among the 10 leading East Asian economies (see Table 3.15). It is projected that, by 2020, China's per capita

Table 3.14. China's FDI flow and stock in 2005, 2006 and 2007

Region	2005				2006				2007			
	Flow (USD10,000)	Proportion	Stock (USD10,000)	Proportion	Flow (USD10,000)	Proportion	Proportion, Stock (USD10,000)	Proportion	Flow (USD10,000)	Proportion	Stock (USD10,000)	Proportion
Total	1,226,117	–	5,720,562	–	1,763,397	–	7,502,555	–	2,650,609	–	11,797,050	–
Asia	448,417	0.37	4,095,431	0.72	766,325	0.43	4,797,805	0.64	1,659,315	0.63	7,921,793	0.67
Southeast Asia	15,771	0.01	125,615	0.02	33,575	0.02	176,228	0.02	96,808	0.04	395,317	0.03
Africa	39,168	0.03	159,525	0.03	51,986	0.03	255,501	0.03	157,431	0.06	452,183	0.04
Europe	–	–	127,293	0.02	59,771	0.03	226,982	0.03	154,043	0.06	445,854	0.04
Latin America	646,646	0.53	1,146,961	0.20	846,874	0.48	1,969,617	0.26	490,241	0.18	2,470,091	0.21
North America	32,084	0.03	126,323	0.02	25,805	0.01	158,702	0.02	112,571	0.04	324,089	0.03
Oceania	20,283	0.02	65,029	0.01	12,636	0.01	93,948	0.01	77,008	0.03	183,040	0.02

Source: http://www.fdi.gov.cn , set out by the author.

GDP will rise to USD3,000 from the current USD800 and its total GDP will grow to 4 trillion U.S. dollars from the current USD 1 trillion. China by then will become the world third largest economy following the U.S. and Japan. One fact that merits our attention is that China's fast economic growth has evident positive correlations with foreign capital and FDI in particular (see Fig. 3.2). This indicates that the Chinese market has become more attractive to foreign capital. Between 1991 and 2001, 9 East Asian countries and regions including Japan maintained an absolute proportion of investment in China (see Table 3.16). China has been gradually included into the industrial division of labor pattern of East Asia and has become a key link in the regional industrial cycle of East Asia.

A study by McKinnon and Schnabl (2003) shows that the Chinese economy has not only grown at the fastest speed but has also grown more stably than other East Asian economies in the last 20 years, and indicates that "China has served as a stabilizer for the integration of the Asian region". We use the same method to measure and estimate the GDP growth rate of East Asian economies and the changes between 1988 and 2007, and the estimation results are shown as Table 3.17. When it comes to the coefficient of variation of the annual growth rate, Mainland China is 0.27, the lowest in the region of East Asia. The coefficient of variation is 0.67 after East Asian economies besides Mainland

Fig. 3.2 The growth of China's GDP and inward FDI

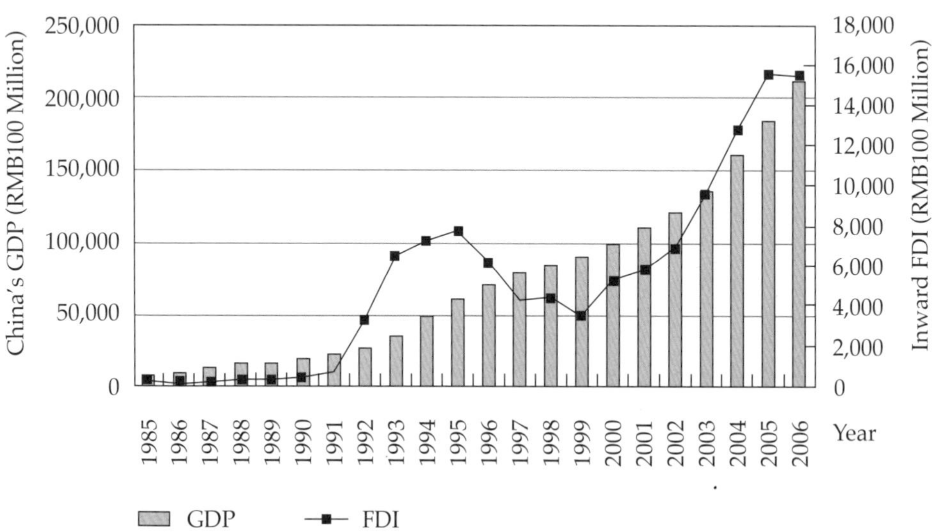

Source: *China Statistical Yearbook 2008*, set out by the author.

China and Japan are totaled up (EA1). The figure will drop to 0.60 if Mainland China is included (EA2), but the coefficient of variation of the overall output growth will rise to 0.62 if Japan is added (EA3). Evidently Mainland China mainland played a significant role in stabilizing the economic growth of East Asia while the involvement of Japan increased the instability of the economic growth of East Asia.

The deepening development of regional economic cooperation requires that at least one nation within the region must be able to serve as the "regional stabilizer" to ensure the overall steady development of the region. In the past, Japan as an economic power could play this role. But the above analysis in effect tells us that Japan has long been slowing down since the late 1980s and has failed to maintain the momentum of stable development, thus it often causes economic instability within the region. In recent years, Chinese economic development indicates that its growing economic strength and steady growth trend are making it become the stabilizer for the growth of the East Asian economy.

Table 3.15. Comparison of GDP growth among East Asian countries and regions (%)

Year	Mainland China	Japan	Hong Kong	Taiwan	South Korea	Singapore	Thailand	Malaysia	Indonesia	The Philippines
1993	13.5	0.3	6.1	7.0	5.5	12.7	8.2	9.9	7.3	2.1
1994	12.7	1.0	5.4	7.1	8.3	11.4	9.0	9.2	7.5	4.4
1995	10.5	1.9	3.9	6.4	8.9	8.0	9.2	9.8	8.2	4.8
1996	9.6	3.4	4.5	6.1	6.8	7.5	5.9	10.0	8.0	5.8
1997	8.8	1.8	5.0	6.7	5.0	8.4	-1.4	7.3	4.5	5.2
1998	7.8	-1.1	-5.0	4.6	-6.7	0.3	-10.5	-7.4	-13.1	-0.6
1999	7.1	0.1	3.4	5.4	10.9	6.4	4.4	6.1	0.8	3.4
2000	8.0	2.8	10.2	5.9	9.3	9.4	4.6	8.3	4.8	4.4
2001	7.3	0.4	0.6	-2.2	3.1	-2.4	1.9	0.4	3.3	3.2
2002	8.0	0.3	2.3	3.5	6.0	2.2	5.2	4.2	3.7	4.6
2003	7.3	0.5–0.7	2.0	3.7	4.0	2.3	5.0	4.3	3.4	4.0
2004	7.6	1.3–1.6	4.0	3.9	5.3	4.2	5.5	5.1	4.0	4.5

Source: Japan's *Toyo Keizai Statistics Monthly*, Issue 4, 2003; ADB, *Asian Development Outlook* 2003.

Table 3.16. The status of East Asia, the EU and the U.S. in China's paid-in FDI

Year	East Asia		The EU		The U.S.		Total Amount	
	Amount (USD100 Million)	Proportion	Amount (USD100 Million)	Proportion	Amount (USD100 Million)	Proportion	Amount (USD100 Million)	Proportion
1991	37.48	80.33	2.66	5.70	3.31	7.09	46.66	100.00
1992	99.00	87.68	2.68	2.37	5.19	4.60	112.91	100.00
1993	233.33	84.02	6.90	2.48	20.68	7.45	277.71	100.00
1994	278.98	82.18	15.44	4.55	24.91	7.34	339.46	100.00
1995	302.35	79.97	21.52	5.69	30.84	8.16	378.06	100.00
1996	327.14	77.64	27.37	6.50	34.44	8.17	421.35	100.00
1997	338.08	74.70	41.71	9.22	32.39	7.16	452.57	100.00
1998	308.25	67.80	39.79	8.75	38.98	8.57	454.63	100.00
1999	264.85	65.69	44.79	11.11	42.16	10.46	403.19	100.00
2001	291.67	62.22	41.83	8.92	44.33	9.46	468.78	100.00
2007	407.46	54.50	38.38	5.13	26.16	3.50	747.68	100.00

Notes:

1. East Asia includes Japan, the Four Asian Tigers namely Taiwan, Hong Kong, Singapore and South Korea, Indonesia, Malaysia, the Philippines and Thailand; Data of the EU between 1991 and 1996 refer to that of France, Germany, Italy, Belgium, Luxembourg, Spain, Austria, Finland, Ireland, Britain, Denmark and Sweden but excludes that of Greece and Portugal.

2. Data between 1991 and 1996 include direct investment and other investment, data between 1997 and 2001 all refer to FDI.

Source: *China Statistical Yearbook*, all issues.

Table 3.17 Changes in the annual output growth rate of East Asian countries and regions

Countries and Regions	Mean Value	Standard Deviation	Coefficient of Variation
Mainland China	9.83	2.67	0.27
Hong Kong	4.44	3.31	0.75
Indonesia	4.96	4.67	0.94
South Korea	6.07	3.65	0.6
Malaysia	6.69	4.05	0.6

(Cont'd)

Countries and Regions	Mean *V*alue	Standard Deviation	Coefficient of *V*ariation
The Philippines	3.98	2.32	0.58
Singapore	7.23	3.75	0.52
Taiwan	5.71	2.23	0.39
Thailand	5.92	5.03	0.85
Japan	2.03	2.00	0.98
EA1	5.62	3.75	0.67
EA2	6.09	3.64	0.60
EA3	5.68	3.51	0.62

Source: According to relevant data collected, where data of Taiwan are from the ADB and other data are from the World Bank.

China becomes the hub in the East Asian industrial labor division

Entering the 1990s, East Asian economies have become increasingly interdependent in trade, investment and finance. The economic integration of East Asia as a whole has been extended both in breadth and depth. On the one hand, the geographical scope of economic integration within the region keeps expanding, China has been gradually included into the regional integration process in recent years, and the economic links between some new members of ASEAN and other economies also keep growing; on the other hand, regional economic integration also keeps deepening in degree. When we look at the economic development of East Asia in recent years, we can see that China has increasingly become the hub in the East Asian industrial division of labor.

The basic landscape of East Asian economic development in recent years

First, the correlation of the economies within the region in economic fluctuation keeps rising. This phenomenon has shown up since the early 1980s, especially with the appreciation of the Japanese yen in 1985 and after Japan added industrial transfer and FDI to other East Asian economies. East Asian countries have increasingly diverged from the U.S. (see Fig. 3.3).

Second, regional trade keeps expanding and China's position has become more and more important in East Asian trade. At the moment the proportion of trade between East Asian economies in the total regional trade has surpassed

Fig. 3.3. Relative coefficient of East Asian economies' GDP growth rate and U.S. GDP growth rate

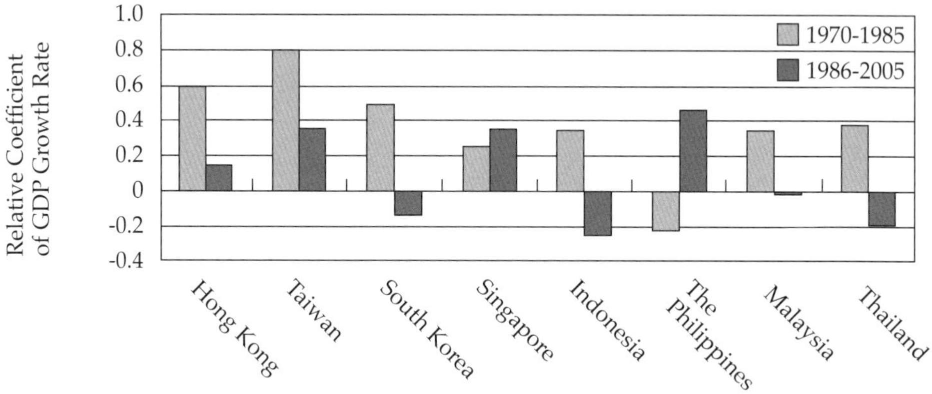

50% while the proportion of trade with the U.S. has shrunk from one third to one fourth. The interdependency rate of East Asian economies in trade also continues to grow steadily (see Table 3.18). The measure and estimation of the trade intensity of East Asia and the EU in 1999 by Goto (2002) show that this index in East Asia was 5.51, much higher than that of the EU's 2.35 and also indicate the inter-dependence of East Asian countries in trade. In addition, from the perspective of each country's dependency rate on export, we can see that during the 21 years between 1985 and 2005, China's proportion in the foreign trade of other East Asian economies keeps mounting. Chinese Hong Kong is the highest and its dependency rate on Mainland China reached 45% in 2005. The dependency rate of Japan on China also increased from 7.1 % in 1985 to 13.4% in 2005. Other East Asian countries also show the same situation, among which South Korea saw the fastest growth from having no inter-dependent relations with China to the 21.8% dependency rate in 2005. Other cases such as Singapore and ASEAN-4 also had a dependency rate of 8.4% and 11.7% respectively in 2005. We can see that China has become more and more important in the regional production system of East Asia.

Third, regional FDI keeps growing in scale and the capital amount flowing into China keeps rising. Not only Japan maintains a huge FDI to East Asia, the FDI between other East Asian economies i.e. ANIES (Asian Emerging Industrial Economies), ASEAN and China have also seen rises by leaps and bounds. Of which, FDI flowing to China has far surpassed the flow between other economies after 1990 (see Fig. 3.4).

Before 1985, economic fluctuations in open East Asian economies were close to those of the U.S. and maintained a high degree of consistency with Japan. There are two reasons: first, during this period, the U.S. and Japan were consistent in their economic cycles and the East Asian economies that had a close relationship with the two would not be affected by a difference of

Table 3.18. The dependency rate between East Asian economies on export (1985–2005)

Exporters	Year	Japan, Mainland China, South Korea, Hong Kong, Singapore, ASEAN-4					
Japan	1985		7.1	4.0	3.7	2.2	4.2
	1990		2.1	6.1	4.6	3.7	7.7
	1995		4.9	7.1	6.3	5.2	12.1
	2000		6.3	6.4	5.7	4.4	9.5
	2005		13.4	7.8	6.1	3.1	9.0
Mainland China	1985	22.3		0.0	26.2	7.5	2.7
	1990	14.7		0.7	43.3	3.2	2.9
	1995	19.1		4.5	24.2	2.3	3.7
	2000	16.7		4.5	17.9	2.3	3.7
	2005	11.0		4.6	16.3	2.2	4.1
South Korea	1985	15.0	0.0		5.2	1.6	3.4
	1990	18.6	0.0		5.6	2.7	4.8
	1995	13.0	7.0		8.1	5.1	7.5
	2000	11.9	10.7		6.2	3.3	7.2
	2005	8.5	21.8		5.5	2.6	5.7
Hong Kong	1985	4.2	26.0	1.8		2.8	3.6
	1990	5.7	24.7	2.3		3.2	4.0
	1995	6.1	33.3	1.6		2.8	3.6
	2000	5.5	34.5	1.9		2.3	3.3
	2005	5.3	45.0	2.1		2.1	3.1
Singapore	1985	9.3	1.4	1.2	6.3		20.5
	1990	8.7	1.5	2.2	6.5		20.9
	1995	7.8	2.3	2.7	8.6		26.6
	2000	7.5	3.9	3.6	7.9		24.8
	2005	5.5	8.6	3.5	9.4		28.8
ASEAN-4	1985	32.7	1.7	8.1	1.6	8.7	
	1990	25.9	2.3	6.2	3.2	10.8	
	1995	18.3	2.9	3.5	4.3	12.8	
	2000	15.7	5.2	4.4	3.9	10.3	
	2005	12.4	11.7	4.1	4.3	10.6	

Source: *IMF*, Direction of Trade Statistics, calculated by the author.

economic cycle between the U.S. and Japan; second, the regional production network had yet to take shape completely and close links in economic structure had yet to take shape among East Asian economies. After the signing of the "Plaza Accord" in 1985, the regional production network featuring "FDI-Trade" in East Asia was phased in and it has boosted the integration process of East Asia. On the one hand, the appreciation of the Japanese yen has helped pick up

Fig. 3.4. FDI Flow between China, ANIES and ASEAN in different periods

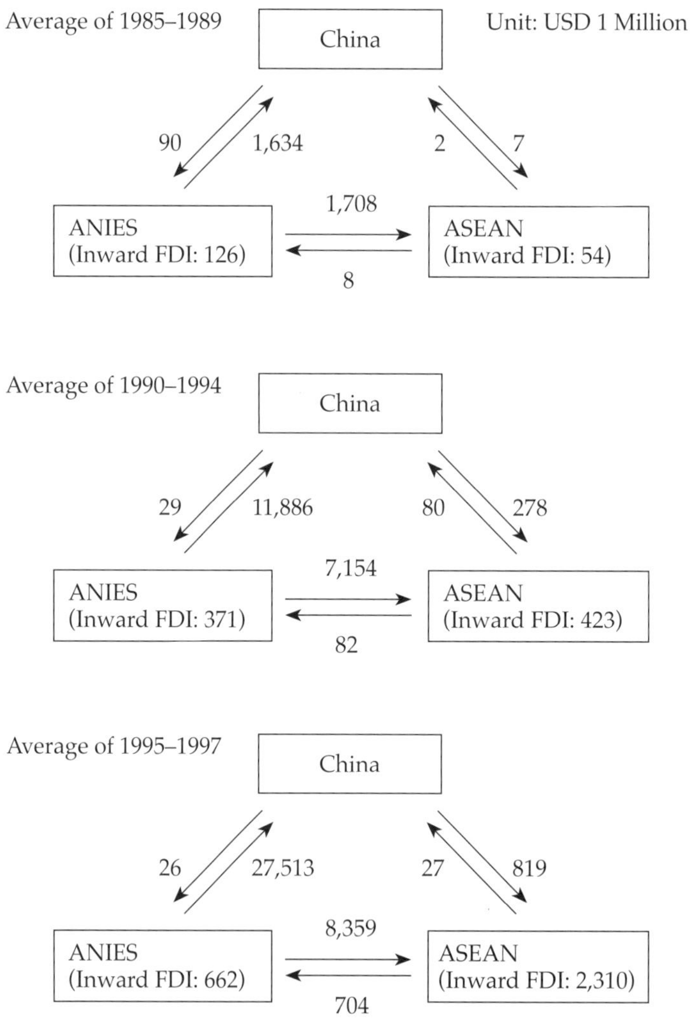

Source: Isogai and Shibanuma, 2000.

Japan's FDI in East Asia and the "Four Tigers" of East Asia have enhanced their direct investment in the region after "graduation," which has resulted in closer connections in trade, investment and finance within the region; on the other hand, trade between East Asian economies and the U.S. is mainly inter-industry trade while trade within the region is mainly intra-industry trade. The former stresses the professionalism of export products of different nations, which will lead to the deviation of the economic cycle among partners; but intra-industry trade tends to strengthen the synchronism of the economic cycle among trade partners (Zebregs, 2004). Studies by Frankel and Rose (1998), and Shin and Wang (2003) also indicate that the improvement of trade intensity between two economies may also strengthen the correlations in economic cycle. As such we find that the East Asian economies see remarkable improvement in synchronism with Japan and China while deviating from U.S. economic fluctuations. The research by Guan Zhixiong (2000) shows that the related coefficient of East Asian nations and regions as a whole and U.S. economic growth dropped from 0.731 between 1971 and 1984 to –0.193 between 1985 and 1998. In the meantime, they have demonstrated more and more outstanding consistency with Japan in economic cycle.

Changes of the role of East Asia in the world industrial chain and the impact on global economic imbalance

Different from the regional production network between Germany and Eastern Europe and between the U.S. and Mexico, East Asia has always been short of a market provider for end products within the region. This role has been seized by the U.S. The U.S. boasts the world broadest and most open single country market and used to unilaterally open the market to its allies during the Cold War period, which promoted the realization of "development by invitation" in the East Asian region. This historical opportunity combines with the high saving tradition of East Asia, phasing in a typical export-driven economic development strategy. The "export and investment-driven" growth pattern has become the basis for the economic development of East Asia and laid a foundation for the current economic relations within the region of East Asia and between East Asia and the U.S. Before 1997, the proportion of the U.S. current account deficit in its GDP was basically controlled below 2% and its growth rate was relatively moderate. But since 1997 the U.S. current account deficit started to expand and its proportion in the GDP keeps rising year by year, especially after entering the 21st century. By the end of 2005 the figure reached USD804.95 billion, accounting for 6.4% of the GDP.[9] At the moment the deficit is equivalent to three fourths of the surplus of leading surplus-running countries. In this sense, the U.S. current account imbalance is also regarded as global economic imbalance. Among major countries worldwide, the current account of the Eurozone and countries including Britain, Canada, New Zealand and Australia is basically balanced, and the deficit is mainly concentrated in the U.S. while the surplus is typically concentrated in East Asia, including Japan, China, the East Asian "Four Tigers" and ASEAN nations. In 2005 the U.S. ran a trade deficit of USD782.74 billion, more than 97% of the current account deficit. According to statistics of the USBureau of Economic Analysis, the U.S. ran the largest trade deficit against China in the year, recording USD201.6 billion, and the second largest trade deficit of USD84.7 billion against Japan. China, Japan the East Asian "Four Tigers" and ASEAN countries ran a trade surplus of USD335.2 billion against the U.S., taking up 42.8% of the total U.S. deficit and becoming the leading source for its deficit.

It is clear that Asia as the leading source for the U.S. economic imbalance has its intrinsic factors. In the wake of the Asian Financial Crisis, East Asian countries were still concerned. They generally settled for the exchange rate system that pegs to the currency of the "central country" and reinforced the control of capital account after the financial crisis, and thus accumulated a large quantity of official foreign exchange reserve. This phenomenon is rather similar to the relations between Western Europe, Japan and the U.S. under the Bretton Woods System, thus Dooley et al. dubbed it the "Resurgent Bretton Woods System". We have noticed that, on the one hand, this so-called "Resurgent Bretton Woods System" is different from the original Bretton Woods System and it is not implemented artificially by some institutional arrangement. Rather it is a spontaneous formation and development of the relations between East Asia and the U.S. On the other hand, the "Revived Bretton Woods System" has evident regional and local features. It is precisely because of the combination of this structure and the economic takeoff of East Asia that has resulted in the asymmetric balance between East Asia and the U.S.

China becomes the hub of the entire East Asian industrial labor division

A correlated four-level industrial cycle and trade cycle have taken shape globally at the moment: the U.S. imports capital goods from other developed countries and consumer goods from emerging industrialized and developing nations, and runs a huge deficit; other developed countries export capital goods to the U.S., import consumer goods from emerging industrialized and developing economies, and ultimately run more or less a surplus in current account (the Eurozone kept running a surplus for most of the time before 2004); emerging industrialized and developing nations import capital goods from developed countries, export consumer goods to them and run a certain surplus; countries enjoying rich resources such as oil exporters export energy and raw materials to leading commodity producers and thus run a surplus. It is this structure that has led to the U.S. economic imbalance. Here, China becomes one of the major sources for the U.S. current account surplus and plays a role that is different from the past in the East Asian industrial system. On the one hand, we should note that China's position is clearly different from that of past Japan in the industrial system of the entire East Asia and even the world. Therefore we need to look carefully at China's position in trade. China is the same as Japan in mid-1990s, importing primary goods for domestic production, but Japan at that time ran a surplus against the U.S. by leveraging on the comparative advantages of domestic producers in the manufacturing industry and its export goods were capital goods including parts and components as well as semi-finished goods towards the mid-1990s. But at this point, China imports more capital goods from East Asian countries, especially from Japan and South Korea, and capitalizes on processing trade to export end consumer goods to developed nations such as the U.S. and to some emerging industrialized economies. According to statistics of the Ministry of Commerce, 54.6% of China's exports and 41.5% of imports were contributed by the processing trade in 2005. The processing trade has become the basic model of foreign trade and the leading source of trade surplus for China. Thus China is now at the lower end of the third level of the above mentioned global division of labor system and its position is higher than resource exporters but lower than other emerging countries, and it belongs as a processing place for end consumer goods. On the other hand, we need to note that China plays a key role at this level. China's advantages in areas such as labor costs have been an advantageous point among emerging markets, making the end products that are provided originally by emerging and other developing countries to end product markets such as the U.S. concentrate in China for the final processing and production. Consequently China has replaced other East Asian economies in export to the U.S., but China will have more demand for parts and components as well as intermediate goods if its export capacity in processing export becomes stronger, which has expanded China's import of capital goods from developed countries and other East Asian economies. As such, China has become the most critical capital goods market within the region. A new "triangle trade" pattern has taken shape, that is the East Asian regional division of labor has generated the picture that East Asian emerging

Table 3.19. The standard deviation of East Asian currencies to RMB, the U.S. Dollar and Japanese Yen after standardization

		RMB	Hong Kong Dollar	New Taiwan Dollar	Japanese Yen	Korean Won	Malaysian Dollar	Philippine Peso	Singapore Dollar	Thai Baht
Standard Deviation of the Exchange Rate to RMB	2000.1–2005.7	0	0.0018	0.039	0.0701	0.0746	0.0028	0.0868	0.0313	0.0521
	2005.8–2008.6	0	0.0534	0.0338	0.0411	0.0651	0.0146	0.0506	0.0187	0.0684
Standard Deviation of the Exchange Rate to the U.S. Dollar	2000.1–2005.7	0.0019	0.0015	0.0383	0.0697	0.0744	0.0025	0.0863	0.031	0.052
	2005.8–2008.6	0.0497	0.0029	0.0286	0.0473	0.042	0.0549	0.0937	0.0616	0.1057
Standard Deviation of the Exchange Rate to Japanese Yen	2000.1–2005.7	0.0684	0.0673	0.0511	0	0.041	0.0664	0.1154	0.0436	0.0406
	2005.8–2008.6	0.0413	0.0497	0.0299	0	0.0756	0.0483	0.0814	0.0514	0.1034

Note: As the Macau Pataca is pegged to the Hong Kong dollar it is not listed separately.
Source: Calculated according to the data on the website of the Census and Statistics Department of Hong Kong.

economies (including some developed countries) export capital goods to China (typically parts and components, and intermediate goods as well as some raw materials), and process and assemble them in China and then export the final finished products to developed nations.[10] This is sufficient to illustrate that China in effect serves as the hub of industrial division of labor in the entire East Asian region.

The RMB's regional influence

The RMB has demonstrated a certain influence in the currency and exchange rate in East Asia while playing its critical role in the real economy. We can see from Table 3.19 that, as with Hong Kong dollar and Malaysian dollar, the RMB before its exchange rate system reform also adopted the system that pegs to the U.S. dollar. The standard deviation between these three currencies and the U.S. dollar is quite small in terms of exchange rate. In this connection, the implications of RMB exchange rate fluctuation in neighboring countries was rather small during this period and its relative influence simply demonstrated the influence of the U.S. dollar in the East Asia region. For this reason we only look at the difference between the Japanese yen and the U.S. dollar in terms of the impact of exchange rate fluctuations in East Asian currencies. During this period the standard deviation of the Taiwan dollar and Singapore dollar to the U.S. dollar was obviously smaller than the changes to the Japanese yen, reflecting that the management floating system adopted by these two economies more often than not took the U.S. dollar as reference while only the standard deviation of South Korean won and Thai baht to Japanese yen is smaller among these currencies. The Japanese yen is also a key currency for trade and investment in East Asia, but its regional influence is far from that of the Japanese regional economy.

After the reform of the RMB exchange rate, the RMB as an important referential currency turns up again in East Asia and the currency package of all economies became more diversified. Hong Kong continues to implement the policy of pegging its dollar to the U.S. dollar and the standard deviation of the Taiwan dollar, Korean won and Japanese yen to the U.S. dollar has decreased significantly, demonstrating that the U.S. dollar still has a strong influence on the region while the influence of the Japanese yen keeps weakening. During this period, the changes in the RMB's position merit more attention and the standard deviation of Taiwan dollar, Japanese yen, Korean won, Philippine peso and Singapore dollar to RMB exchange rate fluctuations has decreased substantially, indicating that the influence of the RMB keeps growing after its independence from the U.S. dollar. But the standard deviation of the Malaysian dollar,

Philippine peso, Singapore dollar and Thai baht to the RMB is much smaller than that to the U.S. dollar and Japanese yen, and the fluctuation of Japanese yen to the RMB is smaller than that to the U.S. dollar, showing the strong influence of the RMB in East Asia during the early days of RMB exchange rate fluctuations. This has laid a strong and realistic foundation for strengthening regional currency cooperation and realizing RMB internationalization through regionalization (see Fig. 3.5).

Advantages and Obstacles of the Chinese Economic Policy and System at the Current Stage

China as a large emerging country is still in its development stage, but it has always had the courage to take international responsibilities and contributes its part in the development of the international community. China has started to strengthen trade ties with neighboring countries since its economic takeoff in the 1980s. During this process, China has optimized the method of frontier trade settlement in the unofficial form under the preconditions of stable development, which has boosted border trade settlement in RMB and created favorable conditions for RMB regionalization. Towards the end of 2008, official documents fully affirmed the regionalization and charted the future course. China has also

Fig. 3.5. The scatter diagram of East Asian currencies to the RMB, the U.S. Dollar and Japanese Yen after RMB exchange rate reform

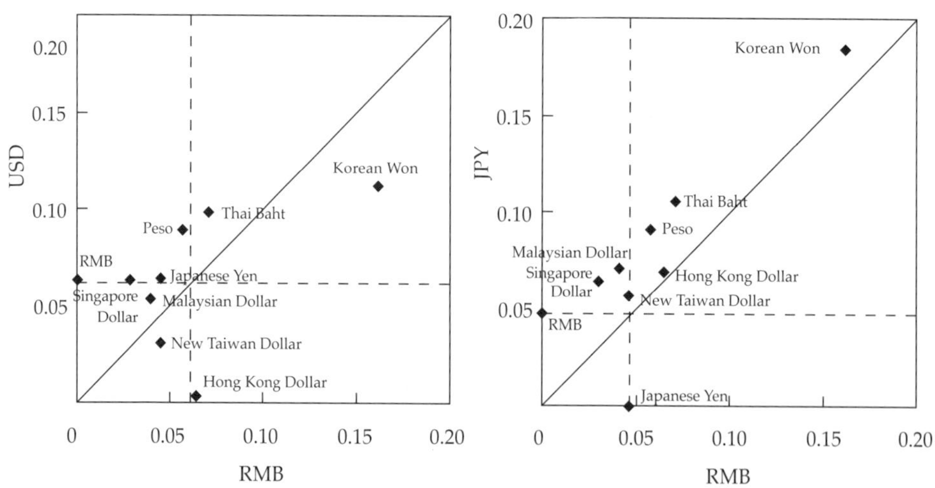

been committed to institutional setup in boosting regionalization, but there are still many obstacles due to the limitation of its strength.

Measures adopted by China in boosting regionalization in recent years

The status quo of border trade settlement in RMB — taking Xinjiang and Xishuangbanna in Yunnan as examples

With China's accession to the WTO and its increasingly developed border trade, the RMB has been widely accepted by merchants in Hong Kong, Taiwan and neighboring nations. It has become the instrument for border trade valuation and settlement and has started to show its functions as a regional currency. Objectively speaking, the flow and use of the RMB outside the border are formed spontaneously and it still far from performing the functions of an international currency in the real sense. That said, as the reform of the exchange rate formation mechanism deepens, the RMB has started to play the role of a regional currency-to-be to some extent and has been recognized by more and more countries and regions. We will take Xinjiang and Xishuangbanna in Yunnan as examples to make a comparative analysis.[11]

The status quo of Xinjiang border trade settlement in RMB

By the end of 2006, the total border trade of Xinjiang accounted for 71.2% of its total foreign trade volume and its foreign trade development was mainly driven by border trade. The frontier trade of Xinjiang mainly includes three forms, namely small-scale frontier trade, fairs among the inhabitants of border areas, and tourist shopping. As the demand increases and time goes by, the variety and amount of commodities for tourist shopping have increased by a large margin and have evolved into the export behavior of the combination of cash and spot exchange. The people's government of Xinjiang Uygur Autonomous Region included the export business of the tourist shopping trade in the management of small-scale border trade in 2002 in order to promote a regulated development of the tourist shopping trade. At the moment there are four major settlement modes for border trade: bank settlement, cash settlement, the model in which import are substituted for exports or vice versa, and the model of settlement in the private foreign exchange market. Of these the proportion represented by the latter two models is larger. In the following text we will focus on taking bank settlement and cash settlement as examples to analyze the performance of the RMB as the means of payment.

In terms of bank settlement, the bank channel for using RMB for settlement has yet to be opened. This mode is typically used by large-scale regular border trade companies and the proportion is about 40% of the total border trade. In Xinjiang the settlement channel for border trade is now basically smooth with the exception of the channel with Afghanistan and Western Mongolia. Commercial banks in Xinjiang have built correspondent banking relationship with 55 foreign banks in neighboring countries via their headquarter banks and established bank settlement relationship for intermediary banks and banks of neighboring countries via U.S. and European banks. For instance, 80% of the frontier trade between Xinjiang and Kazakhstan is done through the transfer remittance of international financial institutions such as U.S. banks while 20% is done through direct remittance of overseas branches of the Bank of China and the Industrial and Commercial Bank of China. But considering the low credit standing of commercial banks of neighboring countries and risks in settlement, the cooperation in the settlement in domestic currency between commercial banks within the region and commercial banks of neighboring countries has yet to start. Commercial banks as financial businesses are not enthusiastic about opening bank channels for settlement in domestic currency because of the requirement for maximizing profits. In this sense the RMB does not have a formal settlement channel within the banking system while the U.S. dollar is used as the major currency for bank settlement.

When it comes to cash settlement, the U.S. dollar still takes a leading role. The frontier trade between Xinjiang and neighboring countries are concentrated in the five Central Asian countries with individual trade at the core. The trade model includes tourist shopping and the fairs among habitants in border areas. The U.S. dollar is freely convertible within its border, using cash in trading can avoid higher taxes and fees, and both sides have poor confidence in each other and stick to the traditional trading model of collection and delivery in both cash and goods, so the U.S. dollar is used in most border trade. In addition, border posts are far from cities and backward in economy, and have fewer outlets of financial institutions, which has resulted in the leading position of U.S. dollar in cash settlement. Both sides rarely settle for domestic currency in settlement.

In recent years the inflow of U.S. dollar cash has shown a sharp increase with the rapid development of the tourist shopping trade. At present only Mongolia uses more Chinese RMB cash for frontier trade settlement, all other countries use U.S. dollar cash for trade settlement. This can be manifested by foreign traders entering China with cash and then converting their cash into RMB while some of them may have with them cash in foreign currencies and use this for valuation and settlement in the market. Accordingly the proportion of RMB cash in trade settlement is rather small and is mainly used for personal entry-exit expenses.[12]

The status quo of Xishuangbanna border trade settlement in RMB

Xishuangbanna is at the forefront for cooperation in the Great Mekong Sub-region (GMS) and the only region with international gateways by water, land and air in Yunnan province. It borders Laos and Burma and represents a crucial passageway and the window of China to South Asia. In recent years the RMB has become a major currency for the valuation and settlement in economy and trade between Xishuangbanna and neighboring countries with its stable value, as China's comprehensive national strength increases and reform and opening up deepens. According to statistics of the State Administration of Foreign Exchange (SAFE) Xishuangbanna Branch, its total foreign trade volume recorded USD97.21 million in 2004, USD98.43 million in 2005 and USD128.86 million in 2006. Of this the total foreign trade volume settled in RMB accounted for 87.73%, 82.50% and 59.87% in 2004, 2005 and 2006 respectively. The verified foreign exchange of small-scale border trade stood at USD45.4282 million, USD54.2110 million and USD43.8746 million in 2004, 2005 and 2006 respectively. 93.62%, 95.09% and 86.98% of which was in RMB.

The settlement model for the border trade of Xishuangbanna in RMB includes cash settlement and transfer settlement. The RMB has become a leading currency for frontier trade settlement because the currencies of countries such as Laos and Burma are unstable and easily depreciate while the RMB is stable and keeps strengthening. In 2006, 65% of the export of small-scale border trade was settled in RMB. On top of that, in accordance with the *Provisions on Administration of Foreign Exchange in Border Trade* and *Regulations on Implementing the Administration of Foreign Exchange in Border Trade of Yunnan*, businesses and individuals from neighboring countries can open special accounts for border trade settlement in RMB in banks in Chinese border areas and use the accounts for the collection and payment of border trade settlement, but the capital outflow of their accounts must be in the form of transfer. On 1 January 2004 Yunnan Province implemented the trial policy on tax rebate (exemption) for small-scale border trade settlement in RMB, providing that goods exported to Laos, Burma and Vietnam are settled in the form of bank transfer and cash and the rebate amount is calculated based on 70% and 40% of the rebate rate. As of 1 October 2004, the rebate rate for export goods settled in RMB through bank transfer rose from the regulated 70% to 100%. The implementation of this policy has greatly enhanced the enthusiasm of businesses of Xishuangbanna to use RMB for export settlement to Burma and Laos. The export-earned foreign exchange using RMB transfer for settlement rose from USD159,500 in 2004 to USD4.3641 million in 2005 and to USD8.762 million in 2006. In 2006, 20% of the export of small-scale border trade was settled by RMB transfer.[13]

We can see from the above analyses that China's practice in settling border trade in RMB has accumulated experience for the expansion of domestic currency settlement function and scope and expanded China's trade with neighboring countries and the scale and scope of RMB settlement to some extent. This a beneficial step for RMB regionalization. At the same time, we can also see problems faced by China in relevant policies and the real currency enforcement of neighboring countries. Few countries except Mongolia choose to settle frontier trade with China in RMB, demonstrating that there is still a long way before the RMB realizes regionalization.

Public trust and the RMB's international influence

Since the outbreak of the Asian Financial Crisis in 1997, the international credibility of China's monetary authority has increased significantly and its capacity in bilateral and multilateral coordination with other East Asian countries and regions has improved dramatically. The promise made by the Chinese government not to "depreciate the Chinese RMB" amid the Asian Financial Crisis avoided competitive currency devaluation within the East Asia region, stabilized the confidence of investors, stimulated the flowing back of international capital to East Asia, drove the economic recovery of the region and greatly improved public trust of the RMB in East Asia. It should be noted that China started to implement a floating, manageable exchange rate based on the balance between market supply and demand and in reference to a package of currencies on 21 July 2005. At the same time the Chinese government has been actively supportive of strengthening the ASEAN 10+3 cooperation framework within the region in the aftermath of the financial crisis and has put forward many constructive proposals. In particular after the signing of the CMI in May 2005, China has inked a number of bilateral currency swap agreements with countries such as Thailand, Japan and South Korea successively and became actively involved in the CMI multilateral process in 2008.

In general, the RMB has started to show its international influence that can be illustrated by the following aspects.

First, Malaysia followed China's example in implementing a floating and manageable exchange rate system. Within only one hour after the PBOC announced the RMB exchange rate adjustment on 21 July 2005, the Malaysian central bank announced the abolishment of the 7-year long fixed exchange rate system between the ringgit and the U.S. dollar and decided to put in place a floating and manageable exchange rate system immediately, making ringgit stop pegging to the U.S. dollar but floating based on the exchange of a basket of currencies.

Second, starting from December 2005, the Reserve Bank of India would work out and issue Indian new foreign exchange rate indices. Among these new indices the index of Nominal Effective Exchange Rate (NEER) was firstly added to the RMB and the Hong Kong dollar.

Third, the European Central Bank (ECB) incorporated the RMB into the "Reference Exchange Rates" of the euro on 30 March 2005.

Fourth, based on the rapidly increasing demand for investment in China, "E-TRADE Securities," a Japanese online securities dealer, launched the Chinese RMB-Japanese yen linked corporate bonds that pegged the Japanese yen to the RMB exchange rate, the first of its kind.[14]

Policy process of RMB regionalization

The internationalization and regionalization of the RMB have been discussed by the international community for a long time, but former discussions were basically non–governmental ones and there were no clear-cut official policy suggestions. On 10 July 2008, the State Council approved the plan of the PBOC to set up an exchange rate division with functions including "developing the RMB offshore market based on the RMB internationalization process." This was the first time an official document mentioned RMB internationalization, which formally opened the curtain to RMB regionalization.

Against the backdrop of the financial crisis, policies on RMB internationalization were also rolled out successively as part of the efforts to fight against the international financial crisis. On 10 November 2008 the PBOC held a working meeting for bank governors on implementing a moderately relaxed monetary policy, proposing "the exploration of providing medium and long-term financing in export credit". On 8 December 2008, the State Council promulgated suggestions on promoting economic development with finance,"allowing financial institutions to open buyer's credit on export business," "studying the issue of RMB bonds by foreign institutions and enterprises within the border of China and allowing Hong Kong businesses or financial institutions that have more business on the mainland to issue RMB bonds in Hong Kong," and "supporting the development of RMB-related business in Hong Kong, expanding the valuation and settlement of trade in RMB in neighboring regions and reducing exchange rate risk in foreign economic activities." On 12 December the PBOC and the Bank of Korea signed a bilateral currency swap agreement that provides for a liquidity support of RMB180 billion/KRW38 trillion. Both sides agreed to explore the possibility and proportion of changing swap currency into reserve currency. Another important implication of this bilateral agreement is that it was the first time the RMB officially went global.

The executive meeting of the State Council held on 24 December 2008 put forward in the studied and defined policy measures on alleviating difficulties faced by export-oriented businesses and keeping a steady growth of foreign trade the pilot program of using RMB to settle trade in goods between Guangdong and the Yangtze River Delta on the one hand and Hong Kong and Macao on the other and between Guangxi and Yunnan for one part and ASEAN for another. Lu Qianjin (2008) noted that this demonstrated that the central government was consciously pressing forward with RMB internationalization while keeping steady growth of foreign trade and indicated that the central government wanted to gradually move forward with RMB regionalization in trade with Hong Kong, Macao and ASEAN and improve the functions of the RMB in valuation and settlement of foreign trade. In February 2009, RMB regionalization was firstly put into trial in Shanghai. The Bank of Communications and Bank of China Shanghai Branches became the banks for the pilot program and started to use RMB for trade settlement with Hong Kong businesses. The partner banks in Hong Kong are the Hong Kong and Shanghai Banking Corporation and Bank of China Hong Kong. After using RMB in the trade settlement with Hong Kong businesses, a further step to move forward with RMB internationalization is to issue bonds in Hong Kong.

We can see that China has formally defined the standpoint of RMB regionalization and accelerated RMB regionalization through the development of a series of policies.

Institutional setup within the context of RMB regionalization

An essential basis for RMB regionalization is a set of mature and regulated market economic structures and systems. Market economic structure should be the precondition for RMB regionalization while the economic system is the necessary guarantee for the realization of a market economic structure. Once the RMB realizes regionalization, it means the integration of market resources within the region. That means that domestic and foreign resources will integrate under the condition of currency regionalization. As such, foreign economic fluctuations will be rapidly felt by the domestic economy, and the international market and domestic market are fully integrated. In this connection the absence of appropriate institutional arrangements as a guarantee in the domestic market is bound to impact on domestic economic security.

Institutional requirements for RMB regionalization

For any country, only a rational institutional arrangement can create the conditions for its currency regionalization. Based on the closeness of currency relations we divide institutions into two categories: foreign exchange management system and other social systems. Other social systems has a broad meaning, such as property relations and enterprise system.

Requirements of RMB regionalization on the foreign exchange administration system

The foreign exchange administration system includes many aspects, such as exchange rate institutional choice, current account openness, capital account openness and exchange rate formation system. Among these the key for the realization of RMB regionalization is how to realize free convertibility of the RMB. The RMB current account realized convertibility in late 1996 and this created the conditions for RMB liquidity in East Asia. But whether the RMB can be recognized by both the private and public sectors of East Asian countries and regions depends on the openness of the RMB capital account and it determines not only the scale and level of trade settled in RMB by investors and financiers but also the confidence of residents and non-residents in the RMB. According to the IMF's classification standard for capital transaction (43 items), 8 items are now convertible in China, accounting for 18.6% of the number of capital account transactions including business credit between residents and non-residents, non-residents' inward direct investment and direct investment liquidation; 11 items are less restricted, about 25.6%, mainly including residents' outward investment or issue of money market tools, guarantees between residents and non-residents, residents' outward direct investment and non-residents' procurement and sales of immovable property within the border; there are more restrictions on 18 items, about 41.9%; 6 items are severely restricted, taking up 13.9%. The RMB has in fact realized convertibility in capital account. After China's entry into the WTO, that the RMB would speed up the openness of capital account was irreversible. Of course, China's financial sector is still challenged in many ways and the reform of finance is still a long, winding journey. Problems and difficulties in this aspect will become a key factor for holding up RMB regionalization.

The precondition for free convertibility of the RMB is to accomplish equal trading with other currencies under a complete market mechanism. The fixed exchange rate system cannot realize this target. We can suppose that if the RMB is freely convertible under the fixed exchange rate system and the government wants to keep the exchange rate stable then the real currency price would depart significantly from the nominal currency price, which will add more external pressure and even result in grave financial crisis. A supporting credit system with commercial banks at the core should be established, which can speed up the promotion of RMB exchange business overseas. RMB regionalization and internationalization is part of the currency business, including domestic operation and international operations. A sound credit system needs to be established to coordinate these two operations. At present we need to create the conditions for RMB convertibility in economic engagement with countries worldwide. For instance, we need to convert rated RMB into domestic currency in countries with an open tourist industry with China, especially in the East Asian countries. At present the RMB is fully or partially current in Thailand, Vietnam, Burma, North Korea, Mongolia, Russia, Chinese Hong Kong and Taiwan (Burma regulates that Chinese tourists can carry RMB6,000 while entering the country and use them for payment), but only RMB20–30 billion are in circulation in the entire East Asian region, less than 2% of the total issue quantity of RMB1.6 trillion. RMB regionalization is in some sense is only the starting point of its internationalization. At the same time, we need to step up our efforts to promote the convertibility of RMB into domestic currencies in developed countries and provide an enabling soft environment for improving RMB regionalization and internationalization.[15]

Other institutional requirements for RMB regionalization

Collection and allocation of foreign exchange and implemented highly centralized planned management. All foreign exchange earnings were turned over to the central government and foreign exchange payment was based on a planned allocation. After 1979, China adopted the foreign exchange retention system and introduced the market mechanism for allocation of foreign exchange. As the retention proportion increased over time, the role of the market in adjusting foreign exchange revenue and spending continued to improve. In 1994 China realized conditional convertibility of the current account and lifted the restrictions on using foreign exchange in China-invested business trade and non-trade operations related to trade. In December 1996, China accepted the obligation of Article Eighth of the IMF, that is to make RMB current account convertibility a reality and abolish all restrictions on external payment and transfer of current account, and foreign exchange transaction of all current accounts only needs to be based on authentication. After that the Chinese government has continued to simplify the examination process and evidence for the authentication of current accounts, gradually allowed enterprises to retain foreign exchange of current account on demand, carried out management of the annual total amount of individual purchase of foreign exchange, and comprehensively pressed ahead with an import-export verification system and the reform of foreign exchange administration in the service trade.

The RMB capital account becomes more convertible

During the planned economy period China had neither internal debt nor foreign debt and did not welcome foreign investment. Since 1979 China has remained committed to prudent opening up and followed the system of "inflow before outflow, long-term before short-term, direct before indirect, institution before individual" to move forward with the opening up of the capital account in a planned and step-by-step manner by attracting foreign direct investment, borrowing debt from foreign countries moderately, putting in place a qualified foreign institutional investor system and opening up the domestic securities market to the outside world in an orderly way, implementing the "go global" strategy for full-fledged businesses, relaxing restrictions on foreign exchange for overseas investment, enforcing the recall of corporate foreign exchange and restrictions on overseas capital operation of multinational enterprises, and delivering a qualified domestic institutional investor system among other measures. As previously mentioned, among the 43 items of 7 categories of capital account transaction classified by the IMF, those which are seriously regulated and controlled by the Chinese government include free issue or buying and selling of financial derivatives by non-residents, and residents' borrowing from overseas and lending to the outside world. More than 20 items are less restricted or have realized a certain convertibility.

The RMB foreign exchange formation mechanism has become increasingly marketized

Before the reform and opening up, the government was the decision maker for RMB exchange rate and implemented a fixed exchange rate. The exchange rate was only an instrument for accounting. In the early days of the reform and opening up China implemented a dual exchange rate regime with the co-existence of the official exchange rate and swap market exchange rate with the implementation of the foreign exchange retention system. In early 1994 the government unified the official exchange rate and the market exchange rate and implemented a single, floating and manageable exchange rate system that is based on the balance between market supply and demand, and the movement of the exchange rate was determined by the market. In July 2005 the government further improved the exchange rate formation mechanism, no longer pegged the RMB exchange rate to the U.S. dollar, and started to implement a single, floating and manageable exchange rate based on the balance between market supply and demand and in reference to a basket of currencies. The market has strengthened its basic role in exchange rate formation, and the elasticity of the exchange rate has been further enhanced and has played a bigger role in regulating international payments.

The foreign exchange market has been established and developed significantly

During the planned economy period, foreign exchange was under highly centralized administration and there was no foreign exchange market. In the early days of the reform and opening up, China implemented the foreign exchange retention system, and set up and developed the foreign exchange swap market. In 1994 the central government started to practice the policy that banks settled and sold foreign exchange, and established a unified inter-bank foreign exchange market and the bank-to-client foreign exchange settlement and sales market. After the reform of the foreign exchange formation mechanism in July 2005, the central authority continued to improve the trading mechanism of the inter-bank foreign exchange market, expand market players, increase market trading instruments and further straighten out the relations between supply and demand. Currently the market system covers all sorts of foreign exchange transaction tools including spot transactions, forward transactions and swap transactions with the combination of the foreign exchange retail market and inter-bank wholesale market and the mutual supplementation of auction trading and over-the-counter trading.

The foreign exchange statistical and monitoring system keeps improving

In 1981 the Chinese government developed the international payment statistical system, started to formally draw up the balance sheet of international payments in 1982, started to make this public in 1985, began to release reports on China's international payments in 2005, initiated the release of the international investment position in 2006, started foreign debt statistics in 1986, started bank settlement and sales statistics in 1994, started cross-border capital flow statistics in 1996, formally put in place the early warning system for risks of international payments in 2003, and had in place a high frequency debt monitoring and early warning system and market expectation investigation system in 2005. China has now established a monitoring and early warning system for cross-border capital flow in line with international common practice and requirements as well as with the national reality.

The foreign exchange reserve operation and administration system becomes increasingly modernized

In early days of the reform and opening up, China's foreign exchange reserve was rather small in size. After 1994 the government worked to meet the rapidly growing demand for foreign exchange reserves, targeted standardization, specialization and internationalization, improved the reserve operation administration system and operation procedures, and effectively controlled risks of all kinds. China has put in place the management model with investment base at the core, gradually turned to long-term diversified investment management from focusing on short-term liquidity management, established a more mature system for strategic study, investment decision and transaction execution, and shaped a more modernized performance rating, risk management and internal control framework. China has maintained and increased the value of state foreign exchange reserves through active and professional investment and effective control of risks.[16]

Institutional arrangements must be improved and perfected

We can see from the above analysis that China is improving the domestic institutional environment for RMB regionalization and has achieved great results. But there are still many problems that need to be solved, reformed and improved. For instance, the forced settlement of exchange system for current account that lasted for 13 years between 1994 and 2007 was rather over-strict while resolving the shortage of China's foreign exchange, which has greatly increased the foreign exchange reserve and then changed the issue structure of base money of the central bank. Funds outstanding for foreign exchange have become a leading channel for the issue of base money and the institutional source for China's growing inflationary pressure in recent years.[17] Some flaws exist in terms of the management of foreign exchange account for capital account, which have resulted in the settlement of funds of capital account in current account. At the same time as the current management of foreign exchange for capital account basically adopts administrative examination and approval and quota means, and economic means are rarely used, the cost of control increases and the efficiency of administration decreases. More importantly, the foreign exchange market and the RMB exchange rate formation mechanism have yet to be improved.

At present, China's forex market is the inter-bank forex market. Since 1994 great restrictions have remained on transaction players in the foreign exchange market. The foreign exchange market is the only major place for the central bank to intervene in foreign exchange and stabilize the exchange rate. As China's interest rate formation mechanism has yet to realize full marketization and free convertibility has yet to be implemented for capital account, the supply and demand of foreign exchange mainly come from operational transaction settlement and sales of foreign exchange, the elasticity of interest rate of capital flow is rather smaller, and the foreign exchange market does not have the interest rate-exchange rate linkage mechanism that is the "interest rate-capital flow-exchange rate."

It is clear that China's existing system still has room for improvement. We need to seriously review and assess existing foreign exchange administration policy and system, improve and modernize the foreign exchange settlement and sales system and the RMB exchange rate formation mechanism, work to "relax controls over foreign exchange for residents," spread risks and reduce foreign exchange reserve pressures on the one hand and effectively control the orderly flow of funds while preventing capital outflow and decreasing interest arbitrage space on the other. Given the current situation, China must practice foreign exchange administration under capital account in principle, strictly supervise and control the flow of capital account, control foreign debt and relax foreign exchange account for some capital account under safe and controllable preconditions. Only when this system is improved can we expect to develop domestic financial business, expand the overseas financial market, create financial derivatives and then realize RMB regionalization.

Textual Research on China's Position as the Market Provider of East Asia

Empirical evidence for China as a market provider of east asia

Examinations based on the Trade Intensity Index

The Trade Intensity Index reflects the closeness of the trade relationship between two countries. The calculation method is as follows:

$$\mathbf{TII}_{ij} = (X_{ij}/ X_{it}) / (X_{wj}/X_{wt}) \qquad (3\text{–}3)$$

Where X_{ij} refers to the export of country i to country j; X_{it} refers to the total export of country i; X_{wj} refers to the export of the world to country j; X_{wt} refers to the total world export. This index indicates the ratio of the proportion of the export of country i to country j in its total export to the proportion of total world export to country j. If TII_{ij} equals 1, it means the trade relationship between country i and country j is neutral. If TII_{ij} is greater than 1, it indicates a close trade relationship between the countries. If TII_{ij} is less than 1, then the two countries have a distant trade relationship.

We select the trade data of the three years of 1985, 1995 and 2005 to calculate the trade intensity between East Asian economies in those years. In the Table, the figure bolded means the trade intensity between two countries is less than 1. We can see from the comparison of the three years that trade ties between East Asian economies boomed during the decades. In 2005 the trade intensity between all economies was greater than 1 apart from that between Chinese Hong Kong, South Korea, Indonesia, Malaysia and Thailand, between Indonesia and Chinese Hong Kong, and between Thailand and South Korea. In particular, China deeply integrated itself into the trade system of East Asia during this period. By 2005 the trade intensity between all East Asian economies and Mainland China had surpassed 1 (Table 3.20).

It can be seen that the trade intensity between China and other East Asian economies has kept rising over the past decade. But we should also note that, for other countries apart from China, the trade intensity index with the rest of East Asia such as the index between Japan and other East Asian economies is more than 3 and the index of Singapore is as high as 19.58. In fact the trade intensity index can only reflect the changing trend of the economic ties between East Asian economies and more precisely reflects the trade dependence between two countries. It cannot

Table 3.20. Trade Intensity Index between East Asian economies

	Japan	South Korea	Hong Kong	Singapore	Indonesia	Malaysia	The Philippines	Thailand	Mainland China
1985									
Japan	-	2.57	2.46	1.65	2.38	1.98	1.97	2.46	3.30
South Korea	2.27	-	3.44	1.22	1.24	2.38	2.93	1.01	**0.00**
Hong Kong	**0.64**	1.14	-	2.12	2.16	1.19	3.80	1.48	12.10
Singapore	1.41	**0.78**	4.21	-	n.a.	24.72	3.51	8.80	**0.67**
Indonesia	6.99	2.24	1.25	6.58	-	**0.66**	3.94	**0.93**	**0.21**
Malaysia	3.72	3.74	**0.89**	14.62	**0.82**	-	8.81	7.29	**0.49**
The Philippines	2.87	1.03	2.69	4.08	**0.76**	6.04	-	3.84	**0.82**
Thailand	2.02	1.18	2.69	5.98	1.17	8.00	2.75	-	1.77
Mainland China	3.37	**0.00**	17.40	5.69	**0.87**	1.09	4.24	**0.91**	-
1995									
Japan	-	2.69	1.67	2.15	2.85	2.51	2.91	2.97	1.93
South Korea	1.99	-	2.17	2.11	2.85	1.49	2.07	1.23	2.71
Hong Kong	1.99	2.17	-	2.11	2.85	1.49	2.07	1.23	2.71
Singapore	1.19	1.04	2.28	-	n.a.	12.70	2.96	3.85	**0.91**
Indonesia	4.14	2.44	**0.97**	3.43	-	1.44	2.36	1.03	1.49
Malaysia	1.91	1.04	1.43	8.39	1.66	-	1.61	2.59	1.00
The Philippines	2.41	**0.97**	1.26	2.36	**0.92**	1.20	-	3.07	**0.47**
Thailand	2.47	**0.52**	1.33	5.57	1.75	1.75	1.28	-	1.09
Mainland China	2.92	1.71	6.45	**0.97**	1.22	**0.57**	1.26	**0.78**	-
2005									
Japan	-	3.52	2.37	1.82	3.19	2.19	3.80	3.76	2.39
South Korea	1.92	-	2.13	1.53	3.61	1.67	2.80	1.18	3.87
Hong Kong	1.20	**0.96**	-	1.21	**0.89**	**0.85**	2.23	**0.97**	7.99
Singapore	1.24	1.58	3.67	-	19.58	13.67	4.51	4.08	1.53
Indonesia	4.80	3.71	**0.68**	5.36	-	4.14	4.10	2.60	1.38
Malaysia	2.13	1.51	2.28	9.14	4.79	-	3.46	5.34	1.17
The Philippines	3.98	1.51	3.17	3.84	2.35	6.15	-	2.81	1.76
Thailand	3.10	**0.91**	2.17	4.06	7.29	5.41	4.59	-	1.47
Mainland China	2.51	2.07	6.38	1.28	2.23	1.44	1.52	1.02	-

Source: IMF, Direction of Trade, calculated by the author.

reflect the level of economic links of the entire East Asia as trade proportion is different for different countries. In this sense, we need to analyze whether China is expected to become the market provider in East Asia from the perspective of specific changes in inter-regional trade.

Analysis based on changes in inter-regional trade pattern

As of the 1990s, under the influence of China's rising economy and especially the robust growth of its foreign trade, the original trade structure of East Asia has been broken and a new "triangle trade" model with China at the hub is taking shape in East Asia (Li Xiao et al., 2005). China has become an export platform for the region of East Asia over time. China imports capital goods and parts and components from other regional economies and then exports the final processed products to developed countries such as the U.S. Japan and the U.S. still have a larger share of the export to some East Asian economies (ASEAN countries in particular), but their share has decreased significantly over the past 10 years and keeps shrinking in a faster manner; at the same time, China's position as the market provider in East Asia is strengthening, especially for South Korea and Chinese Taiwan, and the proportion of their export to China kept mounting between 2000 and 2006 (see Table 3.21).

The formation process of the new trade pattern of East Asia is coupled with tremendous changes in the export orientation and global market share of the exports of the major East Asian economies. Between 1990 and 2007, the export market for finished products manufactured by Mainland China changed from Asia to Europe and North America while the export market for finished products made by Japan and other East Asian economies changed from Europe and North America to Asia in general (see Table 3.22). On the one hand, this indicates the rapid development of intra-trade in East Asia; on the other, it reflects that China has become a major platform for the exports of East Asia to other regions. We can further see from Fig. 3.6 that a sharp contrast to Japan's declining export share is the sharp increase in the share of Mainland China's exports in the total exports of the Asian-Pacific region (nearly 30%). China has replaced Japan to become the largest exporter in Asia.

In the new "triangle trade" model of East Asia, the central role of China is mainly demonstrated in its trade links and complementation with two leading groups of trade partners. On the one hand, China's trade surplus against the U.S. and the EU picked up rapidly, reaching USD163.3 billion and USD134.2 billion respectively in 2007;[18] on the other China substantially increased its

Table 3.21. Changes of the share of Mainland China, Japan and the U.S. in exports to other economies (%)

Export	Import								
	China			Japan			The U.S.		
	1995	2000	2006	1995	2000	2006	1995	2000	2006
South Korea	7.0	10.2	20.3	13.0	11.3	7.7	18.5	20.9	12.7
Singapore	2.3	3.8	9.6	7.8	7.3	5.4	18.3	16.7	10.0
The Philippines	1.2	1.6	9.3	15.8	13.4	15.6	35.8	27.3	17.3
Thailand	2.9	3.9	8.8	16.6	14.2	12.3	17.6	20.5	14.7
Malaysia	2.6	2.9	7.0	12.5	12.3	8.5	20.8	19.5	18.1
Indonesia	3.8	4.2	7.4	27.1	22.1	18.5	13.9	13.0	11.0
Hong Kong	33.3	34.1	46.7	6.1	5.5	4.9	21.8	23.0	15.0
Taiwan	0.3	2.9	23.1	11.8	11.2	7.3	23.7	23.6	14.4

Source: ADB, *Asian Development Outlook 2007* and *Asian Development Outlook 2008.*

Table 3.22. Export orientation and proportion of major East Asian countries' end products (%)

Export	Import							
	Asia		Europe		North America[a]		Other Regions of the World[b]	
	1990	2007	1990	2007	1990	2007	1990	2007
Mainland China	67.7	40.8	14.7	23.5	10.0	22.9	7.6	10.7
Japan	26.1	42.8	23.0	16.8	36.3	24.9	14.7	15.5
South Korea	34.0	51.4	15.5	16.1	33.4	17.5	17.1	15.0
Singapore	47.1	64.7	17.2	11.3	23.0	11.6	12.8	12.4
The Philippines	34.8	68.5	18.8	10.5	40.2	14.8	6.1	6.2
Thailand	37.8	54.1	25.3	15.5	25.3	14.5	11.7	15.8
Malaysia	58.0	57.1	16.6	13.5	18.1	17.3	7.4	12.2
Indonesia	64.3	60.8	12.8	13.3	13.9	12.5	9.0	13.4
Hong Kong	42.3	64.0	20.3	14.3	27.2	14.2	10.2	7.6
Taiwan	38.2	64.8	18.2	7.0	36.0	13.8	7.5	14.4

Notes: a. The statistical data for North America in the table includes two parts, namely North American countries and Central American countries which are not listed separately, considering that the small economies of scale of Central America will not affect the proportion.

b. The Middle East, South America and Africa are not listed alone but rather included in Other Regions.

Source: IMF, Direction of Trade Statistics CD-ROM, 2008.

Fig. 3.6. **The share of East Asian economies' exports in the total exports of the Asian-Pacific region**

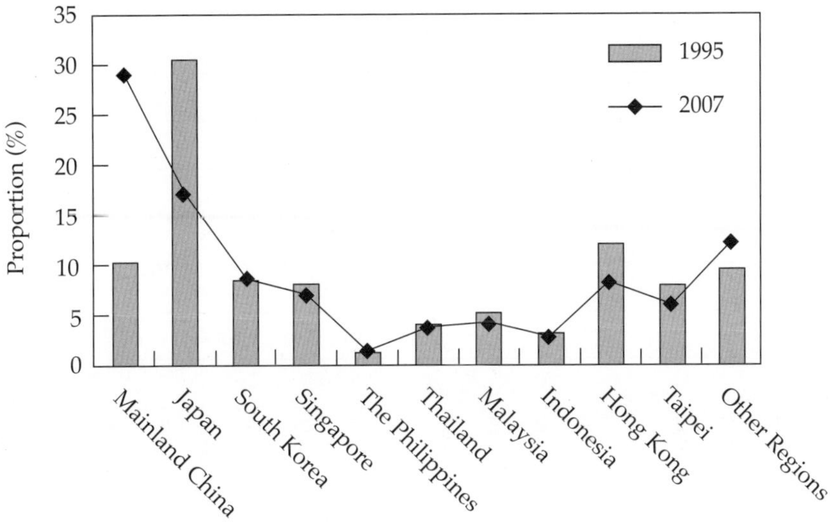

Source: IMF, Country sources, International Financial Statistics CD-ROM, 2008.

imports from its neighboring countries in Asia, which has driven up the exports of emerging East Asian economies to a large extent. We can see from Fig. 3.7 that the growth rate of China's exports to developed countries has changed synchronously with the growth rate of emerging East Asian economies' exports to China. This synchronous change has become more obvious in the wake of the Asian Financial Crisis in 1998. The different model of trade ties between China and its key trade partners demonstrates that an increasingly expanding and strengthening complex cross-border network is taking shape. With the enhancement of China's position as the market provider for East Asia i.e. importing more products from within the region, the RMB's circulating capacity will be further improved in East Asia and the prospect for it to serve as a currency of payment in East Asia is good. This will provide an important foundation for RMB regionalization.

In addition, the China-ASEAN Free Trade Area (CAFTA) that was formally established on 1 January 2010 has also provided an opportunity for RMB regionalization. China and ASEAN countries are now seeing each other as the fourth largest trade partner and a key objective for investment. The

Fig. 3.7. The growth rate of Chinese exports to the U.S., Japan and the EU and that of the exports of the seven emerging East Asian economies to China between 1992 and 2007

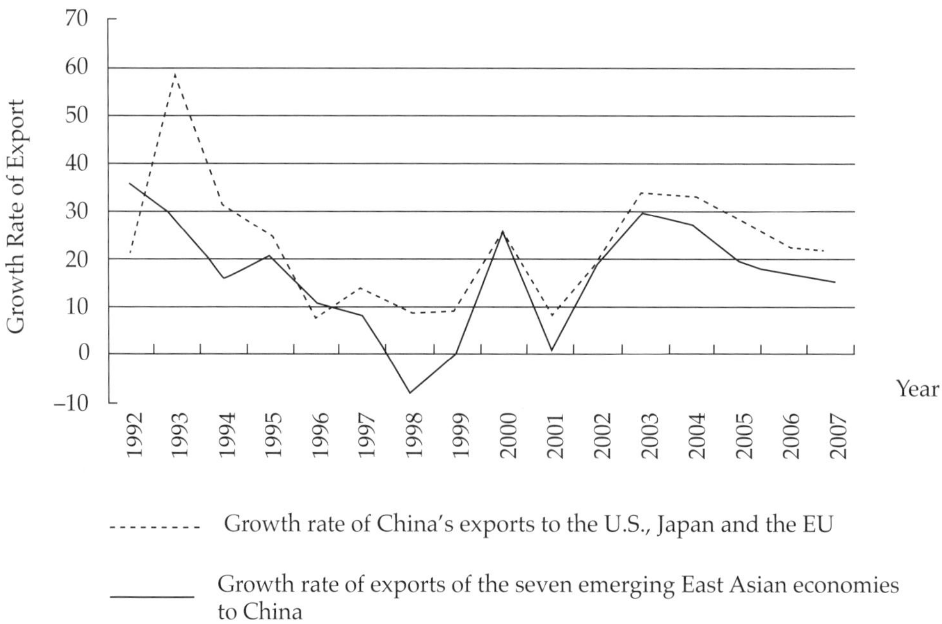

Source: IMF, Direction of Trade Statistics.

establishment of CAFTA has cut back the tariff between China and 6 ASEAN countries to zero for most commodities and the deadline for tax cuts with the new ASEAN-4 is the year of 2015, which means that trade between China and ASEAN countries might see rapid growth. Studies by Roland-Holst (2002) indicate that if China joins the ASEAN Free Trade Area and forms a new trade zone within the region of Asia then it will generate benefits to Asian countries, especially ASEAN countries. It is projected that the export growth rate will surge from 1% to 16%. If the amount of RMB used as a trade settlement currency increases with the growth trade volume between China and ASEAN countries, the circulating capacity of the RMB will undoubtedly be enhanced. The executive meeting of the State Council held on 24 December 2008 decided to implement the pilot program on using RMB for trade settlement with the ASEAN in Guangxi and Yunnan, which has laid a solid foundation for the RMB to become a leading currency within the East Asian trade area.

An empirical analysis of China's position as the market provider in East Asia

It is necessary to make an empirical analysis and forecast of China's position as the market provider in East Asia and examine the macro basis for RMB regionalization from a long-term perspective in order to better assess and predict the prospect of RMB regionalization. Through analyzing the leading source countries for China's imports in East Asia and the coupled examination of the development landscape of these countries, we determined the objectives in the region of East Asia for study to be Japan, South Korea and ASEAN-5.

Model building and data source

Studies of the changes and development trend of China's position as an East Asian market provider can be realized through measuring the changes of the proportion of China's imports from sample countries in the total exports of sample countries. This requires us to make an analysis of the influencing factors for the exports of sample countries. Considering the availability of data and other factors, we select Y, the proportion of the export of sample countries to China in their total export, as a dependent variable and choose the actual growth rate of China's GDP G_C, the actual growth rate of other countries' GDP G_o and the nominal exchange rate of domestic currency against the RMB as independent variables. At the same time, we also add the economic integration dummy variable to measure the implications of regional economic integration for trade orientation. Through analysis, we settle for the following regression model:

$$\mathbf{In}\boldsymbol{Y}_i = \partial_0 + \partial_1\mathbf{In}\boldsymbol{G}_C + \partial_2\mathbf{In}\boldsymbol{G}_{oi} + \partial_3\mathbf{In}\boldsymbol{E}_i + \partial_4\mathrm{In}\boldsymbol{D}_i \qquad (3\text{–}4)$$

Where i represents sample countries, $\boldsymbol{D}_i$ refers to the dummy variable, we can choose 0, 1 respectively through examining whether each country adds WTO or Asia-Pacific Economic Cooperation (APEC). Given that some variables might have time trend, we build the equation after differentiation:

$$\Delta\mathbf{In}\boldsymbol{Y}_i = \partial_0 + \partial_1\mathbf{In}\boldsymbol{G}_C + \partial_2\mathbf{In}\boldsymbol{G}_o + \partial_3\Delta\mathbf{In}\boldsymbol{E}_i + \partial_4\boldsymbol{D}_i \qquad (3\text{–}5)$$

Considering that Chinese economic development just began to take shape after 1985 and China and South Korea established formal diplomatic relations in August 1992, we determined to choose the years between 1985 and 2007 as the time interval for Japan and ASEAN-5 and the years between 1992 and 2007 as the time interval for studies of South Korea. In view of that fact that the unexpected impact triggered by the sharp depreciation of the RMB after the reform of China's exchange rate in 1994 might affect the stability of the data, we omitted the data for that year. All sample data are yearly data, among which the total exports of South Korea and ASEAN-5 during the time interval and their exports to China, the nominal exchange rate of all sample countries' currencies against the U.S. dollar and the data on China's actual GDP growth rate are all taken from the ADB Central Statistical Database. The data on the yearly exports of Japan and its exports to China are all from the UN Commodity Trade Statistics Database. The global GDP, China's GDP and the GDP of sample countries are all from the World Bank Key Development Data & Statistics.

Empirical analysis and its basic conclusion

The nominal exchange rate of the Japanese yen and Korean won against the Chinese RMB can be calculated through using their exchange rate against the U.S. dollar to divide the exchange rate of the RMB against the U.S. dollar; the exchange rate of the currencies of ASEAN-5 against the RMB can be weighted based on the proportion of the trade volume of each of the five countries in their total trade volume and the average exchange rate can be calculated through the weighted average method. According to the time of the accession of Japan, South Korea, ASEAN-5 countries and China to the WTO and APEC, we add two or one dummy variables (D_1 or D_2) in studied objectives respectively.[21] The regression model used by us is:

$$\text{Japan: } \Delta\mathbf{In}Y_{\text{JAP}} = \beta_0 + \beta_1\mathbf{In}\boldsymbol{G}_{chi} + \beta_2\mathbf{In}\boldsymbol{G}_{oth} + \beta_3\Delta\mathbf{In}\boldsymbol{E}_{\text{JAP}} + \beta_4\boldsymbol{D}_1 + \beta_5\boldsymbol{D}_2 \qquad (3\text{–}6)$$

$$\text{South Korea: } \Delta\mathbf{In}Y_{Kor} = \delta_0 + \delta_1\mathbf{In}\boldsymbol{G}_{chi} + \delta_2\mathbf{In}\boldsymbol{G}_{oth} + \delta_3\Delta\mathbf{In}\boldsymbol{E}_{Kor} + \delta_4\boldsymbol{D}_1 \qquad (3\text{–}7)$$

$$\text{ASEAN: } \Delta\mathbf{In}Y_{ASEAN} = \theta_0 + \theta_1\mathbf{In}\boldsymbol{G}_{chi} + \theta_2\mathbf{In}\boldsymbol{G}_{oth} + \theta_3\Delta\mathbf{In}\boldsymbol{E}_{ASEAN} + \theta_4\boldsymbol{D}_1 + \theta_5 D_2 \qquad (3\text{–}8)$$

$$\text{Where: } \quad \boldsymbol{D}_1 = \begin{cases} 0, \text{ before 2001} \\ 1, \text{ after 2001} \end{cases}, \ \boldsymbol{D}_2 = \begin{cases} 0, \text{ before 1991} \\ 1, \text{ after 1991} \end{cases}$$

We make a least-squares estimation through the software Eviews 4.0, and the result is:

$$DInY_{JAP} = -0.438387 + 0.193608\,InG_{chi} - 0.032813\,InG_{oth} + 0.206730\,DInE_{JAP}$$
$$(-1.74) \quad (1.51) \quad (-0.66) \quad (0.91)$$
$$+ 0.05234D_1 + 0.125490D_2 \quad R^2 = 0.5308, \quad \bar{R}^2 = 0.3632$$
$$(0.46) \quad (1.07)$$

$$DInY_{Kor} = -1.593599 + 0.815384\,InG_{chi} - 0.051141\,InG_{oth} + 0.657012\,DInE_{Kor}$$
$$(-2.20) \quad (2.61) \quad (0.49) \quad (1.16)$$
$$-0.270344D_1 \quad R^2 = 0.7050, \quad \bar{R}^2 - 0.5364$$
$$(-1.73)$$

$$DInY_{ASEAN} = -0.453664 + 0.273632\,InG_{chi} - 0.017337\,InG_{oth} - 0.105074\,DInE_{ASEAN}$$
$$(-2.40) \quad (2.95) \quad (-0.34) \quad (-0.55)$$
$$+ 0.106854D_1 - 0.094962D_2 \quad R^2 = 0.4987, \quad \bar{R}^2 = 0.2898$$
$$(1.24) \quad (-0.96)$$

The results of the empirical analysis imply:

First, the growth rate of the Chinese economy is a key variable influencing the proportion of the export of sample countries in their total export, which means that China's economic development has a significant influence on China's position as a market provider in the region of East Asia; by contrast, the economic growth rate of other countries does not have an obvious impact on the export proportion of the sample nations. This can be explained by the fact that the products exported by these sample countries to other countries are not strongly replaceable by those to China and they are complementary to some extent.[22]

Second, the exchange rate can make a great difference in China's share in the exports of Japan and South Korea, which indicates that the exports of Japan and South Korea to China are more likely to be affected by the price factor; yet the exchange rate of the currencies of ASEAN countries against the RMB barely has any influence on their export proportion and this demonstrates their small elasticity of price to Chinese export products.

Third, entering the WTO can give a big boost to the trade of ASEAN nations, but rarely to the exports of Japan to China and even none to the exports of South Korea to China; becoming a member of the APEC can promote the exports of Japan to China, but does not affect the exports of ASEAN economies.

If we suppose that China's GDP growth rate will remain between 7.5 and 10 per cent in the coming 5 years (2008–2012)[23] and other variables influencing the trade volume between China and the sample countries remain unchanged, then we can calculate the changes in the export proportion of the sample countries in their total exports by 2012 through estimating the coefficient of transmission in the equation (see Table 3.23).

Through the above analysis and projection, we can reach three basic conclusions:

First, China's position as the market provider in East Asia will become more important with the steady growth of Chinese economy. This trend has become a reality and is likely to increase. The financial crisis triggered by the U.S. "sub-prime mortgage crisis" has dealt a heavy blow to the global economy, but the impact on China is unlikely to slash China's economic growth rate. On the contrary, China can further improve its position in the economic development of East Asia through giving play to its role as the engine for East Asian economic development.

Second, changes in exchange rate has an evident influence on changes in the export proportion of the sample countries, which is echoed by the research results of Ahearne et al. (2003) and demonstrates that the exchange rate factor can obviously affect the intra-trade orientation of East Asia. Against this backdrop,

Table 3.23. The proportion of exports to China of Japan, South Korea and ASEAN-5 Countries (%)

Country	GDP Growth Rate	Proportion of Exports to China in the Total Export in 2007	Proportion of Exports to China in the Total Exports in 2012	Accumulated Growth Rate
Japan	7.50	15.59	19.34	3.75
	10.0	15.59	24.04	8.45
South Korea	7.50	25.82	32.57	6.75
	10.0	25.82	44.72	18.90
5 ASEAN Countries	7.50	10.93	14.78	3.85
	10.0	10.93	19.57	8.64

RMB appreciation is undoubtedly a key driver for the improvement of China's position as the platform for export in East Asia.

Third, an economic integration organization does not necessarily promote the trade between two members of the organization. Our analysis demonstrates that the accession of South Korea to the WTO and the entry of ASEAN–5 countries to APEC did not result in obvious impact on their exports to China and shows a "blocking" trend. This is probably because of the trade diversion effect between member countries of economic integration organizations. At the same time, both the WTO and APEC are conference-based (or negotiation-oriented) economic organizations and lack a practical and effective role in promoting and safeguarding inter-state trade, so the implications for two specific member nations are not likely to be obvious.

Investigating China's position as the East Asian market provider from the perspective of end products

we can only affirm China's position as the market provider of East Asia from the macro "representation" when it comes to the analysis results of changes in China's proportion in the exports of East Asian economies. We need to make an in-depth examination of whether China can play the role as the market provider in East Asia for the exports of final products if we want to analyze the actual capacity of China to attract local products. That is to examine China's capacity in domestic demand. The formation and expansion of an East Asian end product market represents important preconditions for stable regional economic growth and smooth cooperation in currency and finance. Accordingly, enjoying the strongest capacity to serve as a market provider for end products of East Asia will be an important condition for the RMB to become a currency for regional settlement and then become a key regional currency.

We have examined changes in the proportion of the exports of seven East Asian economies to China[24] in their total export of end products in order to analyze the proportion of China's imported consumption goods from East Asian economies in their total exports to China (see Table 3.24). The statistical results indicate that the U.S. share in the exports of end products by the seven East Asian economies has contracted dramatically since 1999, down by over 6.5 per cent and even 15 per cent (in the case of the Philippines) apart from the nearly 4 per cent in the case of Indonesia; in the meantime, China's share has continued to rise since 1999, up by as high as 6.5 per cent (in the case of Singapore) and as low as 3 per cent in the case of other economies; the share of Japan in the export of most economies has shrunk to some extent, but it still has a larger share in exports of ASEAN nations than China. That said, when we examine the absolute figure of the export proportion of end products, we see China is a far cry from the U.S. Apart from Singapore, the difference in the share of China and the U.S. in the exports of end products of the other six ASEAN countries is more than 15 per cent and even 40 per cent (the Philippines); China is narrowing the gap with Japan and their difference is typically concentrated in ASEAN nations.

The research results demonstrate that China is not now capable of serving as the market provider for end products of East Asia. China more often than not

Table 3.24. Changes of the proportion of China, Japan and the U.S. in the end-product exports of East Asian economies (%)

Export	Mainland China			Japan			The U.S		
	1999	2003	2007	1999	2003	2007	1999	2003	2007
South Korea	2.63	4.14	5.20	16.59	8.49	4.81	30.29	36.62	22.59
Singapore	3.08	4.57	9.34	11.45	6.61	8.52	16.43	14.37	8.62
The Philippines	0.70	1.99	1.04	13.83	11.60	11.01	57.04	47.89	41.97
Thailand	1.43	1.77	2.72	16.73	16.70	11.76	30.97	27.69	20.83
Malaysia	0.59	1.22	2.05	13.18	9.93	5.97	28.25	26.42	18.92
Indonesia	1.47	0.91	1.72	11.62	11.92	7.63	29.97	31.85	33.62
Hong Kong	9.53	11.65	11.95	7.16	8.09	6.61	38.21	36.96	31.53

Note: The end products here include consumer goods, and products with the BEC codes: 112, 122, 51, 522, 61, 62 and 63.

Source: Set out based on relevant data of the UN Commodity Trade Statistics Database.

plays the role as a place for production convergence and an export platform in the regional production network. This is an obvious demonstration of China's export-oriented development strategy. However the position of the U.S. as the regional market provider of East Asia keeps weakening and the development trend of financial cooperation within East Asia is bound to result in the process of "stopping pegging to the U.S. dollar," which will further weaken the status of the U.S. dollar in the East Asian market and its role as the market provider for exports. Japan does not naturally have the capability to become the market provider for end product exports due to the limitation of its market scale. But in recent years, China's share in the end product exports of East Asia has shown a slowly growing trend, indicating its potential to become the market provider for East Asian final products. In addition, China enjoys a huge market and a high economic growth rate among other objective and strong conditions. All these have also determined that China is the potential market provider for regional end products in East Asia.

But we also need to note that although the share of the U.S. in the export of consumption goods from most East Asian economies apart from Singapore has dropped to some extent, its share is still much higher than that of China. It is clear that it is still a long, hard journey for China to become the regional market provider for end products. Beyond that we must anticipate a faster growth rate of China's proportion in the export of end products from East Asian economies in order to meet the realistic requirements for the RMB to serve as a currency for regional settlement. This requires China to adjust its economic structure and adopt strong measures to boost domestic demand in the larger picture of ensuring rapid economic development.

Examination of Economic Cycle Synchronicity between China and Other East Asian Economies

The significance of economic cycle synchronicity

We made an analysis of the advantages and disadvantages for the RMB to become a dominant regional currency in the above text from the aspects of the economic relations between China and other Eastern economies, China's policy and institutional arrangement, and China's position as the potential market provider in East Asia. We need to observe the symmetry of economic impact and the economic cycle synchronicity between China and other East Asian economies if we want to make RMB become the intra-regional "anchor" currency or further make other currencies peg to the RMB, and even form some sort of "RMB Circle."

The examination of the symmetry of economic shock and the economic circle synchronicity is linked to research on currency integration. Based on the traditional theory of OCA, in general we need to understand whether the impact on a region's economy is symmetric, whether its economic cycle is more synchronic, or whether a regulatory mechanism is available to eliminate the asymmetry of economic impact when we judge whether a region meets the standard of an OCA. The traditional theory of OCA mainly probes into the latter and points out that a higher integration degree of factor market means more flexible adjustment of factor price and then whether a region is more likely to realize currency integration as the mechanism for eliminating the asymmetric impact of economic shock depends largely on the adjustment of the factor market. However the indicator for factor market integration in effect demonstrates whether economies within a region are capable of effectively absorbing the asymmetry or flexibly adjusting the impact. The indicator is in nature a passive indicator. Suppose the economic shocks faced by regional economies are symmetric and the economic cycle is synchronic, then there is no necessity to leverage on factor market adjustment to absorb asymmetry and the region will have the key conditions for currency integration. In this sense it is highly relevant to examine the symmetry of economic shocks and the economic cycle synchronicity between China and other East Asian economies to understand the objective of making other currencies peg to the RMB, or the establishment of a currency cooperation arrangement and even a currency region with the RMB at the core.

Economic shock symmetry and regional economic cooperation: comparative research on East Asia and other regions

Review of relevant empirical research literature

Empirical analysis of economic shock symmetry is generally conducted through analyzing economic shock relevance. If the positive correlation of the shock faced by two countries is higher, then the economic shock symmetry between the two economies will be stronger. When it comes to the quantitative analysis of economic shock, the traditional structural model used in the 1980s has been replaced by the dynamic econometric model such as the VAR method firstly created by Sims (1980). Sims and Bernanke (1986) further developed the simplified VAR model into the SVAR method. Following that, Blanchard and Quah (1989) are pioneers in introducing long-term impact effect into the SVAR model and used this model to analyze the total supply and demand shocks in the U.S. economy (output and unemployment are selected as endogenous variables). This has created the conditions for analysis of the relevance of economic shocks between different countries.

Bayoumi and Eichengreen (1993) firstly applied the SVAR model to assess the relevance of economic shocks between European countries and then expanded this application to other regions. They made a comparative analysis of the relevance, scale and adjustment speed of economic shocks between Asian countries, between European countries and between seven regions of the U.S. (Bayoumi and Eichengree, 1994). When it comes to the design of the specific model, they also decomposed economic shocks into supply shock and demand shock, but they selected output and inflation rate as endogenous variables. Their analysis results indicate that the scale of East Asian economic shocks is higher than that of the U.S. while their adjustment speed is faster compared with that of the U.S. There is not much difference in symmetry of shocks. If we divide East Asia into two regions (one region includes Japan, South Korea and Chinese Taiwan and the other includes Chinese Hong Kong, Thailand, Indonesia, Malaysia and Singapore), then the symmetry of economic turbulence in each region surpasses that of the European "German Group" (Germany, Austria, the Netherlands, Belgium, Denmark and Switzerland).

The pioneering analysis of Bayoumi and Eichengree provided a brand new thinking for studying the basic conditions for regional cooperation and even broader economic policy coordination. Since then the SVAR model has been widely applied in analyzing economic shock asymmetry while studying regional cooperation. Yuen et al. (2001) used this method to analyze the economic shock asymmetry in East Asia and made further examination of measuring results through variance decomposition and the examination of stability. Other literature applied this model to analyze other samples, such as member states of the EU (Funke, 1997; Verhoef, 2003), countries in Eastern Europe (Weimann, 2003), Latin America and even South Asia (Saxena, 2003) in different periods. In China Tan Qinghua, Wan Zhihong and Li Xiaojie et al. also adopted this model to study the economic shock relevance within the region of East Asia (Tan Qinghua, 2002; Wan Zhihong, 2003; Li Xiaojie, 2004). What is notable is that most existing documents have applied the Bayoumi-Eichengreen method and the improvement is mainly demonstrated by the expansion of samples and further discussion of measuring results.

In fact the Bayoumi-Eichengreen method (i.e. the Blanchard-Quah method) can still be improved. This model chooses output and price fluctuation as endogenous variables and directly divides economic shocks into the supply shock and the demand shock. The model has included the pure nominal shock and actual demand shock into the domain of demand shocks. Under these two classifications, the nature of demand shock and its message are more complex and ambiguous. They did not independently decompose the turbulence (typically nominal turbulence) brought about by exogenous macro policy changes and classified all shocks that will not have influence in the long run as demand shock, so the measured demand shock in effect includes both the pure stochastic disturbance in real demand and the effects of macro economic policy changes on economic system (Demertzis, 2000). Accordingly, the concluded relevance of demand shock reflects more the mutual influence in currency and coordination in policy but not the symmetry of the actual demand shock felt by countries. In terms of regional economic cooperation, this demand shock is endogenous and a higher degree of policy coordination between economies means stronger relevance of demand shock. This is the important reason for the results of most research that the relevance of demand shock on the EU members is higher than that on East Asia and other regions. Against this background, the demand shock relevance measured by the Bayoumi-Eichengreen model does not quite meet the objective basis for researching currency cooperation and policy coordination as it is the same as the endogenous standard of some optimum currency region. We would prefer the saying that it reflects the results of cooperation to the saying that it reflects the precondition for policy coordination and cooperation. As such, most literature could only focus on supply shock under the preconditions of analyzing regional currency integration and policy coordination. Some redefined the supply and demand shocks in the Bayoumi-Eichengreen model as supply shock and nominal shock (Yuen et al., 2001), but this overlooks the actual demand disturbance reflected by demand shock in the Bayoumi-Eichengreen method and it is featured by one-sidedness. As part of the efforts to reach a more clear-cut conclusion on the basic conditions for regional economic shock symmetry and the currency integration and policy coordination defined by it, it is necessary to further decompose economic shock and differentiate the actual supply and demand shocks from the pure currency shock reflecting policy shock.

In fact, in other research fields, work on this aspect has produced greater achievements. Clarida and Gali (1994) firstly divided economic shocks into real supply shock, actual demand shock and currency shock on the basis of Obstfeld's theoretical model (Obstfeld, 1985) and the two variables SVAR model of Blanchard and Quah. They used the SVAR model with three variables namely output, price and actual exchange rate to examine the factors for the actual exchange rate fluctuation and proved that actual demand shock will have implications for the real exchange rate in both the short and the long-term. Their model has been widely applied and improved in the research field of actual exchange rate. We have adjusted the setting of variables based on the Clarida-Gali-Zhang method, hoping to understand the level of the symmetry of economic shocks between China and other East Asian economies.

Method, model specification and variable selection

First we build a SVAR model containing three endogenous variables namely output $y(t)$, international relative price of commodity $q(t)$ and domestic nominal price $p(t)$ to represent dynamic economic system in order to identify the actual supply, actual demand and currency shocks. When it comes to variable selection, Clarida and Gali (1994) and Zhang et al. (2003) all chose Consumer Price Index (CPI) and the actual exchange rate indicator calculated by nominal exchange rate as $q(t)$. But according to Obstfeld and Rogoff, the indicator calculated based on CPI reflects in effect changes of real exchange rate but not unreal exchange rate i.e. the absolute level of international relative commodity price, so it is not appropriate to match it with output and domestic nominal price. Obstfeld and Rogoff believe that, if we want to examine the international commodity price level, the optimum optional data are relative prices of comparable commodity baskets of different countries provided by the Penn World Table, that is the ratio of the price level of the exact same commodity basket in U.S. dollars after adjustment of each country to the price level of the same variety of commodity basket of the U.S. We here use this as the indicator for the international relative commodity price.

We can write the SVAR model of above three variables into the Vector Moving Average model with the method of matrix iteration. That is to use $y(t)$, $q(t)$ and $p(t)$ to represent unlimited totaling of the real supply shock, the real demand shock and the pure nominal shock i.e. currency shock:

$$X(t) = A_0\varepsilon(t) + A_1\varepsilon(t-1) + \ldots = \sum_{i=0}^{\infty} L_i A_i \varepsilon(t) \tag{3–9}$$

Where L refers to Lag Operation,

$$X(t) = \begin{bmatrix} y(t) \\ q(t) \\ p(t) \end{bmatrix}, \quad \varepsilon(t) = \begin{bmatrix} \varepsilon s(t) \\ \varepsilon d(t) \\ \varepsilon m(t) \end{bmatrix}, \quad \text{then :}$$

$$\begin{bmatrix} y(t) \\ q(t) \\ p(t) \end{bmatrix} = \sum_{i=1}^{\infty} L_i \begin{bmatrix} a_{11i} & a_{12i} & a_{13i} \\ a_{21i} & a_{22i} & a_{23i} \\ a_{31i} & a_{32i} & a_{33i} \end{bmatrix} \begin{bmatrix} \varepsilon s(t) \\ \varepsilon d(t) \\ \varepsilon m(t) \end{bmatrix} \tag{3–10}$$

In the above model, variation processes $y(t)$, $q(t)$ and $p(t)$ are all stationary stochastic processes; $\varepsilon s(t)$, $\varepsilon d(t)$ and $\varepsilon m(t)$ are white noise sequence and refer to the real supply shock, the real demand shock and currency shock respectively. They are all positively correlated to each other, and the covariance is 0:

The shock vector sequence in the SVAR model can not be directly obtained and must be solved by simplified VAR equation, and the simplified model of above mentioned ternary SVAR is:

$$X(t) = B_1X(t-1) + B_1X(t-2) + \ldots + B_nX(t-n) + e(t) \tag{3–11}$$

It can be represented as the unlimited moving average process of residual items:

$$X(t) = [\,I - B(L)]^{-1} e(t) \tag{3–12}$$

Where $e(t) = \begin{bmatrix} ey(t) \\ eq(t) \\ ep(t) \end{bmatrix}$, is the residual vector of the simplified VAR process itself, refers to the turbulence of output, international relative price and domestic nominal price variables. This turbulence comes from structural shocks of economic the system i.e. the supply shock, demand shock and currency shock mentioned above.

Therefore $e(t)$ can represent the linear combination of all shock vectors, and can be represented by:

$e(t) = C\varepsilon(t)$, where $C = \begin{bmatrix} c_{11} & c_{12} & c_{13} \\ c_{21} & c_{22} & c_{23} \\ c_{31} & c_{32} & c_{33} \end{bmatrix}$ is called as transformation matrix.

In order to identify C so as to solve the problem of model identification, constraint conditions need to be preset. We need an equation with four constraint conditions for a two-vector VAR model but nine for a three-vector VAR model. As the supply shock and demand shock are orthometric, after the standardization of the covariance matrix of $\varepsilon(t)$, we will have:

$$\sum \varepsilon(t) = I$$

$$\sum e(t) = C'C \sum \varepsilon(t) = C'C \tag{3–13}$$

As such, we can have three variance constraint conditions and three covariance constraint conditions. We only need to add three long-term constraint conditions based on the principle of the Blanchard-Quah method. Here, according to the nature of the real supply, the real demand and currency shocks, we presume (1) in the long run domestic output is only affected by the supply shock but not by the real demand and currency shocks in the long term; (2) in the long term, the international relative commodity price level has nothing to do with currency shock, but rather is only affected by the real supply and demand shocks; (3) the pure currency shock or nominal shock only impacts domestic nominal price level in the long run. Then in the Formula (3–10),

$\sum_{i=0}^{\infty} a_{12i} = \sum_{i=0}^{\infty} a_{13i} = \sum_{i=0}^{\infty} a_{23i} = 0$, the coefficient matrix $\sum_{i=0}^{\infty} A_i$ is lower-triangular matrix, as thus, we have enough constraint conditions. Because:

$$\begin{aligned} X(t) &= [I - B(L_i)]^{-1} e(t) = \sum_{i=0}^{\infty} D_i e(t) \\ &= \sum_{i=0}^{\infty} D_i C\varepsilon(t) = \sum_{i=0}^{\infty} L_i A_i \boldsymbol{\varepsilon}(t) \end{aligned} \tag{3–14}$$

Therefore, $\sum_{i=0}^{\infty} D_i C = \sum_{i=0}^{\infty} A_i$, as under the balanced state, $X(t) = X(t - i)$, at this point, $\sum_{i=0}^{\infty} D_i [I - B(L)]^{-1} = (I - B_1 - B_2 - \dots - B_n)^{-1}$, accordingly we can solve $\sum D_i$. In this connection, we further identify transformation matrix C. As $e(t) = C\varepsilon(t)$, we can know:

$$\boldsymbol{\varepsilon}(t) = C^{-1}e(t) \tag{3-15}$$

and further solve C^{-1}, which means we can calculate the real supply, the real demand and currency shock sequence and then consider their relevance through the residual sequence in the simplified VAR model. As is pointed out in above text, the higher and more outstanding positive correlations between two economies means shock symmetry and more sufficient fundamental conditions for policy coordination and even currency cooperation.

The data samples we selected include: (1) 10 East Asian economies that are most popular samples of East Asia for researchers at the moment; (2) 11 countries of the Eurozone,[25] which is the sample group that has the highest level of regional economic cooperation and development at this point; (3) the Mercosur, including Brazil, Argentina, Chile, Paraguay, Uruguay and other Mercosur members. We chose these economies just because they have grouped into a regional organization with trade integration. At the same time, some countries used to share insights on practicing dollarization and it includes emerging markets and relatively backward developing countries. These characteristics make it comparable with the region of East Asia. The sampling time is the period between 1980 and 2000, $y(t)$ and $p(t)$ respectively select the GDP and GDP Deflator calculated with fixed price. Data are from the IMF World Economic Outlook database. The international relative commodity price level is from the Penn World Table Version 6.1. All indicators choose the form of natural logarithm. After ADF test most variables are $I(0)$ sequence but there are some $I(1)$ sequence, thus we conducted first-order difference processing.

Empirical results and analysis

We firstly applied Eviews software to estimate the simplified VAR model of each economy. According to the likelihood ratio (LR), Akaike Information Criterion (AIC) and Schwarz Criterion (SC) we choose the lag order of the VAR model as 2, thus we have the variance sequence and transformation matrix C, then we calculate C^{-1}, and then we can obtain the economic shock sequence of each economy (I am not sure I have edited this correctly). The results of relevant analysis of all sequences are shown as Table 3.25 and Table 3.33.

Based on the calculated results, we draw the following conclusions.

(1) In general, the region of East Asia is very different from the Eurozone in structural shock symmetry.

This illustrates that East Asia faces more asymmetry than Europe and has more disadvantages in advancing currency integration. Yet when we compare our calculated results with that concluded by using the two variable SVAR model, we find that they have a big difference in the relevance of currency shock after it was isolated. The relevance of the real supply shock and demand shock of the Eurozone is still higher than of East Asia although it is not that obvious. In particular, they have little difference in the real supply that has greater influence in the long term. The supply shock relevance between some East Asian countries

Table 3.25. Relevance of the real supply shock of 10 East Asian economies

	Mainland China	Japan	South Korea	Hong Kong	Taiwan	Singapore	Thailand	Malaysia	Indonesia
Japan	0.090								
South Korea	0.122	0.417							
Hong Kong	0.258	-0.027	0.504						
Taiwan	0.221	0.159	0.254	0.335					
Singapore	0.192	0.098	0.064	0.443	0.182				
Thailand	-0.027	0.144	-0.037	0.032	0.216	0.130			
Malaysia	0.109	-0.184	0.260	-0.216	0.554	0.500	0.475		
Indonesia	0.033	-0.208	0.280	-0.196	0.440	0.547	0.372	0.574	
The Philippines	0.306	-0.112	0.196	0.050	0.424	0.066	0.310	0.556	0.103

Table 3.26. Relevance of the real demand shock of 10 East Asian economies

	Mainland China	Japan	South Korea	Hong Kong	Taiwan	Singapore	Thailand	Malaysia	Indonesia
Japan	0.178								
South Korea	0.606	0.408							
Hong Kong	0.308	0.287	0.044						
Taiwan	0.337	0.454	0.359	0.441					
Singapore	0.348	0.194	0.356	0.266	0.118				
Thailand	0.018	0.163	0.040	0.182	0.090	0.567			
Malaysia	0.316	0.213	0.298	0.048	0.088	0.567	0.366		
Indonesia	0.316	0.146	0.244	-0.055	-0.495	0.339	0.099	0.195	
The Philippines	0.226	0.147	0.293	0.430	0.389	0.518	0.260	0.621	0.270

Table 3.27. Relevance of the currency shock of 10 East Asian economies

	Mainland China	Japan	South Korea	Hong Kong	Taiwan	Singapore	Thailand	Malaysia	Indonesia
Japan	-0.120								
South Korea	0.089	-0.060							
Hong Kong	0.101	0.751	0.015						
Taiwan	-0.129	-0.099	0.177	-0.106					
Singapore	-0.295	-0.089	0.047	-0.486	0.329				
Thailand	-0.086	0.036	0.602	0.156	0.138	-0.026			
Malaysia	0.316	-0.515	-0.290	-0.311	0.519	0.041	-0.251		
Indonesia	-0.136	0.398	0.503	0.504	-0.211	-0.228	0.825	-0.573	
The Philippines	-0.109	0.130	0.036	-0.103	-0.412	0.302	-0.336	-0.365	-0.138

Table 3.28. Relevance of the real supply shock of 11 countries in the Eurozone

	Germany	France	Austria	Belgium	The Netherlands	Finland	Greece	Ireland	Italy	Portugal
France	0.312									
Austria	0.372	0.407								
Belgium	0.398	0.090	0.345							
The Netherlands	0.764	0.230	0.433	0.472						
Finland	-0.508	0.218	-0.079	0.311	0.015					
Greece	0.508	0.200	0.323	0.117	0.542	-0.340				
Ireland	0.311	0.244	0.208	0.188	-0.022	0.293	0.084			
Italy	0.618	0.503	0.346	0.411	0.751	0.346	0.505	0.287		
Portugal	0.355	0.268	0.296	0.314	0.265	0.328	-0.042	0.084	0.281	
Spain	0.462	0.562	0.445	0.373	0.151	0.193	0.062	-0.168	0.458	0.565

Table 3.29. Relevance of the real demand shock of 11 countries in the Eurozone

	Germany	France	Austria	Belgium	The Netherlands	Finland	Greece	Ireland	Italy	Portugal
France	0.441									
Austria	0.420	0.316								
Belgium	0.462	0.387	0.447							
The Netherlands	0.613	0.433	0.420	0.477						
Finland	0.483	0.316	0.508	0.491	0.528					
Greece	0.517	0.518	0.356	0.463	0.549	0.483				
Ireland	0.445	0.491	0.345	0.339	0.511	0.496	0.498			
Italy	0.437	0.322	0.393	0.357	0.565	0.563	0.495	0.568		
Portugal	0.196	0.377	0.169	0.218	0.272	0.342	0.400	0.414	0.360	
Spain	0.403	0.343	0.472	0.432	0.411	0.574	0.446	0.528	0.520	0.276

Table 3.30. Relevance of the currency shock of 11 countries in the Eurozone

	Germany	France	Austria	Belgium	The Netherlands	Finland	Greece	Ireland	Italy	Portugal
France	0.664									
Austria	0.391	0.361								
Belgium	0.459	0.262	0.552							
The Netherlands	0.342	0.175	0.422	0.531						
Finland	0.229	0.245	0.675	0.295	0.464					
Greece	0.292	0.356	0.6	0.343	0.402	0.436	0.2			
Ireland	0.494	0.563	-0.038	0.393	-0.091	0.311	0.007			
Italy	0.672	0.464	0.657	0.27	0.706	0.296	0.643	-0.155		
Portugal	0.564	0.657	0.45	0.413	0.164	0.285	0.275	0.291	0.352	
Spain	0.605	0.729	0.476	0.367	0.271	0.382	0.463	0.408	0.25	0.611

Table 3.31. Relevance of the real supply shock of four member states of Mercosur

	Argentina	Brazil	Chile	Paraguay
Brazil	0.158			
Chile	-0.107	0.048		
Paraguay	0.201	0.109	-0.033	
Uruguay	-0.197	0.199	0.068	-0.099

Table 3.32 Relevance of the real demand shock of four member states of Mercosur

	Argentina	Brazil	Chile	Paraguay
Brazil	0.441			
Chile	0.077	0.049		
Paraguay	0.184	0.061	0.266	
Uruguay	0.008	0.167	0.566	0.245

Table 3.33. Relevance of the currency shock of four member states of Mercosur

	Argentina	Brazil	Chile	Paraguay
Brazil	0.213			
Chile	-0.007	0.277		
Paraguay	-0.208	-0.108	0.142	
Uruguay	0.208	0.387	-0.290	-0.378

already higher than the average level of the Eurozone.[26] This demonstrates that the evident difference between East Asia and Europe in economic shock relevance reflected by former analyses can be explained by the difference in currency shock but not by the difference in real shocks to a large extent. As currency shock mostly mirrors the influence of macro policy, especially currency policy, it is tempting to say policy coordination between European nations has in itself increased their symmetry of shocks and synchronicity of economic fluctuation. In contrast, East Asian economies obviously lack effective coordination in macro policy and currency policy in particular between each other, which has resulted in a high relevance of real shock and weak and even negative relevance of currency shock. In addition, compared with the Mercosur, East Asia is stronger in the overall symmetry of structural shocks which means East Asia enjoys more space for advancing currency cooperation.

(2) From the perspective of further cooperation in currency, the indicators for shock relevance of some sub-regional group members within East Asia have been approximate to the level of the Eurozone of the same period.

This kind of sub-regional groups can be generally divided into the "Northeast Asia Group" and the "Southeast Asia Group." The "Northeast Asia Group" can be further divided into the "Japan-South Korea Group" and the "Greater China Group" including Mainland China, Hong Kong and Taiwan. Leading members of the "Southeast Asia Group" include Malaysia, Thailand, Indonesia and Singapore. This indicates to a certain extent that conditions are there for a higher level of currency cooperation and even currency integration within this kind of sub-regional group. Among these groups, the "Northeast Asia Group" and especially the "Greater China Group" are closely linked to the RMB. The calculated results show that the relevance between China, Japan and South Korea in supply, demand and currency shocks is rather lower, indicating difficulties for the three to carry out substantial currency cooperation and also for Japan and South Korea to closely link their currencies to the RMB. In the "Greater China Group" the economic shock relevance between Mainland China, Hong Kong and Taiwan is higher than the level between China and Japan, but it is still lower than that within the "Southeast Asia Group." Obviously, in the current situation, conditions are still not mature for the RMB to realize integration and play a leading role in either the "Greater China Group" or the "Northeast Asia Group."

(3) Overall, the related coefficient in shock between China and all other East Asian economies is not high.

In fact it is the same case for Japan, another power in the region. In comparison the real shock symmetry, especially the real supply shock symmetry which does not reflect policy impact in particular, between European leader Germany (including France to some extent) and other economies of the region is clearly higher than that between China and Japan. The real supply shock relevance depends to a certain degree on the similarity of growth pattern and economic structure between different countries. Weak relevance of supply indicates a certain gap between large powers and other economies within a region in terms of economic structure and the driver for their output is different. In East Asia, China and Japan both boast the "full-set" industry system and their economic structure differs from that of other East Asian economies. At the same time Chinese economic volatility is sparked by the rise and fall of domestic demand to a large extent. In this sense, Chinese economic fluctuation is affected little by external shocks but largely by internal shocks. Based on the calculation of Xu Helian et al. by leveraging on the generalized ridge partial least-squares regression (GRPLS) method, the contribution of domestic consumption, government expenditure and labor input to Chinese economic growth is larger than that of export and import contributes little to the growth (Xu Helian et al., 2003). This is clearly different from what is happening in many East Asian economies where economic growth is driven by export in general. As it is difficult to change the economic structure and growth pattern within a short time period, the weak relevance between China and other economies in the region in economic shocks, especially that in the real supply shock, will obviously make it less possible for a unified currency region led by the RMB to be established in East Asia.

But from another point of view, as noted above, the weak relevance between a large economy and other economies in real shocks also reflects that the big power can serve as the stabilizer for the regional economy and its currency can also be the stabilizer for the exchange rate of other currencies of the region when the large country's economy enjoys long-term stability. Table 3.34 tells us that Mainland China's output volatility is higher only than that of Japan and Chinese Taiwan in East Asia and its inflation fluctuation is at a middle level within the region. Since China has been maintainig a quite stable currency policy since the 1990s it is still possible for the RMB to become an intra-regional exchange rate stabilizer to some extent.

Economic cycle synchronicity between China and other East Asian economies: examination based on BBQ method and MSAR method

Apart from the above-mentioned SVAR method, we can also analyze the economic cycle synchronicity between China and the rest of East Asian economies through more specific measuring instruments. Next we use BBQ method and auto regression model MSAR with Markov Switching to examine this issue.

Table 3.34. Standard deviations between real GDP growth rate and inflation rate of East Asian economies (1977–2002)

	Mainland China	Japan	South Korea	Hong Kong	Taiwan	Singapore
Real GDP Growth Rate (%)	2.9896	2.3123	3.9967	4.2169	2.5601	3.2443
Inflation rate (%)	6.1472	2.3182	6.5642	5.8605	4.6787	2.2416

	Thailand	Malaysia	Indonesia	The Philippines
Real GDP Growth Rate (%)	4.664	3.8985	4.5356	3.5684
Inflation rate (%)	4.0729	2.0246	10.4516	10.2977

Data Source: IMF, World Economic Outlook Database.

Sketch of measuring method

The BBQ method

The analysis of economic cycle identified based on turning point concludes that the verification and description of any cycle must isolate the turning points in the time series for the first step, and then divide the turning point data into expansion stage and tightening stage. In so doing, the identification calculation of economic cycle should involve three progressive steps:

First, being able to judge the potential assembly of turning points, such as the peak value and the valley value in the series;

Second, being equipped with a program to ensure alternation of the peak and the valley;

Third, being armed with regulated standards for an array of rules to recombine turning points so as to judge the stage continuity and vibration as well as the complete cycle.

The BB Algorithm of Bry and Boschan (1971) meets the above requirements and it is applicable for obverted value of time series. Later the method was improved by the NBER (National Bureau of Economic Research) and is still being used today. This program includes a number of sub-programs, but the core of its first step is to define partial peak value (valley value). That is the occurrence of $\{y_t > (<) y_{t+k}\}$, $k = 1,\ldots,K$ in the time t, of which, K is usually set as 5. The key standard for the third step is that a stage must last for at least 6 months and a complete cycle must last for 15 months. Growth (Δy_t) cycle follows the same assembly of rules and the input data changes from y_t to z_t. According to the BB Algorithm, the similar first step should set K as 2 when the data frequency is the quarter. For instance: $\{\Delta_2 y_t > 0, \Delta y_t > 0, \Delta y_{t+1} < 0, \Delta_2 y_{t+2} < 0\}$. This setting guarantees that y_t is the partial maximum value of the former and the latter quarters. The quarter frequency version of the BB Algorithm is also called BBQ. We firstly use the improved BBQ Algorithm provided by Harding and Pagan (2002) to set the complete cycle as 4 quarters and measure the economic cycle of selected nations.

The MSAR method

Compared with the economic cycle analysis method identified by turning points that usually does not set a dynamic variable model, the economic cycle measurement based on potential factor model believes that economic cycle fluctuation is the stochastic deviation of some major macro economic variables concerning the long-term balance relationship. In this connection, in the quantitative analysis of economic cycle, the periodicity of economic cycle is more often than not described by the Markov Switching model (MS in short) put forward by Hamilton (1989). The MS model describes different characteristics and natures of economic behavior in different stages and situations or under different mechanisms, and thus can also be called the Regime Switching (RS) model. The MS model or RS model are varying parameter models, but they are different from the general time-varying parameter model. The difference is that the parameter in the MS model depends on the economic condition or regime and the condition and regime in the model are usually identified by economic theory or economic reality, but the RS model is widely applied in studying long-term economic behavior and short-term fluctuation and has become an important method in terms of the state of economic cycle. The initial MS model typically studies a classic economic cycle, that is the economic cycle pattern seeing positive and negative switching of economic growth rate. The

RS model has produced strong results in analyzing the economic cycle of post-war Western countries. But the model is limited in application: the RS model only takes into consideration "economic recession" and "economic expansion," the two totally opposite stages of the economic cycle. The modern economic cycle witnesses more transition between "low growth" and "high growth" in fluctuation but not the alternation of "positive growth" and "negative growth." Here we utilize the auto regression model MS-AR (p) with Markov Switching to measure the economic cycles of selected countries. The specific model is as follows:

$$\Delta y_t = v + \alpha_1 \Delta y_{t-1} + \ldots + \alpha_p \Delta y_{t-p} + u_t \quad (3\text{–}16)$$

In the model, y_t is GDP sequence, Δy_t refers to the logarithmic difference form, t=1, … , T, the error term is compliant to distribution i.e. u_t ~NID (0, $\sigma^2(s_t)$). The adjustment of the mean value of the equation is as follows:

$$\Delta y_t - \mu(s_t) = \alpha_1(y_{t-1} - \mu(s_t)) + \ldots + \alpha_p(y_{t-p} - \mu(s_t)) + \mu_t(s_t) \quad (3\text{–}17)$$

Where $\mu = (I_K - \sum_{j=1}^{p} \alpha_j)^{-1} v$ is the mean value of Δy_t.

For the observable time sequence vector Δy_t, the parameter for the formation process of potential data hinges on the regime variable that is unobservable s_t. Here s_t refers to the possibility of the model in different states. $s_t \in \{1, \ldots, M\}$ complies with the Markov stochastic process with one discrete time and discrete state and can be defined through switching possibility:

$$p_{ij} = Pr(s_{t+1} = j \mid s_t = i), \sum_{j=1}^{M} p_{ij} = 1 \quad \forall i, j \in \{1,\ldots,M\} \quad (3\text{–}18)$$

Variable and data explanations

Based on the initial focus of the research, we give priority to analyzing the synchronicity of the economic cycle of nine East Asian countries and regions: Mainland China, Japan, Chinese Hong Kong, South Korea, Singapore, the Philippines, Indonesia, Thailand and Malaysia. Given the close economic links between East Asia and the U.S. and the huge influence and important position of the U.S. dollar in East Asia, we added the U.S. into our research.

We use the quarter sequence of GDP indices as variables for measuring the economic cycle. The sample period is from the first quarter of 1990 (1990Q1) to the second quarter of 2008 (2008Q2) and the data are from IFS online data

(International Financial Statistics online data). Of which, the data are the fixed price of 1985 for the Philippines, fixed price of 1995 for Indonesia, and fixed price of 2000 for all other countries and regions.

China's 1990Q1–1993Q4 nominal GDP data are from the State Information Center (SIC) and are reduced to the real price of 2000 through CPI. Singapore's 2000Q2–2000Q3 data are from its National Bureau of Statistics, and the 1990–1992 data for Thailand are concluded through decomposing the yearly data by the linear interpolation method provided by Eview5.0. Data for China, South Korea, Singapore, the Philippines, Indonesia, Thailand and Malaysia went through seasonal adjustment by X12 provided by Eview5.0.

The BBQ method uses the natural logarithm sequence of the GDP and the MSAR method utilizes the logarithmic differential sequence.

Analysis of empirical results

Firstly, using the BBQ and MSAR methods to divide the stages of economic cycle of each country, the time sequence concluded combines 0 and 1.0 corresponds to a low economic growth situation while 1 corresponds to the high economic growth situation of the stage. For China, due to the distinct nature of its economic growth, the three-regime form is adopted in building the MSAR model and the two high growth regimes select 1 while the low growth level selects 0.

In the MSAR, the following order p is identified by ACI and SI norms.

Fig. 3.8 presents the stages of the economic cycles of different countries concluded by the BBQ method and the shadow region corresponds to a low economic growth situation. The vertical axis is the natural logarithm of the GDP. Fig. 3.9 presents the stages of the economic cycles of different countries concluded through the MSAR method. The shadow region corresponds to a low growth situation and the vertical axis is the GDP growth rate.

In order to compare the synchronicity of economic cycles between different countries, we have calculated relevant coefficients based on the economic cycle partition results. The related coefficient of the economic cycle between country a and country b is δ_{ab} and $1-\delta_{ab}$ measures the distance between country a and country b in economic cyle. A higher value of $1-\delta_{ab}$ illustrates that country A and country B are not very synchronic in economic cycle. Table 3.35 and Table 3.36 present respectively $1-\delta_{ab}$ that is calculated based on the BBQ and MSAR methods.

However, the distance between Table 3.35 and Table 3.36 is the comparative analysis between nations and fails to demonstrate the intuitive impression

Fig. 3.8. **Classification of economic cycles of different countries or regions based on BBQ (GDP logarithm sequence, the shaded region being the stage of low economic growth)**

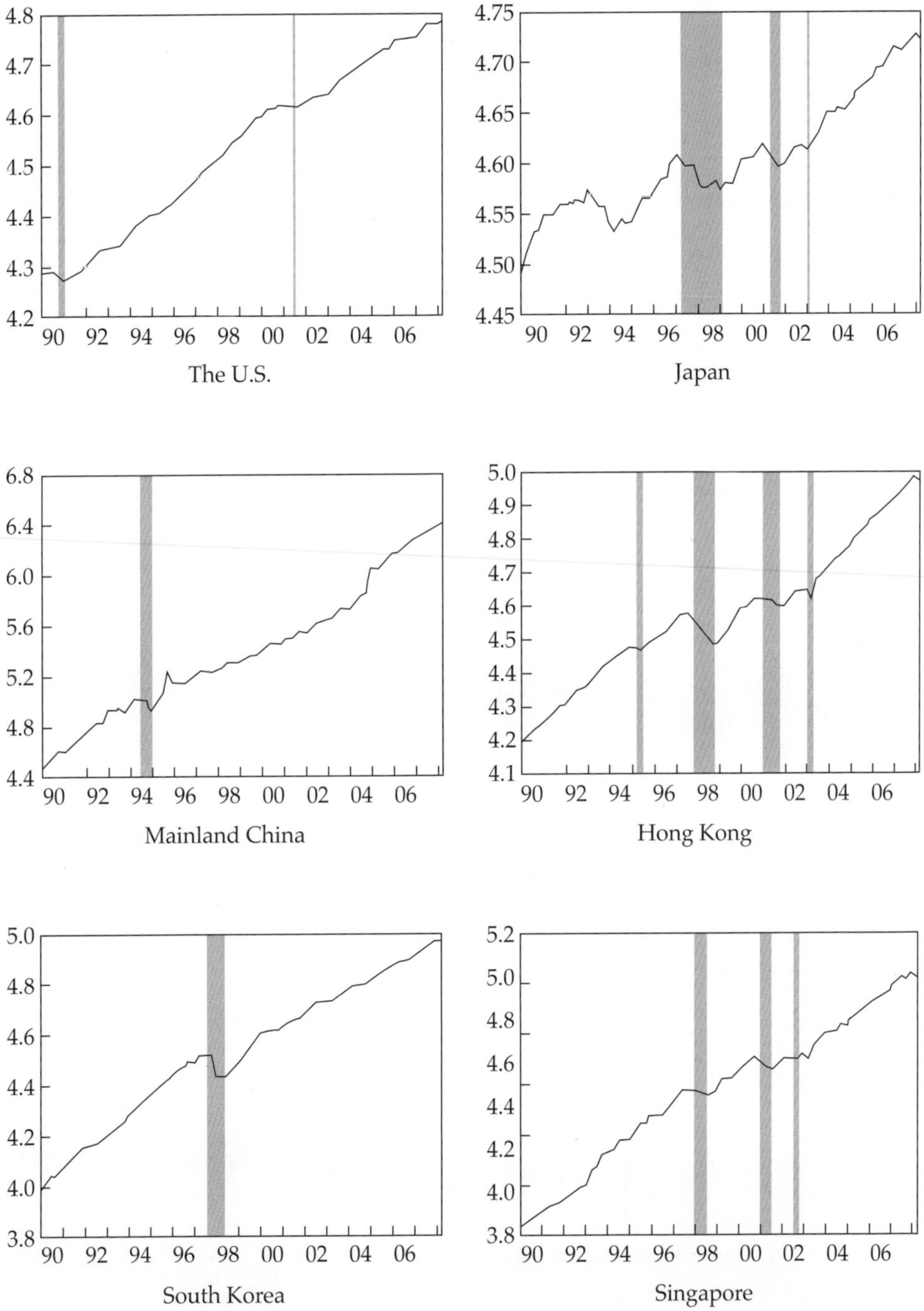

(Cont'd)

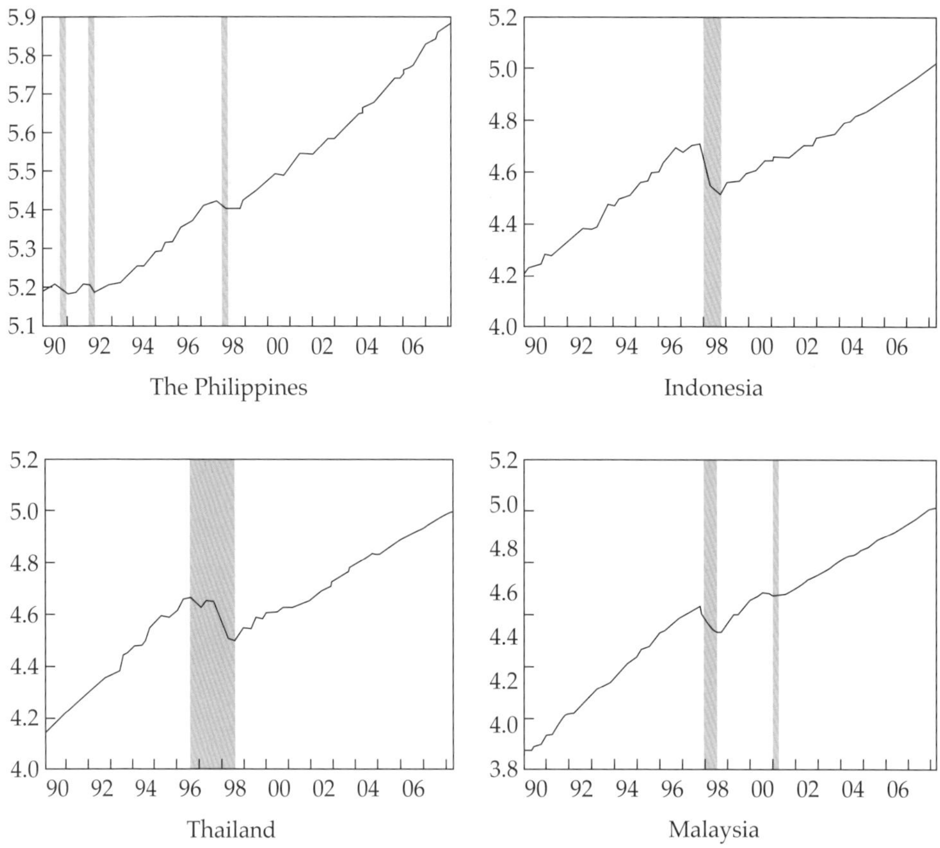

Fig. 3.9. **Classification of economic cycles of different countries or regions (GDP logarithm difference sequence, the shaded region being the stage of low economic growth)**

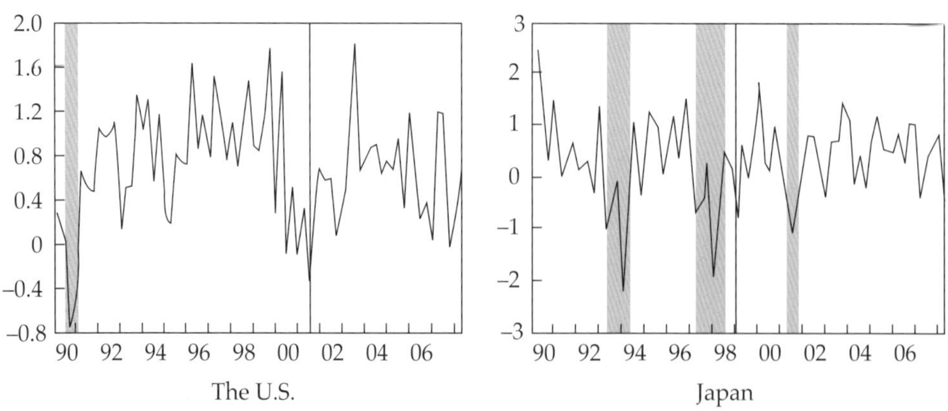

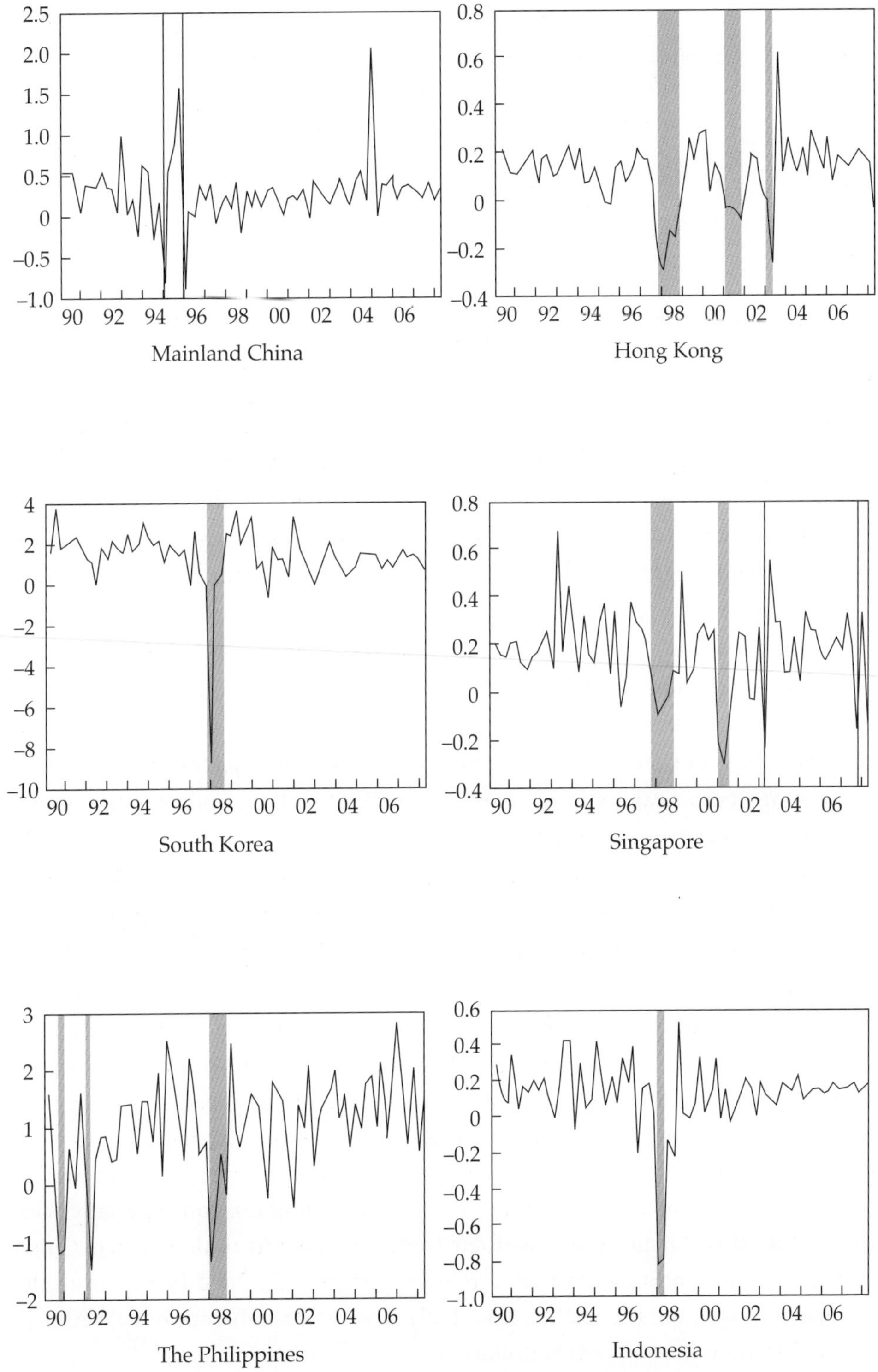
Mainland China
Hong Kong
South Korea
Singapore
The Philippines
Indonesia

(Cont'd)

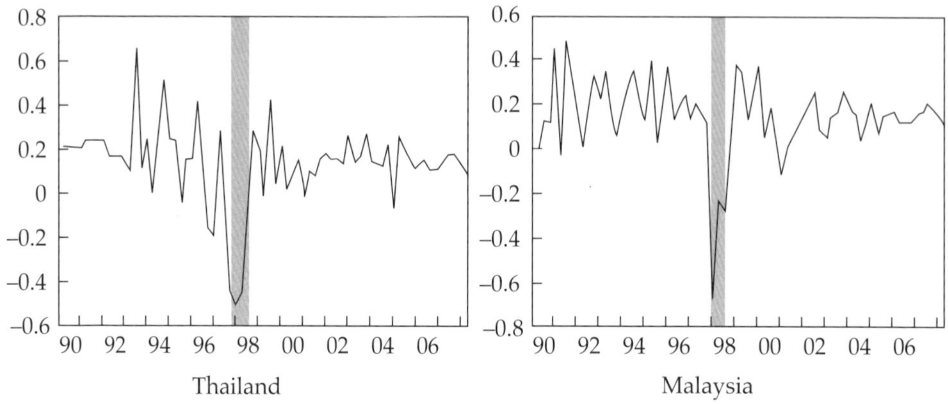

of economic cycle synchronicity. Considering this backward, we use multidimensional scaling to generalize the information of the distance matrix. This method tries to leverage on low dimensional coordinate system to show n-dimensional targets and present the similar distance (Euclidean distance) between targets through setting up a low dimensional chart. This means that under the conditions of a given $n \times n$ dimensional distance matrix, the calculation concludes a $n \times 2$ dimensional matrix. In the concluded multidimensional scaling chart (see Fig. 3.10 and Fig. 3.11), the countries that have a far distance with other countries indicate that their economic cycle synchronicity is poor.

From the empirical analysis results of the BBQ method and MSAR method, we can reach similar conclusions with the above text. Where the economic cycle of most East Asian economies shows a higher degree of synchronicity, China and other East Asian economies differ vastly in economic cycle. In particular, we need to note that the synchronicity between Japan and other East Asian economies in economic cycle is much higher than with China. But the difference between China and the rest of the East Asian economies in economic cycle is already close to the level of the U.S. On the one hand it indicates that it is very difficult to realize RMB regionalization by means of European style currency integration according to traditional currency theories and currency integration models; on the other, considering China's role as the economic stabilizer and its close economic connection with other East Asian economies, and especially with those other than Japan as well as their trade pattern and trade balance, China still enjoys the conditions to play a role in East Asia that is different from the European model, but the RMB is also likely to exert its influence in East Asia in a way that is similar to the U.S. dollar.

Table 3.35. Economic cycle distance of different countries or regions (calculated based on BBQ results)

	The U.S	Japan	Mainland China	Hong Kong	South Korea	Singapore	The Philippines	Indonesia	Thailand	Malaysia
The U.S.	0.000									
Japan	0.905	0.000								
Mainland China	1.042	1.090	0.000							
Hong Kong	0.915	0.336	1.095	0.000						
South Korea	1.042	0.533	1.042	0.555	0.000					
Singapore	0.851	0.563	1.072	0.475	0.630	0.000				
The Philippines	0.559	0.862	1.061	0.877	0.559	0.785	0.000			
Indonesia	1.049	0.457	1.049	0.482	0.443	0.506	0.633	0.000		
Thailand	1.072	0.445	1.072	0.703	0.410	0.701	0.785	0.506	0.000	
Malaysia	1.055	0.534	1.055	0.417	0.509	0.227	0.685	0.350	0.574	0.000

Table 3.36. Economic cycle distance of different countries and regions (calculated based on MSAR results)

	The U.S	Japan	Mainland China	Hong Kong	South Korea	Singapore	The Philippines	Indonesia	Thailand	Malaysia
The U.S.	0.000									
Japan	1.105	0.000								
Mainland China	1.035	1.085	0.000							
Hong Kong	1.087	0.551	1.071	0.000						
South Korea	1.050	0.527	1.040	0.428	0.000					
Singapore	1.082	0.611	1.067	0.277	0.396	0.000				
The Philippines	0.631	0.853	1.059	0.657	0.506	0.757	0.000			
Indonesia	1.035	0.670	1.028	0.602	0.303	0.579	0.522	0.000		
Thailand	1.056	0.467	1.046	0.508	0.112	0.477	0.574	0.381	0.000	
Malaysia	1.043	0.593	1.035	0.509	0.140	0.480	0.410	0.189	0.237	0.000

Fig. 3.10. **Multidimensional scaling chart of economic cycle distance of different countries and regions (based on BBQ method)**

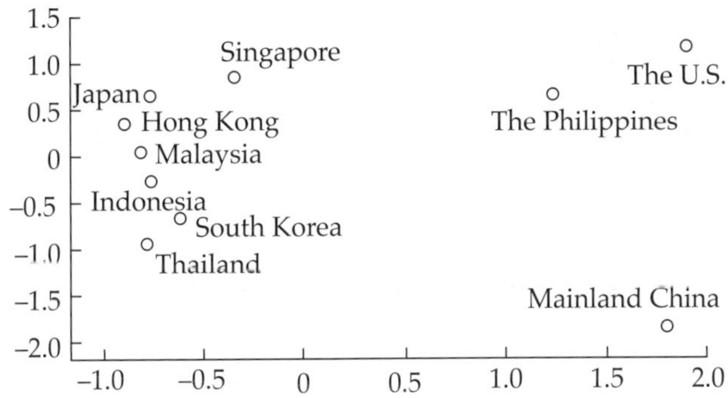

Fig. 3.11. **Multidimensional scaling chart of economic cycle distance of different countries and regions (based on MSAR method)**

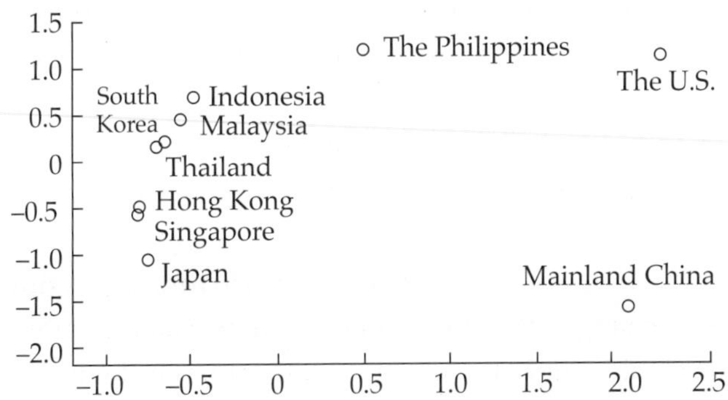

The Possible Role of China in Regional Currency Cooperation—An Examination Based on the OCA Index

We are living in a world where regional currency and financial cooperation keeps strengthening in East Asia. It is necessary to examine what role the RMB can play in a higher level of regional currency cooperation, or how the RMB can press ahead with regional or sub-regional currency cooperation so as to bring its regional currency functions into full play if we want to see the RMB as a regional leading currency and find the way for the RMB to play its function as a regionalized currency. We will combine the OCA index model to analyze the influence of China and other major powers on the East Asian economy, share insights on the possibility for China to engage in a higher level of regional currency cooperation, and exchange views on the practical way for China to become involved in this kind of cooperation.

The OCA Index model

OCA index method and variable selection

It is difficult to comprehensively evaluate the performance of each indicator as the judgment criteria for an OCA in traditional OCA theory is diversified in itself. Bayoumi and Eichengreen (1997) simplified OCA theory on the basis of a general equilibrium model and applied econometric model to create the OCA index method that comprehensively assesses whether specific regions meet the OCA standard.

The essential logic of the OCA index method is that the basic economic factors for exchange rate fluctuation and for the government to join in the common currency area are consistent. That means all variables influencing the entry of a country into an OCA will affect bilateral exchange rate volatility.[27] On this the key to applying OCA theory is to measure the fluctuation ratio of the two countries' nominal exchange rate under the comprehensive influence of various evaluation indicators.

Bayoumi and Eichengreen (1997) firstly built the regression model that explains bilateral exchange rate fluctuation and took bilateral real exchange rate as the explained variable and all evaluation indicators in the OCA theory as the explaining variable. After making regression conclusions of the above-mentioned model, they put the real numerical value or predicted value of explaining variable into the regression model and ultimately draw the predicted value of bilateral exchange rate volatility i.e. the OCA index. When the economic homoplasy among member states within a region is strong and meets the basic standard of OCA theory then the numerical value of the OCA index will be smaller, which means lower integrated costs for maintaining monetary union. It is clear that the OCA index method has enhanced the operability for examining OCA indicators.[28]

The analysis of the accession of EU countries into the EMU made by Bayoumi and Eichengreen through the OCA index method mainly focuses on influencing factors of asymmetry shocks for output, bilateral trade and transaction currency and chose four variables namely difference of output growth, structural difference of export goods, bilateral trade ties and economic scale. Wan Zhihong (2003) added two explaining variables namely inflation rate and exchange rate difference on the basis of above variables in his analysis of the OCA index of East Asia.

Based on former research experiences, we first expanded explaining variables of the model within the framework of the OCA theory while building the OCA index model, and then made a shortlist based on the explaining degree of explained variables by variables of various kinds and the overall significance level. The form of the specifically established OCA index model is:

$$DE_{ij} = \alpha + \sum_{k=1}^{n} \beta_k \bullet W_k \tag{3–19}$$

Of which W_k refers to the k explaining variable, α and β_k are coefficients of the model. The explained variable selected by the model is the fluctuation ratio of bilateral nominal exchange rate DE. The variable is the changing standard deviation of bilateral year-end exchange rate logarithm. The specific presentation is:

$$DE_{ij} = SD(\ln(E_{ij})) \tag{3–20}$$

Where E_{ij} refers to the bilateral year-end nominal exchange rate of the two countries.

The model altogether chooses seven explaining variables, including the influence of asymmetry shocks on output, bilateral trade ties, trade differentiation and price level differentiation. Specifically:

(1). Output growth difference DY. Here the standard deviation of the two countries' real output logarithm difference is used as the indicator for output growth difference. Specifically:

$$DY_{ij} = SD(\ln(Y_i) - \ln(Y_j)) \tag{3–21}$$

Where Y_i refers to the real output of country i. External shocks on the economy will be ultimately reflected by changes of output growth rate. The difference in output growth rate will be naturally small if the two countries' economic cycles are synchronic and the reaction of national output to external shocks is basically the same.

(2). Structural Difference of Export Goods MS. Considering the inconsistency of the standard classification of subdivision industries, we continue to adopt the calculation method of Bayoumi and Eichengreen and use the absolute value of the difference in proportion of agricultural goods, mineral products and industrial products in the total exports of the two economies. Specifically:

$$MS_{ij} = \sum_{n=1}^{3} | X_{i,n} - X_{j,n} | \tag{3–22}$$

Where $X_{j,n} \in [0, 1]$ refers to the proportion of the n industry of country i in the total export goods. More similarity in export sectors between two countries means more symmetric external shocks on them, smaller structural difference in export products of the two countries, and lower costs for the two nations to engage in currency cooperation.

(3). Commodity Trade Intensity TII. This index demonstrates that the two countries' commodity trade ties have exceeded the capability of the world average level, see Formula (3–23) for the specific expression. When the commodity trade intensity between the two nations is stronger, they would have more stable bilateral trade links, and their proceedings on currency cooperation will be enhanced, and they would then have stronger motivation for cooperation.

(4). Bilateral Trade Relations TR. We use the proportion of bilateral commodity trade in *GDP* of the two countries to measure this and the specific expression is:

$$TR_{ij} = \frac{Trade_{i,j} + Trade_{j,i}}{GDP_i + GDP_j} \tag{3-23}$$

Of which, $Trade_{i,j}$ refers to the total exports of country i to country j. Larger indicators for bilateral trade connections illustrate closer trade ties between the two countries. The two economies have more impetus for currency cooperation in order to maintain stable trade relations.

(5). Economic Size SIZE. We adopt the calculation method of Bayoumi and Eichengree and use the mean value of GDP logarithm of the two to express this. Traditional exchange rate regime theory believes that practicing a fixed exchange rate or single currency can generate the most returns for small-scale open economies while the floating exchange rate system fits well to larger scale of countries because the latter pay more costs for giving up autonomous currency instruments.[29]

(6). Trade Tendency Difference MF. We choose the absolute value of the difference of the proportion of the total imports and exports of the two countries in their total GDP to express bilateral trade difference in tendency. Specifically:

$$MF_{ij} = \left[\frac{Trade_i}{GDP_i} - \frac{Trade_j}{GDP_j} \right] \tag{3-24}$$

Of which, $Trade_i$ represents the total commodity imports and exports of country i. Trade tendency difference demonstrates the difference in dependency degree of the national economy of the two countries on import and export trade. A bigger difference in trade tendency means a bigger difference in the influence of exchange rate volatility on their national economy and more costs for currency cooperation between the two.

(7). Difference in Price Index Volatility DPI. One of the critical Convergence Criteria for a country to enter into a currency area is to have a similar level of price fluctuation. But this text adopts the standard deviation of the price index algorithm difference of the two countries as the indicator for difference in price index fluctuation. The specific expression is:

$$DPI_{ij} = SD(\ln(P_i) - \ln(P_j)) \tag{3-25}$$

Of which, P_i represents the CPI of country i. When the volatility of price index between two economies is smaller, the influencing degree of external shocks faced by them is similar. Therefore their costs for carrying out currency cooperation are less.

The East Asian OCA Index Model

As part of the efforts to build the OCA index model of East Asia, we selected nine East Asian economies, Mainland China, Japan, South Korea, Chinese Taiwan, Singapore, Malaysia, Thailand, the Philippines and Indonesia together with the U.S. in the model. The addition of the U.S. is because the U.S. dollar is still playing an irreplaceable role in East Asia and adding it can strengthen the explanation capability of the model across the board. The exclusion of Chinese Hong Kong and Macao in the model is out of the consideration that the Hong Kong dollar and pataca have long been implementing the policy of pegging to U.S. dollar and their addition might make a difference in the effectiveness of the analysis. Another five ASEAN countries are also excluded because they are smaller in economic scale and basically adopt the strategy of following suit with other ASEAN members. Data of the model are typically taken from the ADB, the IMF, the World Bank and the National Bureau of Statistics of each country, and the sample interval of major variables is between 1990 and 2007.

To begin with, we carry out a Granger Causality Tests of variables and measure and calculate whether causality exists between explaining variables and explained variables. We can see from the test results (Table 3.37) that there is no causality between output growth difference DY and the explained variables fluctuation ratio of bilateral nominal exchange rate DE, which is totally different from that of the Eurozone. This reflects that East Asia lacks an internal leading currency and heavily depends on the U.S. dollar in foreign trade. Economic scale SIZE, difference in trade tendency MF and difference in price index fluctuation DPI do not have outstanding causality with explained variables. The three explaining variables of difference in structure of export goods MS, commodity trade intensity TII and bilateral trade relations TR have evident causality with explained variables. Finally, as commodity trade intensity TII and bilateral trade relations TR represent the degree of trade links between two countries and are highly correlated, we only chose one of them according to the significance of the model parameter.

After that, we put all explaining variables into the OCA index model and evaluate the influence of each explaining variable on the overall significance level and the stability of the model one by one. Following the minimization principal of AIC and SC norms, we ultimately establish the explaining variables of the OCA index model as difference in export goods structure MS, commodity trade intensity TII and difference in price index fluctuation DPI, put indicator data into the regression equation, and finally conclude the OCA index mode for East Asia:

$$DX_{i,j} = 0.390481 \bullet MS_{i,j} - 0.00988 \bullet TII_{i,j} + 1.110212 \bullet DPI_{i,j} \qquad (3\text{–}26)$$

Table 3.38 shows that R^2 of the OCA index model (Formula 3–26) reaches 0.79, the logarithm likelihood ratio reaches 47.82, and D-W value is close to 2, indicating that the overall regression of the model has strong results. When it comes to model

Table 3.37. Granger causality tests

Original Hypothesis	Freedom	F-Statistic	P-Value
DY cannot Granger-cause DE	43	0.19517	0.82351
DE cannot Granger-cause DY		0.82042	0.44789
MS cannot Granger-cause DE	43	4.76651	0.01422
DE cannot Granger-cause MS		0.46224	0.63336
TII cannot Granger-cause DE	43	0.24562	0.78345
DE cannot Granger-cause TII		3.61956	0.0364
TR cannot Granger-cause DE	43	0.47927	0.62293
DE cannot Granger-cause TR		14.7266	0.000018
SIZE cannot Granger-cause DE	43	2.15837	0.12947
DE cannot Granger-cause SIZE		0.88629	0.42053
MF cannot Granger-cause DE	43	1.87983	0.16654
DE cannot Granger-cause MF		2.33591	0.11046
DPI cannot Granger-cause DE	43	1.46135	0.24466
SDE cannot Granger-cause DPI		1.23786	0.30143

parameters, the index and coefficient of the difference in export goods structure MS and difference in price index fluctuation DPI have more statistics, P value is close to 0 and enjoys better significance level, the index and coefficient of commodity trade intensity TII is lower in significance level, but considering the symbols of index and coefficient are identical to the economic implications of the indicator and the overall results of the model are good, we retain it.

In order to further test the effectiveness of the model, we exclude the U.S. from the sample countries and only take East Asian economies as samples to observe whether the OCA model will show changes. We carry out Granger Causality Tests of model variables again (see Table 3.39) and find that the causality between difference in output growth DY and explained variable bilateral nominal exchange rate fluctuation DE shows a small improvements but not an obvious one. Other explaining variables and explained variables show somewhat weakening causality, which means the elimination of the U.S. from sample countries will weaken the explaining effects of the model to a large extent.

Table 3.38. Model regression parameter

	Coefficient	*T*-Statistic	*P* -Value
β_1	0.390481	4.628611	0
β_2	-0.00988	-0.94131	0.3519
β_3	1.110212	6.449601	0
R^2		0.793502	
Adjusted R^2		0.783669	
Logarithm Likelihood Ratio		47.82066	
AIC Norm		-1.99203	
SC Norm		-1.87159	
D-W Value		2.195185	

We put explaining variables into the OCA index model and evaluate the influence of each explaining variable on the overall significance level and stability of the model one by one. Following the minimization principal of AIC and SC norms, as with Formula 3-26, we establish the explaining variables of the OCA index model, namely difference in export goods structure MS, commodity trade intensity TII and difference in price index fluctuation DPI, put indicator data into the regression equation and finally conclude the OCA index mode for East Asia:

$$DX_{ij} = 0.381917 \bullet MS_{ij} - 0.008064 \bullet TII_{ij} + 1.062037 \bullet DPI_{ij} \quad (3\text{–}27)$$

Table 3.39. Granger Causality Tests

Original Hypothesis	Freedom	F-Statistic	P-Value
DY cannot Granger-cause DE	34	0.70476	0.50249
DE cannot Granger-cause DY		0.66136	0.52376
MS cannot Granger-cause DE	34	1.80648	0.18223
DE cannot Granger-cause MS		0.2783	0.75907
TII cannot Granger-cause DE	34	0.76562	0.47421
DE cannot Granger-cause TII		1.47514	0.24541
TR cannot Granger-cause DE	34	0.56643	0.5737
DE cannot Granger-cause TR		7.06919	0.00316
SIZE cannot Granger-cause DE	34	1.69195	0.20184
DE cannot Granger-cause SIZE		0.84938	0.438058
MF cannot Granger-cause DE	34	1.2656	0.29719
DE cannot Granger-cause MF		0.49868	0.61244
DPI cannot Granger-cause DE	34	0.68267	0.5132
SDE cannot Granger-cause DPI		0.80025	0.45889

After comparing the model excluding the U.S. (Formula 3–27) and the model (Formula 3–26), we find the significance level and stability of the model excluding the U.S. do not show much change, the significance level of the indicator and coefficient of commodity trade intensity TII drops, but the value of assessment of model parameters is basically the same and the explaining effects of the model does not witness changes. In this sense, we can conclude that the original model 3–26 is more stable and can still be used for OCA index evaluation (see Table 3.40).

The final concluded East Asian OCA index model (Formula 3–26) includes the cost indicator (difference in export goods structure MS and difference in price index fluctuation DPI) and the proceeds indicator (commodity trade intensity TII) for establishing a currency region. The economic implications and regression results of the model are satisfying. When it comes to the structure of the indicator system of the OCA index model, it typically includes trade relations, difference in trade structure and stability of economic growth that are consistent with the current development characteristics of East Asian economies and can effectively illustrate the implications of bilateral currency cooperation for economies of the East Asia region. As such, we can make an in-depth analysis by using them in establishing the OCA index.

Table 3.40. Model regression parameters

	Coefficient	T-Statistic	P -Value
β_1	0.381917	4.679848	0
β_2	-0.00806	-0.80628	0.4259
β_3	1.062037	6.338331	0
R^2		0.829698	
Adjusted R^2		0.819377	
Logarithm Likelihood Ratio		41.79961	
AIC Norm		-2.15553	
SC Norm		-2.02357	
D-W Value		2.265573	

Calculation of the East Asia OCA Index

Based on the previous OCA index model, we can make an assessment of the total costs for and proceeds of currency cooperation among East Asian economies and establish the OCA index for the region. We must build a series of explaining variables in order to project explained variables. We select the difference in price index fluctuation DPI of the years between 1991 and 2000, the difference in export goods structure MS and commodity trade intensity TII of the year 2000 to calculate the OCA index for East Asia for the year 2000, and then choose the difference in price index fluctuation DPI of the years between 1998 and 2007 together with the difference in export goods structure MS and commodity trade intensity TII of the year 2007 to calculate the OCA index for

East Asia for the year 2007. The 1997 Asian Financial Crisis had significant influence on the price index of East Asian economies in 1997 and 1998, but the influence can be effectively eliminated through transforming the logarithm difference of price index. As such there is no need to make adjustment when establishing indicators.

Comparison of the East Asia OCA index between the model with China at the core and the model with the U.S. at the core

In order to evaluate the feasibility that East Asian economies establish monetary cooperation with China as the core and the changing trend of East Asian countries' dependency rate on the leading developed economy the U.S., we here make a comparison of the OCA index of each East Asian economy to China and the U.S. respectively (see Table 3.41).

We can see from the scatter diagram of each East Asian economy's OCA index to China and the U.S. (Fig. 3.12, Fig. 3.13) that their homoplasy with the U.S. was obviously stronger than that with Mainland China in 2000. In particular, the OCA indices of Chinese Taiwan, Malaysia and Singapore to the U.S. are all less than 0.1, indicating that they have remarkable homoplasy, while the OCA indices tof China are evidently larger and it is impossible to establish a currency area.

Since then, their homoplasy to China and the U.S. changed as can be illustrated by the moving trend from the U.S. area to the Chinese area. By 2007, except for individual economies, the homoplasy of the whole of East Asia to the U.S. had weakened significantly. At that time only the OCA indices of the Philippines and Thailand were less than 0.1 and showed an obvious homoplasy.

Table 3.41. OCA index to Mainland China and the U.S.

	Mainland China		The U.S.	
	2000	2007	2000	2007
Indonesia	0.452	0.679	0.403	0.659
Malaysia	0.227	0.146	0.070	0.131
The Philippines	0.332	0.122	0.125	0.093
Singapore	0.270	0.100	0.070	0.129
Thailand	0.263	0.145	0.169	0.086
Taiwan	0.256	0.010	0.063	0.109
South Korea	0.170	0.045	0.103	0.123
Japan	0.335	0.068	0.122	0.171

In this sense, the dependency rate of the region of East Asia on the outside world (especially the U.S.) keeps dropping while the homoplasy to the region keeps growing, which has created the necessary preconditions and guarantee for monetary cooperation in East Asia.

Fig. 3.12 Scatter diagram of OCA to Mainland China and the U.S. in 2000

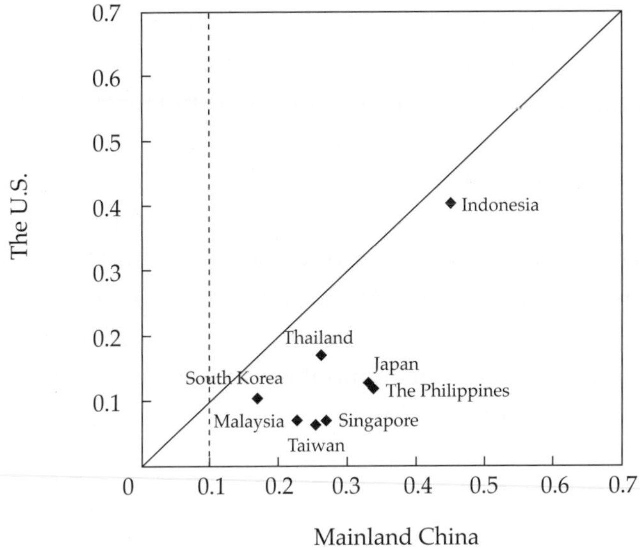

Fig. 3.13 Scatter diagram of OCA to Mainland China and the U.S. in 2007

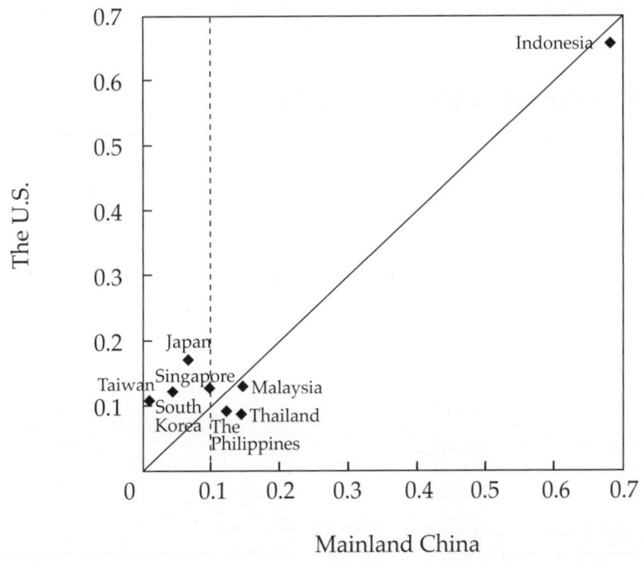

Comparison of the East Asia OCA index between the model with China at the core and the model with Japan at the core

After comparing China and the U.S. we need to focus on whether an appropriate core country exists if the currency area is established in East Asia on the one hand and what role China can play in East Asian monetary cooperation on the other.

We can find through comparing the OCA index with China at the core and with Japan at the core respectively (Table 3.42) that the homoplasy of East Asian economies with both China and Japan is not significant in 2000. Only Chinese Taiwan and Singapore have a smaller OCA index with Japan (Fig. 3.14), illustrating that neither China nor Japan is capable of establish a currency area with themselves at the core at the moment.

By 2007, the homoplasy of East Asian economies had strengthening with with Mainland China and Japan. The number of economies with OCA index smaller than 0.1 had increased significantly (Fig. 3.15) and it is more remarkable with Mainland China. That said, we can see from the scatter diagram of OCA to Mainland China and Japan that their homoplasy with China and Japan is obviously different. That is neither of the two countries have an absolute advantage in attracting East Asian economies to join a currency area with themselves at the core. Learning from the experience of the euro, it's more feasible for China and Japan to jointly establish a currency area in East Asia through cooperation.

We can see from the OCA index in the year 2007 that the OCA index of Chinese Taiwan and South Korea was smaller than 0.1 to China. The figure is obviously smaller than that of other countries and regions. For Mainland

Table 3.42. OCA index to Mainland China and Japan

	Mainland China		Japan	
	2000	2007	2000	2007
Indonesia	0.452	0.679	0.484	0.656
Malaysia	0.227	0.146	0.18t7	0.179
The Philippines	0.332	0.122	0.162	0.203
Singapore	0.270	0.100	0.094	0.133
Thailand	0.263	0.145	0.285	0.216
Taiwan	0.256	0.010	0.054	0.043
South Korea	0.170	0.045	0.168	0.078
Japan	0.335	0.068		

China, Japan, South Korea, Chinese Taiwan, Chinese Hong Kong and Macao, significant benefits will be generated from taking the lead to establish a currency area in the region from the perspective of economic homoplasy. But considering that these six parties have yet to establish an integrated free trade circle and form a close partnership, and they lack sufficient political consensus, there are still many difficulties ahead in establishing a currency area.

Fig. 3.14. Scatter diagram of OCA to Mainland China and Japan in 2000

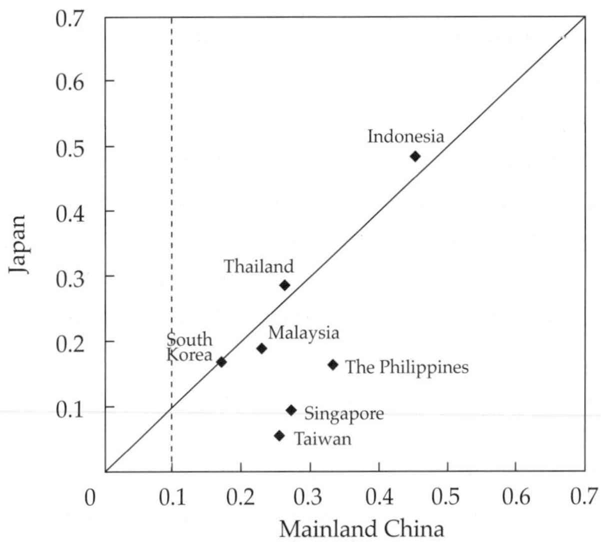

Fig. 3.15. Scatter diagram of OCA to Mainland China and Japan in 2007

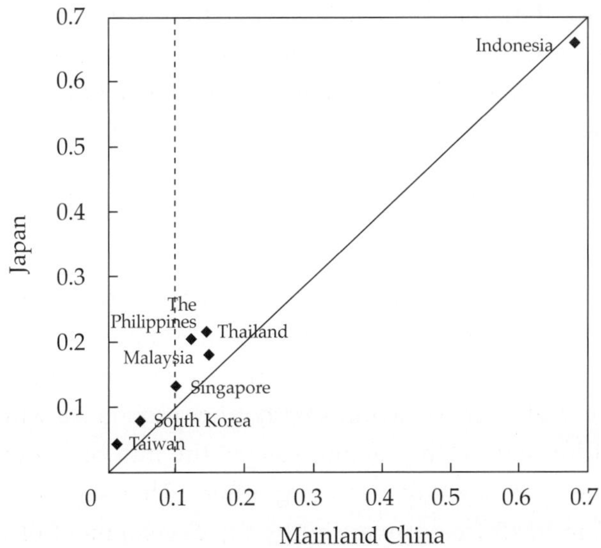

We also noticed that the OCA index between China, Japan and East Asian economies remains high although it has decreased. Only that between Singapore and China reaches 0.1. As ASEAN as an integrated community has established free trade areas with China and Japan respectively, the homoplasy with each of the ASEAN members should be taken into consideration when trying to attract them to join in a currency area.

Evaluation of the East Asian OCA index

Based on the above analyses of the OCA index, we can draw the following conclusions on China's possible role in engaging in a higher level of regional currency cooperation in East Asia.

First, compared with the Eurozone, the time is not mature for East Asia to establish a currency area. On the one hand, the OCA index between East Asian economies is still larger than that of the Eurozone, thus East Asia does not have conditions for the establishment of a currency area and the intra-regional homoplasy leaves much room for improvement. On the other hand, the homoplasy of East Asia and the U.S. is weakening but is not weaker than that of East Asia and China, and East Asia still relies heavily on the outside. Therefore it is not attractive for the economies to set up a currency area.

Second, China is still not in a position to become the core of a currency area. From the perspective of the changes of the OCA index with China at the center, the homoplasy between other economies and China keeps increasing. But China does not have a stronger attractiveness for the region than Japan, so it remains elusive for China to advance the establishment of a currency area alone. It is more practical and feasible for China to boost cooperation with Japan, the only developed economy of the region, to jointly establish a currency area from the perspective of the OCA index.

Summary

At the current stage, both advantages and obstacles are there for RMB regionalization. Based on general theories of currency internationalization, China is in a position to realize its currency regionalization from the perspectives of its economic scale, economic links with other economies within the region, economic position within the region, role as the hub of regional division of labor and stable currency policy, among others. That said, China leaves much to be desired in RMB free convertibility, the development of the foreign exchange market and domestic financial market, institutional setup, the popularity of the RMB within the region and its position in the international currency system. This indicates that RMB regionalization cannot be realized overnight and it must be advanced step by step in line with the reality.

In the long run, China enjoys the position to serve as the potential market provider in East Asia and this position will become more important with the steady growth of the Chinese economy. This is an advantage for the RMB to realize wide-ranging and multi-tiered regionalization. But from another perspective, China is not at the moment capable of serving as the market provider for end products in East Asia and it more often than not plays the role as the region for production convergence and platform for export in the regional production network. China still has a long way to go before it becomes the market provider for finished products in East Asia. It is necessary to increase the proportion of the export of end products from other East Asian economies to China at a faster speed in order to meet the realistic demand for the RMB to serve as the regional settlement currency.

In terms of the possibility for RMB regionalization through some kind of regional currency integration, SVAR analysis results demonstrate that the weak relevance between China and the rest of East Asia in economic shocks, especially in real supply shock, will make it less possible to establish a unified currency area led by the RMB in East Asia within a certain period. Having said that, as has already been stated above, the weak relevance of real shocks between a large power whose economy is in long-term stability and other economies also demonstrates that the large economy can be a stabilizer for the regional economy and its currency can serve as a stabilizer for the exchange rate of other currencies of the region. From this point of view it is still possible for the RMB to become in part a regional stabilizer for the exchange rate. The empirical analysis results of the BBQ method and MSAR method indicate that the RMB is still facing great difficulties in realizing regionalization via the European style currency integration according to traditional currency integration theories and models. But China is well-positioned to play its part in the East Asia region through a model or a way that is different from that of Europe and its currency is also likely to exert its influence in East Asia in a way that is similar to the U.S. dollar.

The examinations based on the OCA index show that the homoplasy of the entire East Asia with the U.S. is obviously weakening while the homoplasy of East Asia with China is strengthening, which has provided a necessary guarantee for China to become actively involved in currency cooperation and to play a critical role in the region. But we should be clear that China and

Japan do not boast absolute merits to attract other East Asian economies to a currency area with the RMB and Japanese yen at the core. China and Japan must cooperate closely as they seek to promote a higher level of regional monetary cooperation.

It is clear that East Asia is likely to blaze a trail in monetary cooperation with distinctive characteristics that is different from that of Europe and the U.S. The context and prospect of this distinctive model is yet to be clarified, but what is certain is that it lies in close cooperation among the countries and regions of East Asia. For this, both China and Japan as two powers of East Asia bear great responsibilities.

4

Chapter

Development Direction for RMB Regionalization

As mentioned above, RMB internationalization is not only necessary but also inevitable for China while regionalization is the only path for RMB internationalization. We can find through analysis that a series of favorable conditions exist although RMB regionalization is facing some obstacles. Furthermore, considering past experiences in and lessons from the internationalization of various currencies and the characteristics of the existing international monetary system, the RMB as the currency of a large developing country also needs to explore unique ways of regionalization rather than follow the internationalization model of some other currencies in line with its own actual development needs and the new international context.

Entering the 21st century, the influence of the RMB keeps growing in neighboring countries and regions, which has been especially reflected by its widespread use in cross-border flow and frontier trade. The international financial crisis in 2007 has also provided an opportunity for RMB regionalization in some sense. Within this context China has continuously introduced a host of measures, such as promoting pilot projects for cross-border trade settlement in RMB, developing the RMB bond market and expanding currency swap with other East Asian countries. This signifies that RMB regionalization has started to move forward steadily. Against this backdrop, it is highly relevant to act on a realistic basis and focus on non-institutionalization and institutionalization to press ahead with RMB regionalization through appropriate and effective channels.

The Overall Principle of RMB Regionalization

In the light of China's current situation and the characteristics of the regional and even the international financial environment, we need to be committed to the following four principles for RMB regionalization.

Moving forward the rmb regionalization in a progressive manner

In the current circumstances, the RMB does not have the foundation for becoming a leading currency in East Asia in the short term although some preconditions for its regionalization have taken shape. The improvement of the international status of the RMB is a long-term and progressive procedure and will not happen overnight, thus we need to follow through a regulated, orderly and steady principle in going forward.

In specific terms, first and foremost, the economic strength of a nation is one of the defining factors for the internationalization of its currency (Huang Meibo,

2001). That means that the precondition for the RMB to become a key currency in East Asia is that China's economic strength can support this behavior. When we examine the economic aggregate, Chinese economic scale as continued to grow in recent years but China's GDP at the moment is only one tenth of that of the U.S. and about the same as that of Japan. When it comes to the per capita GDP, the gap is even more salient. Taking 2004 as an example, China's per capita GDP was only one fifth of that of Japan, less than one sixth of that of the U.S. and even only three fourths of that of Thailand.[1] Obviously, the realization of RMB regionalization needs China's economic strength to increase further.

Second, a larger trade scale of an economy means more possibilities for the currency of the country to flow in international trade and for it to be accepted and recognized by the two parties of the trade, as noted in the discussions in the first chapter about the theory of currency internationalization. From this perspective China has become one of the major market providers of East Asia, but it has yet to become the central market of the region. East Asian economies are now still depending more on the U.S. market. In the meantime, the U.S. also represents the most important export market for China, which has made it difficult for East Asian currencies including the RMB to escape the influence of U.S. dollar and this is also one of the major obstacles for the RMB to realize regionalization. As part of the efforts to overcome this difficulty and seek to create the conditions for RMB regionalization, we need to enhance the role of the Chinese domestic market in driving China's economic growth and further expand the share and effects of the Chinese market in the East Asian regional market.

Third, RMB regionalization is bound to be closely linked with the openness and development of China's financial market. The development of the financial market of a nation directly determines the openness of the financial market and then affects the internationalization process of the currency of the economy. If the soundness of the domestic financial system and the openness of the financial market are far from meeting the requirements for adopting the internationalization of the domestic currency and the country blindly delivers impractical internationalization principles for the domestic currency, then this will easily result in inflationary financial bubbles and economic recession (Ba Shusong, 2007). At the moment the development of the Chinese financial market is at a lower level and is rather vulnerable, which means it is far from meeting the requirements for the RMB to become the leading currency in East Asia, especially during the process of RMB regionalization when a large quantity of RMB will flow overseas at a fast speed. This will require a higher level of financial supervision and regulation in China. In this sense, the regionalization process of the RMB must rely on the development and improvement of the Chinese financial market and financial supervision system.

In addition, RMB regionalization is also a process of the East Asian economies accepting the RMB over time and it involves more other complex factors, and cannot be realized at one stroke.

Specifically speaking, the steps and procedures of RMB regionalization must be designed according to the status quo of RMB regionalization and internationalization and its gap with international currencies. Table 4.1 and Table 4.2 list respectively the functions of an international currency in a general sense and the functions of an international currency that have been borne by the RMB. We can see from the tables that the RMB is still far behind regionalized and internationalized currencies in terms of the three major functions namely medium of exchange, unit of account and store of value.

Table 4.1. Functions of an international currency

	Private Use	Official Use
Medium of Exchange	Vehicle Currency: (1)Trade of commodities; (2) Financial transaction	Intervention currency of foreign exchange market
Unit of Account	Invoice currency	Anchor currency pegging to the exchange rate
Store of Value	Investment International reserve currency	

Source: Xu Qiyuan and Liu Lizhen, 2008.

Table 4.2. RMB's functions as an international currency

	Private Use	Official Use
Medium of Exchange	(1) Border trade; (2) Foreign exchange transactions (small in scale)	Nil
Unit of Account	Border Trade	Nil
Store of Value	RMB savings and bonds in Hong Kong	Reserve currency of Cambodia, the Philippines and Nepal

Source: Set out based on Xu Qiyuan and Liu Lizhen, 2008.

On these grounds, considering China's economic, financial and political landscape and the rest of Asia, RMB regionalization should follow a path from neighboring countries to the rest of the region and its currency functions should follow the order from medium of exchange, unit of account and store of value. Specifically speaking, RMB regionalization can be divided into the following four stages or levels.

Stage one, steadily moving ahead with the circulation of the RMB in neighboring countries, creating the conditions for promoting the functions of the RMB as a settlement currency for part of the trade between China and neighboring economies, increasing the market popularity of the RMB in trade between neighboring countries and China, and at the same time actively and prudently carrying out the establishment of the RMB offshore financial market and international bond market so that the RMB takes on the functions of an investment currency within a specific range.

Stage two, based on the above, through official settlement agreements between China and neighboring countries and even between more East Asian economies, promoting use of the RMB in general trade settlement between China and the rest of the East Asian economies, fully leveraging on measures such as currency swap agreements to facilitate official transaction of the RMB by the central banks of other East Asian economies with China's central bank and to make the RMB become an official reserve currency for other East Asian economies to a certain degree, and gradually improving the convertibility of the RMB in official transactions. In addition, gradually opening the domestic financial market, relaxing restrictions on capital account and improving the RMB backflow mechanism to make the RMB play the functions of an investment currency at a broader and higher level.

Stage three, promoting other East Asian economies to spontaneously take the RMB as a kind of "anchor" currency in terms of exchange rate arrangement so as to establish the RMB as an intervention currency for the foreign exchange market of East Asian countries through the reform, adjustment and development of the domestic economy and the transformation of the foreign trade pattern.

Stage four, boosting regional monetary cooperation in East Asia; on the one hand, capitalizing on the regional financing arrangement to enhance the attractiveness of the RMB as a reserve currency and intervention currency; on the other hand, realizing the position of the RMB as an "anchor" currency at the institutional level through gradual advancement of sub-regional cooperation on exchange rate, properly coordinating the relationship with key currencies such as the Japanese yen and U.S. dollar, and ultimately making the RMB the leading or one of the leading currencies within the region.

Strengthening cooperation and coordination with other East Asian economies

The process of RMB regionalization is filled with economic frictions of various kinds and might encounter the influence and obstruction of all sorts of political factors as well.

Trade and investment are the two essential channels for advancing currency circulation. Investment abroad cannot be taken as a key passage for RMB regionalization as China has insufficient capital. In this sense it is highly relevant to facilitate overseas circulation of the RMB by means of trade. At the moment, trade between China and other East Asian economies is still challenged in many ways, especially by trade frictions triggered by the homoplasy in export structure and target market, which is harmful for the process of RMB regionalization. Trade frictions in other aspects (such as trade interest allocation) will also put a brake on the development of RMB regionalization.

Analyzed from the political perspective, the right to issue currency has always been regarded as one of the important symbols of national sovereignty. The nature of RMB regionalization is to realize substitution for other regional currencies. Obviously, it is destined to be a long, hard journey for a currency to realize substitution of other regional currencies in East Asia amid "sovereignty expansion." On top of that, economic players more usually have inertia in selecting a valuation and settlement currency (for instance, within a certain time period after the euro made its debut, residents of the Eurozone were still used to thinking in their old currencies), and the objective existence of a U.S. dollar area in East Asia and the current position and influence of the Japanese yen are bound to trigger competition between the RMB, Japanese yen and U.S. dollar and add to the costs and difficulties of RMB regionalization.

International cooperation and coordination can weaken and eliminate certain differences and contradictions to a large extent, which is highly relevant for China that is in the middle of an economic boom. In recent years, as the Chinese economic growth rate has kept picking up, some countries argue that China's economic growth will jeopardize the economic development of other countries and the entire world. These negative arguments in some sense have damaged the external environment for China's economic development. But China has in effect disproved this point through international cooperation and coordination. We take cases of China and ASEAN countries to examine the necessity of cooperation and coordination. Before the signing of the China-ASEAN Free Trade Agreement, China attracted abundant foreign capital through its huge market and cheap labor, which had a certain influence on the attractiveness of

ASEAN countries for foreign capital and led to the re-emergence of the "China Threat Theory." But after the entry into force of the China-ASEAN Free Trade Agreement, ASEAN countries have witnessed a rapid increase of exports to China and the increase of foreign capital, which have finally eliminated their worries about China's rise. Evidently, strengthening cooperation and coordination with other East Asian counterparts is for China an essential principle in the strategy of RMB regionalization.

Integration of market spontaneous evolution and institutional arrangement

As is well known, from the ending of the Second World War to the founding of the Jamaica System, the internationalization strategy of the U.S. dollar mainly relied on the international system framework built by the Bretton Woods System and this global institutional arrangement propelled the global expansion of the U.S. dollar. The current strong position of the U.S. dollar can be understood as the resetting of the U.S. dollar system and it is the reflection of economic players' inertial dependence on the U.S. dollar. The internationalization strategy of the euro also owes its success to the various institutions established in the Eurozone and they paved the way for the euro to be internationalized. The success of the internationalization strategy of the euro and the U.S. dollar are sufficient proof of the driving force of institutional arrangement for currency internationalization.

The circulation of the RMB in neighboring countries is the results of spontaneous market force or we can say that it is a result driven by governments at their convenience on the basis of natural evolution. However the RMB is naturally weak in the international currency system led by the U.S. dollar, thus it is not sufficient for the RMB to naturally become a regionalized currency only by relying on institutional development. In other words, spontaneous market evolution is not enough for the RMB to realize regionalization. We need more relevant institutional arrangements to press ahead with RMB regionalization. The establishment of an institutional framework will lead to path dependence and self-strengthening effects and exert great influence on the expectation and actions of individuals and businesses both inside and outside the region. Once the vested interests are identified, it will become the driving force for currency integration at an even higher level. In this connection it is necessary to seek intra-regional institutional arrangements during the process of market spontaneous evolution so as to advance RMB regionalization. RMB regionalization needs to be advanced at both the non-institutional level and the institutional level.

Rmb regionalization needs to rely on East Asian currency and financial cooperation

As stated above, RMB regionalization needs not only sustaining marketization but also the enhancement of monetary and financial cooperation between East Asian countries (regions). The reasons behind the emphasis that RMB regionalization strategy needs to be supported by East Asian monetary and financial cooperation are that on the one hand, East Asian monetary and financial cooperation represents the external environment for the implementation of the RMB regionalization strategy and RMB regionalization cannot be separated from the arrangement and restriction of East Asian monetary and financial cooperation; on the other hand, East Asian monetary and financial cooperation as an institutional arrangement of the region has two outstanding features in itself—it is voluntary and universal. These two characteristics have determined that this cooperation plays a key role in the RMB regionalization process.

Of course, the Asian Financial Crisis in 1997 is the main driver for the broad acceptance of East Asian currency and financial cooperation as the formal institutional arrangement within the region in the middle of the "sovereignty expansion stage." Asian economies are keenly aware of the drawbacks of the existing international currency system due to the financial crisis. These countries and regions decided to sacrifice some political sovereignty in order to safeguard their own interests and get rid of the negative impact of the U.S. dollar regime in East Asia through building regional institutional protection. It is clear that East Asian monetary and financial cooperation is the voluntary and autonomous behavior of East Asian countries and regions and it has overcome part of the political discrepancies and conflicts between relevant countries and regions. In this context, the RMB regionalization strategy is undoubtedly a path for cutting political costs for RMB regionalization if it is supported by East Asian monetary and financial cooperation.

East Asian currency and financial cooperation as a bilateral or multilateral institutional arrangement between different economies has produced substantive progress. Many East Asian countries and regions have engaged in the cooperation. It is predictable that more and more countries and regions will join in the cooperation as their financial cooperation keeps expanding and deepening. Ultimately, a clearer development prospect for regional financial cooperation will be outlined and this trend can be vaguely observed from the currency swap framework between East Asian economies. This institutional framework that is gradually shaped is bound to offer a convenient channel for the circulation of strong currencies. Given that, advancing RMB regionalization with the support of East Asian monetary and financial cooperation can not only save costs for RMB regionalization but also accelerate the regionalization process.

All in all, regional monetary cooperation is undoubtedly the optimal path in the current conditions no matter whether it is aimed at surmounting international political divides or finding a shortcut for currency regionalization.

Prompting the RMB in Neighboring Countries: Using the RMB as a Settlement Currency and Building the RMB Offshore Market

Promoting RMB cross-border circulation and expanding the pilot program for RMB-denominated trade settlement

As previously mentioned, the total volume of trade between China and neighboring countries has shown an upward trend for years running as China's national strength keeps increasing and its role as the market provider in East Asia grows more apparent. The RMB has been widely used for frontier trade settlement and daily payment due to optimistic expectations for Chinese economic landscape and the reality of RMB appreciation. At the moment, RMB cross-border circulation is typically seen in two areas: border trade and outbound tourism. In recent years, border trade between China and neighboring countries and regions has gained momentum. In 2006, according to statistics of China's National Bureau of Statistics, the frontier trade volume surpassed USD89.67 billion between China and its 14 adjacent countries and regions (excluding Chinese Hong Kong and Taiwan) and continues to surge. In addition, a large proportion of frontier trade is settled in RMB. The retention time of RMB in borders is relatively longer and it functions as a valuation currency and a medium of exchange within a certain range. Beyond that, China's outbound tourism has boomed in recent years and Southeast Asian countries and regions such as Thailand, Malaysia, Singapore and South Korea are singled out by Chinese tourists. Accordingly, a large amount of RMB have been taken out of the country for use on consumption. This kind of RMB circulation driven by border trade and tourism is typically limited to countries and regions having dynamic border trade activities with China and seeing concentrated Chinese tourists in terms of geography, and this can be deemed as the preliminary manifestation of RMB regionalization. At the current stage, the top priority is to adopt measures to advance this kind of cross-border circulation in line with the characteristics of current RMB cross-border circulation so as to lay a market foundation for neighboring countries to accept the RMB.

In 2005 the PBOC set up the research team for cross-border RMB cash flow and made an investigation of the cross-border flow of RMB in cash in Hong Kong and Macao as well as neighboring countries. The team generalized through investigation and analysis that RMB cross-border flow has the following basic characteristics:

First, the amount of RMB retention in neighboring countries and regions keeps growing but it is still small in scale as a whole. In 2004 the quantity of RMB retained in neighboring countries and Hong Kong as well as Macao only accounted for one per cent of the circulating RMB in cash of the year.

Second, RMB cross-border flow is large in scale and its total cross-border flows posted RMB771.3 billion in 2004. Among which 390.6 billion RMB was outflow and RMB380.7 billion was inflows, indicating a net outflows of RMB9.9 billion in general, especially in Hong Kong and Macao which witnessed large inflow and outflow. In 2004 the total inflow and outflow of RMB in Hong Kong and Macao registered RMB752.2 billion, taking up 97.5 per cent of the total.

Third, among the total cross-border flow of RMB in cash in 2004, RMB760.3 billion was under non-trade items, about 97 per cent of the total, illustrating that the RMB was mainly used for tourism and visiting families and friends; RMB11.7 billion was under border trade items, accounting for only 2 per cent of the total.

It is clear that the absolute size of RMB cash in circulation is larger in neighboring countries and regions, but the cross-border flow is concentrated in Hong Kong and Macao and non-trade flows, such as flows for tourism and visiting families and friends, dominate the circulation which is only the demonstration of RMB in fulfilling its function as a daily means of payment. The share of cross-border flows of RMB functioning as a valuation currency and trade settlement currency is quite small and drawbacks exist from the institutional perspective. As such, we cannot only depend on market spontaneous evolution to advance RMB cross-border flow at the current stage. Rather we must take active measures to promote the use of the RMB as a settlement currency for border trade on the one hand; on the other hand, we must modernize the settlement mechanism for border trade between China and bordering economies from the institutional perspective and bring the RMB overseas flow into normalized channels. This is not to artificially boost the circulation and settlement of the RMB in neighboring countries. Rather it is to reduce institutional obstacles and create facilitating conditions for the circulation of the RMB in neighboring countries through institutional arrangements so as to make it easier for the RMB to become a choice for trade settlement between Chinese and foreign businesses on the market.

In fact, China has taken some strong measures in this regard. A good start is the release of the *Notice on Issues about Using RMB as a Valuation Currency for Trade by Domestic Institutions* by China's State Administration of Foreign Exchange on 3 March 2003. Since the signing of the *Agreement on Border Trade Settlement between the People's Bank of China and the Central Bank of the Russian Federation* between China and Russia on 22 August 2002, the PBOC has inked agreements on domestic currency for border trade settlement with eight countries, such as Russia, Vietnam, Mongolia and North Korea, which have played an active role in increasing the proportion of RMB in border trade settlement and advancing RMB regionalization. In view of the above situation, the following measures should be adopted to further press ahead with the use of the RMB in evaluation and settlement for border trade.

First, China needs to carry out further consultations with neighboring countries to enter into more bilateral or multilateral agreements on domestic currency settlement for border trade and further refine the contents of relevant agreements so as to set a stage in policy for use of the RMB in settlement for border trade, expand the range of RMB use, and improve its acceptability.

Second, China needs to work harder in expanding the pilot program for RMB-denominated settlement for border trade from some areas of frontier provinces to the entire region of frontier provinces in the south.

Third, Chinese commercial banks in border areas need to actively strengthen connections and cooperation with their counterparts in neighboring countries and regions, and establish mechanisms for communication and exchanges. On the basis of deepening bilateral understanding they could mutually select banks that are strong in finance and credit standing to boost business cooperation, set up correspondent banking relationships, and facilitate the development of border trade settlement in domestic currency.

In addition, in December 2008, the State Council decided to launch the pilot program for RMB-denominated settlement for trade in goods in Guangdong and the Yangtze River Delta with Hong Kong and Macao and in Guangxi and Yunnan with ASEAN, which has given a big boost to the popularity of the RMB in neighboring countries. The pilot program for RMB-denominated settlement for general cross-border trade was launched in 2009. On 8 April 2009, the Standing Committee of the State Council decided to launch the program in Shanghai and the cities of Guangzhou, Shenzhen, Zhuhai and Dongguan in

Guangdong Province. The tentative range in the four cities of Guangdong is for the trade in goods with ASEAN countries. At present, the Bank of China and Bank of Communications have been chosen as the banks for the pilot program. 365 enterprises in Shanghai and Guangdong have been singled out for the implementation of the program. In July 2009 the PBOC issued the *Regulations on the Pilot Program for RMB-Denominated Settlement for Cross-Border Trade* and its rules for the implementation. Relevant regulations on export tax rebate have also been promulgated. Towards the end of 2009, Shanghai had carried out 118 cases of RMB-denominated settlement for cross-border business with a total value of RMB2.135 billion. According to statistics of the Finance Affairs Office of the People's Government of Guangdong Province, the entire province had handled 567 cases of RMB-denominated settlement for cross-border business with a total value of RMB5.655 billion by mid-February 2010.

Entering 2010, restrictions on the program have been further relaxed. First, the pilot business is not restricted in overseas territory. The Chinese government has agreed not to impose restrictions on overseas territory for cross-border trade settlement in RMB any more. Second, the pilot program for import trade settlement in RMB is opened across the board and all enterprises in cities singled out for the program can use the RMB for cross-border trade settlement so long as they are qualified for foreign trade business. In the meantime, the number of businesses for the pilot program has been increased. At the moment Guangdong has submitted the list of the second batch of 3,293 enterprises for the pilot program to the relevant authorities for approval and has meanwhile started to screen the third batch of businesses for the program. Moreover based on the business needs put forward some time before by businesses that were singled out for the pilot program, relevant departments have made it clear that enterprises in the program are allowed to use RMB for cross-border trade settlement and to try direct investment in cross-border settlement for capital accounts.

Under this enabling policy environment, efforts need to be made in the following three aspects in order to further advance RMB cross-border settlement.

First, we need to further improve relevant institutional arrangement, improve the convenience of RMB purchase and sale, inter-bank capital lending, overseas retention and backflow, increase availability of the RMB in settlement, and reduce transaction costs for RMB settlement.

Second, on the basis of the consultations on revising the *Settlement Agreement on Clearing of RMB Business* between the PBOC and Bank of China Hong Kong, China needs to promote the central bank and commercial banks to sign more and better clearing agreements with overseas financial institutions, try to sign official agreements on RMB settlement with neighboring countries, and provide a more convenient system for RMB cross-border settlement. At the same time China can consider the launch of the pilot program for bilateral domestic currency settlement over time with countries that have already reached currency swap agreements with China and promote the use of the RMB as a settlement currency for general trade through providing mutual convenience.

Third, on the basis of continuously improving the system for the pilot program and absorbing experiences in the existing pilot program, China needs to further expand the domestic territorial scope, business scope and trade scope for the pilot program and increase the attractiveness of use of the RMB in settlement.

Improve RMB exit-entry management and strengthen supervision of RMB overseas circulation

Promoting RMB circulation overseas and even facilitating RMB settlement for foreign trade require further improvement and modernization of the RMB exit-entry management mechanism. The PBOC announced in December 2004 that given that RMB regionalization in neighboring countries and regions has become a reality, China's monetary policy, including RMB issue in cash, the plan for withdrawing RMB from circulation and the liquidity arrangements for foreign exchange reserves, need to take into consideration the above changes and make corresponding adjustment. To this end the PBOC has implemented some institutional arrangements such as expanding the maximum amount of RMB that can be carried out of the country by a citizen, increasing the upper limits of RMB that can be carried in or out by Chinese or foreign citizens from RMB6,000 to RMB20,000, supporting the RMB UnionPay Card to go global, and working harder to boost international cooperation in bank card business.

On this basis, regulations on RMB exit-entry need to be further adjusted and improved. For instance, the upper limit for the amount of RMB for residents and non-residents to take in or out of the country is RMB20,000. This amount is too much for general tourists but obviously insufficient for businessmen. China can try for improvement in the following aspects: improving regulations for bilateral trade businessmen on carrying RMB in cash in and out of the border for border trade, allowing the issue of certificates to non-residents for carrying RMB out of the border within the limit of the total amount of the special settlement account opened in China, and issuing certificates to domestic businesses for carrying RMB out of the border for border trade so long as they have a real background in trade. All these measures can help to promote RMB regionalization.

At the same time, when the RMB is used in international settlement involving RMB overseas convertibility for current account that is convertibility for non-residents, then popularizing the RMB in neighboring countries might bring new risks and challenges to domestic financial institutions, which will pose a greater challenge to China's supervision and control in this regard. The specific demonstrations are in the following four aspects.[2]

First, abundant RMB circulation outside the supervision and regulation system. This will not only affect the effectiveness of the implementation of domestic policy instruments such as the currency policy but also provide a means for speculators.

Second, overseas debts and creditor's debt in RMB. The result of using domestic currency for international settlement is the formation of debts and creditor's debts overseas. For example, Chinese businesses need to pay in RMB for importing foreign goods when RMB is used for trade settlement. Their payments will be transferred through the clearing of a banker's agency to their foreign trade partners, namely the account of the exporters, which will result in the phenomenon that foreign enterprises hold RMB. To China, these payments constitute the overseas RMB debts . This poses three questions: first, does this RMB resulting from international settlement belong to current account or capital account? Second, can it be converted into free foreign exchange and does the exchange happen inside or outside China? Third, when RMB inflows are used in direct investment, can they enjoy the same preferential policies as foreign investment and can earnings on the investment be converted into free foreign exchange and be remitted abroad?

Third, foreign exchange administration. For a long time China's foreign exchange administration has been designed on the condition of cross-border payments with foreign exchange and much monitoring work is carried out based on business foreign exchange income and expenses and related foreign exchange settlement and sales. A case in point is that the import and export cancellation after verification system is designed on the basis that business export trade must receive foreign exchange and import trade must pay foreign exchange. A possible phenomenon after using the RMB for international settlement is that RMB will be received and paid for exports and imports. Against this backdrop, difficulties might occur in operation of the current cancellation after verification system for import and export as the source of the RMB might be confused. In particular when there is confusion between the channel for payment and domestic payment after repeated transfers of foreign exchange. Issues related to the cancellation after verification system for import and export also include the foundation and certificate for export tax rebate and reporting balance of international payments, among others.

Fourth, domestic and foreign clearing arrangements. As with other freely convertible currencies, when the RMB is used for settlement through the main channels for international settlement (letter of credit, collection and type of remittance), there will be certain requirements for international settlement of banks and domestic clearing channels. In the specific settlement process, using RMB for international settlement will involve issues where domestic clearing channels undertake RMB-denominated international settlement business and agent bank accounts.

In view of above questions, the RMB cross-border trade system and supervision arrangement must be equipped with a support system.

Firstly, RMB cross-border circulation should be included into the formal financial service system such as commercial banks so as to reduce risks brought to dealers by unsupervised circulation, more timely and precisely access all kinds of information on RMB overseas, closely monitor changes in RMB circulation overseas and avoid the outflow or backflow of RMB on a large scale. The normalization of RMB circulation across the border can not only incorporate RMB cross-border circulation and conversion from institutions such as the money-changers into the formal financial monitoring system such as commercial banks but also provide a convenient and secure channel for RMB outflow and backflow that can be monitored and improve the convenience of the RMB international settlement service.

Secondly, the operation channel for RMB creditor's rights should be properly set up. As the phenomenon of holding RMB overseas is bound to occur after using the RMB as international settlement, it ought to control the development of the RMB's overseas market during the preliminary stage of using RMB for international settlement on a large scale so as to win time for the monetary authority to control the RMB overseas market and transactions gradually if we seek to fend off risks against the backdrop of insufficient experience in management and supervision. Specifically, we can allow RMB external claims to be used for paying for imports from China, to enter the Chinese financial market and make direct investment in China through entrusted financial service business, and to be freely traded in the RMB offshore market to realize RMB backflow by allowing free convertibility of RMB claims generated from international settlement in RMB.

Thirdly, designing scientific and rational settlement channels and working together with neighboring countries to build a convenient mechanism for trade settlement in RMB in a bid to cut back institutional obstacles during the settlement process.

Lastly, strengthening the comprehensive management of RMB overseas circulation, establishing the mechanism for cooperation and coordination among relevant departments, such as the customs, tax, economic and trade, bank, tourism, foreign exchange and foreign affairs departments, and setting up a statistical and monitoring system for the method, channel and scale of use of the RMB in international settlement and overseas circulation.

Building a RMB offshore financial market and settlement center in Hong Kong

There is a need to set up a RMB offshore trading market in due course and directly realize the convertibility of the RMB for capital account against the current background that the RMB for capital account is not freely convertible as we seek to further create the conditions for the RMB to serve as a trade settlement currency in neighboring countries or regions and set the stage for the deepening development of RMB regionalization further down the road.

The enhancement of the international status of the RMB lies in the cultivation and development of its offshore market. The demand for RMB has increased to some extent with the advancement of its internationalization, thus the emergence and growth of a RMB offshore market for providing non-residents with the means of investment or raising funds in RMB will inevitably become a reality. There is an urgent need to set up a rational mechanism for RMB backflow in Hong Kong as it is the region with the most retention of RMB outside of Mainland China. At the same time, Chinese Hong Kong as an international financial center boasts a strong financial market, relevant laws and regulations, preferential policy measures, and sound and modernized telecommunication and financial facilities. Therefore we can consider the establishment of a RMB offshore trading market in Hong Kong. Apart from opening an investment channel for RMB holders overseas to resolve problems in the operation of RMB claims overseas to some extent, the establishment of the offshore market can help the Chinese authorities have a clear picture of the amount of RMB in circulation and the changes in circulation outside China on the one hand; on the other hand, the establishment of the offshore market will also accumulate experience for the opening up a domestic RMB financing market down the line and help the formation of a totally marketized indicator system for the RMB exchange rate which will be a reference for the adjustment of the domestic foreign exchange market. In the meantime, in the current difficult situation regarding the direct connection between the domestic RMB settlement channel and the foreign settlement system, it will be a positive step to set up a RMB settlement center in Hong Kong.

The Chinese monetary authority has been considering these two aspects. In July 2008 the PBOC decided to set up a new exchange rate agency as an internal organization in accordance with the *Regulations on Organizational Setup and Staffing within in Responsibilities of the People's Bank of China* and one of its functions is to "develop the RMB offshore market in line with the process of RMB internationalization." By the end of 2008, the central government had rolled out 14 measures on supporting Hong Kong's financial stability and economic development, allowing fully-fledged enterprises to use the RMB for trade payment in Hong Kong. In January 2009 the PBOC signed the agreement on currency swap with the Hong Kong Monetary Authority and the clearing agreement with the RMB clearing banks such as the Bank of China Hong Kong, stipulating that capital support will be provided if needed. We can regard these measures as the preparation for building Chinese Hong Kong into a RMB settlement hub in the future.

From the perspective of the development landscape of RMB-related business in Chinese Hong Kong in recent years, Chinese Hong Kong has some advantages for setting up a RMB offshore market and settlement center. The Chinese government opened the scope of RMB business operations of Hong Kong Bank in three stages, namely in November 2003, November 2005 and January 2007 respectively. The Hong Kong Bank is already able to operate five items of RMB-related business, including deposit, exchange, remittance, credit card and check, the business of exchanging the RMB of businessmen of seven industries into Hong Kong dollar and RMB cash deposit business; on top of that, five mainland banks have issued RMB22 billion in bonds in Hong Kong since the central government started to allow mainland financial institutions to issue RMB financial bond on 14 January 2007. Chinese Hong Kong has by now established a well-operated RMB real-time settlement system and accumulated rich experience in RMB settlement. The State Council released the *Suggestions of the State Council on the Current Promotion of Economic Development through Finance*, further allowing Hong Kong enterprises or financial institutions that have more businesses on the mainland to issue RMB bonds in Hong Kong so as to expand the main body of RMB bond issue from domestic banks to Hong Kong banks and enterprises and increase the dealing in and amount of RMB bonds issued in Hong Kong over time. On 28 September 2009 the Ministry of Finance issued 6 billion RMB in bonds in Hong Kong. This was the first time for the Chinese government to issue RMB-denominated sovereign debt outside the mainland and can be deemed another breakthrough in terms of RMB bond issue in Hong Kong.

Expanding the issue of RMB bonds in Hong Kong can obviously help Hong Kong develop into a RMB offshore center. After issuing RMB bonds in Hong Kong, Hong Kong enterprises or financial institutions that have more businesses on the mainland could remit the cash earned from bond issue through the RMB real-time settlement system to the mainland, which will improve the economics of scale of the RMB real-time settlement system and lay a solid foundation for further development of RMB-related business in Hong Kong, such as allowing full-fledged companies to use the RMB for trade settlement. This step also represents a major breakthrough in RMB offshore business in Hong Kong.

Of course, what needs to be noted is that the establishment of a RMB offshore market will make people face two markets, namely the internal RMB market and the external RMB market: one is the free and open RMB offshore market outside of China based on the market mechanism and the other is the RMB market inside China that is relatively controlled and its interest rate has yet to be fully marketized. The two markets are bound to impact on and influence each other, which will have great implications for the development of Chinese macro regulation policies and the delivery of monetary and fiscal policies and add to the difficulties in maintaining China's monetary policy independence. This is also an issue that must be taken seriously and handled properly by the monetary authority while establishing a RMB offshore market.

Promoting the RMB to become a settlement currency and a reserve currency for general trade through official settlement agreements signed between China and East Asian economies

After realizing the use of the RMB for border trade settlement and the establishment of a RMB offshore market, we can consider further making the RMB become a settlement currency for general trade (block trade) between China and other economies in the region and promote the RMB to play the function of trade settlement in East Asia. This can be realized through efforts in the following three aspects:

First, continuing to boost the trade links between China and the rest of the East Asian economies and expanding China's capacity to attract exports of other economies in order to enhance the attractiveness of the RMB in trade settlement.

Second, leading other East Asian economies to accept the RMB as a settlement currency for general trade through intensifying economic diplomacy with them and through comprehensive official settlement agreements.

Third, encouraging the RMB to become a reserve currency for other economies in some sense through extending intra-regional currency swap arrangements and other RMB financing arrangements so as to create the conditions for the RMB to play the function of an international currency.

In addition, we can also further press ahead with RMB regionalization by means of realizing the use of the RMB for valuation through facilitating connections between the central bank of China and the central banks of other East Asian countries.

Gradually opening up the domestic financial market to improve the RMB backflow mechanism

As the RMB comes to play the functions of a settlement currency and a reserve currency in a larger scope, it is difficult to meet the huge demand for RMB in investment just by setting up a RMB offshore market. In this sense, we need to open up the domestic financial market in a prudent and orderly way, put in place a diversified RMB backflow mechanism such as a RMB-denominated capital market, further shore up the confidence in holding RMB overseas and provide non-residents who are willing to hold RMB with more sufficient liquidity and a broader investment environment in a bid to move forward RMB regionalization towards a higher level.

Specifically speaking, in the preliminary stage, we can try to allow overseas RMB to be invested in the mainland in order to cut risks and realize conditional convertibility of the RMB for some capital accounts. In the meanwhile, China needs to work together with countries within the region to establish an Asian bond market, give full play to the role of Hong Kong as a region with a strong financial infrastructure and issue RMB-denominated bonds to expand the scope for the use of the RMB. China can further expand the domain for RMB bond issuance and circulation internationally on the basis that mainland institutions issue RMB bonds in Hong Kong.

Beyond that, China can further open up its bond market and improve the development of the bond market. Towards the end of 2005, China's bond market had a total of RMB4.18 trillion but the size is still too small in the light of China's GDP and the financing scale of the entire financial system. Moreover China has insufficient liquidity. At present China should open the bond market wider to the rest of the Asian governments, other international organizations, and credible banks and enterprises so as to promote reform with opening up. Beyond that, China needs to draw on international bond markets' experiences in institutional regulation, operation mode, credit rating, guarantee, payment and settlement, and oversight system among other financial infrastructures and the financial technologies of international bond markets in the structure of variety and time limit as we seek to boost the reform of the domestic bond market and the building of the talent pool, technologies, information and other financial infrastructures and increase the attractiveness of the Chinese bond market. Specifically, China can now gradually relax the limitations on the issue of RMB bonds by other East Asian economies and foreign institutions in China, that is panda bonds. In fact China has made some efforts in this respect. For instance, in October 2005, the International Financial Corporation (IFC) and the ADB obtained the approval of the Chinese government to issue RMB1.13 billion and RMB1 billion in RMB bonds respectively in China's inter-bank bond market. The issue of RMB bonds by foreign institutions in China can increase the credibility and influence of the RMB in the global capital market and shore up the confidence of investors in the RMB, which will make a positive difference in alleviating the pressure of RMB appreciation.

Moreover, during the process of RMB regionalization, the free convertibility of the RMB and a rational exchange rate formation mechanism depend on an effective foreign exchange market. The transaction size and type of China's foreign exchange market are far from meeting the market demand compared with the scale of China's huge import and export trade, capital liquidity and economic scale. Therefore one of the top priorities at the moment remains to speed up the development of the foreign exchange market while moving forward with RMB regionalization.

Feasibility Analysis of the RMB Becoming the Regional Anchor Currency

One of the key functions of an international currency is to become the anchor currency for the exchange rate of other currencies. If the RMB could play some functions of an anchor currency as it becomes a trade settlement currency and an investment currency in neighboring countries and even the entire region, then it will be another crucial process for RMB regionalization. The questions we are interested in are whether other East Asian economies could spontaneously take RMB as the "anchor" for their exchange rate arrangement and what measures China will take to facilitate the market to go for the RMB as the anchor currency. In particular, given that the current global financial turmoil is posing new challenges to East Asian countries' exchange rate policy, the above questions need to be further examined.

Composition changes of the RMB implicit currency package and its linked relationship with East Asian currencies

In order to analyze the possibility of the RMB becoming the regional "anchor" currency, we firstly need to observe the fluctuation of its exchange rate and its relationship with other East Asian currencies and major international currencies since the exchange rate reform on 21 July 2005 (Li Xiao and Ding Yibing, 2009). We here settle for the implicit currency package regression method that was firstly developed by Frankel and Wei Shangjin (Frankel and Wei, 1994) and was later adopted by most exchange rate researchers. According to statistics of the PBOC, and including the U.S. dollar, euro, Japanese yen and Korean won into the implicit currency package, using the daily exchange rate data of all currencies against the Swiss franc (the data are from www.oanda.com, the structure regression equation is as follows:

$$\Delta S_{\text{chkt}} = a_0 + a_1 \Delta S_{\text{uskt}} + a_2 \Delta S_{\text{eukt}} + a_3 \Delta S_{\text{jpkt}} + a_4 \Delta S_{\text{krkt}} + u_t \quad (4\text{-}1)$$

Where S_{chkt}, S_{uskt} , S_{eukt} ,S_{jpkt} and S_{krkt} respectively refer to the logarithm of daily exchange rate of the RMB, the U.S. dollar, Euro, Japanese Yen, Korean Won against the Swiss Franc, Δ refers to the first-order difference, and all exchange rate data passed the test for stability at the first-order difference. a_1, a_2, a_3, a_4 represent the weighting of the above mentioned four currencies in the RMB implicit currency package respectively.

Table 4.3. indicates that from the "exchange rate reform" in 2005 to mid-2008, the weighting of the U.S. dollar in the RMB implicit currency package kept dropping, the implicit weighting of the euro and Japanese yen rose to some extent, but the Korean won was not included in the RMB reference currency package in that it just had some influence on the RMB exchange rate in the early stage of the "exchange rate reform." In general this trend is similar to that of other East Asian currencies with the exception of Japanese yen. The research of Eiji Ogawa et al. (2008) demonstrates that the U.S. dollar is still the most important external currency influencing the exchange rate of other economies since 2001, but most East Asian currencies have weakened their connections with the U.S. dollar in a progressive and minor way. What merits our attention is that the weighting of the U.S. dollar in daily changes of the RMB exchange rate has picked up significantly while the status of other leading currencies has declined since the outbreak of the global financial crisis triggered by the U.S."sub-prime mortgage crisis" in September 2008. The reasons behind this phenomenon might include:

First, there is a need to keep a generally stable exchange rate of the RMB

Table 4.3. Weight of different currencies in the implicit currency basket of RMB daily exchange rate (%)

		a_1 (U.S. Dollar)	a_2 (Euro)	a_3 (Japanese Yen)	a_4 (Korea Won)	Adjusted R^2	D.W. *Value*
2005.7.21–2006.7.21	Coefficient (%)	101.50	–3.40	0.30	1.30	0.9335	2.1173
	t-value	59.5891	–0.7240	0.1789	1.9063		
2006.7.21–2007.7.21	Coefficient (%)	91.9	–0.60	3.10	–0.20	0.9424	1.9770
	t-value	56.8414	–0.1940	1.8929	–0.6093		
2007.7.21–2008.9.15	Coefficient (%)	88.2	7.80	1.00	–0.60	0.9458	2.1211
	t-value	53.0173	2.6875	0.6477	–0.9512		
2008.9.16–2008.11.24	Coefficient (%)	99.40	5.30	–0.20	–0.20	0.9806	1.8357
	t-value	44.2653	2.0209	–0.1485	–3.6712		

against he U.S. dollar in order to avoid external shocks brought about by global financial turmoil.

Second, there is a need to guard against the fluctuation of the U.S. dollar-denominated reserve value as the monetary authority is holding a large quantity of dollar assets and is increasing the holding of the U.S. government bonds.

Third, one of the factors for the picking up of the weighting of the U.S. dollar might be the strengthening trend of the U.S. dollar exchange rate and the still solid international status of the U.S. dollar during the same period.

In addition, another possibility is that, as happened after the financial crisis in 1997, the RMB actively maintains a stable exchange rate against the U.S. dollar to stabilize the regional exchange rate environment and prevent grave consequences triggered by competitive depreciation.

We will use the related coefficient of the exchange rate of different currencies against the U.S. dollar to examine the linked relationship between the RMB and other East Asian currencies considering that our attention is on exchange rate changes but not on non-exchange rate fluctuation. At the same time, we will analyze the linked relationship by stages in consideration of the exchange rate changes of the RMB against other East Asian currencies and the changes in the external economic and financial environment.

We can see from Table 4.4 to Table 4.7 that the RMB remained highly stable in its exchange rate against the U.S. dollar and it was less correlated with the fluctuation of other East Asian currencies, while some East Asian currencies witnessed exchange rate fluctuation after the crisis in 1997 and before the reform of the RMB exchange rate. After the reform in 2005, the RMB exchange rate maintained a moderate tendency of "breaking away from U.S. dollar" during a period of two years; it also showed a fairly high frequency of volatility with other East Asian currencies, but since mid-2007 the correlations with the exchange rate changes of other East Asian currencies against the U.S. dollar decreased obviously and to a negative value in terms of its correlated coefficient with the Korean won and Thai baht, while only the related coefficient with the Singapore dollar increased in some way; at the same time, the correlations among other East Asian currencies in exchange rate changes also decreased to different extents. That might indicate that the East Asian monetary authorities adopted their exchange rate policies basically on their own under the threat of external shocks during this period. What merits our special attention is that the related coefficient of exchange rate between the RMB and other East Asian currencies dropped to a negative value when the other East Asian currencies devalued against the U.S. dollar and showed a higher degree of consistency in changes after the worsening of the global financial turmoil in September 2008. This is similar to what happened in the relationship between the RMB and other East Asian currencies during a period of time after the outbreak of the crisis in 1997. Moreover we need to emphasis that the Japanese yen and other East Asian currencies did not show stable connections during the same period, indicating that Japanese exchange rate policy was basically adopted in Japan's own way and witnessed huge and frequent fluctuations with other East Asian currencies.

The inconsistency between the RMB and other East Asian currencies in exchange rate after September 2008 has twofold implications: first, it might be the result of the fact that each adopted exchange rate policies in their own way; second, the RMB maintained a stable exchange rate against the U.S. dollar while other East Asian currencies depreciated dramatically, which means RMB is likely to serve as the "anchor" for stabilizing the regional exchange rate. If we say the stable exchange rate of the RMB against the U.S. dollar reflects the credibility of the RMB in policy, then the relatively stable exchange rate of the RMB against the U.S. dollar at the moment is the result of market choice and thus has more significance.

When it comes to the influence of RMB exchange rate changes on other East Asian currency exchange rates, we can use the above-mentioned implicit currency package to examine the relationship between the RMB exchange rate and other East Asian currencies after its exchange rate reform in 2005 by stages based on the same stages for calculating the aforementioned relevant coefficients. As the relevant coefficients of the logarithm first-order of the

Table 4.4. Relative coefficient matrix of the exchange rate of the RMB and other East Asian currencies against the U.S. Dollar between 1 July 1997 and 20 July 2005

	China	South Korea	Thailand	Malaysia	Indonesia	The Philippines	Singapore
South Korea	–0.2475						
Thailand	0.0120	0.6511					
Malaysia	–0.2124	0.5666	0.5782				
Indonesia	–0.0520	0.4987	0.5879	0.7467			
The Philippines	0.4513	0.0011	0.4927	0.4046	0.4846		
Singapore	0.0108	0.4513	0.7139	0.6041	0.6401	0.51990	
Japan	–0.0235	0.6115	0.3618	0.1244	0.3106	–0.23710	0.2642

Table 4.5. Relative coefficient matrix of the exchange rate of the RMB and other East Asian currencies against the U.S. Dollar between 21 July 2005 and 21 July 2007

	China	South Korea	Thailand	Malaysia	Indonesia	The Philippines	Singapore
South Korea	0.8142						
Thailand	0.9718	0.8660					
Malaysia	0.9267	0.8312	0.9353				
Indonesia	0.6577	0.8810	0.7391	0.6879			
The Philippines	0.93770	0.8682	0.9412	0.8749	0.8174		
Singapore	0.88170	0.9454	0.9352	0.8789	0.8599	0.9023	
Japan	–0.71570	–0.46990	–0.64270	–0.58480	–0.48220	–0.76610	–0.5057

Table 4.6. Relative coefficient matrix of the exchange rate of the RMB and other East Asian currencies against the U.S. Dollar between 21 July 2007 and 16 September 2008

	China	South Korea	Thailand	Malaysia	Indonesia	The Philippines	Singapore
South Korea	–0.8711						
Thailand	–0.6032	0.7335					
Malaysia	0.6321	–0.27340	0.0682				
Indonesia	0.0961	0.0976	–0.03520	0.2888			
The Philippines	0.09400	0.2580	0.6035	0.7191	0.0894		
Singapore	0.8836	–0.61810	–0.30870	0.8800	0.2378	0.4108	
Japan	0.7598	–0.54760	–0.20630	0.8355	0.0521	0.5021	0.8586

Table 4.7. Relative coefficient matrix of the exchange rate of the RMB and other East Asian currencies against the U.S. Dollar between 16 September 2008 and 24 November 2008

	China	South Korea	Thailand	Malaysia	Indonesia	The Philippines	Singapore
South Korea	–0.2015						
Thailand	–0.1220	0.6826					
Malaysia	–0.1995	0.9040	0.8118				
Indonesia	–0.3572	0.7354	0.8448	0.8578			
The Philippines	–0.1602	0.8937	0.8631	0.9497	0.9013		
Singapore	–0.2303	0.9460	0.7813	0.9657	0.8414	0.9567	
Japan	0.1095	–0.8998	–0.8018	–0.9053	–0.7757	–0.9308	–0.9405

exchange rate of the RMB and U.S. dollar against the Swiss franc were as high as 0.9663, 0.9723 and 0.9884 within the three stages since then, we calculated the implicit currency packages including the U.S. dollar, euro and Japanese yen and including the RMB, euro and Japanese yen in order to avoid multi-collinearity problems. The results are shown in Table 4.8 to Table 4.10.

We can draw the following two conclusions based on Tables 4.8 to 4.10:

First, when it comes to the relationship between the RMB and other East Asian currencies, the influence of the RMB on the exchange rate of other East Asian currencies is almost equal to the influence of the U.S. dollar on East Asian currencies under the circumstances that the RMB remains stable against the U.S. dollar. At the same time, noticeably, the dollar parameter significance and the

Table 4.8. Implicit weight of the U.S. Dollar, Euro, Japanese Yen and RMB in the frequent fluctuations of some East Asian currencies between 21 July 2005 and 21 July 2007

	U.S. Dollar	Euro	Japanese Yen	RMB	Adjusted R^2
Korean Won	0.54(4.15)	0.80(2.54)	0.19(1.35)		0.07
		0.84(2.70)	0.19(1.35)	0.53(4.24)	0.07
Thai Baht	0.67(14.88)	0.37(3.43)	0.29(6.01)		0.43
		0.45(4.13)	0.30(6.22)	0.62(14.40)	0.42
Malaysia Ringgit	0.80(5.16)	0.59(1.55)	0.08(0.50)		0.07
		0.61(1.64)	0.07(0.41)	0.82(5.50)	0.07
Rupiah	0.67(11.29)	0.39(2.72)	0.07(1.05)		0.25
		0.48(3.33)	0.09(1.32)	0.62(10.70)	0.24
Philippines Peso	0.84(16.56)	0.31(2.48)	0.01(0.24)		0.79
		0.40(3.22)	0.03(0.48)	0.79(16.12)	0.74
Singapore Dollar	0.60(40.21)	0.31(8.60)	0.22(13.48)		0.84
		0.39(9.92)	0.24(13.24)	0.55(34.80)	0.80

Note: Inside brackets are t-value, same as below.
Source: http://www.oanda.com

Table 4.9. **Implicit weight of the U.S. Dollar, Euro, Japanese Yen and RMB in the frequent fluctuations of some East Asian currencies between 21 July 2007 and 15 September 2008**

	U.S. Dollar	Euro	Japanese Yen	RMB	Adjusted R^2
Korean Won	0.84(7.55)	0.50(2.45)	−0.08(−0.72)		0.29
		0.60(2.93)	−0.01(−0.10)	0.81(6.70)	0.27
Thai Baht	1.02(10.16)	0.06(0.31)	−0.30(−2.97)		0.33
		0.06(0.35)	−0.27(−2.73)	1.08(10.08)	0.32
Malaysia Ringgit	0.16(5.43)	0.62(1.55)	0.11(0.50)		0.23
		0.63)3.10)	0.13(1.16)	0.64(5.31)	0.22
Rupiah	0.65(7.84)	0.54(3.60)	−0.01(−0.13)		0.34
		0.66(4.31)	0.06(0.73)	0.59(6.54)	0.31
Philippines Peso	0.86(12.36)	0.62(4.91)	−0.08(−1.22)		0.54
		0.71(5.48)	−0.02(−0.28)	0.84(10.95)	0.52
Singapore Dollar	0.61(23.17)	0.46(9.64)	−0.03(−0.95)		0.81
		0.48(9.73)	0.00(0.00)	0.63(21.72)	0.80

Note: Inside brackets are t-value, same as below.
Source: http://www.oanda.com

Table 4.10. **Implicit weight of the U.S. Dollar, Euro, Japanese Yen and RMB in the frequent fluctuations of some East Asian currencies between 16 September 2008 and 24 November 2008**

	U.S. Dollar	Euro	Japanese Yen	RMB	Adjusted R^2
Korean Won	1.35(2.66)	0.17(0.28)	−1.19(−3.34)		0.25
		0.31(0.50)	−1.05(−2.85)	1.01(1.92)	0.21
Thai Baht	0.85(7.31)	0.04(0.28)	−0.08(−0.96)		0.51
		0.02(0.15)	−0.08(−0.89)	0.83(6.86)	0.48
Malaysia Ringgit	1.07(7.00)	−0.13(−0.71)	−0.20(−1.89)		0.45
		−0.17(−0.91)	−0.22(−1.98)	1.08(6.97)	0.44
Rupiah	0.31(1.09)	0.55(1.56)	0.17(0.83)		0.05
		0.56(1.57)	0.18(0.90)	0.27(0.93)	0.05

(Cont'd)

Philippines Peso	0.97(10.53)	0.43(3.81)	−0.05(−0.82)		0.74
		0.39(3.41)	−0.07(−0.99)	0.98(10.52)	0.74
Singapore Dollar	0.75(12.79)	0.25(3.44)	−0.11(−2.76)		0.79
		0.23(2.96)	−0.12(−2.64)	0.75(11.89)	0.77

Note: Inside brackets are t-value, same as below.
Source: http://www.oanda.com

overall goodness of fit in the regression equation containing the dollar but not the RMB are generally higher than the the RMB parameter significance and the overall goodness of fit in the regression equation containing the RMB but not the dollar apart from few cases. This indicates that it is the dollar and not the RMB that is taken as the real "anchor" currency by other East Asian currencies at the current stage from the statistical perspective. In other words, the potential functions of the RMB as an "anchor" currency could only be realized by maintaining a stable relationship with the U.S. dollar.

Second, in terms of the relationship between the RMB and other East Asian currencies, the implicit weighting of the U.S. dollar in the exchange rate of other East Asian currencies shows a slightly downward trend, and the connection between other East Asian currencies and the U.S. dollar keeps weakening when there are no external shocks. But when external shocks occur, the connection between most East Asian currencies and the U.S. dollar strengthens while their exchange rate shows different changes against the dollar except in a few cases like the rupiah. In fact, since the onset of the global financial tsunami, the U.S. dollar weighting has seen different degrees of recovery in the implicit currency package of the RMB and other East Asian currencies except the rupiah.

Conditions for the RMB to become the Anchor currency

The aforementioned changing trend of the RMB exchange rate and the changes in the linked relationship between the RMB and other East Asian currencies (including the exchange rate changes of other East Asian currencies and the changes in their interlinked relationship) are of great significance in understanding the possibility and channels for the RMB to become the regional "anchor" currency.

The RMB enjoys the potential to become the regional anchor currency

Firstly, the exchange rate changes of the RMB against other East Asian currencies between 2005 and 2007 demonstrate that the position of the U.S. dollar in the realistic exchange rate of East Asian economies has fallen on the one hand under normal circumstances; on the other hand, formal cooperation in the exchange rate arrangement did not exist, but the exchange rate of East Asian currencies including the RMB (excluding the Japanese yen) still retained strong links. This means that East Asian economies did show a trend of "breaking away from the U.S. dollar" in their exchange rate and policy arrangements (refer to Ogawa and Yoshimi, 2008) on the one hand; on the other part, spontaneous demand did exist in the market in driving consistent exchange rate changes of the East Asian currencies based on the close economic links within East Asia. This demand is reflected by exchange rate changes and the dramatic rising links between other East Asian currencies and the RMB. This signifies that East Asian currencies have a demand for maintaining relatively stable relations with the RMB with the declining influence of the U.S. dollar on East Asian currencies under normal circumstances.

Secondly, the rising economic status and strength of China will also make other countries spontaneously demand a stable exchange rate against the RMB. In fact a new "triangle trade" pattern in which China imports capital goods and parts and components from other East Asian countries and then exports finished products to external markets such as the U.S. has taken shape in the East Asia region (Li Xiao et al., 2005; refer to Fig. 4.1),[3] reflecting the deepening development of the East Asian production network with China as the hub. This points to a stronger demand by other East Asian countries for a stable exchange rate against the RMB to some extent, which will add to the possibility for the RMB to become the regional "anchor" currency.

It is still difficult for the RMB to replace the U.S. dollar to be the dominate anchor currency in East Asia under the current conditions

Favorable conditions for the RMB to become the regional "anchor" currency exist as mentioned above, but apparent difficulties still exist for the RMB to spontaneously become the anchor currency in the current stage.

First, the exchange rate changes of East Asian currencies between 2007 and 2008 indicate that the consistency of exchange rate changes driven by market force spontaneously does not necessarily mean coordination in exchange rate policy within the region of East Asia and falling dependence on leading external

Fig. 4.1. The growth rate of China's exports to the U.S. and Japan and the growth rate of exports of the seven East Asian economies' to China between 1981 and 2007 (%)

Source: *IMF*, Direction of Trade Statistics.

currencies. On the one hand, countries may respond to external shocks on their own, which has resulted in a growing trend of exchange rate fluctuations and greater deviation degree of East Asian currencies. On the other hand, external turbulence may also drive East Asian countries to strengthen the connections of their currencies with the U.S. dollar (even if it is the connection at a high frequency data level) and lead to a reverse in the existing trend of "stopping pegging to the U.S. dollar." In effect, no matter if it is the market spontaneous result or an intentional policy choice, the RMB has played its role as a regional exchange rate stabilizer through maintaining a relatively stable exchange rate against the U.S. dollar.

Second, other East Asian countries will have a stronger demand for a stable exchange rate of their currencies against the RMB with the increasing pivotal role of China in the East Asian division of labor system, but this demand finally points to the U.S. dollar at the current stage. In other words, with the growing competitive pressure of China on other East Asian countries and the increasing share of China in the export of East Asian nations, we can expect to see a growing influence of the RMB on other East Asian currencies and demand from other East Asian countries for coordination with the RMB in exchange rate. But as long as the trade model whereby China imports capital goods and components and parts from East Asian countries and then exports end products to markets such as the U.S., and the structure of the regional production network, remain unchanged, the influence of the RMB exchange rate within the region will only be the "shadow" of the U.S. dollar. A more essential condition for the RMB to become the key regional currency is that China must play the role of a "market provider" in absorbing exports of regional end products, gradually replace the U.S. market to some extent, and make other East Asian countries focus more on a stable exchange rate of their currencies against the RMB. In so doing, if China cannot change the current economic growth model that depends heavily on external markets, the RMB can only play the role of a potential anchor currency through the U.S. dollar and cannot become a regional key currency independently.

In fact, China's proportion in other East Asian countries' exports of end products (end consumer goods) has indeed showed an upward trend (see Table 4-11) while the market share of the U.S. has fallen slowly in most cases. This indicates that China has some potential to become a market provider for the finished products of East Asian countries (with the signing and implementation of the free trade agreement between China and ASEAN countries, the status of China as the largest internal "market provider" in the East Asia region will be greatly improved). But we also need to note that, apart from Singapore, the proportion occupied by the U.S. in the end products exported from most East Asian countries has dropped but it is still larger than that of China. It is obvious that for China to become a regional market provider for end products is by no means something that can be realized overnight, which means the currencies of most East Asian countries including China might still need to maintain relatively close links with the U.S. dollar for quite some time.

Preparations for the RMB to Become the anchor currency

First, considering China's economic development trend and its economic ties with the rest of East Asia at the current stage and for quite some time going forward, China needs to take into account regional cooperation on the RMB exchange rate policy if it seeks to make the RMB the regional "anchor" currency. Within the context that the real economy of East Asia countries is inter-linked, economic integration keeps increasing and the Chinese economy plays an ever more important role, any moves in RMB exchange rate policy would have a

Table 4.11. Changes of the share of exports of East Asian end products[1] to China and the U.S. (%)

Exporter	Importer							
	China				The U.S.			
	1995	1999	2003	2007	1995	1999	2003	2007
Japan	2.09	0.90	2.38	3.84	42.08	47.78	43.92	37.67
South Korea	2.21	2.63	4.14	5.20	24.09	30.29	36.62	22.59
Singapore	1.46	3.08	4.57	9.34	14.14	16.43	14.37	8.62
The Philippines	0.78	0.70	1.99	1.04	47.08	57.04	47.89	41.97
Thailand	2.72	1.43	1.77	2.72	20.84	30.97	27.69	20.83
Malaysia	0.89	0.59	1.22	2.05	25.64	28.25	26.42	18.92
Indonesia	0.72	1.47	0.91	1.72	25.03	29.97	31.85	33.62

Notes: 1. End products in the statistics here include consumer goods and products with the BEC code : 112, 122, 51, 522, 61, 62 and 63;
2. Given the shortage of the data for the Philippines for 1995, we input the data for 1996 instead so as to observe the changing trend.

Source: *UN Commodity Trade Statistics Database.*

significant impact on the East Asia region. In contrast, the economic development of East Asia and the trend of other East Asian economies' currencies and exchange rate policies will inevitably rein in China's decisions on exchange rate policy. Thus the Chinese government must take into consideration the regional background and its due responsibilities in adopting the RMB exchange rate policy and any "unilateral" adjustment, such as the implementation of free floating, will bring about greater risks for both China and the rest of the East Asian economies.

Specifically, considering regional factors in RMB exchange rate policy at the current stage, two approaches can be taken. One is to realize some degree of joint action with other East Asian currencies and the other is to gradually become the regional exchange rate stabilizer through maintaining a relatively stable exchange rate with the U.S. dollar. The RMB can make a choice between the two approaches in line with the changes in specific economic environment and external conditions. For example, between 2005 and 2007, the RMB maintained consistency of exchange rate changes against the U.S. dollar and other East Asian currencies but it also maintained a relatively stable exchange rate against the U.S. dollar while facing external financial turmoil and the depreciation of other East Asian currencies.

Second, when it comes to the exchange rate arrangement and adjustment of the RMB against the U.S. dollar, it is inadvisable to either recover the absolutely stable exchange rate against the U.S. dollar or to dramatically adjust the exchange rate against the dollar at the current stage. The former action will not help to meet the China's requirements for adjusting the exchange rate for the purpose of internal balance, and the latter action will interrupt China's connections both within the region and outside the region, and weaken the RMB's influence on other currencies of the region. In this sense an important strategic choice for RMB exchange rate policy and regionalization should be maintaining an adjustable and relatively stable exchange rate against the U.S. dollar for some time in the future. Of course, this relatively stable exchange rate and adjustment must take into consideration changes in the economic environment both inside and outside the region and the appeals of other economies in exchange rate policy.

In short, the characteristics of the East Asian division of labor network and the foreign economic and trade relation model have determined that East Asian countries need some degree of exchange rate stability under external impact. At the moment, this spontaneous exchange rate stability demand is in nature taking the U.S. dollar as the ultimate goal. But the RMB naturally has some indirect influence on the exchange rate of other East Asian currencies given that it is closely linked with the U.S. dollar in high frequency of exchange rate fluctuations; at the same time, the close trade and industrial ties between China and other East Asian economies also call for a relatively stable exchange rate of the RMB against the U.S. dollar within a certain period of time. Furthermore, the credibility of the RMB will be greatly improved if it can maintain stability amid the current financial turbulence. In this context a relatively stable exchange rate of the RMB against the U.S. dollar could help the RMB to be accepted as the "anchor" currency by the market over time against the background of lacking an institutionalized exchange rate coordination mechanism.

As mentioned before, whether the RMB can finally shake off the influence of the U.S. dollar and become the "anchor" currency in East Asia depends in the final analysis on whether China can replace the U.S. to become a market provider for regional end products. It is possible given the current development landscape, but it will be a long process as it relies on a continuous and steady growth of the Chinese economy, rapid increase of national income, and the transformation of the economic growth pattern.

Promoting the RMB to Become a Regional Leading Currency through Regional Monetary and Exchange Rate Cooperation

Apart from creating the conditions to encourage East Asian economies to spontaneously take the RMB as the "anchor" currency, becoming actively involve in and effectively leveraging on the framework for regional monetary and exchange rate cooperation will also boost RMB regionalization. This can be discussed from the two perspectives of non-exchange rate cooperation and exchange rate cooperation.

Facilitating Regional Monetary and Financial Cooperation from the Perspective of Non-exchange Rate Cooperation

Actively Carry out Currency Swap and Promote Official Use of the RMB

In the context of the current global financial turbulence, East Asia has started a new wave of the signing of bilateral currency swap agreements and the multilateralization of the CMI has been initially launched. Being active in currency swap and domestic currency swap arrangements in particular will not only create an enabling international environment for RMB regionalization and further expanding its influence but also boost the application of the RMB by other East Asian monetary authorities in official trading, which will help the RMB to become a reserve currency. As things stand, some neighboring countries such as Cambodia, the Philippines and Nepal have already taken the RMB as their official reserve currency or one of the freely convertible currencies of their central banks. Considering the close and strengthening economic links between China and other East Asian economies, currency swap arrangements are destined to improve the enthusiasm of other economies to settle for the RMB as their official reserve currency.

In effect, this initiative is well underway. By the end of 2008 China had inked some currency swap agreements with some East Asian countries and regions as part of the regional currency and financial cooperation strategy. As of December 2008, Mainland China had signed currency swap agreements with the central banks and monetary authorities of the Hong Kong Special Administrative Region, South Korea, Malaysia, Indonesia, Belarus and Argentina with a total value of RMB650 billion (see Table 4.12), about 5 per cent of China's total foreign exchange reserves. In the meantime the PBOC is holding discussions about reaching bilateral currency swap agreements with the central banks of other countries with similar demands.

The currency swap agreements signed by China in this round have two obvious characteristics. First, they lay emphasis on coordinating the implementation of RMB regionalization strategy i.e. to follow the path through neighboring countries to the rest of the world; second, the effects of these agreements are different. For instance, the swap agreements signed with South Korea, Malaysia and Indonesia are mainly for the convenience of mutual investment and trade settlement, the agreement reached with Argentina is to realize the functions of the RMB serving as a currency for trade payment and settlement, and the one inked with Belarus is to take the RMB as a reserve currency. It is evident that the measures adopted by the Chinese monetary authority to press ahead with RMB internationalization have been directional from the very beginning and the currency swap agreements signed with other East Asian economies are undoubtedly the most important ones. Four of the six agreements were reached with East Asian economies, accounting for 86.2 per cent of the total value. This demonstrates to some extent that East Asia still represents a priority for China to advance currency swap arrangements. There is no doubt that expanding the scope and scale of RMB swap arrangements on this basis has a positive significance.

Strengthening regional oversight cooperation and controlling risks in RMB regionalization

RMB regionalization inevitably signifies RMB transnational circulation and transaction and the internationalization of Chinese financial institutions and financial market. This will bring more international risks to domestic financial institutions and the RMB transaction network. It is far from enough to fend off these risks only by enhancing domestic financial supervision and regulation.

Table 4.12. Currency swap agreements signed by China since the end of 2008

Date	Swap Partner	Scale (RMB100 Million)
12 December 2008	South Korea	1,800
20 January 2009	Hong Kong	2,000
8 February 2009	Malaysia	800
11 March 2009	Belarus	200
24 March 2009	Indonesia	1,000
29 March 2009	Argentina	700

Source: http: / /www.sina.com.cn, 02-04-2009.

It is necessary to reinforce international cooperation in financial oversight and regulation in order to further improve China's capacity to deal with international risks.

On top of that, as RMB regionalization deepens, the externality of RMB currency and exchange rate policies will keep increasing. This calls for the coordination of possible conflicts in policy targets between China and other East Asian economies so as to make the RMB better able to take on responsibilities as a regional currency. Specifically speaking, we can take into consideration the following two aspects to strengthen regional cooperation in financial oversight and regulation:

First, facilitating the establishment of bilateral and even regional economic cooperation organizations. At the bilateral cooperation level, leveraging on and further expanding Chinese supervision authority to sign bilateral memorandums of supervision cooperation with the financial watchdogs of other East Asian countries and regions, and further capitalizing on bilateral economic partnership agreements within the region to carry out cooperation in oversight and regulation. At the regional level the most important thing is to take advantage of the currently established East Asian economic monitoring mechanism and extend it to financial oversight cooperation, and utilize the CMI and ABMI frameworks to phase in institutionalized regional financial oversight cooperation arrangements while moving forward with regional reserve cooperation and regional bond market establishment.

Second, active involvment in and fulfillment of international agreements on financial supervision, such as the New Basle Capital Accord, Core Principles for Effective Banking Supervision and relevant regulations of the WTO that are highly relevant for boosting regional cooperation in financial supervision and improving the internationalization level of China's financial oversight.

Engaging in Regional Financial Market Setup and Creating the Conditions for Regional Circulation of RMB Assets

At the moment, East Asian countries and regions are actively working to build a regional financial market and a regional bond market in particular. Being active in this process is of great importance to promoting the regional circulation of RMB assets and facilitating the RMB to play the function of regional investment currency. While developing the bond market denominated by international currencies such as the U.S. dollar, China needs to gradually create the conditions to establish a bond market denominated in the currencies of the region, especially the RMB or the currency package containing the RMB.

This will also help reduce risks in liquidity, exchange rate and fundamentals faced by other East Asian economies when using the RMB for trade settlement or taking the RMB as a reserve currency.

The path for the RMB to engage in regional exchange rate cooperation

Actively engaging in regional cooperation at the non-exchange rate level is of great significance to the RMB in playing the functions of the regional settlement currency, investment currency and reserve currency, but institutionalized exchange rate cooperation is more important for the RMB to become the regional leading currency and the "anchor" currency for exchange rate arrangements. As mentioned above, conditions are not mature for institutionalized exchange rate cooperation throughout East Asia in the current conditions. That said, China enjoys the conditions to progressively carry out exchange rate cooperation at different levels by starting from regional cooperation in line with the closeness of trade and investment ties with neighboring economies and the impact of the exchange rate on trade and investment. We conclude from Table 4.13 that the order in which China should establish exchange rate cooperation arrangements with neighboring economies is: first, implement institutionalized exchange rate cooperation with economies that have close links with China in trade and investment and that are vulnerable to exchange rate impact; second, build up a partnership with economies that have close connections with China but suffer little from exchange rate shocks; and last, establish connections with economies that have general connections with China and feel little impact from exchange rate shocks. That is the order of 1 → 2 → 3 → 4 in Table 4.13.

The objectives in considering cooperation on exchange rate are the major East Asian economies, specifically Chinese Hong Kong, Macao, Taiwan, Japan, South Korea, Singapore, Malaysia, the Philippines and Thailand. Considering the currently limited quota and scope of Mainland China's foreign investment, we settle for the investment propensity of East Asian countries and regions to China for measuring their investment contacts. This is specifically represented by the ratio of the share of East Asian economies' investment in Mainland China to the proportion of their GDP in the world total, reflecting that the share of their investment in China in the total output value is higher than the world

Table 4.13. Relations between two economies and the impact of exchange rate shocks

		Impact of Exchange Rate Shocks	
		Small	Large
Bilateral Trade or Investment Relations	General	4	3
	Close	2	1

Source: http: / / www.sina.com.cn, 02-04-2009.

average level. See Table 4.14 for specifics.

Within the context that heuristics indicators for evaluating the implications of exchange rate shocks for trade and investment cannot be found, we build the model from long-term and short-term perspectives and take the implications for trade and investment when the exchange rate fluctuates at 1 per cent as the evaluation indicator by referring to the exchange rate parameters in the model.

Table 4.14. The investment propensity of East Asian economies in China in 2005

Countries or Regions	Investment in China (RMB100 Million)	GDP (RMB100 Million)	Investment Propensity in China
The World	603.25	447954.5	1
Hong Kong	179.49	1777.83	74.97
Macau	6	115.79	38.48
Taiwan	21.52	3559.58	4.49
Japan	65.3	45339.65	1.07
South Korea	51.68	7914.27	4.85
Singapore	22.04	1166.93	14.03
Malaysia	3.61	1307.7	2.05
The Philippines	1.89	983.66	1.43
Thailand	0.96	1762.22	0.4

Source: Calculated from the data released on the website of Invest in China.

Long-term Model

In the long run, we observe that there is a rather stable relationship between the export (or investment) and GDP, and relative exchange rate fluctuation of two countries or regions. We have simplified the export (or investment) model for analysis convenience and it can be represented by the following equation from a national perspective:

$$EX_t = \gamma \cdot \mathrm{GDP}_{Ft}^{\alpha} \cdot exp\{ ß \cdot V_t \} \quad (4\text{–}2)$$

$$IM_t = \gamma \cdot \mathrm{GDP}_{Dt}^{\alpha} \cdot exp\{ ß \cdot V_t \} \quad (4\text{–}3)$$

$$\mathrm{FDI}_t = \gamma \cdot \mathrm{GDP}_{Dt}^{\alpha} \cdot exp\{ ß \cdot V_t \} \quad (4\text{–}4)$$

$$V_t = \frac{RATE_t - RATE_t{-}1}{RATE_t{-}1} \times 100 \quad (4\text{–}5)$$

In the equation, GDP_D and GDP_F refer to domestic and foreign GDP respectively, EX and IM represent domestic export to foreign countries and domestic import from foreign countries respectively, FDI represents foreign investment in the country, RATE refers to the relative exchange rate of the two countries and V refers to the exchange rate fluctuations of the two countries.

In order to build a model for the relationship between trade (or investment), GDP and exchange rate fluctuation of China and the rest of the East Asian economies, we adjusted the indicators for China and the other nine East Asian economies and determined to build the model with China's export logarithm ln(EX), China's import logarithm ln(IM), China's attracted investment logarithm ln(FDI), China's GDP logarithm $\ln(\mathrm{GDP}_D)$, other economies' GDP logarithm $\ln(\mathrm{GDP}_F)$ and the exchange rate fluctuation ratio of two countries V 6. The exchange rate fluctuation ratio of two countries is calculated by converting one unit of RMB into foreign currencies. The sample interval is between the first quarter of 2003 and the third quarter of 2007 (the time interval of several indicators of the economies is shortened properly based on data availability), the exchange rate fluctuation ratio is the mean value of the first quarter, and unit root test is carried out for indicators sequence and the first-order sequence respectively to judge the stability of the data, see Table 4.15 and Table 4.16 for specific data.

Through the unit root test we conclude that, at the 1% significance level, major indicators for all economies are non-stationary sequence and the first-order difference sequence is stationary and can be judged as first-order single sequence. In order to judge the co-integration relationship of all indicators, we build the following regression equation based on long-term relations:

Table 4.15. Unit root test of the index sequence for East Asian economies

	ln(*EX*)	ln(*IM*)	ln(FDI)	*V*	GDP
Hong Kong	–2.40092 (0.1576)	p–3.578099 (0.0176)	–3.28743 (0.0447)	–1.58428 (0.4697)	–2.53684 (0.127)
Macao	–1.24156 (0.6269)	–0.64788 (0.8359)	–2.94719 (0.0744)	–1.58428 (0.4697)	0.047332 (0.9482)
Taiwan	–1.07924 (0.6827)	–0.02591 (0.9357)	–3.36609 (0.0398)	–3.73735 (0.0127)	p–1.161367 (0.6669)
Japan	p–6.620921 (0)	p–1.732957 (0.3991)	–0.85196 (0.7582)	–3.12964 (0.0433)	–2.51257 (0.1299)
South Korea	–1.11863 (0.674)	–2.64387 (0.1138)	–3.57293 (0.0322)	–3.75117 (0.0131)	p–0.122766 (0.9178)
Singapore	0.0306 (0.9421)	–2.85871 (0.0819)	–3.05275 (0.0671)	–4.76958 (0.0018)	p–0.281686 (0.9549)
Malaysia	–1.52928 (0.4824)	p0.303734 (0.9691)	–3.80294 (0.0207)	–6.6689 (0)	0.753732 (0.9814)
The Philippines	p–1.149515 (0.6641)	–1.45639 (0.5167)	–3.61453 (0.027)	–1.39289 (0.5592)	–0.46445 (0.8314)
Thailand	–1.54527 (0.4824)	0.991753 (0.9923)	–3.66514 (0.0254)	–1.22529 (0.636)	–0.80468 (0.7519)
Mainland China					p–2.49962 (0.1318)

Note: The default is the ADF test value, the figure with p in front of it represents the Phillips–Perron test value, and the numerical value inside the bracket is the probability of rejecting the null hypothesis.

Source: Calculated from the data released on the websites of Hong Kong Census and Statistics Department, Macao Statistics and Census Service, Japan Statistics Bureau, the Ministry of Commerce of the People's Republic of China and ASEAN.

Table 4.16. Unit root test of the first-order difference of index sequence for East Asian economies

	$\Delta\ln(EX)$	$\Delta\ln(IM)$	$\Delta\ln(\text{FDI})$	ΔV	ΔGDP
Hong Kong	–15.6414 (0)	p–7.252656 (0)	–6.28138 (0.001)	–6.57363 (0.0001)	–10.7561 (0)
Macao	–7.5749 (0)	–4.91423 (0.0013)	–3.82698 (0.0017)	–6.57363 (0.0001)	–5.84978 (0.0003)
Taiwan	–5.86868 (0.0009)	–5.74778 (0.0047)	–4.46708 (0.0006)	–4.14591 (0.0078)	p–10.76506 (0)
Japan	p–4.780615 (0.0017)	p–6.254579 (0.0001)	–3.26268 (0.0047)	–5.32079 (0.0007)	–3.58691 (0.0014)
South Korea	–7.61186 (0)	–6.01315 (0.0007)	–5.23287 (0.0047)	–4.75342 (0.002)	p–3.354346 (0.0479)
Singapore	–6.33803 (0.0005)	–6.52069 (0.0018)	–4.47229 (0.0007)	–5.4986 (0.0005)	p–5.414906 (0.0077)
Malaysia	–13.8633 (0)	p–4.30801 (0.0065)	–4.44971 (0.0096)	–6.14531 (0)	–3.94085 (0.04)
The Philippines	p–8.479453 (0)	–6.16821 (0.0006)	–4.47618 (0.0093)	–9.92477 (0)	–5.48667 (0.0072)
Thailand	–2.93577 (0.0068)	–5.42198 (0.0022)	–3.97397 (0.0016)	–7.33297 (0)	–6.89883 (0.0042)
Mainland China					p–14.11544 (0)

Note: The default is the ADF test value, the figure with p in front of it represents the Phillips-Perron test value, and the numerical value inside the bracket is the probability of rejecting the null hypothesis.

Source: Calculated from the data released on the websites of the Ministry of Commerce of the People's Repubilc of China and ASEAN.

Export equation:

$$\text{In}(EX_t) = c_0 + c_1 \cdot \text{In}(\text{GDP}_{Ft}) + k_1 \cdot V_t + \mu_t \tag{4–6}$$

Import equation:

$$\text{In}(IM_t) = c_0 + c_1 \cdot \text{In}(\text{GDP}_{Dt}) + k_1 \cdot V_t + \mu_t \tag{4–7}$$

Investment equation:

$$\text{In}(\text{FDI}_t) = c_0 + c_1 \cdot \text{In}(\text{GDP}_{Dt}) + k_1 \cdot V_t + \mu_t \tag{4–8}$$

After estimating above equations, we conclude the parameter estimated value and the residual error sequence of the export, import and investment equations of the economies $\hat{\mu}_t$. Unit root test is carried out for the residual error sequence of the equations. We can see from the conclusion of Table 4.17 that the residual error sequence of most equations rejects the null hypothesis at the 1% significance level, and the residual error sequence of all equations rejects the null hypothesis at the 5% significance level, thus we can confirm that μ_t is the stationary sequence, there are con-integration relations between indicators of the three equations for all economies, and can build an error correction model.

Table 4.17. Unit root test of regression equation residual and the estimated value of exchange rate fluctuation parameter

	Export Equation		Import Equation		Investment Equation	
Countries or Regions	Unit Root Test Value of Residual	Coefficient k_1	Unit Root Test Value of Residual	Coefficient k_1	Unit Root Test Value of Residual	Coefficient k_1
Hong Kong	–4.71368 (0.0022)	0.039387 [1.31602]	p–3.20904 (0.003)	–0.04685 [–1.0546]	–3.88814 (0.0013)	–0.00229 [–0.055]
Macau	–3.79256 (0.0009)	0.090955 [1.57129]	–2.68016 (0.0105)	0.210217 [1.73313]	–3.63101 (0.0024)	0.136913 [1.2176]
Taiwan	p–5.36414 (0.0009)	0.021883 [0.93281]	p–2.73983 (0.01)	0.006832 [0.49066]	–3.01673 (0.0068)	–0.05415 [–1.8643]
Japan	–4.77226 (0.0083)	0.031146 [3.00567]	–2.95216 (0.0061)	0.01266 [1.51252]	–3.29633 (0.004)	0.078584 [2.26483]
South Korea	–5.12569 (0.0002)	0.01146 [2.09873]	p–3.03642 (0.0053)	0.011429 [1.15604]	–3.0361 (0.007)	–0.04717 [–1.0502]
Singapore	–3.22233 (0.0072)	–0.00082 [–0.0902]	–3.02173 (0.0054)	0.001041 [0.09261]	–3.60995 (0.0022)	0.058393 [1.91626]
Malaysia	–2.58224 (0.0196)	0.030176 [3.36359]	p–2.98079 (0.0059)	0.016065 [0.77023]	–3.34442 (0.0037)	–0.10987 [–1.9504]
The Philippines	–2.77069 (0.0132)	0.028854 [3.74377]	p–3.31906 (0.0029)	–0.0127 [–0.626]	–3.04231 (0.0064)	–0.01909 [–0.7515]
Thailand	–2.57131 (0.02)	0.01765 [0.78706]	p–3.18609 (0.0038)	–0.01796 [–1.3655]	4.31626 (0.0006)	0.037982 [0.58229]

Note: the default is the ADF test value, the figure with p in front of it represents the Phillips-Perron test value, the numerical value inside the bracket "( )" is the probability of rejecting the null hypothesis, and the data inside bracket "[ ]" is the t-value.

As all indicators meet the first-order stationary, we build a first-order difference error correction model for each economy, and make error correction term $ecm_t = \hat{\mu}_t$. The specific form is:

Export equation:

$$\Delta \ln(EX_t) = b_0 + b_1 \cdot \Delta \ln(GDP_{Ft}) + k_2 \cdot \Delta V_t + \lambda \cdot ecm_{t-1} + \varepsilon_t \qquad (4\text{–}9)$$

Import equation:

$$\Delta \ln(IM_t) = b_0 + b_1 \cdot \Delta \ln(GDP_{Dt}) + k_2 \cdot \Delta V_t + \lambda \cdot ecm_{t-1} + \varepsilon_t \qquad (4\text{–}10)$$

Investment equation:

$$\Delta \ln(FDI_t) = b_0 + b_1 \cdot \Delta \ln(GDP_{Dt}) + k_2 \cdot \Delta V_t + \lambda \cdot ecm_{t-1} + \varepsilon_t \qquad (4\text{–}11)$$

After estimating the above equations, we conclude the estimated value and significance level of all parameters. We especially focus on the adjusted R^2 of the overall significance indicators of equations, coefficient k_2 of exchange rate fluctuation difference and error correction term coefficient λ, refer to Table 4.18 for specific evaluation results.

For the long-lasting balanced error correction model, when exchange rate fluctuation is 1% at stage t–2, the implications for export, import and investment at stage t is $\lambda \cdot (k_2 - k_1)$, and the specific percentage is calculated with the data of the third quarter of 2007, see Table 4.19 for the results.

Short-term model

The long-term model is featured by containing more variables and long time slot for examination, but the estimated results of the model might be affected as variables are incomplete and the data are difficult to be accessed. Therefore we again build a *V*AR model of export, import, investment and exchange rate fluctuation to evaluate the impact of short-term exchange rate shocks on variables.

We select Chinese export logarithm ln(EX), Chinese import logarithm ln(IM), China's attracted investment logarithm ln(FDI) and the exchange rate fluctuation ratio of two countries V to build the *V*AR model. The specific form of the model is:

Table 4.18. Estimated value of parameters of the Error Correction Model

Countries or Regions	Export Equation			Import Equation			Investment Equation		
	Coefficient k_2	Coefficient λ	$\overline{R}^2$	Coefficient k_2	Coefficient λ	$\overline{R}^2$	Coefficient k_2	Coefficient λ	$\overline{R}^2$
Hong Kong	0.058265 [3.2735]	−2.13785 [−7.4332]	0.8657	−0.00298 [−0.0577]	−0.80572 [−3.177]	0.601	−0.00513 [−0.16]	−1.39161 [−3.315]	0.9083
Macau	0.083193 [1.3798]	−1.10723 [−4.4838]	0.5459	−0.00934 [−0.111]	−0.15715 [−0.799]	0.0408	0.214016 [2.5196]	−1.32881 [−3.371]	0.6008
Taiwan	0.02248 [2.2382]	−0.52458 [−2.0619]	0.4272	0.009863 [1.223]	−0.1871 [−0.5]	0.4744	−0.05418 [−2.315]	−0.62403 [−2.13]	0.6737
Japan	0.003343 [1.3118]	−0.08727 [−1.4624]	0.6662	0.002821 [1.0478]	−0.10239 [−0.9516]	0.759	0.056888 [1.4583]	−0.59448 [−1.036]	0.1097
South Korea	0.009572 [2.44]	−1.67832 [−4.5609]	0.7274	0.01036 [2.5638]	−0.07102 [−0.398]	0.4909	−0.7715 [−2.564]	−0.77289 [−2.089]	0.5263
Singapore	−0.00752 [−1.706]	−1.34644 [−5.1754]	0.9437	0.006291 [0.8955]	−0.42592 [−1.8054]	0.6043	0.081142 [2.4813]	−1.0701 [−3.141]	0.6702
Malaysia	0.037071 [6.1452]	−0.98227 [−2.3603]	0.9531	0.032526 [3.4912]	−0.17313 [−0.676]	0.6841	−0.13144 [−3.157]	−1.30144 [−3.244]	0.7353
The Philippines	0.030594 [4.562]	−1.04451 [−1.8103]	0.738	0.002546 [0.5361]	−0.07992 [−0.526]	0.2507	−0.01315 [−0.807]	−1.04462 [−2.732]	0.5398
Thailand	0.033243 [1.3868]	−0.59262 [−1.0297]	0.4781	0.005789 [0.916]	−0.16064 [−0.63]	−0.277	0.013115 [0.2103]	−1.36299 [−3.862]	0.6087

Table 4.19. Influence of exchange rate fluctuation based on Error Correction Model

Countries or Regions	$\lambda \cdot (k_2 - k_1)$			Percentage of Influence (%)			
	Export Equation	Import Equation	Investment Equation	EX	IM	EX+IM	FDI
Hong Kong	–0.04036	–0.03535	0.00395	4.12	3.6	7.72	0.4
Macao	0.00859	0.0345	–0.10246	0.86	3.51	4.37	10.79
Taiwan	–0.00031	0.00057	0.00002	0.03	0.06	0.09	0
Japan	0.00243	0.00101	0.0129	0.24	0.1	0.34	1.3
South Korea	0.00317	0.00008	0.02317	0.32	0.01	0.33	2.34
Singapore	0.00902	–0.00224	–0.02434	0.91	0.22	1.13	2.46
Malaysia	–0.00677	–0.00285	0.02807	0.68	0.29	0.97	2.85
The Philippines	–0.00182	–0.00122	–0.00621	0.18	0.12	0.3	0.62
Thailand	–0.00924	–0.00381	0.03389	0.93	0.38	1.31	3.45

Note: The percentage of the influence of exchange rate on variables is absolute value.

Trade Model:

$$\begin{cases} \text{In}(\text{EX}_t) = c_1 + \sum a_i \bullet \text{In}(EX_{t-i}) + \sum b_i \bullet \text{In}(IM_{t-i}) + \sum k_i \bullet V_{t-i} + \varepsilon_{1t} \\ \text{In}(\text{IM}_t) = c_2 + \sum d_i \bullet \text{In}(EX_{t-i}) + \sum e_i \bullet \text{In}(IM_{t-i}) + \sum m_i \bullet V_{t-i} + \varepsilon_{2t} \\ V_t = c_3 + \sum p_i \bullet \text{In}(EX_{t-i}) + \sum q_i \bullet \text{In}(IM_{t-i}) + \sum r_i \bullet V_{t-i} + \varepsilon_{3t} \end{cases} \quad (4\text{–}12)$$

Investment Model:

$$\begin{cases} \text{In}(\text{FDI}_t) = c1 + \sum ai \bullet \text{In}(\text{FDI}_{t-i}) + \sum hi \bullet Vt\text{-}i + \varepsilon_{1t} \\ Vt = c_2 + \sum b_i \bullet \text{In}(\text{FDI}_{t-i}) + \sum s_i \bullet V_{t-i} + \varepsilon_{2t} \end{cases} \quad (4\text{–}13$$

The sampling interval of indicators is between January 2003 and September 2007 (the interval of FDI data is between January 2005 and September 2007) and the exchange rate fluctuation ratio is the average value of one month. We make a seasonal adjustment of the data of indicators ln(EX) and ln(IM) with the X12 software package of the Census Bureau of the U.S. Department of Commerce, use the TRAMO/SEATS method to eliminate the influence of seasonal factors in ln(FDI), and conclude a stationary time sequence. While building the *VAR* model we carried out unit root test to ensure the overall stability of the model and made a Johansen co-integration test to determine the co-integration relationship between variables and to guarantee the effectiveness of the analysis of the *VAR* model. We follow through the minimum principle of AIC criterion and SC criterion to confirm the lag order. We ultimately conclude the *VAR* model of the nine East Asian economies and we focus on the overall effects and exchange rate fluctuation ratio first-order lag order of the trade model and investment model. Table 4.20 shows that the logarithm natural function value of the trade model is bigger while the logarithm natural function value of the investment model is smaller, which demonstrates that the fitting effect of the trade model is better and the significance level is high.

The exchange rate at stage *t*-1 of the trade model and the investment model fluctuates at 1% and its influence on the export, import and investment at stage *t* are k_1, m_1 and h_1 respectively. The specific influence is calculated with the data of September of 2009. See Table 4.21.

Table 4.20. Estimated value of parameters of the VAR model

Countries or Regions	Trade Model			Investment Model	
	k_1	m_1	Likelihood Function Value	h_1	Logarithm Likelihood Function
Hong Kong	0.012069 [0.47729]	–0.01718 [–0.33948]	172.6627	0.136615 [2.10319]	32.62012
Macao	0.002225 [0.04472]	–0.00533 [–0.04489]	63.3089	0.288339 [2.41200]	–2.21212
Taiwan	–0.00754 [–0.71439]	–0.00719 [–0.98802]	53.21393	–0.11512 [–3.18421]	–44.404
Japan	0.009524 [2.14396]	0.001769 [0.44102]	40.814	0.013377 [0.82962]	–56.5984
South Korea	–0.006 [–1.10785]	–0.00523 [–1.53063]	64.88169	0.007646 [0.25132]	–67.5161
Singapore	0.000902 [0.05907]	4.87E–05 [0.00498]	54.57155	0.081184 [1.60692]	–43.509
Malaysia	–0.01207 [–0.80908]	–0.00127 [–0.10187]	83.9455	–0.12313 [–1.12904]	–50.2771
The Philippines	0.007441 [0.94490]	–0.01008 [–1.42155]	64.03855	–0.04794 [–1.37240]	–68.2755
Thailand	–0.00033 [–0.04125]	0.000254 [0.05752]	42.55577	–0.006 [–0.09654]	–91.2475

Note: The data inside brackets "[ ]" are *t*–value.

Comprehensive analysis

Through the above analysis we can conclude the influence of the trade intensity, investment orientation and exchange rate shocks of the nine East Asian leading economies and China on trade and investment. Putting the above data into Table 4.15 can obtain the path choice of China in exchange rate cooperation

Table 4.21. Influence of exchange rate fluctuation based on the VAR model

Countries or Regions	Country or Region Percentage of Influence (%)			
	EX	IM	EX+IM	FDI
Hong Kong	1.21	1.73	2.94	14.64
Macao	0.22	0.53	0.75	33.42
Taiwan	0.76	0.72	1.48	12.2
Japan	0.96	0.18	1.14	1.35
South Korea	0.6	0.52	1.12	0.77
Singapore	0.09	0	0.09	8.46
Malaysia	1.21	0.13	1.34	13.1
The Philippines	0.75	1.01	1.76	4.91
Thailand	0.03	0.03	0.06	0.6

Note: The percentage of the influence of exchange rate fluctuation is absolute value.

with East Asian economies during its reform of the exchange rate. According to the table of exchange rate fluctuation influence calculated from the long-term model (error correction model) and the short-term model (*VAR* model), we can respectively conclude the path choice for currency cooperation determined by trade and investment. See Table 4.22 and Table 4.23 for specifics.

We observe on the basis of analyzing the above two tables that the path for exchange rate cooperation between China and the major East Asian economies can be divided into four stages:

The first stage is to carry out exchange rate cooperation with Chinese Hong Kong and Taiwan and build a "Chinese currency circle." Chinese Hong Kong and

Table 4.22. Development direction for exchange rate cooperation (Long-term model)

		Impact of Exchange Rate Shocks	
		Small	Large
Bilateral Trade or Investment Relations	General	Singapore, Malaysia, Thailand	-
	Close	Chinese Taiwan, Japan, South Korea, The Philippines	Hong Kong, Macao

		Impact of Exchange Rate Shocks	
		Small	Large
Bilateral Investment Relations	General	Japan, The Philippines	-
	Close	Hong Kong, Taiwan	Macao, South Korea, Singapore

Table 4.23. Development direction for exchange rate cooperation (Short-term model)

		Impact of Exchange Rate Shocks	
		Small	Large
Bilateral Trade or Investment Relations	General	Singapore, Malaysia, Thailand	-
	Close	Macao, Taiwan, Japan, South Korea, The Philippines	Hong Kong

		Impact of Exchange Rate Shocks	
		Small	Large
Bilateral Investment Relations	General	Japan, Thailand	Malaysia, The Philippines
	Close	South Korea	Hong Kong, Macao, Taiwan, Singapore

Macao have maintained close links with Mainland China in trade and investment. They are China's special administrative regions and enjoy the favorable conditions in economy, politics and culture that are necessary for exchange rate cooperation.

The second stage is to engage in exchange rate cooperation with South Korea and Chinese Taiwan based on the first stage and build the pan China currency rim. Both the Mainland and Taiwan are part of one China and have close trade and investment links. They will enjoy strong potentials for exchange rate cooperation after reaching common ground in politics. South Korea has a similar cultural background with China and both China and South Korea are at the same development level. On top of that, South Korea has a close economic and trade ties with China and is one of the closest foreign partners of China.

The third stage is to cooperate with Japan, Singapore and the Philippines in currency based on the first two stages and establish regional monetary cooperation led by China and Japan. The cooperation between China and Japan in exchange rate will be a major breakthrough in the development of an exchange rate cooperation mechanism for East Asia at a time when neither country as the most influential powers in East Asia can establish a regional leading currency in East Asia alone.

The fourth stage is to carry out cooperation with Malaysia and Thailand based on the third stage, strengthen currency coalition with the ASEAN and gradually set up an integrated monetary cooperation system in East Asia. ASEAN countries are key trade and investment partners of China and Japan alike. Enhancing monetary cooperation with ASEAN serves the long-term interests of both China and Japan and contributes to the consolidation of their relationship in currency coordination.

Reform and Restructuring of China's Economic and Financial System

RMB regionalization is by no means the process of waiting for other East Asian economies to spontaneously accept the RMB as the "anchor" currency for settlement, investment and reserve, and cannot be realized only through advancing institutionalized regional currency and financial cooperation. China needs to restructure its trade and economy while ensuring fast economic growth as it seeks to make the RMB take on responsibilities as a regionalized currency in the real sense. In addition, China also needs to adopt strong measures to boost domestic demand, gradually open up the domestic market, drive the reform of the financial sector and relax controls over the capital account in an active, prudent and progressive manner.

Trade and economic restructuring

Comparisons of the trade structure of China, Japan and the U.S.

China and Japan represent the two most influential countries in East Asian monetary cooperation. The analysis of the status as the market provider for end products demonstrates that China and Japan differ little in strength but vastly in trade structure. We can see from Table 4.24 that China's trade structure has remained basically unchanged since the 1990s and it shows only a moderately changing trend. China still imports semi-finished product and exports end products[4] in general. But Japan has restructured its trade as of the 1980s, from assembly and productive trade[5] into overall production-based trade, that is to export domestically manufactured parts and components and capital goods while importing processed goods and consumer goods. If we examine the proportional changes of China and Japan in finished product imports, then we can see that Japan's proportion of imports of finished consumer goods kept rising before 2003 while China's proportion kept declining. In addition, China's proportion is far lower than that of Japan in this regard.

The U.S. still plays the role of a market provider for end products in East Asia, which is also the fundamental reason why the U.S. dollar serves as the settlement currency in the region. China must be able to replace the U.S. to become the market provider for end products in East Asia if it wants to make the RMB the regionalized currency in the region. We can see clearly from

Table 4.24. Comparative analysis of the trade structure of China and Japan (%)

Export	China		Japan		
	1990	2003	1980	1990	2003
Primary Products	9.5	2.3	0.7	0.4	0.6
Processed Products	23.2	16.9	24.7	17.5	20.7
Parts and Components	4.1	15.1	13.8	22.9	32.6
Capital Goods	12.6	23.8	28.2	35.6	25.8
Consumer Goods	50.5	41.9	32.5	23.6	20.4

(Cont'd)

Import	China		Japan		
	1990	2003	1980	1990	2003
Primary Products	10.0	11.9	58.7	30.1	19.9
Processed Products	37.9	34.5	24.6	31.8	25.2
Parts and Components	16.1	27.2	2.2	6.4	15.3
Capital Goods	27.8	21.8	5.9	7.5	13.2
Consumer Goods	8.2	4.6	8.6	24.1	26.4

Source: Quote from Susumu Okamoto, Spiral Pattern of Development and Triangular Trade Structure as a Regional Manufacturing Platform, RIETI BBL Seminar, 2005.

comparing the trade structure of China and the U.S. that the U.S. trade structure has always been stable and that it mainly exports processed goods and parts and components while importing consumer goods; when it comes to the trade structure in China, we can see that it is the other way around as analyzed above (see Table 4.25). This reflects to some degree why China's trade surplus against the United States is a structural trade surplus similar to that between Japan and the U.S. in the 1980s. If we focus on the import of end products, we can see that China's proportion in consumer goods import was only 4.5 per cent (2007),

Table 4.25. Comparative analysis of the trade structure of China and the U.S. (%)

Export	China			The U.S		
	1995	2001	2007	1995	2001	2007
Primary Products	5.2	3.4	1.1	8.4	5.2	7.7
Processed Products	27.6	21.8	23.8	25.0	24.5	28.5
Parts and Components	7.2	14.0	17.4	28.9	31.5	24.8
Capital Goods	12.0	18.4	28.0	21.3	22.9	22.2
Consumer Goods	48.0	42.4	29.7	16.4	15.8	16.8

(Cont'd)

Import	China			The U.S		
	1995	2001	2007	1995	2001	2007
Primary Products	9.8	12.3	19.9	8.8	9.8	15.6
Processed Products	44.2	37.7	27.8	21.6	21.8	23.8
Parts and Components	14.5	25.3	29.5	21.3	17.3	14.3
Capital Goods	25.9	20.3	18.3	18.2	18.2	16.7
Consumer Goods	5.6	4.4	4.5	30.1	32.9	29.5

Note: The BEC code of products included in primary products is 111, 21 and 31; the BEC code of products included in processed products is 121, 22 and 32; the BEC code of products included in parts and components is 42 and 53; the BEC code of products included in capital goods is 41 and 521; the BEC code of products included in consumer goods is 112, 122, 51, 522, 61, 62 and 63. This classification is made by referring to the method of Broad Economic Categories of the UN Statistics Division.

Source: Set out according to relevant data of the *UN Commodity Trade Statistics Database.*

about one seventh of that of the U.S. That means China lags far behind the U.S.

Compared with that of the United States and Japan, China's trade structure does not serve its interests of becoming a market provider for finished products of East Asian countries. In this connection, China must restructure its trade, transform the production model that is defined by low value chain and processing trade, and gradually transform the trade pattern into one of exporting intermediate products and importing finished products.

The trend of China's trade structural reform in the near term

The transformation from the extensive economic model to the intensive economic pattern also corresponds to economic and trade restructuring. China's economic restructuring in recent years indicates that the original trade structure is being restructured slowly (see Table 4.25, Fig. 4.2). The proportion of semi-finished products in China's imports keeps declining and correspondingly the proportion of finished products in China's exports keeps shrinking. Statistics show that China is gradually transforming its original processing model of trade and production, but not substantially, thus China needs to make a fundamental transformation and further adjustment of its industrial structure for future development. The outbreak of the U.S. "sub-prime mortgage crisis" has provided China with opportunities for economic and trade restructuring. The global financial crisis has inevitably exerted a major negative impact on China's foreign trade, but China's exports are mainly labor-intensive products and low price products that have little income elasticity from the perspective of trade structure, thus the demand for these commodities might increase amid economic downturn and decrease of residents' income. At the same time, China has partially alleviated the influence of the changing international economic landscape on Chinese exports through adopting measures to increase the export rebate rate of some industries and improve the foreign trade environment. In this connection, Chinese foreign trade is facing both challenges and favorable conditions for restructuing amidst the international financial crisis. The crisis is also positively driving the upgrading of China's trade structure and making its products more competitive and high-tech. This will enhance the rights to choose means of payment for trade and the influence of the currency, and help advance RMB internationalization.

Fig. 4.2. **China's exports of end products and imports of intermediate products**

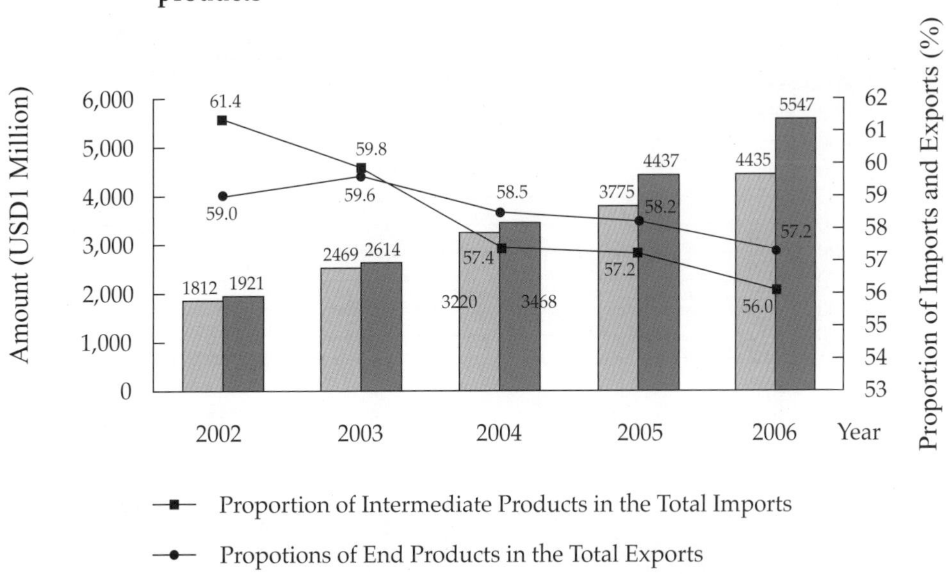

Source: Quoted from 2007 JETOR White Paper on International Trade and Foreign Direct Investment, Fig. I-13.

Expanding domestic demand and improving people's consumption level

Comparison of consumption level between China, Japan and the U.S.

China still has a long way to go to catch up with the developed countries in per capita GDP, although it has maintained the world highest growth rate in the recent decade. We can clearly see the large gap between China and the U.S., Japan and South Korea through comparing their GDP level and the changing trend (see Fig. 4.3). This demonstrates that China's per capital disposable income is still at a lower level which will damage the fast growth of domestic consumer spending. This national condition has determined that China must guarantee a rapid increase of national income (especially per capita income) if it seeks to boost domestic demand.

Fig. 4.3. Comparison of per capita GDP between China, Japan, South Korea and the U.S. (1980–2007)

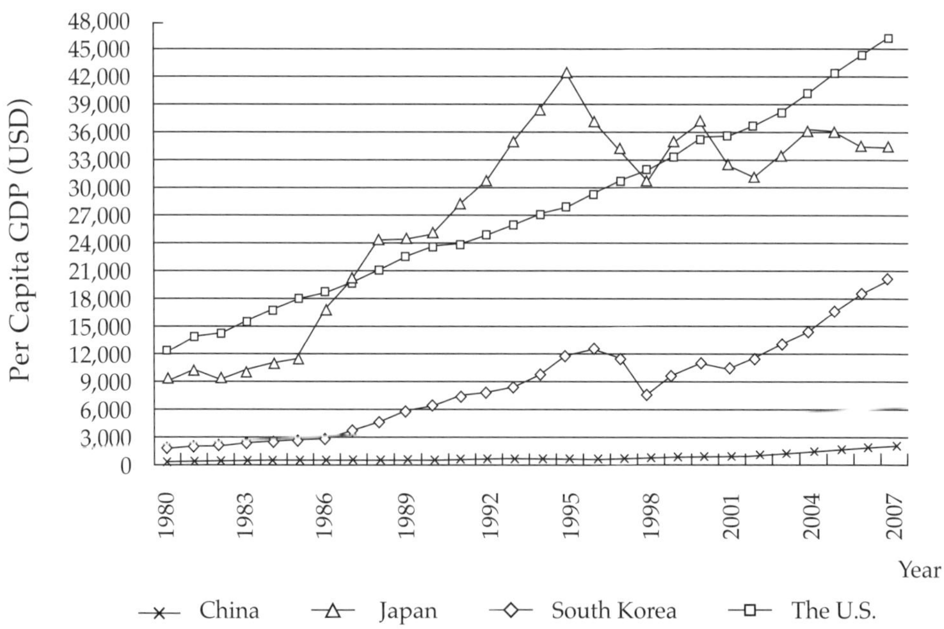

Note: The data of 2006 onwards for China and South Korea and that of 2005 onwards for Japan are predicted data.

Source: International Monetary Fund, World Economic Outlook Database.

We made comparative analyses of the consumption expenditures of China, Japan and the U.S. as part of the effort to examine the level of China's domestic demand. The analysis results show that the proportion of China's consumer spending in its GDP is obviously lower than that of the U.S. and Japan. In 2007, the consumer spending of the U.S. accounted for 70.33 per cent of its GDP, almost twice as much as that of China; and when it comes to the proportion of final consumption expenditure in the GDP (consumption rate) in 2007, Japan and the U.S. recorded as much as 74.45 per cent and 86.35 per cent respectively while China registered only 52.04 per cent, demonstrating a downward trend as with the proportion of consumer spending in the GDP (see Table 4.26). China's consumption rate is clearly lower than that of Japan and the U.S., which is reflected by its lower level of consumer spending. In this sense China must improve the consumer spending level and consumption propensity for expanding domestic demand. Given China's special urban-rural dual structure, we will further examine Chinese people's living standard and consumption structure so as to find a practicable road for improving the overall resident spending level.

China's household consumption level and consumption structure

China's dual structure has resulted in a huge gap between urban and rural dwellers in per capita disposable income and the gap has kept widening since the 1990s (see Fig. 4.4). Income is the function of consumption and the divide of per capita discretionary income between the urban and rural residents has further resulted in the gap in per capita consumption level. In 2006 the per capita consumption level of farmers was less than one third of that of urban residents (see Fig. 4.5). We can see from further examination of the structure of China's consumption spending that the proportion of government expenditure in final consumption expenditure remained almost unchanged, but the proportion of urban resident consumption spending rose sharply while the proportion of rural resident consumption spending fell dramatically. As of 1990, the proportion of urban household consumption spending surpassed that of rural residents and the gap keeps growing (see Fig. 4.6).

The current disparity between China's urban and rural areas in living standards has something to do with the urbanization process after the reform and opening up and the economic development strategy that rural areas support urban areas. China must narrow the gap between urban and rural areas if it wants to increase people's consumption level across the board as

Table 4.26 The proportion of consumption expenditure1 of China, Japan and the U.S. to GDP (%)

Year	China			Japan			The U.S.		
	Proportion of Residents' Consumption Expenditure to GDP	Proportion of Government Consumption Expenditure to GDP	Proportion of Total Consumption Expenditure to GDP	Proportion of Residents' Consumption Expenditure to GDP	Proportion of Government Consumption Expenditure to GDP	Proportion of Total Consumption Expenditure to GDP	Proportion of Residents' Consumption Expenditure to GDP	Proportion of Government Consumption Expenditure to GDP	Proportion of Total Consumption Expenditure to GDP
1995	46.05	11.44	57.49	55.40	15.01	70.41	67.14	18.54[2]	85.68
1999	47.58	12.57	60.14	56.90	15.93	72.83	67.78	14.39	82.18
2003	41.67	15.11	56.78	57.47	18.05	75.52	70.28	15.84	86.13
2007	37.49	14.55	52.04	56.89	17.56	74.45	70.33	16.02	86.35

Notes: 1.The consumer spending part of consumption spending includes that of non-profit institutions serving households (NPISHs);
2. Statistics onthe U.S. government consumption expenditure in 1995 include government consumption and investment.

Source: Calculated based on relevant data of *IFS Database* of the IMF.

China's potential in consumption is in the countryside. Both the Party and the government have clearly recognized this issue and made it clear at the 16th National Party Congress, stating that that cities starting to fund rural areas and improving the living standard of the rural population should be put at the top of the agenda of further development. At the 17th National Party Congress convened on 15 October 2007, General Secretary Hu Jintao spelled out the target of quadrupling the per capita GDP by 2020 compared with that of 2000, that is to increase the per capita GDP from USD856 in 2000 to USD3,500 in 2020; he also proposed attaching importance to the fairness of "primary distribution of the national income," working to expand the middle-class population to half of the total population by 2020, and basically eliminating poverty. The Congress also identified the two policy visions of narrowing regional gaps and income gaps. These policies will contribute to improve the overall income and consumption level of Chinese people, which will undoubtedly make a great difference in boosting domestic demand.

Fig. 4.4. The trend of the per capita disposable income for urban dwellers and the per capita net income for rural residents in China

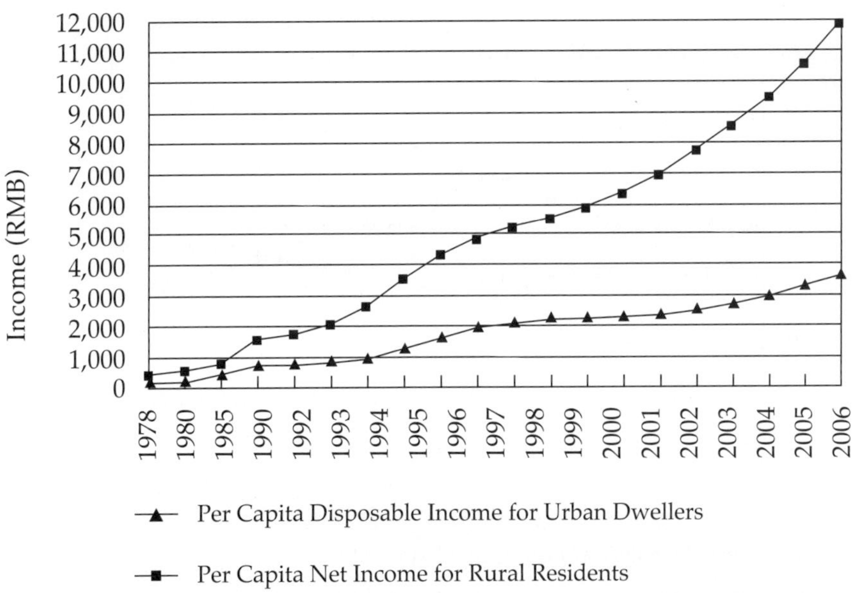

Source: *China Statistical Yearbook* 2007.

Fig. 4.5. The trend of China's per capital consumption expenditure between 1978 and 2006

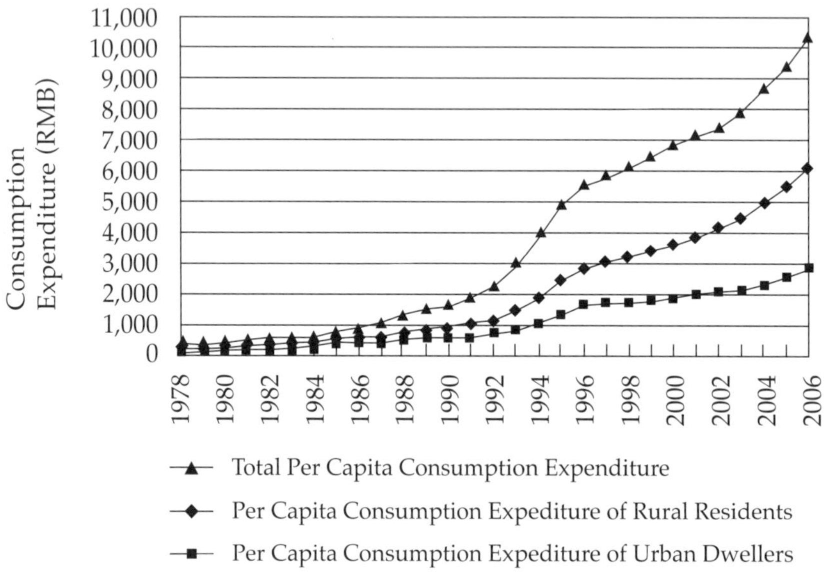

Source: *China Statistical Yearbook* 2007.

Fig. 4.6. The trend of China's total consumption expenditure between 1978 and 2006

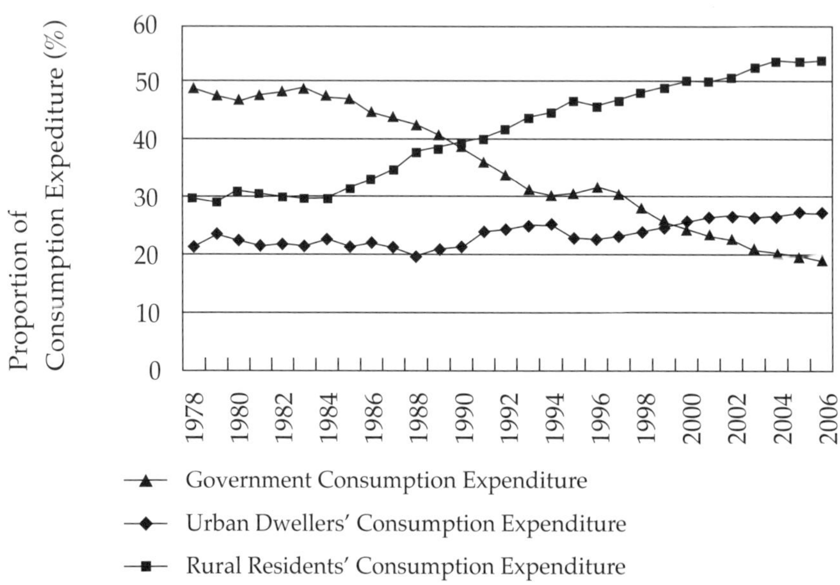

Source: *China Statistical Yearbook* 2007.

Examination of the openness of the chinese market

Comparative analysis of the openness of the market in China, Japan and the U.S.

At the moment 70 per cent of China's GDP comes from foreign trade, representing the highest level in the world (the figure is only around 30 per cent for Japan and the U.S.) and reflecting the fact that China's economic growth depends heavily on foreign trade (refer to Table 4.27). Since China's trade structure in itself goes against the development of domestic demand, the excessively high dependency ratio on foreign trade also suggests that China's domestic resources are excessively consumed by its trade partners, which will put a brake on China's long-term economic growth and on it becoming a market provider for the end products of East Asia. We can see from Table 4.28 that final consumption spending and net export contribute little to GDP growth, thus China must focus on restructuring its trade while lowering its dependency ratio on foreign trade, increasing the contribution rate of domestic demand (final consumption) to the GDP, and gradually transforming the trade-driven economic model into a domestic-oriented economic pattern in future reform.

Trade expansion effects of tariff exemption after the establishment of the Free Trade Area (FTA) between China and ASEAN

China and ASEAN signed the *China-ASEAN Comprehensive Economic Cooperation Framework Agreement* in November 2002. The agreement stipulates that the tariff for most normal products between the two sides be cut to zero before 2010. On 1 January 2010, the China-ASEAN FTA (CAFTA) was formally established and became the world's third largest FTA following the U.S. and the EU.

Lai Mingyong and Li Jingchi (2007) analyzed the long-term influence of China's exemption of the tariff for the original ASEAN-6 in 2010 on China's macro-economy based on the Chingem model (a Chinese static CGE model). Their studies show that the complete exemption of tariffs for ASEAN has helped reduce the dependence of economic growth on net export and has increased import and export amounts. Imports grew by 2.85 per cent while exports rose by 1.41 per cent, and the trade surplus has shown a declining trend; at the same time, the tariff exemption will also promote the upgrading of the import and export commodity mix and the development of the service industry, but some sectors of the agriculture and manufacturing industries will be negatively affected.

JETOR (2007) utilized the GTAP (Global Trade Analysis Project) model to analyze the economic effects after the establishment of the East Asian FTA and concluded that the establishment of CAFTA has boosted the GDP growth of both China and ASEAN, but the positive effect on ASEAN is more remarkable; if the ASEAN10+3 FTA could be established in the future, then it will give a strong boost to the growth of the GDP of countries within the region (see Table 4.29).

With the implementation of the CAFTA, the status of China as the largest "market provider" of the region of East Asia will be improved significantly. Beyond that, the pilot program that was planned to be implemented for using the RMB as the settlement currency for the trade in goods between Guangxi and Yunnan in China for one part and ASEAN for another will have a constructive significance for the RMB to circulate and gradually replace the U.S. dollar to become a major settlement currency within the region.

Pushing forward the financial system reform

RMB regionalization inevitably calls for a matching financial market that is large enough in scale and balanced in structure. Developing the financial market and modernizing the financial system represent not only the necessary conditions for realizing RMB internationalization but also the preconditions for guaranteeing a smooth opening up of capital accounts. Developing the financial market requires further reform, development and establishment of a unified, flexible, highly efficient and large monetary market; further development of the capital market, cultivation of diversified market investment players, and increasing the proportion of direct financing; promotion of the bond market to expand issue main bodies and bond varieties, strengthening of bond rating, guarantee and clearing, among other infrastructure construction, and working

Table 4.27. Comparison of the dependency ratio on foreign trade between China, Japan and the U.S. (%)

Year	China	Japan	The U.S.	Year	China	Japan	The U.S.
1990	35	20	21	2003	57	22	24
1995	44	17	23	2006	72	30	28
2000	44	21	26				

Note: Dependency Ratio on Foreign Trade = Total Import and Export Volume/GDP.

Source: Set out based on relevant data of the World Bank's Key Development Data & Statistics.

Table 4.28. The contribution rate and the pullof the three main types of demand on China's GDP growth between 2000 and 2006

Year	Final Consumption Expenditure		Gross Capital Formation		Net Export of Goods and Services	
	Contribution Rate (%)	Pull (Percentage Point)	Contribution Rate (%)	Pull (Percentage Point)	Contribution Rate (%)	Pull (Percentage Point)
1990	47.8	1.8	1.8	0.1	50.4	1.9
1995	44.7	4.9	55.0	6.0	0.3	0.0
2000	65.1	5.5	22.4	1.9	12.5	1.0
2003	35.3	3.5	63.7	6.4	1.0	0.1
2006	39.2	4.3	41.3	4.6	19.5	2.2

Notes:

1. The data is calculated based on comparable prices;
2. The three major types of demand refer to final consumption expenditure, gross capital formation and the net export of goods and services;
3. The contribution rate refers to the ratio of the increments of the three major types of demand to that of the GDP;
4. The pull refers to the product of the growth rate of the GDP and the contribution rate of the three major types of demand.

Source: *China Statistical Yearbook 2007.*

Table 4.29. Impact of ASEAN 10+3 FTA on the GDP of its members (%)

Country or Region	Intra ASEAN (AFTA)	ASEAN-China	ASEAN-Japan	ASEAN-ROK	ASEAN 10+3
ASEAN	0.9	1.3	1.4	1.0	2.0
Japan	–	–0.01	0.3	–	0.7
China	–0.01	0.4	–0.02	–0.02	1.5
South Korea	–0.01	–0.04	–0.02	0.3	1.6

Note: 1. The assumption of the table is that under the circumstances of the establishment of FTA, tariffs will be exempted and non-tariff measures decreased by 50%;

2. " —" means the impact on GDP is 0.00% i.e. no impact;

Source: Quoted from 2007 JETOR White Paper on International Trade and Foreign Direct Investment, Table II-5.

harder to develop the government bond market. China also needs to enhance the development of commercial banks and state-owned commercial banks in particular, actively press ahead with the modernization drive of commercial banks, strive to become compatible with internationally accepted practices, improve the management mechanism of commercial banks, and strengthen the capacity to fend off risks. At the government level there is a need to intensify and modernize the government financial supervision and regulation system, further improve the monitoring system and legal frameworks of the PBOC (the People's Bank of China), the CBRC (China Banking Regulatory Commission), the CSRC (China Securities Regulatory Commission) and the CIRC (China Insurance Regulatory Commission), maintain the independence of supervisory organizations, and build up the authority of supervisory institutions and improve their monitoring level.

One of the top priorities in deepening the reform of the financial system is to reform the banking system. Given the success story of China's reform and opening up since 1979, we need to attach more importance to the role of RMB regionalization in advancing and driving financial reform at the current stage. China must draw lessons from the "Japanese yen internationalization." That means we should neither sacrifice the reform of the domestic financial system for the external (U.S. dollar) balance nor separate external financial adjustment from internal financial reform. The exchange rate adjustment of the RMB against the U.S. dollar or the reform of the RMB exchange rate system is only part of China's entire financial system reform. China must realize the improvement and effective operation of the entire financial system during the continuous opening up process. Promoting domestic reform with targeted opening up has always been a leading driver for deepening reform in China since 1979. China should take RMB Asianization as a key driver for advancing the reform of the financial system, gradually reform the domestic financial system, move forward with the reform of the governance structure of commercial banks and the marketization of the exchange rate, and establish an open financial market.

Moreover China also needs to accelerate the reform of the interest rate market. The liberalization and marketization of the interest rate and the exchange rate are the preconditions for asset risk pricing and for taking the RMB as trade pricing and settlement currency. In terms of the liberalization and marketization of the interest rate and exchange rate, the liberalization and marketization of the interest rate should come before the liberalization and marketization of the exchange rate as the interest rate is more easily regulated and controlled by the monitoring authority of a country to a certain degree, has a more profound and broader influence than exchange the rate, and can be realized under relatively closed circumstances while opening up.

Opening up the capital account

China's stricter capital control is obviously a major obstacle to the RMB realizing a higher level of regionalization. Progressively relaxing the control over capital account is a precondition for RMB regionalization at a higher level and the RMB regionalization process can also promote the opening up of the capital account. In December 1996, China accepted Article Eight of the IMF, realized the convertibility of the RMB current account and started to proactively prepare for the convertibility of the capital account. Thanks to years of development, as stated above, China has made a great difference in opening up the capital account. What merits our mention here is that Chinese government has been very positive in utilizing foreign direct investment since 1990s, thus relevant authorities have rarely imposed restrictions on this kind of capital inflow during the actual implementation process. In so doing the foreign direct investment in China has been unrestrained to some extent. This means that the openness of China's capital account might be higher than is demonstrated by the relevant regulations.

We need to continue to accumulate experience in the opening up of current accounts and part of the capital account and gradually realize the convertibility of capital account in an active and prudent way under the permissible conditions both at home and abroad. In line with the specific national reality of China, the opening up of capital account can be divided into three stages as follows.

Early stage

This stage is also known as the "active preparation stage." Specifically, it includes: deepening domestic financial system reform, further optimizing the exchange rate mechanism, and making trade liberalization a reality. Deepening the reform of domestic financial system specifically means that China needs to cultivate the short-term monetary market that meets the requirements for opening up the capital account, realize RMB exchange rate marketization, strengthen domestic banks resistance to risks and provide a safe and highly efficient capital allocation environment for the opening up of the capital account. Further optimizing the exchange rate mechanism means expanding the elasticity of the exchange rate system to make the RMB float freely within a broader space and abolishing the system of exchange, settlement and sales to make changes in the exchange rate reflect market supply and demands. Further realizing trade liberalization means providing a more liberal competitive environment for domestic enterprises, enhancing the international competitiveness of businesses and strengthening the capability of the domestic current account to stave off external shocks. On top of that, China also needs to completely open up long-term capital outflow and outward direct investment in particular, abolish the existing examination and approval system, and put in place another examination and authorization system.

Middle stage

This stage is also called the "progressively opening up stage." The opening up in this stage mainly consists of conditionally open up the inflow and outflow of securities investment, especially the inflow and outflow of bond investment. China can first relax the restrictions on domestic institutions to go abroad to issue corporate bonds. For overseas institutions that engage in domestic stock market dealing restrictions on capital amount, shareholding ratio and shareholding time should be adopted but there should be no restrictions on their engaging in the dealing of domestic right of credit type of instruments.

Later stage

This stage is also called the "basically complete opening up stage." China needs to gradually relax the restrictions on overseas residents engaging in domestic securities market dealing, lift the controls over domestic residents engaging in overseas stock market dealing, and prudently open up the trading of financial derivative products according to the development landscape of the domestic securities market. What merits our attention is that there is still a necessity to keep control over domestic financial institution in raising funds overseas.

Coordinating the Relationship between the RMB and the Japanese Yen

The regionalization of the RMB signifies its rising status in the international monetary system and regional monetary system. This process is bound to involve the relationship between the RMB and the Japanese yen — another key currency within the region. Better coordinating this relationship is of great importance to a smooth implementation of RMB regionalization strategy.

Relative status of the RMB and Japanese Yen within the region

In general the Japanese yen has played a critical role in East Asia. That said, its regional influence has weakened apart from its rising status in exchange rate arrangements in East Asia after it went through a long-term economic recession and the Asian Financial Crisis since the 1990s as well as the problems with the "internationalization of the Japanese Yen." In contrast, the position and influence of the RMB in East Asia keep leveling up China's continuous and fast economic growth and the rapid development of foreign trade. RMB regionalization and the repositioning of the Japanese yen in Asia have become unavoidable issues for the East Asian economies.

To begin with, we need to point out that neither China or Japan are in a position to dominate regional currency and financial cooperation alone under the current "U.S. dollar-denominated system." We examined the pressure of competition faced by China, Japan and other East Asian countries on the world market by using the trade Competitive Stress Index (CSI) put forward by Yao Zhizhong (2004) (see Table 4.30). We can see from the table that the CSI of China to other East Asian economies keeps rising basically apart from dropping to the Philippines and Indonesia in 2007 while the CSI of Japan to other East Asian economies has shown a moderately downward trend in 2000. In 2007 the CSI of China to three East Asian economies surpassed 0.78 while the CSI of Japan to other East Asian countries was less than 0.78 with the exception of that to the Philippines. This is totally different from 2004. In addition, when it comes to the number of countries that felt more CSI of China than that of Japan, there were only Indonesia and Thailand in 1992, 1996 and 2000, but Malaysia and the Philippines were added in 2004 and the total number remained four, namely Indonesia, Thailand, Malaysia and South Korea in 2007.

In the meantime, the CSI of other East Asian economies to China and Japan also changed quite differently. On the world market, the CSI of other East Asian economies has dropped significantly to China but increased or slightly increased to Japan. In 2007 the CSI of all other East Asian countries to China was lower than 0.15 while the CSI of only two East Asian countries was lower than 0.15 to Japan apart from South Korea and Singapore whose CSI was 0.24 and 0.164 to China respectively and 0.40 and 0.308 to Japan respectively. This is just the opposite from 2000.

Such being the case, the asymmetry in competitive stress is worsening between China and the rest of the East Asian economies but it is moving towards moderate development between Japan and other East Asian economies.

These East Asian economies are feeling more competitive stress from China than from Japan. The growing pressure of asymmetric competitiveness faced by East Asian economies from China has made them require a more stable exchange rate of the RMB than of the Japanese yen and seeking a stable exchange rate against the RMB has become an essential choice for them.

In addition, China has more potential to become the market provider for end products in East Asia. As shown in Table 4.31, Japan provides more markets for end products within the region of East Asia than China. China takes up 70 per cent of the finished product markets provided by Japan. So if the trade between China and Japan is not included, China provides more end product markets than Japan and the market scale is 1.24 fold that of Japan for another eight East Asian economies. In the meantime, the market scale of capital goods offered by China to the whole of East Asia is already 1.9 times of that of Japan. The market for finished products provided by China to the whole of East Asia has developed rapidly since 2002. The scale of the market provided by China to another eight East Asian economies increased by five fold in 2006 compared with 2001, but the market scale provided by Japan only increased by 16 per cent during the same period. Of course, as mentioned before, whether China can become the leading market provider for finished products in East Asia relies on transforming the economic growth pattern and taking domestic demand as the engine for economic growth.

China would surpass Japan to become the largest economy in East Asia. Experiences in regional monetary integration demonstrate that the monetary integration model of any region has to do with the economic aggregate and changes of the economies in the region. The formation of the euro is based on the relatively balanced economic strength of countries in the Eurozone. This unified currency finally emerged through cooperation among countries in the region under the conditions that no single currency could dominate the monetary integration process alone. The formation of the "dollarization" in the American region is built on the "U.S.-dominated" structure. A strong currency will ultimately become the leading player while the weak currency will leave the game.

The situation in East Asia is that Japan contributed to 70 per cent of the GDP in East Asia in the 1980s, but its proportion has contracted rapidly while China's proportion has picked up since 2000. We make a prediction of the economic scale of the eight East Asian countries down the line based on their GDP growth trend between 1960 and 2007 (see Table 4.32). The results indicate that 60 per cent of the total GDP of East Asian leading countries will come from China in 2040 while

Japan's proportion will shrink to 23.5 per cent. In this sense, East Asia is very likely to shape a China-dominated economic structure that is similar to today's "U.S.-dominated" structure as time goes on.

That being said, what needs to be pointed out is that Asia is not America as the region of Asia has a complicated historical, political and cultural tradition. This has determined that it is difficult for the region to adapt to the "one country-dominated" economic structure. Different from Britain, Japan and the U.S. are obviously not synchronic in economic cycle (business, investment, trade and so on), but they are highly synchronic with other East Asian economies in economic cycle and Japan is unlikely to be independent from the regional financial cooperation like the UK. In this connection, the rapidly increasing economic aggregate of China does not mean China can dominate the regional monetary and financial cooperation. Rather, it just demonstrates that cooperation between China and Japan is absolutely necessary. Generally speaking neither the Japanese yen nor the RMB has the conditions for becoming a regional leading currency on their own. From the perspective of the Japanese yen, it is an international currency, but Japan cannot regain its position as a key trade partner of East Asian economies and the core of the regional division of labor system. Issues faced by Japan in economic growth, industrial and financial structure, market opening up and aging population among others will hinder its efforts to become an essential market provider in East Asia, which will hold back the Japanese yen from becoming a regional single dominant currency. From another perspective, the RMB is not in a position to independently play the role of a regional leading currency at the current stage due to its shortage of free convertibility, vulnerability of the financial sector and the lack of openness of the financial market. All in all, no matter how the position of the RMB and Japanese yen will change in East Asia, neither will independently become the regional leading currency.

The necessity to coordinate the RMB and the Japanese Yen in the light of european experiences

Within the context that neither the RMB nor the Japanese yen could become the regional dominant currency, what relationship should be maintained between the two during the process of RMB regionalization? European monetary integration as the most thorough regional monetary cooperation process with the largest economic scale of member countries could serve as a reference for us to examine the relationship between the RMB and the Japanese yen during the process of RMB regionalization.

Table 4.30. CSI in trade of China and Japan to other East Asian economies in the global market

	Year	Japan	South Korea	Indonesia	Malaysia	The Philippines	Singapore	Thailand		South Korea	Indonesia	Malaysia	The Philippines	Singapore	Thailand
China to Other Countries	1992	0.118	0.515	0.567	0.525	0.591	0.413	0.733	Japan to Other Countries	0.769	0.315	0.626	0.765	0.808	0.556
	1996	0.174	0.461	0.6	0.547	0.725	0.427	0.74		0.807	0.356	0.717	0.803	0.82	0.643
	2000	0.262	0.556	0.663	0.647	0.676	0.529	0.834		0.837	0.462	0.779	0.894	0.873	0.739
	2004	0.424	0.689	0.724	0.768	0.975	0.658	0.857		0.821	0.505	0.724	0.913	0.786	0.745
	2007	0.59	0.788	0.585	0.804	0.655	0.67	0.891		0.769	0.414	0.66	0.902	0.728	0.723
Other Countries to China	1992	0.471	0.465	0.227	0.252	0.068	0.309	0.28	Other Countries to Japan	0.179	0.031	0.075	0.022	0.151	0.053
	1996	0.475	0.396	0.198	0.252	0.099	0.284	0.273		0.225	0.043	0.137	0.04	0.245	0.087
	2000	0.503	0.385	0.165	0.255	0.103	0.292	0.23		0.301	0.06	0.16	0.071	0.251	0.106
	2004	0.405	0.295	0.079	0.164	0.065	0.22	0.139		0.368	0.058	0.162	0.064	0.276	0.127
	2007	0.342	0.24	0.055	0.112	0.065	0.164	0.112		0.405	0.067	0.159	0.072	0.308	0.157

Source: Calculated based on the annual export figures of 261 types of commodities counted according to 3 digit codes of SITC (Rev. 3) by The United Nation Commodity Trade Statistics Database.

Table 4.31. Comparison of the scale of the end-product market of China and Japan for East Asian economies between 1991 and 2006

(USD 1 Billion)

	Market	Country	1991	1993	1995	1997	1999	2000	2001	2002	2003	2004	2005	2006
8 East Asian Economies	Consumer Goods Market	China	2.42	1.48	2.1	1.98	2.26	2.72	2.79	3.19	4.29	5.59	6.44	7.67
		Japan	13.85	15.32	19.05	16.02	15.58	16.06	14.64	13.84	13.85	14.71	14.97	14.11
	Capital Market	China	3.68	2.74	3.81	3.35	3.97	6.65	7.36	13.87	25.67	36.36	40.95	43.79
		Japan	6.85	8.65	15.28	17.38	21.23	28.14	20.27	18.07	20.7	26.23	26.21	26.56
	End-Product Market	China	6.1	4.22	5.91	5.33	6.23	9.36	10.14	17.06	29.96	41.95	47.39	51.46
		Japan	20.7	23.97	34.33	33.4	36.81	44.19	34.91	31.91	34.55	40.94	41.19	40.67
10 East Asian Economies	Consumer Goods Market	China	3.27	3.5	3.83	3.39	3.89	4.65	4.57	5.96	7.67	9.47	10.4	11.99
		Japan	24.26	31.08	45.45	41.52	41.84	48.58	48.17	46.8	50.24	56.3	60.36	62.65
	Capital Market	China	7.02	10.41	11.88	9.69	10.62	15.52	17.11	26.7	45.54	61.46	65.12	71.79
		Japan	3.71	4.71	12.66	15.47	17.88	24.67	22.73	23.12	27.37	32.81	36.98	40.2
	End-Product Market	China	10.29	13.92	15.71	13.08	14.51	20.17	21.68	32.667	53.22	70.93	75.52	83.78
		Japan	27.97	35.79	58.12	56.99	59.72	73.25	70.9	69.92	77.61	89.11	97.34	102.85

Note: The eight East Asian economies include South Korea, Singapore, Hong Kong, Taiwan, Malaysia, Indonesia, The Philippines and Thailand, while the ten East Asian economies is the eight economies plus Mainland China and Japan.

Source: RIETI-TID 2007.

(1) The European monetary integration process has shown fully that the consensus of regional powers in cooperation contributes to the shaping of a stable regional monetary system.

The European monetary integration went through 50-plus years of development from the founding of the European Payments Union (EPU) in 1950 to the final replacement of the currencies of member states by the euro in 2002. This process was far from plain sailing and we can even say that each stage of the process suffered setbacks and repeated stagnations. But European countries finally overcame the difficulties and successfully deepened monetary cooperation. The cooperation between Germany and France, the two great powers within the region, contributed a lot to the process.

First, the common ground on cooperation between Germany and France became the most important engine for European monetary cooperation. During the process of European monetary integration, countries such as Germany and France bargained furiously about a host of specific issues (such as the grid parity system and the package parity system) and also suffered grave frustrations such as the failure of the "Werner Plan" and crisis of the European Monetary System. In addition, France also exited from "The Snake in the Tunnel" twice. That said, all these were policy games on the basis of consensus on cooperation and the priority of their respective interests was to play their roles under the premise of reaching common ground on basic cooperation. Neither Germany nor France wavered in the general course and basic targets of monetary cooperation. That is why the European Monetary System still came into being after the shrinking of "The Snake in the Tunnel" system, the foundation of the European Monetary Institute as scheduled and the smooth implementation of the single currency area plan in 1994 after the consecutive monetary crises between 1992 and 1993.

Second, among all stakeholders, the consensus on cooperation between Germany and France played a pivotal role in the success of European monetary integration. Some small countries like the Netherlands, Belgium and Luxembourg played a more important role in he early days of the integration, but the cooperation between Germany and France had undoubtedly always been central to the European monetary integration. The attitude towards monetary cooperation of Germany and France as the leading players in Europe in terms of economy, trade and currency directly determined success or failure. The failure of the "Werner Plan" and the setbacks in "The Snake in the Tunnel" in 1970s are attributed to the fact that the two nations could not reach a common ground in the plan on monetary cooperation and the coordination of macro-economic policy. Having said that, the successful establishment of the European Monetary

Table 4.32. The scale of East Asian leading countries' GDP and the prediction based on their growth trend

(Unit: USD10 Billion)

Year	Japan	China	Indonesia	South Korea	Malaysia	The Philippines	Thailand	Singapore	The Total GDP of the Eight Countries	The Proportion of Japan (%)	The Proportion of China (%)
1980	105.5	18.9	7.8	6.4	2.5	3.2	3.2	1.2	148.8	70.9	12.7
1985	134.7	30.7	8.7	9.7	3.2	3.1	3.9	1.8	195.7	68.8	15.7
1990	301.8	35.7	11.4	26.4	4.4	4.4	8.5	3.7	396.4	76.1	9
1995	524.8	72.8	20.2	51.7	8.9	7.4	16.8	8.4	711	73.8	10.2
2000	466.7	119.8	16.5	51.2	9.4	7.6	12.3	9.3	692.8	67.4	17.3
2001	409.5	132.5	16	48.2	9.3	7.1	11.6	8.6	642.8	63.720.6	
2002	391.8	145.4	19.6	54.7	10.1	7.7	12.7	8.8	650.8	60.2	22.3
2003	422.9	164.1	23.5	60.8	11	8	14.3	9.3	713.9	59.2	23
2004	460.6	193.2	25.7	68	12.5	8.7	16.1	10.9	795.7	57.9	24.3
2005	455.2	223.6	28.6	79.1	13.8	9.9	17.6	12	839.8	54.2	26.6
2006	437.6	265.8	36.5	88.8	15.6	11.8	20.7	13.7	890.4	49.1	29.9
2007	438.4	320.6	43.3	97	18.7	14.4	24.5	1.2	973	45.1	32.9
2020	772	599.2	51.5	153.3	26.5	35.8	33.9	25	1,697.10	45.5	35.3
2025	871.7	911.6	60.7	184.9	31.7	51.2	39.9	30.1	2,181.90	39.9	41.8
2030	976.1	1,387.00	70.8	219.6	37.4	73.2	46.5	35.7	2,846.30	34.3	48.7
2035	1,085.40	2,110.30	81.6	257.1	43.5	104.7	53.5	41.8	3,778.00	28.7	55.9
2040	1,199.50	3,210.90	93.2	297.7	50.2	149.6	61	48.4	5,110.30	23.5	62.8

Source: Data before 2007 are from the website of the World Bank, while the data for between 2020 and 2040 are predicted values based on the actual growth trend of GDP of different countries. The ratio of the predicted values to the real values is between 0.8–1.2, indicating that the prediction is basicallysignificant.

System in 1979 owed much to their clear-cut attitudes towards cooperation and the unyielding efforts of the leaders of the two countries. Especially after the crisis of the European Monetary System in 1992 when other countries were skeptical about further development of monetary integration, the steadfast cooperation between the two economies helped save the integration process and prompted countries such as Italy to return to the European Exchange Rate Mechanism.[7] It is tempting to say that their cooperation effectively gave play to their role in "regional hegemony" and brought about the regional currency cooperation, the first of its kind (Krugman, 1991).

Drivers for cooperation between powers within the region and changes of their relative status from the perspective of European experiences

As stated above, the collaboration between Germany and France was what underlay the smooth advancement of the European monetary integration after repeated setbacks. Their unswerving consensus represents the key power for conquering obstacles and supporting the partnership. But on the one hand, the political and economic landscape have changed a lot domestically and internationally for the two countries over the past decades, which has not always served the interests of the two in monetary cooperation; on the other hand, conflicts more often than not existed between the two in history, so what is the reason why these two powers could remove all obstacles, put aside old grudges and stick to the partnership amidst the ever-changing environment and conditions?

Generally speaking, multi-lateral cooperation is the result of a mix of factors at play. On top of that, the motivations for the two countries to stick to collaboration also changed during different periods of time. But fundamentally it was based on rational thinking on their respective interests.

Germany did not play a dominant role in the cooperation with France in the days of the integration process, but it realized its targets. As time went on, the status of Germany in economy and politics changed and it had played a leading role in the European economy at least from the ending of the Bretton Woods System. But joining in monetary integration at that moment would potentially jeopardize its autonomous rights in monetary policy and even the monetary policy on controlling inflation.[8] At the same time, the political status of Germany was undergoing gradual normalization and it no longer needed to play its political role through cooperation. Back then, the Germany policy-making authority still adhered to the attitude towards cooperation and the major underpinners include: first, Germany hoped to institutionalize its leading position in the European economy through monetary integration; second, it sought to restrain the depreciation of other currencies through monetary integration; third, it looked to other countries to share responsibilities to provide international reserve currencies and adjust the exchange rate; fourth, it expected to forgo some dominant rights in monetary policy for the support of other countries in its domestic affairs such as the unification of Germany. From the last point of view, it is fair to say that being part of the plan on monetary integration was the compromise made by Germany to France in economy.

When it comes to France, the reason for it to engage in monetary cooperation in the early days was to maintain its leading position in Europe, restrain and contain Germany under the collective leadership system, and restrict the unilateral actions of Germany. But later on, France gradually took second place in the European economic framework with the recovery of the political status and the strengthening of the economy of Germany. At that time France wavered in its attitude towards cooperation and thus exited from "The Snake in the Tunnel" system and stood against the joint floating of the European exchange rate. However, what happened indicates that this instead drove the majority of European countries into the Mark area in the real sense. As part of the efforts to impose influence on German policies, prevent the establishment of a Mark area and control domestic inflation, France joined the European Monetary System. After that France further recognized that it could not maintain an independent monetary policy under the circumstances of relaxing control over the European Monetary System and regional capital flow.[9] It preferred to join the integrated regional currency system rather than play a passive role as a follower while Germany played the dominant role in the marketized European economy as it looked to weaken the leading role of Deutsche Bundesbank in determining the European exchange rate and sought to share the decision-making rights in the monetary policy of the entire region together with other EU countries, especially with Germany. By doing so France could become a "co-manager". It is fair to say that this however was the second best choice.

During the process of European monetary cooperation, the relationship and the relative status of Germany and France went through the evolution from the France-dominant leading—following model to cooperation on the basis of equality and then to the Germany-dominant leading—following model. During this process the position of large countries could change with factors including economic scale, trade scale, monetary policy, political status and the selection of market at play, but whether they would accept this change in status relied on the balance of proceeds and opportunity costs.

Significance of European experiences

We can see from individual cases in Europe that active and effective cooperation between large powers within the region not only have important significance to the formation of a stable and relatively independent currency system in the region but also represents a beneficial choice for large countries. During the process of European economic and financial cooperation, the basis for the common ground reached between Germany and France was rational thinking of their respective political and economic comprehensive interests. Under this precondition, the tense relationship shaped in history could be eliminated through conscious efforts. At the same time, the mutual relationship and position of large economies in cooperation could be transformed as the realistic economic landscape changed under the circumstances of reaching consensus. These conclusions are highly valuable as reference for China and Japan, the two large powers in East Asia, in currency regionalization.

First, existing research indicates that neither the RMB nor the Japanese yen has the conditions to become the sole regional dominant currency in East Asia; second, currency regionalization cannot solely rely on market spontaneous power. Rather, it needs to leverage on the development of regional currency cooperation. Just as Eichengreen (1989) pointed out, a country cannot make its currency an international currency or regional leading currency naturally even if it enjoys the leading position in the economy. It needs different degrees of cooperation with other countries and this cooperation includes both arrangements for promoting market exchanges and arrangements for institutionalization. Last, China and Japan have increasingly close economic and trade ties. When it comes to the changes of the country proportion of Japan's imports and exports between 1997 and 2002, its exports to China increased from 5 per cent to 10 per cent while its imports from China rose from 12 per cent to 18 per cent, representing the highest growth rate; in 2002, China surpassed the U.S. for the first time to become Japan's largest importer (Sasaki, Koga Yuko, 2003). Such close economic and trade ties have shaped an inter-dependent relationship in the economic sector between the two countries, so cooperation serves their respective economic interests better than conflict.

Neither the RMB nor the Japanese yen has the conditions for becoming the regional dominant currency independently in East Asia, but cooperation between China and Japan in the monetary and financial sectors can help the realization of RMB regionalization. Moving forward with RMB regionalization through regional cooperation inevitably requires effective coordination between the two currencies as it is difficult for them to compete with and even replace the U.S. dollar alone within the region and they would benefit little from their competition and pay a heavy price for the competition. Although some studies observe that asymmetric competition pressures exists between China and the rest of the East Asian countries, the experiences of "Japanese yen internationalization" signifies that this asymmetric competition is not enough for the RMB to become a regional leading currency. Rather it might repeat the track of "Japanese yen internationalization" on the one hand; on the other hand, considering what is happening in Japan, the competition between the RMB and the yen would bring about losses to both of them if there is no coordination between the two. RMB regionalization should follow the track of coordinating with Japanese yen.

Coordinating with the Japanese Yen during the Process of RMB regionalization

First, we need to make a choice between regional cooperation and unilateral action for RMB regionalization. In addition, there is a need to draw lessons from "Japanese yen internationalization" and learn from the experiences of the euro. The unilateral actions of Japan and its exchange rate polity that takes little consideration of the economic demand of other economies within the region have become one of the reasons behind the failure of the "Japanese yen internationalization" strategy (Li Xiao, 2005), so it is necessary to learn this lesson.

Second, China and Japan have their respective strong points in the economic, trade, monetary and financial sectors. The effective integration of China's huge potential market and its status as the hub of regional division of labor system for one part and the Japan's advanced level in financial market development and financial technology for another will generate positive effects to both sides and even to the entire region.

Specifically, the RMB could carry out coordination and cooperation with Japanese yen in the following aspects during its regionalization process.

First, with regards to financial regulation, Japan might assist China to strengthen international supervision of RMB circulation overseas and provide beneficial technical support to the reform and development of the Chinese domestic financial market so as to jointly promote the status and role of both the RMB and the yen as regional reserve currencies.

Second, regarding currency swap and reserve, China and Japan could establish a larger scale of RMB/JPY swap arrangement to facilitate their respective currencies to become official reserve currencies.

Third, as regards the building of a regional financial market, both sides could assist each other in the issue and transaction of international bonds valued in the currency of the other side or a currency package including both currencies. In addition, both sides should also work together in advancing the establishment and development of regional bond rating agencies.

Fourth, Japan could offer helpful institutional suggestions and technical support to the establishment of the Shanghai international financial center and RMB offshore financial center, so they could enhance the connections in transaction with the Tokyo International Financial Market and press ahead with the formation and development of an East Asian financial transaction center network.

Fifth, on regional monetary cooperation, the two countries could join hands in the institutionalized building of the CMIM mechanism, push forward the establishment and development of AMF and reinforce regional financial oversight.

Sixth, in terms of exchange rate arrangement, China and Japan could act in line with the reality at the current stage to firstly put in place exchange rate stabilization arrangements excluding each other. In particular, China could consider the setting up of a sub-regional RMB exchange rate stabilization circle and even an East Asian RMB exchange rate stabilization circle excluding the Japanese yen and then take into consideration the inclusion of the Japanese yen into this exchange rate stabilization system. Of course it is necessary for China and Japan to keep in communication on exchange rate policy during this process. As such, the two countries would be able to jointly promote the region of East Asia to realize mutual reinforcement and common development in both economy and finance.

When it comes to the relationship between the RMB and other East Asian currencies, China should give priority to the overall interests of the relevant countries and actively engage in communication and coordination with the countries concerned during the RMB regionalization process so as to give them a share in the benefits of RMB regionalization and avoid a hostile attitude to RMB regionalization. During the process of RMB regionalization we need to recognize both the benefits and the necessary costs. China needs to put the regionalization of the RMB into perspective and act on the principle of "win-win results" and "all-win results" to make great efforts to weaken the negative effects of RMB penetration or currency replacement and make neighboring countries and regions share the benefits of RMB regionalization. Only by doing so can we reach a collective consensus on RMB regionalization and smoothly move forward with RMB regionalization.

Conclusion

In conclusion, RMB internationalization must follow the path of regionalization. According to the current situation of China and the East Asia region, RMB regionalization should start from neighboring areas and extend to the rest of the region in geographical terms and from serving as the medium of exchange, to unit of account and then store of value in terms of function. Specifically, RMB regionalization could be boiled down to four stages or levels for advancement as follows:

First, steadily pushing forward the circulation of the RMB in neighboring countries, creating the conditions for the RMB to play the function of the settlement currency for trade between China and neighboring countries, increasing the market popularity of the RMB in trade between China and neighboring countries and at the same time actively and prudently promoting the establishment of a RMB offshore financial market and RMB international bond market to make the RMB function as an investment currency within specific range.

Second, based on the above work and through official settlement agreements between China and neighboring economies and even more East Asian economies, China should remain committed to promoting the use of the RMB for general trade settlement between China and other East Asian economies, fully leveraging on instruments such as currency swap agreements to facilitate the central banks of other East Asian economies to engage in official transactions with the central bank of China, making the RMB become an official reserve currency for other East Asian economies to a certain degree and gradually advancing the convertibility of the RMB in official transactions; in addition, gradually opening up the domestic financial market, relaxing controls over capital account and improving the RMB backflow mechanism so as to make the RMB take on the functions of an investment currency in a broader range and at a higher level. In the meantime, China needs to consider the establishment of a RMB offshore center in Hong Kong in the light of the process and difficulties of the opening up of capital account, give full play to the status and role of Hong Kong as a financial center and control the risks and stress of RMB circulation overseas within a certain degree and range.

Third, through domestic economic reform, adjustment and development and the gradual transformation of the foreign trade model, promoting other East Asian economies to spontaneously take the RMB as some kind of "anchor" currency in exchange rate arrangement so as to make the RMB an intervention currency for the exchange rate market of other East Asian economies.

Fourth, China need to give a major push to regional monetary cooperation in East Asia and capitalize on regional financing arrangement to increase the attractiveness of the RMB as a reserve currency and an intervention currency on the one hand; on the other hand, it needs to realize the position of the RMB as the "anchor" currency at the institutionalized level and ultimately make the RMB a regional leading currency or one of the regional leading currencies through gradually boosting regional exchange rate cooperation.

RMB regionalization should be advanced at both the non-institutionalized and institutionalized levels, avoiding a unilateralist train of thinking and emphasizing regional cooperation and coordination, especially properly handling the relationship with the Japanese yen, the other major currency within the region. When it comes to promoting RMB regionalization through exchange rate cooperation, China needs to start from the sub-regional level in a progressive manner according to the closeness of connections in trade and investment between China and neighboring East Asian economies and the implications of exchange rate shocks for trade and investment.

As part of the efforts to realize RMB regionalization, China needs to carry out reforms in the following three aspects:

First, China needs to adjust its trade structure while maintaining sustainable and steady economic growth, change the model of production of low-end value chain and processing trade into the trade pattern of exporting semi-finished products and importing finished products.

Second, China needs to narrow the gap between urban and rural areas, between regions, and in national income while increasing residents' income, improving residents' consumption tendencies and boosting domestic demand.

Last, China needs to increase the contribution rate of final consumption to the GDP while cutting China's dependency ratio on foreign trade and gradually transforming the trade-driven economic model into the domestic demand-based economic model.

Afterwords

This book is the collection of all the relevant research results of my research team and myself over the years.

I started to study for a doctoral degree under the tutorship of professor Chi Yuanji in the Economics School of Jilin University in 1991. At the same time, my studying focus on the world economy shifted from the Japanese economy to issues about the "East Asian model" with the rise of the East Asian economy and the rapidly development of the Chinese economy. In my opinion, the so-called "East Asian model" consists of two parts, namely the common "institutional model" within East Asian countries and regions and the specific "regional industrial cycle model" of the region. Accordingly I had my book *East Asian Miracle and Strong Government — Institutional Analysis of the East Asian Model* published on the basis of my doctoral dissertation in 1996. In 1998, my paper under the title of "*On the Industrial Cycle Mechanism in East Asia*" was published on the *World Economy*, Issue 3. My book *East Asian Industrial Cycle and Chinese Industrial Rejuvenation* was published in 2000. These research results have evoked great repercussions in the academic community both at home and abroad. In particular, *East Asian Miracle and Strong Government — Institutional Analysis of the East Asian Model* has been designated by some colleges and universities as one of the required textbooks or reference books for post graduates majoring in economics and it still enjoys a very high citation rate in CSSCI.

It is on this basis, in the wake of the outbreak of the Asian Financial Crisis in 1997, that I set up a research team together with my first doctoral student Ding Yibing who is now a Professor (doctoral supervisor) of the Economics School of Jilin University and other young teachers. We started to study issues about regional monetary and financial cooperation in East Asia in response to malpractices and imbalances exposed by the crisis. In 1999 we wrote a paper in collaboration about the necessity and feasibility of setting up a monetary cooperation system in East Asia and submitted the paper to a well-known Chinese journal for publication, but it failed to be published due to the "too sensitive" issues contained even though it was highly recognized by editors and went through the final reading and editing procedures.

In 2000 I was invited by the Japan Foundation to serve as a Distinguished Professor in the School of Economics of Kwansei Gakuin University for 10 months. I took advantage of this period to make an in-depth study and adjustment of my research achievements that had failed to be published in China and wrote the paper *"Building a Regional Monetary System in East Asia and the Japanese Yen's 'Asianization'"* together with Hirayama Kenjiro, Professor of Kwansei Gakuin University. This paper was highly valued by the *World Economic Review,* a famous publication in the Japanese economic community, and was published in four consecutive issues (November and December of 2001, January and April of 2002). When I came back to China in August 2001 I found that studies on issues about monetary cooperation in East Asia had started to become the "hotspot" of the Chinese academic community. It was obvious that the Chinese government had decided to actively engage in regional monetary and financial cooperation under the framework of the "Chiang Mai Initiative".

Entering the 21st century, as China's economic strength increases, research on RMB internationalization has attracted great attention. However the domestic academic community still remains divided over the path choice for a large developing country's currency internationalization. Some scholars observe that RMB internationalization should move towards internationalization directly and that there is no necessity to move forward through regionalization. Our studies indicate that it is impossible for any currency to realize internationalization directly under the current "U.S. dollar regime" in terms of both theory and practice. Rather, a currency must firstly become a regional "key currency" through regional monetary and financial cooperation and then try to realize internationalization on this basis. In this sense, the RMB must draw lessons from European monetary integration and "Japanese Yen Internationalization" and blaze a trail of regionalization or Asianization. On this we individually or collectively wrote and had published a host of theses, including *On Specific Measures for Monetary Cooperation in East Asia East Asian Monetary Cooperation in the New Century: China's Status and Role* and *Difficulties and Strategic Adjustment of "Japanese Yen Internationalization"*. On top of that, we took the lead in putting forward and systematically demonstrating the necessity and feasibility as well as path selection of RMB regionalization. In 2006, Ding Yibing and I published *Asia's Transcendence — Building an East Asian Monetary System and "RMB Asianization"* on the basis of relevant periodic research results. The book has a evoked strong response and was awarded with second prize (humanities and social sciences) of Higher Learning University Outstanding Scientific Research Achievement by the Ministry of Education in September 2009.

During the process of our relevant studies we deeply feel that it is not easy to persist in long-term independent research in the scientific spirit and it is even more difficult to gain a precise and timely understanding of issues at the forefront of research but not to go with the stream of the so-called "hotspot." Before 2005 we attended many domestic academic conferences and delivered speeches to elaborate our own viewpoints, but we were taunted on some occasions as some academicians lacked understanding and argued that regional monetary and financial collaboration in East Asia was infeasible; before 2009 I went to many countries including Japan and South Korea for academic meetings or to deliver special academic reports on RMB internationalization and I still remember the headshakes and expressions of some foreign scholars or audiences. Yet the Chinese government decided to launch the pilot program of using the RMB for border trade settlement in the end of 2008. In particular, after the Chinese government made the determination to carry out the pilot program of using RMB for cross-border trade settlement, academic research achievements about issues including East Asian monetary and financial cooperation and RMB regionalization have sprung up. In Japan the academic circle has also changed its "prejudice" about RMB internationalization and regionalization. Starting from 2009 I have been invited many times by Japanese academic publications (such as *International Finance*) to write relevant theses; at the end of May of 2009, when I was invited by Japan Chuo University to participate in an international academic conference and deliver a report on RMB regionalization, I personally felt the attitude changes of some scholars and audience at the event. Following that, I was invited to join in a collaborative research project by Professor Eiji Shiomi, head of the Economic Research Institute of Japan Chuo University, Professor Seiichi Nakajo of the School of Economics of Chuo University and Kamikawa Takao, Professor of the School of conomics of Yokohama National University.

In 2005 I obtained the support of the National Social Science Fund Project "Research on RMB Regionalization" (Approval Number: 05BGJ004). On the basis of numerous preliminary research results, my research team and I made further painstaking and systematic research and accomplished the research work on schedule in 2009. This research was reviewed by the National Social Science Fund and rated as "Excellent". This book is composed on the basis of these research results. We would like to express our sincere thanks to the National Social Science Fund and its anonymous review experts.

Our research team consists of my doctoral students, post-doctors and young teachers of the School of Economics of Jilin University and the Northeast Asian Studies Academy of Jilin University. This book quotes or refers to some results of the doctoral dissertations of Li Junrui and Liu Chong. Post-doctor Yu Zhen and doctoral candidates including Fu Jinghui, Feng Yongqi, Ma Yechi and Zhou Xuezhi also contributed their parts in compiling the book. I will not list all the names as each chapter of the book is collected work with repeated modification by Professor Ding Yibing and myself. Therefore I would like to extend my thanks to all contributors for their hard work in compiling the book.

I sincerely hope that the book can serve as a modest spur to promote further studies on the relevant issues. The comments of our readers are welcomed.

To conclude, I wish to sincerely thank the editor in charge for the highly efficient work in the publication of the book.

Li Xiao
Dong Rong Building of Jinlin University
February 2010

Notes

Chapter 1

1. Mukund Raj, "Currency Competition—Survival of the Fittest (2003)," http://econwpa.wustl.edu:8089/eps/mac/papers/0309/0309010.pdf.
2. Jiao Jijun, "A Study on RMB Internationalization," doctoral dissertation of Liaoning University (2004). Currently there is no unified and authoritative definition of RMB internationalization since academic opinion is not in agreement.
3. "The Euro As an International Currency," http://www.europarl.eu.int/workingpapers/econ/101/chap1-en.htm#a.
4. Patricia S. Pollard, "The Creation of the Euro and the Role of the Dollar in International Markets," *The Federal Reserve Bank of St. Louis* (September/October 2001); ECU Institute, *International Currency Competition and the Future Role of the Single European Currency* (Kluwer Law International, 1995).
5. ECU Institute (See note 4 above).
6. Barry Eichengreen, "The Euro as a Reserve Currency," *Journal of Japanese and International Economics* 12 (1998): 483–506.
7. Cipolla, *Money, Prices, and Civilization in the Mediterranean World, Fifth to Seventeenth Century* (New York: Gordian Press, 1967). Quoted from Gerald P. Dwyer Jr. and James R. Lothian, "The Economics of International Monies," *Federal Reserve Bank of Atlanta Working Paper* 2003–37 (December 2003).
8. Gerald P. Dwyer Jr. and James R. Lothian, "The Economics of International Monies," *Federal Reserve Bank of Atlanta Working Paper* 2003–37 (December 2003).
9. Tavlas, George S., "The International Use of Currencies: The U.S. Dollar and the Euro," *Finance & Development* 35 (June, 1998): 46–49, http://www.imf.org/external/pubs/ft/fandd/1998/06/tavlas.htm. Gerald P. Dwyer Jr. and James R. Lothian, "The Economics of International Monies," *Federal Reserve Bank of Atlanta Working Paper* 2003–37 (December 2003).
10. Andrew Walter, *World Power and World Money: The Role of Hegemony and International Monetary Order* (Harvester Wheatsheaf, 1991).

11. Eiji Ogawa and Yuri Nagataki Sasaki, "Inertia in the Key Currency," *Japan and the World Economy* 10 (1998): 421–439.
12. For details on network externality and relevant concepts, please refer to Liebowitz, and S. Margolis, "Network Externality," *The New Palgraves Dictionary of Economics and the Law* (MacMillan, 1998).
13. ECU Institute, *International Currency Competition and the Future Role of the Single European Currency* (Kluwer Law International, 1995).
14. Mundell Robert, "A Theory of Optimum Currency Areas," *American Economic Review* (1961): 51.
    McKinnon Ronald, "Optimum Currency Areas," *American Economic Review* (1963): 53.
    Kenen Peter, *The Theory of Optimum Currency Areas: An Eclectic View* (Chicago: University of Chicago Press, 1969).
    Fleming, J. M., "On Exchange Rate Unification," *Economic Journal,* Vol. 81 (1971),.
    Corden, "Monetary Integration," *Essays in International Finance* (Princeton: Princeton University Press, 1972).
15. Jiang Boke and Zhang Qinglong, "Currency Internationalization: An Academic Review of its Terms and Impacts," *New Finance* Vol. 8 (2005).
16. Huang Yanjun: *HK Dollar-RMB Integration: Significance, Conditions and Prospects* (Beijing: China Social Sciences Press, 2003).
17. K. Dowd and D. Greenaway, "Network Externalities and Switching Costs," *Economic Journal* (1993).
18. Chen Yulu and Bian Weihong, "Monetary Union Theory: Progress of Optimum Currency Areas Measures," *Studies of International Finance* Vol. 2 (2004).
19. Kiyotaki and Wright, "On Money as a Medium of Exchange," *Journal of Political Economy* 97 (1989): 927–954.
20. Kiyotaki and Wright, "A Contribution to the Pure Theory of Money," *Federal Reserve Bank of Minneapolis Research Department Staff Report* 123 (August 1989).
21. Matsuyama, Kiminori, Nobuhiro Kiyotaki and Akihiro Matsui, "Toward a Theory of International Currency," *Review of Economic Studies* 60 (1993): 283–307.
22. Lu Lei, "Macroeconomics and Monetary Economics—A Review of Nobuhiro Kiyotaki's Academic Ideas," *Comparative Studies* Vol. 6 (2003).
23. Shi Shouyong, "Money and Prices: A Model of Search and Bargaining," *Journal of Economic Theory* 67 (1995): 461–496.

Trejos, Alberto and Randall Wright, "Search, Bargaining, Money and Prices," *Journal of Political Economy* 103 (1995): 118–141.

24. Noritaka Kudoh, "A Search–Theoretic Model of Money as a Store of Value (2003)," http://www2.ipcku.kansai-u.ac.jp/~kudoh/MyResearch/store.pdf.
25. Peter Rupert, Martin Schindler, Andrei Shevchenko and Randall Wright, "The Search—Theoretic Approach to Monetary Economics: A Primer (2000)," http://www.ssc.upenn.edu/~rwright/courses/rssw.pdf.
26. See note 22 above.
27. See Victor E. Li (2001).
28. Hiroyuki Oi, Akira Otani and Toyoichirou Shirota (2003) believe that the importance of the invoice currency is quite extensive. Exporters' choice of the invoice currency for export products—to adopt PCP or LCP—is of great influence on the transmission of monetary currencies, the optimum monetary policy rules and the optimum exchange rate system.
    Hiroyuki Oi, Akira Otani and Toyoichirou Shirota, "The Choice of the Invoice Currency in International Trade: Implications for the Internationalization of the Yen," *IMES Discussion Paper Series* 2003-E-13 (October 2003).
29. Sven Grassmann, "A Fundamental Symmetry in International Payments Pattern," *Journal of International Economics* 3 (1973): 105–106.
30. Richard Friberg, "On the Role of Pricing Exports in a Third Currency," *Stockholm School of Economics Working Paper* No. 128 (1996).
31. Richard Friberg, "In Which Currency Should Exporters Set Their Prices?," *Journal of International Economics* 45 (1998): 59–76.
32. The general preference to use local currency as the invoice currency has been verified and tested as an empirical law by many scholars, including Page (1977,1981), Carse et al. (1980), Magee and Rao (1980), San Paolo Bank of Turin (1990), S. Black (1990, 1993), Thygesen et al. (1995), and Tavlas (1996b). The analytical model to explain whether to choose local currency or vehicle currency as the invoice currency has been further developed by many scholars, including Magee and Rao (1980), Rao and Magee (1980), Bilson (1983), Donnenfeld and Zilcha (1991), and Ahtiala and Orgler (1995). Quoted from *The Geography of Money* (Southwest University of Finance and Economics Press, 2004) by Benjamin J. Cohen, 154.
33. Devereux, Michael B. and Charles Engel (2001): "Endogenous Currency of Price Setting in a Dynamic Open Economy Model," mimeo.

34. Quoted from Jiang Boke and Zhang Qinglong, "Currency Internalization: Academic Review of its Terms and Impact," *New Finance* Vol.8 (2005).
35. Shin-ichi Fukuda and Masanori Ono, "The Choice of The Invoice Currency under Uncertainty: Theory and Evidence from Korea," *CIRJE Discussion Paper* CIRJE-F-271 (2004).
36. Mukund Raj, "The impact of agriculture on exchange rates (2002)". Mukund Raj, "Currency Competition—Survival of the Fittest (2003)," http://econwpa.wustl.edu:8089/eps/mac/papers/0309/0309010.pdf.
37. Tavlas, G., "On the international use of currencies: The case of the D.M.," *IMF Working Paper* (1990).
38. Baron, D., "Fluctuating Exchange Rates and the Pricing of Exports," *Economic Inquiry* 14 (1976): 425–438.
39. Giovannini, Alberto, "Exchange Rates and Traded Goods Prices, *Journal of International Economics* 24 (1988), 45–68.
40. J. Bilson, *The Choice of An Invoice Currency in International Transactions, in Economic Interdependence and Flexible Exchange Rates*, J. Bhandari and B. Putnam, Eds. (MIT Press, Cambridge, MA., 1983), 384–401,
41. Hartmann, "The Future of the Euro as an International Currency: A Transactions Perspective," *London School of Economics Financial Markets Group Special Papers* (November 1996).
42. Saeed Samiee and Patrik Anckar, "Currency Choice in Industrial Pricing: A Cross-National Evaluation," *Journal of Marketing* Vol. 62 (1998), No. 3.
43. Quoted from Jiang Boke and Zhang Qinglong, "Currency Internalization: An Academic Review of its Terms and Impact," *New Finance* Vol. 8 (2005).
44. Li Jing and He Fan, "Cost-benefit Analysis on and Path Choices of RMB Internationalization," Doctor Cafe website.
45. Menzie Chinn and Jeffrey Frankel, "Will the Euro Eventually Surpass the Dollar as Leading International Reserve Currency? NBER conference on G7 Current Account Imbalances: Sustantialbility and Adjustment," post-conference draft.
46. See note 43 above.
47. Paul Krugman, "Who is Afraid of the Euro?," *Fortune* (1998.4.27): 8.
48. See note 45 above.
49. See note 43 above.
50. Zhou Wengui and Xiao Yaofei, *International Monetary System* (Guangzhou: Sun Yet-sen University Press, 2003).
51. The "Washington Consensus" refers to the "consensus" reached at the seminar on economic regulations and reforms in Latin America that was held by the Institute for International Economics in Washington in 1990.

Government officials from the U.S. and Latin American countries and representatives from the financial sector, enterprises, experts, scholars and international financial institutions presented the seminar. John Williamson, head of the Institute for International Economics, believed that participants in the seminar reached a consensus on the economic policies adopted and to be adopted by Latin American countries and stated 10 recommendations, namely strengthening fiscal policy discipline, controlling fiscal deficits and reducing inflation, redirecting public spending from subsidies ("especially indiscriminate subsidies") toward broad-based provision of key pro-growth, pro-poor services; reforming taxation system, broadening tax base, adopting interest rates marketization, adopting competitive exchange rates, implementing trade liberalization; liberalizing restrictions on foreign direct investment, privatizing state enterprises, loosening government regulation and protecting private property rights etc. Such recommendations were later called the "Washington Consensus".

52. In terms of the amount of attracted foreign capital, these countries are arranged in order: China, Mexico, Brazil, South Korea, Malaysia, Argentina, Thailand, Indonesia, Russia, India and Hungary.
53. The *Chiang Mai Initiative* executed in May 2000 is deemed as the official start of the monetary and financial cooperation in East Asia.
54. "Hegemony" as used here, including "financial hegemony", means of international political and economic significance. It is a neutral concept, being neither commendatory nor derogatory but expressing or reflecting an objective reality.
55. From early August 2008 to early May 2009, the USD index rose by nearly 15%. Moreover after the outbreak of the financial crisis, the prices of real estate and other assets in the U.S. plummeted and capital prices fluctuated substantially, yet the inflow of international capital into the U.S. financial market never stopped. In 2008 investment in bonds other than U.S. government bonds reduced considerably, yet that in U.S. government bonds reached USD 508.065 billion, far exceeding that of USD 230.330 billion in 2007. In 2008 there was still a surplus of USD 546.590 billion in the U.S. capital account (the deficit in its current account was USD 673.265 billion). The website of the U.S. Department of Commerce: http://www.bea.gov/.
56. Philipp Hartmann and Otmar Issing, "The International Role of the Euro," *Journal of Policy Modeling* 24 (2002): 315-345.

57. John F. Crown, *A History of Money from AD 800 (Chinese Edition)* (Beijing: The Commercial Press, 2002).
58. See note 57 above.
59. P. Deane and H. J. Habakkuk, "The Take-Off in Britain," paper submitted to the September 1960 meeting of the International Economic Association at Constance. Quoted from C. P. Kindleberger, "Foreign Trade and Economic Growth: Lessons from Britain and France, 1850 to 1913 (1961)".
60. H. J. Habakkuk, *Free Trade and Commercial Expansion, 1853-1870* (Cambridge History of the British Empire, 1940). Quoted from C. P. Kindleberger, "Foreign Trade and Economic Growth: Lessons from Britain and France, 1850 to 1913 (1961)".
61. Paul Kennedy, *The Rise and Fall of the Great Powers: Economic Change and Military Conflict from 1500 to 2000* (London: Unwin Hyman, 1988).
62. Walt W. Rostow, *The World Economy: History and Prospect* (London: Macmillan, 1978).
63. Paul Krugman, Richard N. Cooper and T. N. Srinivasan, "Growing World Trade: Causes and Consequences," *Brookings Papers on Economic Activity* (1995), Vol. 1995, No. 1, 25th Anniversary Issue.
64. A.G. Kenwood and A.L. Lougheed, *The Growth of the International Economy: 1820-1990 (Chinese Translation)* (Beijing: Economic Science Press, 1997).
65. See note 64 above.
66. Charles P. Kindelberger, *World Economic Primacy: 1500-1990* (Beijing: Commercial Press, 2003).
67. See note 64 above.
68. See note 64 above.
69. Andrew Walter, *World Power and World Money: The Role of Hegemony and International Monetary Order* (Harvester Wheatsheaf, 1991).
70. Williams David, The Evolution of the Sterling System, in C. R. Whittlesey and J. S. G. Wilson (eds.) (1968).
    Triffin Robert, *Our International Monetary System: Yesterday, Today, and Tomorrow* (New York: Random House, 1968).
    Marcello de Cecco, *Money and Empire: The International Gold Standard, 1890-1914* (Oxford: Blackwell (1974).
71. Zheng Weimin, *Decline or Renaissance: The United States in the Global Economy* (Social Sciences Academic Press, 1998).
72. See note 71 above.
73. Barry Eichengreen, "Sterling's Past, Dollar's Future: Historical Perspectives on Reserve Currency Competition," *NBER Working Paper* 11336 (2005).

74. Zhou Lin and Wen Xiaozheng, *Currency Internationalization* (Shanghai: Shanghai University of Finance and Economics Press, Jan 2001), 55.
75. The so-called "liberalization in principle" refers to being based on the liberalization of foreign exchange, foreign trade and other foreign transactions; the so-called "control on occasions" refers to carrying out the least necessary control or regulation on foreign trade.
76. Li Ping et al., *Monetary Cooperation and Coordination in East Asia* (China Financial and Economic Publishing House, 2004).
77. Yu Tongshen, "Dollarization, Currency Regionalization and Financial Security of Developing Countries," *Forum of World Economics and Politics* Vol.3 (2002).
78. Kong Xiangyi, "European Financial System: World Paradigm," *Modern Bankers* Vol.3 (2005).
79. Huang Yanjun, *HK Dollar—RMB Integration: Significance, Conditions & Prospects* (Beijing: China Social Sciences Press, 2003), 42.
80. Sun Jian, Wei Xiuhua and Tang Aipeng, "Strategic Path Choice of Internationalization of the RMB Based on the Developmental Process of Three Main Currencies", *Asia-Pacific Economic Review* Vol.2 (2005).
81. The Portuguese hegemony in the 16th century, the Dutch hegemony in the 17th century, the rise and fall of the British hegemony in the 18th and the 19th centuries, and the emergence of the U.S. hegemony in the 20th century all prove this point—almost all the challengers failed. During WWII, when challenging the traditional hegemony of Britain in Europe, Germany suffered an utter defeat; and Japan paid a painful cost for challenging the sphere of influence of the U.S. in the Pacific Ocean. After WWII the Soviet Union failed in challenging the hegemony of the U.S. before its collapse. On the contrary, the U.S. shared enormous benefits from its cooperation with Britain before becoming the new hegemony, creating a helpful prerequisite for launching the USD onto the world stage through post-WWII international treaties.

Chapter 2

1. In his essay "On RMB Internationalization", Liang Qinxing (2003) defines RMB internationalization as: the process during which the legal tender of the People's Republic of China i.e. the RMB, with the expansion of China's merchandise and services trade on the foreign markets, gradually serves as the medium of circulation, means of payment, means of storage and measure of value abroad in such forms as regular account,

capital account, overseas currency free convertibility on the basis of its functions as a local currency; it is the inevitable result of the expansion of international trade in China. RMB internationalization is the process of the RMB developing from a local currency into a regional currency and then an international currency.

2. In his book *Exchange Rates under the East Asian Dollar Standard – Living with Conflicted Virtue* McKinnon points out that conflicted virtue usually appears in countries with larger exports than imports, such as East Asian countries currently. Exerting pressures on such creditor countries with the tradition of high savings would push them into a dilemma: deflation in the case of local currency appreciation; threats of trade sanctions from countries that exert the pressure.
3. Li Xiao et al. (2003) define RMB regionalization as the process during which the RMB participates in institutional cooperation in the monetary and financial fields in East Asia, and struggles to become a key currency in the region. It is an indispensable and crucial step towards RMB internationalization and is determined by China's current domestic and foreign economic and financial environment.
4. AMU is part of "The Optimal Exchange Rate Regime for East Asia", a research project led by Ito Takatoshi, a professor from Tokyo University, Japan, and its specific preparation was completed by the Japanese scholar Eiji Ogawa. The ACU (Asian Currency Unit is also known as the Asian Monetary Unit but was put forward by the Asian Development Bank, announced to the public by Kawai Masahiro, a special adviser to the governor of Asian Development Bank and director of ADB Regional Cooperation Division, and officially released to the public in June 2006. The two Asian monetary units have more or less identical ways of preparation.
5. Foreign scholars also have some ideas on the currency basket when discussing the exchange rate cooperation arrangements in East Asia, but most of them pay less than due attention to the RMB, either placing the U.S. dollar at the core position (McKinnon, 1998, 2000a, 2000b) or advocating the currency basket pegged to the U.S. dollar and the Yen (Benassy-Quere, 1999; Rajan, 1999; Ito Takatoshi et al., 2000) or the currency basket pegged to the U.S., dollar, Yen and euro (Kawai and Takagi, 2000; Williamson, 2000) before proposing different ideas on exchange rate cooperation in East Asia.
6. In her essay Exchange Rate Cooperation Models and Choice Analysis in East Asia, Liu Lizhen (2006) classifies the opinions of Chinese and

foreign scholars on exchange rate cooperation in East Asia into three types: 1) "external currency anchor"-based exchange rate cooperation i.e. the U.S. dollar standard in East Asia, which has long been advocated by U.S. scholar McKinnon; 2) "internal currency anchor"-based exchange rate cooperation, which can be further divided into three models i.e. the exchange rate target zone model, the regional hard currency standard model, and regional currency substitution, all of which are unfeasible in the author's opinion; 3) "mixed currency anchor"-based exchange rate cooperation i.e. pegging to the common currency basket composed of currencies in and outside East Asia, which is actively promoted by the author.

7. As reported by Nihon Keizai Shimbun on 9 January 2009, according to the statistics released by the Japanese Ministry of Finance, as of the end of December 2008 foreign exchange reserves in Japan had hit 1,030.647 billion USD, while the latest Treasury International Capital (TIC) released by the U.S. Treasury Department showed that the total amount of Japanese investment in U.S. treasury bonds was 578.3 billion USD, which accounted for over half of the foreign exchange reserves in Japan. According to the statistics of the People's Bank of China, as of December 2008, foreign exchange reserves in China had reached 1,946.030 billion USD. Meanwhile Treasury International Capital (TIC) released by the U.S. Treasury Department showed that, as of the end of December 2008, the U.S. treasury bonds held by China reached 696.2 billion USD, making China the first of all countries in terms of the total amount of held U.S. treasury bonds; and that the total amount of Chinese investment in U.S. treasury bonds accounted for over 30% of the foreign exchange reserves of China.
8. Data are from the State Administration of Foreign Exchange of China.
9. Treasury International Capital (TIC) released by the U.S. Treasury in November 2008 showed that as of the end of September 2008, China held 585 billion USD in U.S. treasury bonds and had taken the place of Japan in becoming the largest creditor of the U.S.; Japan used to hold the largest amount of U.S. treasury bonds but had seen two consecutive months of reduction in the amount of U.S. treasury bonds it held, which reduced from 586 billion USD to 573.2 billion USD. Britain ranked third, and saw a reduction in 1.5 billion USD of the U.S. treasury bonds it held, which made the total amount of U.S. treasury bonds it held 355 billion USD.
10. The "Yen–USD Committee" set up in 1984 is thought to be a typical case in which the U.S. forced, openly and secretly, Japan to appreciate the Yen.

11. Data are from the Almanac of China's Finance and Banking 2007.
12. Data are from the Almanac of China's Finance and Banking 2007 and are obtained by calculation.
13. Data are from the Almanac of China's Finance and Banking 2007.
14. Data are from http://www.chinabond.com.cn.
15. The ratio of industrial added value is the share of added value per unit output value; data are from http://www.most.gov.cn.
16. Under the "U.S. dollar system," the U.S. dollar has become the main settlement and reserve currency in the foreign trade of most economies in East Asia, including China, making it more difficult for China and other economies in East Asia to use the RMB in trade settlement or for other economies to adopt the RMB as a reserve currency.
17. Available at the website of The Central People's Government of China, http://www.gov.cn/gzdt/2009-02/24/content_1241525.htm
18. Dr. Zhang Bin from the Institute of World Economics and Politics, Chinese Academy of Social Sciences, has made a detailed analysis of the ACU development background, functions, preparation method etc. (Zhang Bin, 2005)
19. Available at the website of The Central People's Government of China, http://www.gov.cn/gzdt/2009-02/24/content_1241525.htm
20. Data are from the website of the People's Bank of China, http://www.pbc.gov.cn/diaochatongji/tongjishuju/
21. In the recent announcement made by the Treasury Department of the United States, as of the end of 2008 the amount of U.S. treasury bonds held by China had increased to 727.4 billion USD from the past 696.2 billion USD, and China was still the largest holder of US treasury bonds. The data also showed that, as of the end of November 2007, the amount of U.S. treasury bonds held by China had exceeded 700 billion USD, being 713.2 billion USD. It indicated that, in December 2007, the net increment of U.S. treasury bonds held by China was 14.2 billion USD. In all months, the U.S. treasury bonds held by China increased the most in October 2007, being 65.9 billion USD (available at people.com.cn on March 2, 2009).
22. The last intervention in the price of U.S. treasury bonds by the Federal Reserve can be traced back to the 1960s, when the Federal Reserve bought T-bonds and sold out treasury bills for long and in large amounts in order to affect the yield curve, fight against economic recession, and eliminate trade deficits. The Federal Reserve announced the latest decision on saving the market in the context that the interest rate had

reduced to the zero range (0~0.25%) and that the U.S. economic recession had become increasingly severe. The so-called quantitative easing refers to the intentional creation of new liquidity for the economic system through various ways by the central bank so as to encourage expenditure and loans. Generally speaking, only when interest rate and other regular instruments are no longer effective will the monetary authority take such an extreme action.

23. Zheng Muqing, "On the Economic Effect of RMB Internationalization," *China International Finance Society* Vol. 7 (1995).
24. Data are calculated based on the China Statistical Yearbook 2008. East Asia here includes the 10 ASEAN member states, Japan, South Korea, Mongolia, Hong Kong, Macau and Taiwan.
25. Calculated with the statistics provided by WTO International Trade Statistics 2008. The main 13 countries in East Asia include the 10 ASEAN member states, China, Japan and South Korea.
26. Data are from the State Administration of Foreign Exchange of China, http://www.safe.gov.cn.
27 Of China's foreign investments in 2006 the Cayman Islands ranked first at 44.4%, followed by Hong Kong. The data are calculated according to the data released on the website of Invest in China.
28. Liu Lizhen, Xu Qiyuan et al., *Exploration of RMB Internationalization* (People's Publishing House, 2006), 26–27.
29. Data were mentioned by Ma Delun, the former Deputy Secretary of the State Administration of Foreign Exchange of China, in his speech "Present and Prospects of the Opening up of the Capital Account in China" at the high-profile forum International Capital Strategy in China. Information is available at the website of the State Administration of Foreign Exchange of China, http://www.safe.gov.cn/.
30. Data are available at the website of the State Administration of Foreign Exchange of China, http://www.safe.gov.cn.
31. Bank for International Settlements (BIS).
32. On November 5 2008, at the executive meeting of the State Council presided over by Chinese Premier Wen Jiabao, ten measures for enlarging domestic demand were determined with a total investment of about 4 trillion yuan. Of which it was clearly proposed to improve the income of urban and rural residents, especially low-income groups of people, and boost consumption growth. The measure was good for transforming the Chinese economic pattern and improving the contribution of domestic demand to the GDP.

33. In case of deviation of the real RMB exchange rate from the nominal RMB exchange rate, or the spot exchange rate and interest rate from the expected exchange rate and interest rate, it will provide opportunities of interest arbitrage for international speculators, stimulate the flow of short-term speculative capital, and may lead to "herd behaviour", affecting the economic and financial stability in China.
34. Capital flight refers to the flight of capital to another country to seek a greater degree of security for such reasons as physical monetary instability or concern about possible instability, confiscatory taxation, wars and revolutions etc.

Chapter 3

1. In this sense, the so-called Japanese yen internationalization is the development process from an incomplete international currency to a complete international currency; while the failure of the Japanese yen internationalization means that it failed to meet the target of becoming a completely internationalized currency and it still functions as an incomplete international currency. If we make a comparison of the different "internationalization" paths of the Japanese yen and the Deutschmark, we will find a phenomenon with profound theoretical significance and practical value: The Deutschmark played a role similar to a completely internationalized currency before the emergence of the euro due to the development of economic integration, especially the existence of the European Monetary System (EMS) – a regional monetary system. But obviously, the role of the Japanese yen in Asia cannot be compared with that of the Deutschmark in Europe. In this connection, the Deutschmark in effect chose a path towards internationalization through becoming a regional key currency first compared with the internationalization of Japanese Yen.
2. Bergsten (1997) believes that five key factors are at play for a currency to become an international currency: (1) potential economic and international trade scale; (2) economic independence from external restrictions; (3) no foreign exchange control; (4) the breadth, depth and liquidity of the capital market of the country; (5) the economic strength, stability and international status of the country. Yasuyoshi Masuda (1998) observes that five preconditions are needed for a currency to become internationalized: (1) a certain scale of economic aggregate, trade and capital flow; (2) price stability; (3) surplus of current account payment

and pure creditor nation; (4) no foreign exchange control and capital trade restrictions; (5) enjoying a free, open and developed financial market. David Hare (Hu Dinghe, 1995) pointed out that six conditions must be there for a country to play a central role in the international monetary system: (1) the currency issuing country must maintain close trade ties with other countries; (2) it must enjoy a huge and open capital market; (3) it must enjoy economic stability and have a low inflation rate; (4) it must be less dependent on foreign trade and can isolate its domestic economy from external economic fluctuations; (5) the currency issuing country must be a huge net creditor nation and can provide international floating assets at any time; (6) the central bank of the country must be financially strong and can serve as the lender of last resort in the world. Lei Zhiwei (2000) argues that whether a currency can become an influential international currency depends on three basic conditions: the first is the "basic factor" - whether the currency is freely convertible; the second is the "scale factor" - the size of the currency in the national and regional economy, foreign trade and foreign financial trading; the third is the "risk factor" - whether the currency is stable both internally and externally and what is the risk degree of holding or dealing in the currency.

3. Cheng Xianping, "Review and Foresight of the Progress of RMB Convertibility," *China's Administration for Foreign Exchange* Issue 10 (1999).
4. Zhao Chunming and Li Xiaoying, "Analysis of Monetary Cooperation and the Core Status of the RMB in East Asia," *Journal of Contemporary Asia-Pacific Studies* Issue 2 (2007).
5. Li Jing, Guan Tao and He Fan: "The Status Quo of Transnational Circulation of the RMB and Its Impact on China's Economy," *Management World* Issue 9 (2004).
6. Zheng Xiaozhou, "RMB: From 'Unpopular' to 'Fully Circulated'", *Shanghai Securities News* (2007-6-29).
7. Zhong Wei, "The Status Quo, Problems and Countermeasures of RMB Circulation in Neighboring Countries," *Management World* Issue 1 (2008).
8. Wang Yafan, Guan Tao and Wen Jiandong, *Moving Towards RMB Convertibility: Practice of China's Progressivism* (The Publishing House of Economic Science, 2002).
9. "Economic Report of the President, 2005," World Economic Outlook database, 1980–2005.

10. Li Xiao, Ding Yibing and Qin Tingting, "The Promotion of China's Position in East Asian Economy: Study Based on Trade Orientation," *Forum of World Economics and Politics* Issue 5 (2005).
11. Wang Guifen and Zhou Guiyi, "Primary Investigation of Frontier Trade and RMB Regionalization," *Heilongjiang Finance* Issue 10 (2006).
12. Research group for *Xinjiang Finance* Society, "Studies on RMB Regionalization and the Expansion of Border Trade Settlement in RMB—Studies on Promoting RMB Regionalization in Countries Bordering Xinjiang," Xinjiang Finance Supplementary Issue (2007).
13. The research group of SAFE Xishuangbanna Branch, "Status Quo, Problems and Countermeasures of Using the RMB for Xishuangbanna Border Trade Settlement," *Times Finance* Issue 12 (2007).
14. Zheng Lingyun, "RMB Regionalization and the Expansion of Its Functions in Frontier Trade Settlement," *International Trade* Issue 7 (2006).
15. Yang Song and Wang Lina, "Legal Advancement of RMB Regionalization," *Journal of Liaoning University (Philosophy and Social Science Edition)* Issue 3 (2007).
16. Hu Xiaolian, "Process and Experience of the Reform of China's Foreign Exchange Administration System," *China Finance* Issue 7 (2008).
17. Xiao Fengjuan, "Review and Outlook of the Reform of China's Foreign Exchange Administration System," *International Trade* Issue 7 (2008).
18. Data source: Statistical Communiqué of National Economy and Social Development of China (2007).
19. The executive meeting of the State Council also determined to implement the program in Guangdong and the Yangtze River Delta for trade settlement with Hong Kong and Macao. The leading reason behind the implementation of the pilot program is to alleviate difficulties faced by export-oriented businesses and maintain a steady growth of foreign trade. The international exchange rate fluctuates drastically during financial crisis, so most enterprises will be happy if the RMB with a more stable exchange rate can be used for settlement. Evaluations by a number of media and scholars observe that this move is an important step for the RMB to move forward towards internationalization.
20. The 5 ASEAN economies refer to the 5 countries that have a relatively higher level of economic development and a relatively larger trade volume with China, namely Malaysia, the Philippines, Thailand, Indonesia and Singapore. On the one hand, we only choose ASEAN-5 because of their representative export trade. In 2003, the imports of the ASEAN-5 accounted for 93% of the total of ASEAN in 2003. On the other

hand, it is because some small ASEAN economies do not have complete economic data.

21. Japan, South Korea and ASEAN-5 entered the WTO simultaneously in January 1995 and China made entered in December 2001; Japan, South Korea and ASEAN-5 became members of the APEC in 1989 while China only became a member of it in 1991. In this sense, when selecting dummy variables, the year of 2001 and 1991 are taken for the demarcation points for Japan and ASEAN-5. When it comes to the dummy variable for South Korea, the year of 2001 when it entered the WTO is taken as the demarcation point.
22. According to the statistical data released by the ASEAN Secretariat, the exports of ASEAN to China are typically mineral fuels such as petroleum and natural gas as well as non-food raw materials such as timber and paper pulp while the exports of China to ASEAN are mainly general mechanical products including vehicles and electromechanical appliances, and textile garments.
23. According to the statistics released by the ADB, China's GDP recorded a growth rate of 11.4 per cent in 2007, hitting a new high in recent years. It might be very difficult for China to reach this again in the future; meanwhile, China Quarterly Update issued by the World Bank on November 25 2008 projected that China's GDP growth rate would be around 7.5 per cent in 2009 and this is mainly based on the driving force of China's four trillion RMB investment package in fixed assets in 2009 in GDP. This text settles for the growth rate of 7.5 and 10 per cent to make a predictive analysis according to different situations.
24. According to the standard of classification of the UN Data Department, within the context of BEC classification, final products include two categories namely capital goods and consumption goods. Here we only take into consideration consumption goods according to the requirements for analysis and these include: 112 Food and beverages, primary, mainly for household consumption; 122 Food and beverages, processed, mainly for household consumption; 51 Passenger motor cars; 522 Other non-industrial transport equipment; 61 Durable consumer goods n.e.s; 62 Semi-durable consumer goods n.e.s; 63 Non-durable consumer goods n.e.s.
25. As the economy of Luxembourg is small in scale, we omitted Luxembourg from the 12 countries of the Eurozone.

26. If we compare the results concluded by Bayoumi and Eichengreen (1994) based on earlier data of Europe (1962-1989), the gap would be smaller between the two.
27. T. Bayoumi and B. Eichengreen, "Exchange rate volatility and intervention: implications of the theory of optimum currency areas," *Journal of International Economics* Vol.45 (1998).
28. T. Bayoumi and B. Eichengreen, "Ever Closer to Heaven? An Optimum — currency-area Index for European Countries," *European Economic Review* Vol. 41 (1997).
29. Wan Zhihong, "Studies on the Economic Foundation for Monetary Cooperation in East Asia — Perspective of Optimum Currency Area Theory," *Nankai Economic Studies* Issue 3 (2003).

Chapter 4

1. All data are from the National Bureau of Statistics and the comparison of per capita GDP adopts the PPP method.
2. Mainly refers to "Report on Research on Using RMB for the Region's International Settlement (2009)" of the research group of the Bank of Communications.
3. Between 1981 and 1995 the related coefficient between the export growth rate of the seven East Asian economies of Chinese Hong Kong, South Korea, Singapore, Thailand, Malaysia, Indonesia and the Philippines to China and the export growth rate of China to the U.S. and Japan is -0.256 96, but this figure rose to 0.904493 between 1995 and 2007.
4. Semi-finished products here include processed goods, components and parts while finished products only include consumer goods.
5. The assembly and productive trade structure of Japan in the 1980s refers to the fact that it typically imported raw materials and exported finished consumer goods. It is this trade structure that resulted in Japan's structural trade surplus with the U.S.
6. Stagnations and hesitations were quite common during the European integration process, which is called "euro-sclerosis" (Fabrice Larat, 2005).
7. During this period, on the one hand, the French monetary authority changed its previous position of resolutely upholding independent monetary policy in the mid-1980s and bore heavy losses of unemployment to follow suit with Germany, which turned out to be the most critical factor for the successful operation of the European Monetary System. On

the other hand, Germany also contributed abundant resources to support the French franc. In order to shore up the confidence of investors in the European exchange rate mechanism, the Germany monetary authority even deviated from its consistent monetary policy to claim that the Deutsche Bundesbank would purchase any currency that deviated from exchange rate parity so as to assume all or part of the losses on released exchange rate parity.

8. In fact the European Central Bank after the emergence of the euro in 1999 used to carry out an expansionary monetary policy that resulted in accelerated money supply and rising inflation rate within the Eurozone. This obviously goes against the consistent principles of the Deutsche Bundesbank. It is this that made the Deutsche Bundesbank and the Ministry of Finance prefer to maintain the greatly shrinking scale of "The Snake in the Tunnel" to join in the proposed European Monetary System in the late 1970s.

9. For instance, in early 1980s when Mitterrand had just taken office, he tried to adopt an expansionary monetary policy to cut back the interest rate but as with West Germany, the majority of European countries settled for a stable monetary policy that led to big outflows of French capital and it ultimately gave up the expansionary policy.

References

English Materials

Ahearne, Alan G., John G. Fernald, Prakash L. and John W. S. 2003. China and Emerging Asia: Comrades or Competitors?. FRB International Working Paper No. 789.

Alexius A. 2000. Supply Shocks and Real Exchange Rates. Sveriges Riksbank (mimeo).

Bacchetta P. and Wincoop E. 2002. A Theory of the Currency Denomination of International Trade. International Finance Discussion Papers 747, Board of Governors of the Federal Reserve System (U.S.). 159.

Baron D. 1976. Fluctuating Exchange Rates and the Pricing of Exports. *Economic Inquiry* 14: 425–438.

Barro, Robert J. 1986. Reputation in a Model of Monetary Policy within Complete Information. *Journal of Monetary Economics* Vol.17.

Bayoumi T. and Eichengreen, B. 1993. Shocking Aspects of European Monetary Unification. In F. Torres and F. Giavazzi, eds., *Adjustment and Growth in the European Monetary Union*. Cambridge: Cambridge University Press.

— 1994. One Money or Many? Analyzing the Prospects for Monetary Unification in Various Parts of the World. *Princeton Studies in International Finance* 16. International Finance Section, Princeton University.

— 1998. Exchange Rate Volatility and Intervention: Implications of the Theory of Optimum Currency Areas. *Journal of International Economics* Vol.45.

— 1997. Ever Closer to Heaven? An Optimum-currency-area Index for European Countries. *European Economic Review* Vol. 41.

Bergsten C. F. 1996. The Dilemma of the Dollar: The Economics and Politics of the United States. *International Monetary Policy* (2nd ed.). Sharpe.

— 1997. The Dollar and the Euro. *Foreign Affairs* Vol. 76 No. 4: 83–95.

Bernanke, B.S. 1986. Alternative Explanations of the Money-Income Correlation. *Carnegie-Rochester Conference Series on Public Policy* 25.

Bhattacharya, A., Swati G. and W. Jos J. 2001. Has the Emergence of China Hurt Asian Exports?. *Applied Economics Letters* Vol. 8:217–221.

Bilson, J. 1983. The Choice of an Invoice Currency in International Transactions. In *Economic Interdependence and Flexible Exchange Rates* (J. Bhandari and B. Putnam, Eds.). MIT Press, Cambridge, MA, 384–401.

Black, Stanley W. 1990. The International Use of Currencies. *The Evolution of the International Monetary System* (edited by Yoshio Suzuki , Junichi Miyabe, and Mitsyaki Okabe). University of Tokyo Press:175–194.

Blanchard, O. J. and D. Quah. 1989. The Dynamic Effects of Aggregate Supply and Demand Disturbances. *American Economic Review* 79.

Bourguinat, H. 1985. *L'économie mondiale à découvert*. Paris: Calmann-Lévy.

Bry, G. and C. Boschan. 1971. *Cyclical Analysis of Time Series: Selected Procedures and Computer Programs*. New York: NBER.

Cipolla. 1967. *Money, Prices and Civilization in the Mediterranean World, Fifth to Seventeenth Century*. New York: Gordian Press.

Clarida, R. and Gali J. 1994. Sources of Real Exchange Rate Fluctuations: How Important are Nominal Shocks?. *Carnegie Rochester Series on Public Policy* 41.

Corden. 1972. Monetary Integration. *Essays in International Finance*. Princeton: Princeton University Press.

de Cecco, Marcello. 1974. *Money and Empire: The International Gold Standard, 1890-1914*. Oxford: Blackwell.

Deane, P. and H. J. Habakkuk 1960. The Take-off in Britain. Paper submitted to the September 1960 Meeting of the International Economic Association at Constance.

Demertzis M., Hallett A. H. and Rummel O. 2000. Is the European Union aNatural Currency Area, Or Is It Held Together by Policy Makers. Weltwirtschaftliches Archiv 136(4).

Devereux, Michael B. and Charles E. 2001. Endogenous Currency of Price Setting in a Dynamic Open Economy Model. Mimeo.

Dooley, Michael, David F.-L. and Peter G. 2003. An Essay on the Revived Bretton Woods System. NBER Working Paper No.9971.

Dowd, K. and Greenaway D. 1993. Network Externalities and Switching Costs. *Economic Journal*.

Dwyer, Gerald P. Jr. and James R. L. December 2003. The Economics of International Monies. Federal Reserve Bank of Atlanta Working Paper 2003–37.

ECU I. 1995. *International Currency Competition and the Future Role of the Single European Currency*. Kluwer Law International.

Eichengreen, B. 1989. The Comparative Performance of Fixed and Flexible Exchange Rate Regimes: Interwar Evidence. NBER Working Papers 3097.

— 1998. The Euro as a Reserve Currency. *Journal of the Japanese and International Economics* 12: 483–506.

— 2005. Sterling's Past, Dollar's Future: Historical Perspectives on Reserve Currency Competition. NBER Working Paper 11336

Eichengreen, B., Yeongseop Rhee and Hui Tong. 2007. China and the Exports of Other Asian Countries. *Review of World Economics* Vol.143, Issue 2: 201–226.

Emerson, M. and others. 1992 .5. *One Market One Money*. Oxford University.

Flemming J. M. 1971. On Exchange Rate Unification. *Economic Journal* Vol.81.

Frankel, J. and Wei S. J. 1994. Yen Bloc or Dollar Bloc? Exchange Rate Policies of the East Asian Economies. Takatoshi Ito and Anne O. Krueger, eds., *Macroeconomic Linkage: Savings, Exchange Rates and Capital Flows*. Chicago: University of Chicago Press.

Frankel, J. and Andrew R. 1998. The Endogeneity of the Optimum Currency Area Criteria. *Economic Journal*Vo1.108, Issue 1:1009–1025.

Frankel, J. and Goldstein M. 1999. The International Role of the Deutsche Mark , in Deutsche Bundesbank (Ed.). *Fifty Years of the Deutsche Mark: Central Bank and the Currency in Germany Since 1948*. Oxford: Oxford University Press. 685–792.

Friberg R. 1996. On the Role of Pricing Exports in a Third Currency. *Stockholm School of Economics Working Paper* No. 128.

Fukuda, Shin-ichi O. and Masanori. 2004. The Choice of Invoice Currency under Uncertainty: Theory and Evidence from Korea. *CIRJE Discussion Paper* CIRJE-F-271.

Funke, M. 1997. The Nature of Shocks in Europe and in Germany. *Economica* 64.

Giovannini, A. 1988. Exchange Rates and Traded Goods Prices. *Journal of International Economics* 24: 45–68.

Grassman, S. 1973. A Fundamental Symmetry in International Payments Pattern. *Journal of International Economics* 3:105–106.

Goto J. 2002. Economic Preconditions for Monetary Cooperation in East Asia. Kobe University (mimeo).

Habakkuk, H. J. 1940. Free Trade and Commercial Expansion, 1853–1870. *Cambridge History of the British Empire II.*

Haberler, Gottfreid. 1970. The International Monetary System: Some Recent Devlopments and Discussions. *Approaches to Greater Flexibility of Exchange Rates*. Princeton: Princeton University Press. 115–123.

Hamilton J. D. 1989. A New Approach to the Economic Analysis of Non-Stationary Time Series and the Business Cycle. *Econometrica* 57: 357–384.

Hartmann, P. 1998. *Currency Competition and Foreign Exchange Markets: The Dollar, the Yen and the Euro*. U.K.: Cambridge University Press.

References

Hartmann, P. 1996.The Future of the Euro as an International Currency: A Transactions Perspective . London School of Economics Financial Markets Group Special Papers, November.

Hartmann, P. and I. Otmar. 2002.The International Role of the Euro. *Journal of Policy Modeling* 24, 315–345

Harding D. and A. Pagan. 2002. Dissecting the Cycle: A Methodological Investigation. *Journal of Monetary Economics* 49(2). 365–381,

Hiroyuki O., O. Akira and S. Toyoichirou. 2003. The Choice of Invoice Currency in International Trade: Implications for the Internationalization of the Yen. *IMES Discussion Paper Series* 2003-E-13, October.

Ingram, James C. 1969. Comment: The Currency Area problem. Monetary Problems of the International Economy, 95–100.

Isogai, Takashi and Shunichi S. 2000. East Asia's Intra- and Inter-Regional Economic Relations: Data Analyses on Trade, Direct Investment and Currency Transactions. Bank of Japan, International Department Working Paper Series 00-E-4.

Ito. 2008. The Influence of the RMB on Exchange Rate Policy in Other Economies. In M. Goldstein and N. Lardy, Debating China's Exchange Rate Policy, 239–258.

JETRO. 2007. International Trade and Foreign Direct Investment: Increasing Utilization of Asian FTAs and Growth Strategies for Japanese Companies. JETRO White Paper.

Kenen, Peter. 1969. *The Theory of Optimum Currency Areas: An Eclectic View*. Chicago: University of Chicago Press.

Kennedy, Paul. 1988. *The Rise and Fall of the Great Powers: Economic Change and Military Conflict from 1500 to 2000*. London: Unwin Hyman.

Krugman, P. 1991. Target Zones and Exchange Rate Dynamics. *Quarterly Journal of Economics*, CVI, 669–682.

Krugman P., Richard N. Cooper and T. N. Srinivasan. 1995. Growing World Trade: Causes and Consequences. Brookings Papers on Economic Activity, Vol. 1995, No. 1, 25th Anniversary Issue.

— 1998. Who is afraid of the Euro?. *Fortune*, 1998.4.27.

Kiyotaki, Wright. On money as a medium of exchange" , *Journal of Political Economy* 97, pp927-954,1989.

— 1989. A Contribution to the Pure Theory of Money. *Federal Reserve Bank of Minneapolis Research Department Staff Report* 123, August.

Kudoh, Noritaka A. 2003. Search-Theoretic Model of Money as a Store of Value, http://www2.ipcku.kansai-u.ac.jp/~kudoh/MyResearch/store.pdf.

Maehara, Y. 1993. The Internationalization of the Yen and Its Role as a Key Currency. *Journal of Asian Economics*, 4(1). 153–170.

McKinnon, R. 1963. Optimum Currency Areas. *American Economic Review*, 53.

– 1979. *Money in International Exchange: The Convertible Currency System.* Oxford University Press.

Matsuyama et al. 1993. Toward a Theory of International Currency. *Review of Economic Studies* 60, 283–307.

Menzie C. and Jeffrey Frankel. 2005. Will the Euro Eventually Surpass the Dollar as Leading International Reserve Currency?. NBER conference on G7 Current Account Imbalances: Sustantialbility and Adjustment, post-conference draft.

Mundell, Robert A. 1961. Theory of Optimum Currency Areas. *American Economic Review*, 51.

— 1998. The Euro and the Stability of the International Monetary System. Paper prepared for Conference on the Euro as a Built-In Stabilizer in the Economic System, Luxembourg, December 3–4.

Nakagawa, T. 2004. Internationalization of the RMB (Yuan) and Its Impact on East Asia. Institute for International Policy Studies (Tokyo).

Ng, Francis and Y. Alexander. 2002. Production Sharing in East Asia: Who Does What for Whom and Why?. World Bank Staff Paper.

Ng, B. K. 2007. The Economic Rise of China: Threats and Opportunities from the Perspective of Southeast Asia. *The Copenhagen Journal of Asian Studies* 25, 9–27.

Obstfeld, M. 1985. Floating Exchange Rates: Experience and Prospects. *Brookings Papers on Economic Activity* 2.

Ogawa E. and N. S. Yuri. 1998. Inertia in the Key Currency. *Japan and the World Economy* 10, 421–439.

Ogawa, Yoshimi. 2008. Widen Deviations among East Asian Currencies. RIETI Discussion Paper Series 08-E-010.

Okamoto, Susumu. 2005. Spiral Pattern of Development and Triangular Trade Structure as a Regional Manufacturing Platform. RIETI BBL Seminar.

Persuad A. and S. Spratt. 2004. The New RMB Bloc (mimeo). June.

Pollard, Patricia S. 2001. The Creation of the Euro and Role of the Dollar in International Markets. The Federal Reserve Bank of St. Louis, September/ October.

Raj, Mukund. 2002. Impact of Agriculture on Exchange Rates.

— 2003. Currency Competition—Survival of the fittest. http://econwpa.wustl.edu:8089/eps/mac/papers/0309/0309010.pdf.

Roland-Holst D. 2002. An Overview of the PRC's Emergence and East Asian Trade Patterns to 2020. ADB Institute Research Paper Series No.44.

Roland-Holst D., Jean-Pierre Verbiest,and Fan Zhai. 2005. Growth and Trade Horizons for Asia: Long-term Forecasts for Regional Integration. ADB ERD Working Paper Series No.74.

Rostow, Walt W. 1978. *The World Economy: History and Prospect*. London: Macmillan.

Rupert P. et al. 2000. The Search-Theoretic Approach to Monetary Economics: A Primer. http://www.ssc.upenn.edu/~rwright/courses/rssw.pdf.

Samiee et al. 1998. Currency Choice in Industrial Pricing: A Cross-National Evaluation. *Journal of Marketing* Vol. 62, No. 3.

Sarr, Abdourahmane and L. Tonny. 2002. Measuring Liquidity in Financial Markets. *IMF Working Paper* 02/232.

Saxena, S. C. 2003. Is the Euro Area a Role Model for Asia?. University of Pittsburgh (mimeo).

Schlote, Werner. 1952. *British Overseas Trade*. Oxford.

Selgin, G. 2000. World Monetary Policy after the Euro. *Cato Journal* Vol. 20, No.1.

Shams, R. 2002. Is it Time for a World Currency?. HWWA Discussion Paper 167.

Shi, S. Y. 1995. Money and Prices: A Model of Search and Bargaining. *Journal of Economic Theory* 67, 461–496.

Shin, Kwanho and W. Yunjong. 2003. Trade Integration and Business Cycle Synchronization in East Asia. *Journal of Asian Economics* Vol. 13, Issue 6, 767–785.

Sims, C. A. 1980. Macroeconomics and Reality. *Econometrica*, 48.

— 1986. Are Forecasting Models Usable for Policy Analysis?. *Federal Reserve Bank of Minneapolis Quarterly Review*, 1–16.

Swoboda, Alexander. 1968. *The Euro-Dollar Market: An Interpretation, Essays in International Finance, no. 64*. International Finance Section, Princeton University.

Tavlas, George S. 1990. On the International Use of Currencies: The Case of the D.M.. *IMF Working Paper*.

— 1991. *On the International Use of Currencies: The Case of the Deutsche Mark, Essays in International Finance No.181*, Princeton University.

— 1998. The International Use of Currencies: The U.S. Dollar and the Euro. Finance & Development 35, June: 46–49. http://www.imf.org/external/pubs/ft/fandd/1998/06/tavlas.htm.

Trejos, Alberto and W. Randall. 1995. Search, Bargaining, Money and Prices. *Journal of Political Economy* 103, 118–141.

— 1996. Toward a Theory of International Currency: A Step Further. PIER Working Paper 97–115.

Triffin Robert. 1968. *Our International Monetary System: Yesterday, Today, and Tomorrow*. New York: Random House.

Verhoef, Bastiaan A. 2003. The (A)symmetry of Shocks in the EMU, De Nederlandsche Bank Staff Reports, No. 106.

Walter, A. 1991. World Power and World Money: the Role of Hegemony and International Monetary Order" , Harvester Wheatsheaf, 1991.

Weimann, M. 2003. OCA Theory and EMU Eastern Enlargement—An Empirical Application. Deutsche Bank Research, Working Paper, No.8.

Weiss, John. 2004. People's Republic of China and its Neighbors: Partners or Competitors for Trade and Investment?. ADB Institute Discussion Paper Series No.13.

Williams, D. 1968. *The Evolution of the Sterling System*, in C.R. Whitlesey and J.S.G Wilson (eds.). Essays in Money and banking. Oxford: Oxford University Press.

Yeh, K. C. and J. Plasmans. 2002. Establishing an Exchange Rate Mechanism with Chinese Characteristics: An Option for Taiwan, China, and Hong Kong to Prevent a Next Currency Crisis?, in *Asian Crisis IV*. Taipei: National Taiwan University.

Yuen, H. 2001. Optimum Currency Area in East Asia: A Structural VAR Approach. ASEAN Economic Bulletin, 18 (2).

Zebregs, H. 2004. Intra-Regional Trade in Emerging Asia. IMF Policy Discussion Paper, PDP/04/1.

Zhang, Z., K. Sato and M. McAleer. 2003. Is East Asia an Optimum Currency Area?. IMMMs Achieve, 2.

Chinese Materials

Ba Shusong 巴曙松. 2003. Ba Xianggang dazao cheng Renminbi li'an zhongxin 把香港打造成人民幣離岸中心 (Developing Hong Kong to be a RMB Offshore Center). Shanghai & Hongkong Economy, Issue 10.

— 2006. Zhongguo jinrong gaige ruhe shiying guoji hua中國金融改革如何適應國際化 (How China's Financial Reform Is Adapted to Internationalization). Finance & Economy, Issue 2.

— 2007. Renminbi guoji hua de san ge jieduan 人民幣國際化的三個階段 (Three Stages of the Internationalization of RMB). Beijing News, Jun 20.

Bergsten C. Fred, (C.弗雷德· 伯格斯坦). 2002. Ouyuan yu Meiyuan qianzai de "tongzhi diwei zhi zheng" 歐元與美元潛在的"統治地位之爭" (The Potential Competition of the Euro and U.S. Dollar for Ruling Position). Economics News, NO.478; International Financing Review, March 1.

Cai Yiping 蔡乙萍. 2005. Dong Ya huobi hezuo de biyao xing ji ke xing xing fenxi 東亞貨幣合作的必要性及可行性分析 (The Necessity and Feasibility Analysis on the Currency Cooperation in East Asia). Market Modernization, Issue 5.

References

Cao Honghui 曹紅輝. 2006. Guoji hua zhanlue zhong de Renminbi quyu hua 國際化戰略中的人民幣區域化 (The Regionalization of RMB in the Strategy for Internationalization). China Finance, Issue 5.

Cao Honghui 曹紅輝 and Hu Zhihao 胡志浩. 2007. Yazhou zhaiquan de ji zhi huobi yu Renminbi de guoji hua 亞洲債券的計值貨幣與人民幣的國際化 (Bonds Evaluation Currency in Asia and RMB Internationalization). Studies of International Finance, Issue 10.

Cao Xiaoheng 曹小衡. 2008. Liang an jingji yiti hua de jinzhan yu qianjing 兩岸經濟一體化的進展與前景 (The Progress and Prospect of Cross-Straits Economic Integration). Asia-Pacific Economic Review, Issue 2.

Cao Yong曹勇. 2005. Renminbi guoji hua lun gang 人民幣國際化論綱 (Theses on RMB Internationalization). Journal of Henan Institute of Financial Management, Issue 4.

Cha Yonggui 查勇貴. 2005. Dui Renminbi guoji hua de moshi xuanze yu guojia zhanlue 對人民幣國際化的模式選擇與國家戰略 (The Model Choice of and National Strategy for the RMB Internationalization). Journal of Guangdong Institute of Public Administration, Issue 5.

Chen Hong陳虹. 2004. Riyuan de guoji hua zhi lu 日元國際化之路 (The Internationalization Path of Japanese Yen). World Economy and Politics, Issue 5.

Chen Yanyan 陳岩岩, Tang Aipeng唐愛朋and Sun Jian孫健. 2005. Renminbi guoji hua guocheng zhong huobi zhenghe de ke xing xing fenxi人民幣國際化過程中貨幣整合的可行性分析 (The Feasibility Analysis on Monetary Integration in the Process of RMB Internationalization). Studies of International Finance, Issue 7.

Chen Yulu 陳雨露. 2003. Dong Ya huobi hezuo zhong de huobi jingzheng wenti 東亞貨幣合作中的貨幣競爭問題 (The Problem of Currency Competition in East Asian Monetary Cooperation). Studies of International Finance, Issue 3.

Chen Yulu 陳雨露 and Bian Weihong 邊衛紅. 2004. Huobi tongmeng lilun: Zui you huobi qu hengliang biaozhun de jinzhan 貨幣同盟理論: 最優貨幣區衡量標準的進展 (Theory of Monetary Union: The Progress of Measurement Criteria for the Optimum Currency Area). Studies of International Finance, Issue 2.

Chen Yulu 陳雨露, Wang Fang 王芳 and Yang Ming 楊明. 2005. Zuowei guojia jingzheng zhanlue de huobi guoji hua: Meiyuan de jingyan zhengju—Jian lun Renminbi de guoji hua wenti 作為國家競爭戰略的貨幣國際化: 美元的經驗證據—兼論人民幣的國際化問題 (*Currency Internationalization* as a National Competition Strategy: The US Dollar's Empirical Evidence—and a Study on the RMB Internationalization Issues). Economic Research, Issue 2.

Cheng Xianping 程憲平. 1999. Renminbi ke duihuan jincheng huigu yu qianzhan 人民幣可兑換進程回顧與前瞻 (The Review and Preview of the RMB Convertibility Progress). China's Foreign Exchange Management, Issue 10.

Cheng Engui 程恩富 and Zhou Zhaoguang周肇光. 2003. Guanyu Renminbi quyu hua he guoji hua keneng xing fenxi 關於人民幣區域化和國際化可能性探析 (The Feasibility Analysis of the RMB Regionalization and Internationalization). Journal of Shandong Institute of Finance and Economics, Issue 3.

— 2004. Zhu bu tuijin Renminbi de quyu hua he guoji hua 逐步推進人民幣的區域化和國際化 (The Gradual Advances of the RMB Regionalization and Internationalization). Exploration and Free Views, Issue 4.

— 2007. Dong Ya Quyu Hezuo: Riben de chufa dian yu suqiu ji dui Zhongguo de jiejian yiyi東亞區域合作: 日本的出發點與訴求及對中國的借鑒意義 (TheRegional Cooperation in East Asia: Japan's Initial Goal and Appeal and the Reference for China). Asia & Africa Review, Issue 1.

Chown, John F., (約翰·F·喬恩). 2002. Huobi Shi: Cong Xiyuan 800 nian qi (Zhong yi ben) 貨幣史:從西元800年起 (中譯本)(A History of Money: From AD 800 Onwards (Chinese Version)). Beijing: The Commercial Press.

Cohen, Benjamin J. 1971. *The Future of Sterling as an International Currency*. London: Macmillan; New York: St. Martin's Press.

— 1998. *The Geography of Money*. Ithaca: N.Y. Cornell University Press.

Comprehensive Research and Development Institute (綜合研究開發機構). 2002. *Dongya huobi zhengce de hezuo ji qi shenhua* 東亞貨幣政策的合作及其深化 (East Asian Monetary Policy Cooperation and Deepening). *Comprehensive* Research and Development Institute.

Dai Jinping戴金平. 2004. Dong Ya de huobi jinrong hezuo de jingji zhengzhi jichu fenxi東亞的貨幣金融合作的經濟政治基礎分析 (The Analysis of the Economic and Political Base of East Asian Monetary and Financial Cooperation). Nankai Economic Studies, Issue 3.

Dai Jinping 戴金平 and Xiong Xingmei 熊性美. 2001. Dong Ya huobi hezuo de jieduan queding he xingtai xuanze 東亞貨幣合作的階段確定和形態選擇 (The Stage Identification and Form Choice of Monetary Cooperation in East Asia). Nankai Economic Studies, Issue 8.

Dai Jinping 戴金平 and Wan Zhihong 萬志宏. 2005. Dong Ya diqu huobi jinrong hezuo de jingji jichu yanjiu東亞地區貨幣金融合作的經濟基礎研究 (The Study of the Economic Base of East Asian Monetary and Financial Cooperation). Journal of Yunnan University, Issue 2.

Ding Jianping丁劍平. 2003. Guanyu xian xing de Renminbi huilu jizhi de ke chixu xing yanjiu 關於現行的人民幣匯率機制的可持續性研究 (The Study of the

Sustainability of the Existing RMB Exchange Rate Mechanism). Studies of International Finance, Issue 5.

— 2006. Jin yi bu zengqiang Renminbi huilu tanxing 進一步增強人民幣匯率彈性 (The Further Enhancement of RMB Exchange Rate Flexibility). World Economy, Issue 3.

Ding Jianping 丁劍平and Yang Fei楊飛. 2007. Renminbi huilu canzhao huobi lanzi yu Dong Ya huobi liandong de yanjiu人民幣匯率參照貨幣籃子與東亞貨幣聯動的研究 (The Study of the Currency Basket for RMB Exchange Rate Reference and East Asian Currency Linkage). Studies of International Finance, Issue 7.

Ding Yibing 丁一兵and Li Xiao李曉. 2004. Guanyu Dong Ya quyu huobi hezuo de yanjiu: Wenxian zong shu 關於東亞區域貨幣合作的研究: 文獻綜述 (The Literature Reviews of the Studies of Monetary Cooperation in East Asia). Contemporary Asia-Pacific Studies, Issue 6.

Ding Yibing 丁一兵. 2006. Dong Ya huobi hezuo de xin jinzhan 東亞貨幣合作的新進展 (The New Progress of the Monetary Cooperation in East Asia). World Economy, Issue 3.

Dong Jihua 董繼華. 2008. Jing wai Renminbi liutong guimo guji—Jiyu ji du ziliao de xie zheng fenxi 境外人民幣流通規模估計—基於季度資料的協整分析 (The Estimation of RMB Circulation Scale Overseas—Cointegration Analysis based on Quarterly Data). Modern Economic Science, Issue 1.

Dong Mu 東木. 2001. Dui Renminbi guoji hua wenti de sikao 對人民幣國際化問題的思考 (The Reflections on RMB Internationalization). Finance Teaching and Research, Issue 5.

Eiji Ogawa (小川英治) and Yao Zhizhong 姚枝仲. 2004. Lun ding zhu yi lanzi huobi de huilu zhidu 論釘住一籃子貨幣的匯率制度 (On Exchange Rate System of Pegging to a Currency Basket). World Economy, Issue 6.

Fan Aijun 范愛軍 and Xiao Dandan肖丹丹. 2005. Renminbi guoji hua guandian ping shu ji qi zouxiang fenxi 人民幣國際化觀點評述及其走向分析 (The Reviews of the Perspectives on RMB Internationalization and Its Trend Analysis). Reform, Issue 1.

Fang Guozhi 方國志. 2008. Renminbi zai ASEAN liutong de xian zhuang ji celue 人民幣在ASEAN流通的現狀及策略 (The Status Quo of and Strategy for RMB Circulation in ASEAN). South China Finance, Issue 5.

Gao Haihong 高海紅. 2008. Dang qian quan qiu meiyuan benwei: Wenti ji Dong Ya quyu jiejue fang'an 當前全球美元本位: 問題及東亞區域解決方案 (The Current Global US-Dollar Standard: Issues and Solutions in East Asia). World Economy and Politics, Issue 1.

Guan Jian 關鍵. 2006. Renminbi yu Lubu xian chao zai Zhong E bianjing diqu liutong zhuangkuang bijiao 人民幣與盧布現鈔在中俄邊境地區流通狀況比較 (The Comparison of the Circulation Conditions between the RMB and the Ruble on the China-Russian Border). Heilongjiang Finance, Issue 12.

Guan Zhixiong 關志雄. 2000. Yazhou gaobie ding zhu Meiyuan de huilu zhidu 亞洲告別釘住美元的匯率制度 (Asia Says Goodbye to Pegging to the Exchange Rate System of the US Dollar). International Economic Review, Issue of March and April.

Guo Hua 郭華. 2006. Dong Ya huobi hezuo zhong Zhong Ri huobi Jingzheng li bijiao 東亞貨幣合作中中日貨幣競爭力比較 (The Comparison of the Competitiveness between China's and Japan's Currencies in the East Asian Monetary Cooperation). Finance Teaching and Research, Issue 4.

Guo Shuqing 郭樹清. 2003. Zhongguo de wai hui zhengce he wai hui guanli tizhi gaige 中國的外匯政策和外匯管理體制改革 (China's Foreign Exchange Policy and Management System Reform). Caijing Magazine, Issue 7.

Han Jiyun 韓繼雲. 2008. Renminbi guoji hua de biyao xing he celue xuanze 人民幣國際化的必要性和策略選擇 (The Necessity and Strategic Choice of RMB Internationalization). China Real Estate Finance, Issue 2.

Han Minchun 韓民春 and Yuan Xiulin 袁秀林. 2006. Jiyu maoyi shijiao de Renminbi "quyu hua" de weiguan jingji fenxi 基於貿易視角的人民幣"區域化"的微觀經濟分析 (Micro-economic Analysis of RMB "Regionalization" based on Trade). Journal of International Trade.

He Fan 何帆. 2004. Meiyuan guoji hua de lishi ji qishi 美元國際化的歷史及啟示 (The History and Inspirations of the US Dollar Internationalization). Doctor's Café.

He Fan 何帆 and Li Jing 李婧. 2005. Meiyuan guoji hua de lujing, jingyan he jiaoxun 美元國際化的路徑、經驗和教訓 (The Path, Experience and Lessons of the US Dollar Internationalization). Social Science Front, Issue 1.

He Huigang 何慧剛. 2005. Dong Ya huobi hezuo yu Renminbi guoji hua 東亞貨幣合作與人民幣國際化 (The Monetary Cooperation in East Asia and RMB Internationalization). Finance and Investment, Issue 8.

— 2005. Ouyuan moshi he Meiyuan moshi hua bijiao fenxi ji qi dui Dong Ya huobi hezuo de qishi 歐元模式和美元模式化比較分析及其對東亞貨幣合作的啟示 (The Comparative Analysis of the Euro and the US Dollar Modes and Its Inspirations to East Asian Monetary Cooperation). Finance and Investment, Issue 11.

— 2007. Dong Ya quyu huobi hezuo de moshi he lujing xuanze 東亞區域貨幣合作的模式和路徑選擇 (The Mode and Path Choices of Monetary Cooperation in

East Asia). Research on Economics and Management, Issue 7.

— 2007. Ziben zhanghu kaifang, huilu zhidu yu Renminbi guoji hua 資本帳戶開放、匯率制度與人民幣國際化 (The Opening Up of Capital Accounts, the Exchange Rate System and the RMB Internationalization). Social Science Journal, Issue 3.

He Jia 賀佳 and Mai Fu 邁夫. 2005. Renminbi guoji hua xin lun 人民幣國際化道路新論 (A New Discussion on the Path of RMB Internationalization). Heze University Journal, Issue 4.

He Xiyou 何喜有. 2005. Hanguo de Dong Ya jinrong hezuo zhanlue ji qi dui Zhongguo de qishi 韓國的東亞金融合作戰略及其對中國的啟示 (The South Korean Strategy for East Asian Financial Cooperation and Its Inspirations to China). Journal of Fudan University, Issue 3.

Hiroshi Okuda (奥田宏司). 2002. *Meiyuan tizhi yu Ouyuan, Riyuan* 美元體制與歐元、日元 (U.S. Dollar Regime, the Euro and the Japanese Yen). Japanese Economics Publishing House.

Hu Dinghe 胡定核 and Cheng Haiyong 程海泳. 1996. Renminbi guoji hua de tiaojian 人民幣國際化的條件 (The Conditions for RMB Internationalization). Development Forum, Issue 1.

Hu Xiaolian 胡曉煉. 2008. Zhongguo wai hui guanli tizhi gaige de licheng he jingyan 中國外匯管理體制改革的歷程和經驗 (The Processes and Experiences of China's Foreign Exchange Management System Reform). China Finance, Issue 7.

Hu Zaiyong 胡再勇. 2004. Renminbi chengwei Yazhou chubei xing huobi xian zhuang yanjiu 人民幣成為亞洲儲備性貨幣現狀研究 (The Study on the Status Quo of RMB to Become a Reserve Currency in Asia). Economic Survey, Issue 11.

Hua Min 華民. 2006. Quan qiu jingji shi heng de chufa jizhi ji Zhongguo de xuanze 全球經濟失衡的觸發機制及中國的選擇 (The Trigger Mechanism of Global Economic Imbalance and China's Choice). International Economic Review, Issue of March and April.

Huang Meibo 黄梅波. 2001. Huobi guoji hua ji qi jueding yinsu—Ouyuan yu Meiyuan de bijiao 貨幣國際化及其決定因素—歐元與美元的比較 (The *Currency Internationalization* and Its Deciding Factors—The Comparison between the Euro and the US Dollar). Journal of Xiamen University (Philosophy and Social Sciences Edition, Issue 2.

Ishimi Tetsu (石見徹) and Masahiro Kawai (河合正弘). 1990. *Jichu huobi yu guoji huobi tixi* 基礎貨幣與國際貨幣體系 (The Base Currency and the International Monetary System). *Collections on Economics*. Tokyo University.

Jia Huiyan 賈輝豔. 2005. Li An Renminbi shichang yu Renminbi de guoji hua jincheng 離岸人民幣市場與人民幣的國際化進程 (The Offshore Market and the Internationalization Progress of RMB). Journal of Beijing Institute of Economic Management, Issue of March.

Jia Yanning 覃延寧. 2004. Renminbi zai ASEAN quyu hua fazhan de xianzhuang ji jianyi 人民幣在ASEAN區域化發展的現狀及建議 (The Status Quo of and Suggestions for yjr RMB Regionalization Development in ASEAN). South China Finance, Issue 9.

Jia Yongjia 賈永嘉. 2005. Renminbi guoji hua de tiaojian he shixian tujing de tantao 人民幣國際化的條件和實現途徑的探討 (Discussions on the Conditions and Realization Path for RMB Internationalization). Journal of Hebei University of Science and Technology, Issue 4.

Jiang Boke 姜波克. 1994. Renminbi Guoji hua wenti tantao 人民幣國際化問題探討 (Discussions on RMB Internationalization). Economic Review, Issue of May.

Jiang Boke 姜波克 and Zhang Qinglong 張青龍. 2005. Huobi guoji hua: Tiaojian yu yingxiang de yanjiu zong shu 貨幣國際化: 條件與影響的研究綜述 (The Currency Internationalization: Reviews of the Studies on Its Conditions and Influences). New Finance, Issue 8.

Jiang Ling 姜凌. 1997. Renminbi guoji hua lilun yu shijian de ruo gan wenti 人民幣國際化理論與實踐的若干問題 (Some Questions about the Theory and Practice of RMB Internationalization). World Economy, Issue 4.

Jiao Jijun 焦繼軍. 2004. Renminbi guoji hua yanjiu 人民幣國際化研究 (The Study on RMB Internationalization). Doctoral Dissertations of Liaoning University.

Jing Xuecheng 景學成. 2002. Lue lun wen jian de huobi zhengce he zhichi jingji zengzhang de cuoshi 略論穩健的貨幣政策和支持經濟增長的措施 (Brief Discussion on the Prudent Monetary Policies and Measures of Supporting Economic Growth). Journal of Financial Research, Issue 4.

Kamikawa Takao (上川孝夫) and Imamatsu Eietsu (今松英悦). 1997. *Riyuan de zhengzhi jingji xue—Yazhou yu shijie tixi* 日元的政治經濟學—亞洲與世界體系 (Political Economy of the Japanese Yen—Asia and the World System). Dōbunkan.

Kan Jingyang 闞景陽. 2006. Renminbi jing wai liutong ji guoji hua yanjiu 人民幣境外流通及國際化研究 (A Study on RMB Overseas Circulation and Internationalization). Finance Theory and Teaching, Issue 2.

Ke Meishui 柯美水. 1996. Renminbi ziyou duihuan yu guoji hua wenti de zai sikao 人民幣自由兑換與國際化問題的再思考 (Re-thinking of the Free Convertibility and Internationalization of RMB). Journal of Chongqing Business School, Issue 9.

Kenwood, A. G. (肯伍德) and A. L. Lougheed (洛赫德). 1997. *Guoji jingji de chengzhang: 1820–1990 (Zhong yi ben)* 國際經濟的成長: 1820–1990 (中譯本) (The Growth of the International Economy: 1820-1990, Chinese Version). Beijing: Economic Science Press.

Kindleberger, Charles P. (查理斯·P.金德爾伯格). 1991. *Xi Ou jinrong shi (Zhong yi ben)* 西歐金融史（中譯本）(A Financial History of Western Europe, Chinese Version). Beijing: China Financial Publishing House, 1991.

Kong Xiangyi 孔祥毅. 2005. Ouzhou jinrong tixi: Shijie de fanshi 歐洲金融體系: 世界的範式 (European Financial System: The Paradigm of the World). Modern Bankers, Issue 3.

Kwan Chi Hung 關志雄. 2003. *Yazhou huobi yiti hua yanju—Riyuan qu fazhan qushi* 亞洲貨幣一體化研究—日元區發展趨勢 (Studies on Monetary Integration in East Asia—Development Trend of the Yen Bloc). Beijing: China Financial & Economic Publishing House.

Lai Mingyong 賴明勇 and Li Jingchi 李鏡池. 2007. Quanmian jianmian ASEAN guanshui dui Zhongguo hongguan jingji he chanye yingxiang de ke jisuan yiban junheng 全面減免 ASEAN 關稅對中國宏觀經濟和產業影響的可計算一般均衡 (The Computable General Equilibrium of the Effects of Across-the-Board Tariff Reduction on China's Macroeconomy and Industry). South China Journal of Economics, Issue 3.

Larat, Fabrice (拉哈). 2005. *Ouzhou yiti hua shi 1945–2004 (Zhong yi ben)* 歐洲一體化史1945–2004 (中譯本) (The History of European Integration 1945–2004 (Chinese Version)). Beijing: China Social Sciences Publishing House.

Li Chong 李翀. 2002. Lun Renminbi de quyu hua 論人民幣的區域化 (On RMB Regionalization). Hebei Academic Journal, Issue 5.

Li Daokui 李稻葵. 2006. Zhongguo yinggai jujue Yayuan 中國應該拒絕亞元 (China Should Reject an Asian Dollar). Foreign Business, Issue 6.

Li Daokui 李稻葵 and Liu Linlin 劉霖林. 2008. Shuang gui zhi tuijin Renminbi guoji hua 雙軌制推進人民幣國際化 (The Double-track System Advancing the RMB Internationalization). China Finance, Issue 10.

Li Fuyou 李富有. 2004. *Quyu huobi hezuo: Lilun, shijian yu Yazhou de xuanze* 區域貨幣合作: 理論、實踐與亞洲的選擇 (Regional Monetary Cooperation: Theory, Practice and Asia's Choice). Beijing: China Financial Publishing House.

Li Huamin 李華民. 2003. Jiyu Renminbi xingzhi de Zhongguo huobi guoji hua zhanlue 基於人民幣性質的中國貨幣國際化戰略 (China's Strategy for *Currency Internationalization* Based on the Nature of RMB). Economic Management, Issue 3.

Li Jianjun 李建軍 and Tian Guangning 田光寧. 2003. San da huobi guoji hua de lujing bijiao he qishi 三大貨幣國際化的路徑比較與啟示 (The Comparison and Inspirations of the Internationalization Path among Three Major Currencies). Shanghai Finance, Issue 9.

Li Jing 李婧. 2005. Zhongguo dui Yazhou huobi he jinrong hezuo de xuqiu yu gonggei 中國對亞洲貨幣和金融合作的需求與供給 (China's Demand and Supply of Asian Monetary and Financial Cooperation). Research On Economics and Management, Issue 2.

Li Jing 李婧. 2006. *Zhongguo ziben zhanghu ziyou hua yu huilu zhidu xuanze* 中國資本帳戶自由化與匯率制度選擇 (China's Capital Account Liberalization and Choice of Exchange Rate Regime). Beijing: China Economic Publishing House.

Li Jing 李婧, Guan Tao 管濤 and He Fan 何帆. 2004. Renminbi kuajing liutong de xian zhuang yiji dui Zhongguojingji de yingxiang 人民幣跨境流通的現狀以及對中國經濟的影響 (The Status Quo of RMB Cross-border Circulation and Its Influence on the Chinese Economy). Management World, Issue 9.

Li Ping 李平 and Liu Peizhi 劉沛志. 2003. Dong Ya diqu huobi hezuo guodu jiduan de jiben gouxiang—Dong Ya diqu huilu xietiao jizhi 東亞地區貨幣合作過渡階段的基本構想—東亞地區匯率協調機制 (The Basic Conception of East Asian Monetary Cooperation at the Transitional Stage—The Exchange Rate Coordination Mechanism in East Asia). World Economy and Politics, Issue 12.

Li Ping, et al. 李平等. 2004. *Dong Ya diqu huobi hezuo yu xietiao* 東亞地區貨幣合作與協調 (Monetary Cooperation and Coordination in East Asia). Beijing: China Financial & Economic Publishing House.

Li Qiansheng 李前勝 and Hu Xihong 胡曦虹. 2004. Lun Renminbi guojia hua de shixian tiaojian he fazhan jincheng 論人民幣國家化的實現條件和發展進程 (On the Realization Conditions and Development Process of RMB Nationalization). Business Studies, Issue of December.

Li Xiao 李曉. 2005. "Riyuan guoji hua" de kunjing ji qi zhanglue tiaozheng "日元國際化"的困境及其戰略調整 (Difficulties of "Japanese Yen Internationalization" and Its Strategic Adjustment). World Economy, Issue 6.

— 2009. Quan qiu jinrong weiji xia Dong Ya huobi jinrong hezuo de lujing xuanze 全球金融危機下東亞貨幣金融合作的路徑選擇 (The Path Choice of East Asian Monetary and Financial Cooperation under the Global Financial Crisis). Northeast Asia Forum, Issue 5.

References

Li Xiao 李曉 and Ding Yibing 丁一兵. 2002. Lun Dong Ya huobi hezuo de juti cuoshi 論東亞貨幣合作的具體措施 (On Specific Measures on East Asian Monetary Cooperation). World Economy, Issue 11.

— 2003. Dong Ya quyu huobi tixi de goujian: Biyao xing, ke xing xing yu lujing xuanze 東亞區域貨幣體系的構建:必要性、可行性與路徑選擇 (The Establishment of East Asian Monetary System: The Necessity, Feasibility and Path Choice). Social Science Front, Issue 4.

— 2004. Xin shiji Dong Ya quyu huobi hezuo: Zhongguo de diwei yu zuoyong 新世紀東亞區域貨幣合作:中國的地位與作用 (East Asian Monetary Cooperation in the New Century: China's Status and Function). Jilin University Social Science Journal, Issue 2.

— 2005. Xian Jieduan de Dong Ya jinrong hezuo: Mianlin de tiaozhan ji zhengce jianyi 現階段的東亞金融合作: 面臨的挑戰及政策建議 (East Asian Financial Cooperation at the Current Stage: Challenges and Policy Suggestions). International Economic Review, Issue of May – June.

— 2006. Jingji chongji duichen xing yu quyu jingji hezuo: Dong Ya yu qita quyu de bijiao yanjiu 經濟衝擊對稱性與區域經濟合作: 東亞與其他區域的比較研究 (Economic Shock Symmetry and Regional Economic Cooperation: A Comparative Study among East Asia and Other Regions). Jilin University Social Science Journal, Issue 4.

— *Yazhou de chaoyue* 亞洲的超越 (Asian Transcendence). Beijing: Contemporary China Publishing House.

— 2009. Renminbi huilul biandong qushi ji qi dui quyu huobi hezuo de yingxiang 人民幣匯率變動趨勢及其對區域貨幣合作的影響 (The Changing Trend of the RMB Exchange Rate and Its Influences on Regional Monetary Cooperation). Studies of International Finance, Issue 3.

Li Xiao 李曉 and Dai Jinping 戴金平, ed.. 2006. *21 Shiji Chuqi Dong Ya huobi hezuo yu Renminbi guoji hua* 21 世紀初期東亞貨幣合作與人民幣國際化 (Monetary Cooperation in East Asia and RMB Internationalization in the Early 21st Century). Changchun: Jilin University Press.

Li Xiao 李曉, Li Junjiu 李俊久 and Ding Yibing 丁一兵. 2004. Lun Renminbi yazhou hua 論人民幣亞洲化 (On RMB Asianization). World Economy, Issue 2.

Li Xiao 李曉, Ding Yibing 丁一兵 and Qin Tingting 秦婷婷. 2005. Zhongguo zai Dong Ya jingji zhong diwei de tisheng: Jiyu maoyi dongxiang de kaocha 中國在東亞經濟中地位的提升:基於貿易動向的考察 (The Promotion of China's Status in East Asian Economy: Examinations Based on Trade Tendency). The Forum on World Economy and Politics, Issue 5.

Li Xiaojie 李曉潔. 2004. Yazhou huobi lianmeng ke xing xing yanjiu—Dong Ya shiji chanchu bodong de chongji fenxi 亞洲貨幣聯盟可行性研究—東亞實際產出

波動的衝擊分析 (The Feasibility Study of Asian Monetary Union—The Analysis on the Shock of the Actual Output Fluctuations in East Asia). Journal of Finance and Economics, Issue 6.

Li Yang 李揚 and Cao Honghui 曹紅輝. 2005. Yazhou zhaiquan shichang fazhan yanjiu 亞洲債券市場發展研究 (A Study of the Development of Asian Bond Market). Japanese Studies, Issue 1.

Li Yao 李瑤. 2003. Fei guoji huobi, huobi guoji hua yu ziben xiangmu ke duihuan 非國際貨幣、貨幣國際化與資本項目可兌換 (The Non-International Currency, *Currency Internationalization* and Capital Accounts Convertibility). Journal of Financial Research, Issue 8.

Li Yao 李瑤 and Chen Bingcai 陳炳才. 2003. Zhu bu tuijin de jincheng—Fei guoji huobi yu ziben xiangmu ke duihuan 逐步推進的進程—非國際貨幣與資本項目可兌換 (A Step-by-Step Process—A Non-International Currency and Capital Accounts Convertibility). International Trade, Issue 6.

Li Zhuo 李卓. 2005. *Ouzhou huobi Yiti hua de lilun yu shijian* 歐洲貨幣一體化的理論與實踐 (Theory and Practice of European Monetary Integration). Wuhan: Wuhan University Press.

Liang Qinxing 梁勤星. 2003. Dui Renminbi guoji hua wenti de sikao 對人民幣國際化問題的思考 (Reflections on RMB Internationalization). Southwest Finance, Issue 7.

Ling Xingguang 凌星光. 2002. Shi lun Renminbi shengzhi he Zhongguo guoji huobi zhanlue 試論人民幣升值和中國國際貨幣戰略 (On RMB Appreciation and China's International Currency Strategy). Management World, Issue 3.

Liu Aiwen 劉愛文. 2005. Renminbi de guoji hua zhi lu 人民幣的國際化之路 (A Road to RMB Internationalization). Business Studies, Issue 18.

Liu Houjun 劉厚俊 and Ma Shusheng 馬樹生. 2006. Zhuzhong cong fei shengchan maoyi lingyu tuijin Dong Ya hezuo 注重從非生產貿易領域推進東亞合作 (Focusing on Advancing East Asian Cooperation via Non-Productive Trade Sector). Asia-pacific Economic Review, Issue 4.

Liu Lizhen 劉力臻 and Xie Chaoyang 謝朝陽. 2003. Dong Ya huobi hezuo yu Renminbi huilu zhidu xuanze 東亞貨幣合作與人民幣匯率制度選擇 (East Asian Monetary Cooperation and the Choice of RMB Exchange Rate System). Management World, Issue 3.

Liu Lizhen 劉力臻 and Xu Qiyuan 徐奇淵 et al. 2006. Renminbi guoji hua tansuo 人民幣國際化探索 (Exploration of RMB Internationalization). Beijing: People's Publishing House.

Liu Qun 劉群. 2006. Quyu huobi yu shijie huobi: Renminbi qianjing panduan yu jueze fenxi 區域貨幣與世界貨幣: 人民幣前景判斷與抉擇分析 (Regional

Currency and World Currency: An Analysis on Judgment and Choice of RMB Prospect). Academic Forum, Issue 9.

Liu Zhenlin 劉振林. 2006. *Dong Ya huobi hezuo yu Renminbi zhidu xuanze yanjiu* 東亞貨幣合作與人民幣匯率制度選擇研究 (Studies on Monetary Cooperation in East Asia and Choice of RMB Exchange Rate Regime). Beijing: China Economic Publishing House.

Lu Hao 盧皓. 2007. Zhong-Mian, Zhong-Lao bianjing Renminbi liutong zhuangkuang diaocha yu sikao中緬、中老邊境人民幣流通狀況調查與思考 (Investigation and Thinking of RMB Circulation in Border Areas Between China and Burma and Between China and Laos). Times Finance, Issue 9.

Lu Lei 陸磊. 2003. Hongguan jingji xue he huobi jingji xue—Qinglong Xinhong de xueshu sixiang shuping 宏觀經濟學和貨幣經濟學—清瀧信宏的學術思想述評 (Macroeconomics and Monetary Economics—Review of Nobuhiro Kiyotaki's Academic Thoughts). Comparison, Vol. 6.

Luo Junchong 羅俊翀 and Zhou Yu'e 周聿峨. 2008. Zhong Ri zai Dong Ya huobi lingyu de boyi yu jingzheng 中日在東亞貨幣領域的博弈與競爭 (The Game and Competition between China and Japan in the East Asian Monetary Area). Mondern Japanese Economy, Issue 1.

Ma Ronghua 馬榮華 and Rao Xiaohui 饒曉輝. 2007. Renminbi de jing wai xuqiu guji 人民幣的境外需求估計 (The Estimation of Overseas Demand for RMB). Studies of International Finance, Issue 2.

Marx, Karl 馬克思. 1975. *Ziben lun* 資本論 (Das Kapital). Vol. 1. Beijing: People's Publishing House.

Mckinnon Ronald, (羅奈爾得· 麥金農)and Gunther Schnabl (甘瑟· 施納布林). 2003. Zhongguo shi Dong Ya diqu de wending liliang haishi tongsuo yali zhi yuan? —Jian lun yu he xiong zhang bu ke jian de 中國是東亞地區的穩定力量還是通縮壓力之源？—兼論魚和熊掌不可兼得 (Is China a Stabilizer or a Source of Deflationary Pressure in East Asia?—On "You Cannot Burn the Candle at Both Ends"). Comparison, Issue 7.

McKinnon, Ronald (麥金農) and Gunther Schnabl (施納布林). 2003. *Dongya jingji zhouqi yu huilu anpai (Zhong yi ben)* 東亞經濟週期與匯率安排（中譯本） (Economic Cycle and Exchange Rate Arrangement in East Asia, Chinese Version). Beijing: China Financial Publishing House.

McKinnon, Ronald (麥金農) and Kenichi Ohno (大野健一). 1999. *Meiyuan yu Riyuan—huajie Mei Ri liang guo de jingji chongtu (Zhong yi ben)* 美元與日元—化解美日兩國的經濟衝突（中譯本） (U.S. Dollar and Japanese Yen—Resolving Economic Conflict between the United States and Japan, Chinese Version). Shanghai: Shanghai Far East Publishers.

Mundell (蒙代爾). 2003. *Huilu yu zui you huobi qu* 匯率與最優貨幣區 (Exchange Rate and Optimum Currency Areas). *Mengdaier jingji xue wenji di wu juan (Zhong yi ben)* 蒙代爾經濟學文集第五卷（中譯本）(Selected Works on Economics of Robert Mundell, Vol. 5, Chinese Version). Beijing: China Financial Statistics Publishing House.

Maurice Obstfeld (奧博斯特弗爾德) and Kenneth Rogoff (若戈夫). 2002. *Gao ji guoji jinrong xue jiaocheng (Zhong yi ben)* 高級國際金融學教程 (中譯本) (Lectures on Advanced International Finance, Chinese Version). Beijing: China Financial Publishing House.

Pan Liquan 潘理權. 2000. Guoji huobi tixi gaige yu Renminbi guoji hua 國際貨幣體系改革與人民幣國際化 (The *International Monetary System* Reform and RMB Internationalization). East China Economic Management, Issue 4.

— 2004. Renminbi jie ru guoji huobi tixi tanxi 人民幣介入國際貨幣體系探析 (An Analysis on RMB Getting Involved in the International Monetary System). China Urban Finance, Issue 4.

Qi Shaozhou 齊紹洲. 2007. Zhongguo–ASEAN Xianghu maoyi yicun du yu jianli Dong Ya huobi de lujing xuanze 中國–ASEAN 相互貿易依存度與建立東亞貨幣區的路徑選擇 (The Mutual-Trade Dependency Rate of China-ASEAN and Path Choice of Establishing the East Asian Currency Area). Journal of International Trade, Issue 4.

Qian Fengyuan 錢鳳元, Zhang Cuiwei 張翠微 and Zou Jianlun 鄒劍倫, ed. 2000. *Da liuzhuan guoji huobi fengyun lu* 大流轉國際貨幣風雲錄 (Big Circulation of International Currencies Events). Beijing: Economic Daily Press.

Qiao Guiming 喬桂明. 2008. Renminbi Quyu liutong wenti yanjiu—Jiyu Shouyi yu chengben de hongguan fenxi 人民幣區域流通問題研究 (Studies on RMB Regional Circulation—Macro-Analysis Based on Costs and Profits). Suzhou University Journal, Issue 3.

Qiu Danyang 邱丹陽. 2005. Zhongguo–ASEAN ziyou maoyi qu: Zhongguo heping jueqi de diyuan jingji xue sikao 中國–ASEAN 自由貿易區:中國和平崛起的地緣經濟學思考 (China-ASEAN Free Trade Area: Geo-economics Thinking on China's Peaceful Rise). Contemporary Asia-Pacific Studies, Issue 1.

Qiu Xuewei 丘雪薇. 2005. Renminbi Yazhou hua tiaojian fenxi yu celue 人民幣亞洲化條件分析與策略 (Analysis on the Conditions of RMB Asianization and Its Strategy). Reformation & Strategy, Issue 11.

Research Team for RMB Internationalization 人民幣國際化研究課題組. 2006. Renminbi guoji hua de shiji, tujing ji qi celüe 人民幣國際化的時機、途徑及其策略 (The Time, Path and Strategy of RMB Internationalization). China Finance, Issue 5.

Sasaki (佐佐木仁) and Koga Yuko (古賀優子). 2003. Dui Zhongguo jin chu kou de kuoda yu biandong 對中國進出口的擴大與變動 (The Expansion and Changes of Imports and Exports of China). Economic Scanning of the Investigation and Statistical Bureau of the Bank of Japan, Issue of July.

Research Team of the Bank of Communications 交通銀行課題組. 2009. Renminbi yong yu quyu xing guoji jiesuan yanjiu baogao 人民幣用於區域性國際結算研究報告 (A Research Report on Using RMB for Regional International Settlement).

Research Team of Xinjiang Finance Society 新疆金融學會課題組. 2007. Renminbi quyu hua yu bian mao jiesuan tuozhan wenti yanjiu—Dui zai Xinjiang zhoubian guojia tuixing Renminbi quyu hua wenti yanjiu 人民幣區域化與邊貿結算拓展問題研究—對在新疆周邊國家推行人民幣區域化問題研究 (The Study of the RMB Regionalization and Border-Trade Settlement Expansion—The Study of Promoting the RMB Regionalization in Countries Bordering Xinjiang). Xinjiang Finance, Supplementary Issue.

Shen Guobing 沈國兵. 2004. Riyuan yu Renminbi: Quyu nei huobi hezuo yihuo huobi jingzheng 日元與人民幣:區域內貨幣合作抑或貨幣競爭 (The Yen and the RMB: Monetary Cooperation or Competition within the Region). Journal of Finance and Economics, Issue 8.

Shi Jianhuai 施建淮. 2007. Zhongguo ziben zhanghu kaifang: Yiyi, jinzhan ji pinglun 中國資本帳戶開放: 意義、進展及評論 (The Opening-Up of China's Capital Accounts: Significance, Progress and Review). International Economic Review, No. November–December.

Subject Team of State Administration of Foreign Exchange Xishuangbanna Prefecture Center Branch 國家外匯管理局西雙版納州中心支局課題組. 2007. Yunnan Sheng Xishuangbanna Zhou bian mao shiyong Renminbi ji jia jiesuan de xian zhuang, wenti ji duice 雲南省西雙版納州邊貿使用人民幣計價結算的現狀、問題及對策 (The Status Quo, Problems and Countermeasures of Using RMB for Valuation and Settlement for Border Trade in Xishuangbanna Prefecture of Yunnan). Times Finance, Issue 12.

Sun Jian 孫健, Wei Xiuhua 魏修華 and Tang Aipeng 唐愛朋. 2005. Cong san da huobi fazhan licheng kan Renminbi guoji hua zhanlue de lujing xuanze 從三大貨幣發展歷程看人民幣國際化戰略的路徑選擇 (Looking at the Path Choice of RMB Internationalization Strategy from the Development Process of Three Major Currencies). Asia–Pacific Economic Review, Issue 2.

Sun Jie 孫傑. 2007. Shenhua Yazhou jinrong hezuo de tujing: Riben de zuoyong ji yingxiang 深化亞洲金融合作的途徑:日本的作用及影響 (The Road to Deepening Asian Financial Cooperation: Japan's Role and Influence). World Economy and Polities, Issue 5.

Tan Qinghua 譚慶華. 2002. Dui Dong Ya huobi yiti hua de zai kaocha: Yi ge jiyu jingji chongji xiangguan xing de shizheng yanjiu 對東亞貨幣一體化的再考察:一個基於經濟衝擊相關性的實證研究 (Re-examination of the East Asian Monetary Integration: An Empirical Study Based on Economic Shocks Correlation). World Economic Papers, Issue 5.

Tao Shigui 陶士貴. 2002. Renminbi quyu hua de chubu gouxiang 人民幣區域化的初步構想 (The Preliminary Conception of RMB Regionalization). Management Modernization, Issue 5.

Tetsuji Murase (村瀨哲司). 2000. *Yazhou anding huobi quan* 亞洲安定貨幣圈 (A Zone of Asian Monetary Stability). Keiso Shobo.

Tong Jiadong 佟家棟 and Cheng Xinxuan 成新軒. 2001. Ouyuan de quyu hua yu guoji hua yanjiu 歐元的區域化與國際化研究 (A Study of the Euro Regionalization and Internationalization). Nankai Economic Studies, Issue 6.

Wan Zhihong 萬志宏. 2003. Cong hongguan jingji duichen xing kan Dong Ya diqu huilu hezuo de jichu 從宏觀經濟對稱性看東亞地區匯率合作的基礎 (Looking at the Foundation for East Asian Exchange Rate Cooperation from the Macro-Economic Symmetry Perspective). Nankai Economic Studies, Issue 3.

Wan Zhihong 萬志宏 and Dai Jinping 戴金平. 2003. Huobi qu de dongtai zui you juece: Jiantan Dong Ya huobi hezuo wenti 貨幣區的動態最有決策:兼談東亞貨幣合作問題 (The Dynamics of the Currency Area Is Most Determining: With the Discussion on East Asian Monetary Cooperation). World Economy, Issue 10.

— 2005. Dong Ya huobi hezuo de xianshi jichu—Cong zui you huobi qu zhishu jinxing jiedu 東亞貨幣合作的現實基礎—從最優貨幣區指數進行的解讀 (Realistic Foundations for East Asian Monetary Cooperation—Interpretation from Optimum Currency Area Index). Social Sciences In Guangdong, Issue 3.

Wang Guifen 王桂芬 and Zhou Guiyi 周貴義. 2006. Chu tan bian mao jiesuan yu Renminbi quyu hua 初探邊貿結算與人民幣區域化 (A Primary Exploration of Border-Trade Settlement and the RMB Regionalization). Heilongjiang Finance, Issue 10.

Wang Xiaoqing 王曉青. 2006. Jiyu Yazhou huobi danwei de Renminbi guoji hua wenti de sikao 基於亞洲貨幣單位的人民幣國際化問題的思考 (Thoughts on the RMB Internationalization Based on Asian Monetary Unit). Journal of Nanjing Audit University, Issue 3.

Wang Yafan 王雅范, Guan Tao 管濤 and Wen Jiandong 溫建東. 2002. *Zou xiang Renminbi ke duihuan: Zhongguo jianjin zhuyi de shijian* 走向人民幣可兑換: 中國漸進主義的實踐 (Moving towards RMB Convertibility: Practice of China's Gradualism). Beijing: Economic Science Press.

Wang Yubao 王育寶 and Hu Fangxiao 胡芳肖. 2003. Renminbi guoji hua wenti tanxi 人民幣國際化問題探析 (An Analysis on RMB Internationalization). South China Financial Research, Issue 5.

Wang Sicheng 王思程. 2008. Dui Renminbi guoji hua wenti de ruogan sikao 對人民幣國際化問題的若干思考 (Some Thoughts about RMB Internationalization). Contemporary International Relations, Issue 8.

Wang Zhengbao 王政寶. 1996. Shi lun Renminbi de guoji hua 試論人民幣的國際化 (On RMB Internationalization). Journal of Jinzhou Normal University (Philosophy and Social Sciences Section). Issue 1.

Wei En 緯恩. 2002. Renminbi ruhe zou xiang guoji hua 人民幣如何走向國際化 (How Could the RMB Move Towards Internationalization). China Reform, Issue 3.

Xia Bin 夏斌. 2009. Cong quan qiu tongzhang dao Meiguo jinrong weiji—Ben lun shijie jingji zhouqi de luoji ji Zhongguo duice 從全球通脹到美國金融危機—本輪世界經濟週期的發展邏輯及中國對策 (From Global Inflation to the US Financial Crisis—The Logic of the Development of World Economic Cycle of This Time and China's Countermeasures). New Finance, Issue 4.

Xiao Fengjuan 肖鳳娟. 2008. Zhongguo wai hui guanli tizhi gaige de huigu yu zhanwang 中國外匯管理體制改革的回顧與展望 (A Review and Outlook of the Reform of China's Foreign Exchange Management System). International Trade, Issue 7.

Xie Luoqi 謝羅奇 and Huang Minghua 黃明華. 2006. Yazhou huobi danwei ji gei Zhongguo dai lai de jiyu sikao 亞洲貨幣單位及給中國帶來的機遇思考 (Asian Monetary Unit and Thoughts on Its Opportunities Brought to China). Jinan Finance, Issue 3.

Xu Helian 許和連, Lai Mingyong 賴明勇 and Xu Qingsong 許青松. 2003. Jiyu GRPLS huigui de Zhongguo jingji zengzhang yingxiang yinsu fenxi 基於GRPLS 回歸的中國經濟增長影響因素分析 (An Analysis of the Influencing Factors for Chinese Economic Growth Based on GRPLS Regression). Journal of Management Sciences in China, Issue 12.

Xu Hongshui 徐洪水. 2004. Renminbi guoji hua de lilun fenxi ji zhanlue sikao 人民幣國際化的理論分析及戰略思考 (The Theoretical Analysis and Strategic Thoughts of RMB Internationalization). International Economics and Trade Research, Issue of September.

Xu Mingqi 徐明棋. 2005. Cong Riyuan guoji hua de jingyan jiaoxun kan Renminbi guojihua yu quyu hua 從日元國際化的經驗教訓看人民幣國際化與區域化 (Looking at RMB Internationalization and Regionalization from the Lessons of the Internationalization of the Yen). World Economy Study, Issue 12.

Xu Qiyuan 徐奇淵 and Liu Lizhen 劉力臻. 2006. Zhongguo canyu guoji quyu jingji yiti hua wenti wenxian zongshu 中國參與國際區域經濟一體化問題文獻綜述 (A

Literature Review on China's Involvement in the International Regional Economic Integration). Development & Research, Issue 1.

— 2006. Xianggang Renminbi cunliang guji: M1 koujing de kaocha 香港人民幣存量估計: M1口徑的考察 (An Estimation of the RMB Stocks in Hong Kong: An Examination of M1 Caliber). World Economy, Issue 9.

— 2008. Renminbi guoji hua jincheng: Xianzhuang yu qianjing 人民幣國際化進程:現狀與前景 (The Progress of RMB Internationalization: The Status Quo and Prospects). Conference paper at the Seminar on "Celebrating the 30th Anniversary of the Reform and Opening-Up & Review and Outlook of Chinese Exchange Rate System Reform" (Shanghai), November.

Yang Song 楊松 and Wang Lina 王麗娜. 2007. Renminbi quyu hua de falu tuijin 人民幣區域化的法律推進 (The Legal Advancement for RMB Regionalization). Journal of Liaoning University (Philosophy and Social Sciences Section), Issue 3.

Yang Rong 楊榮 and Chen Jie 陳傑. 2008. Huilu gaige yi lai Zhongguo wai hui shichang de fazhan 匯率改革以來中國外匯市場的發展 (The Development of China's Foreign Exchange Market since the Exchange Rate Reform). The Banker, Issue 11.

Yao Zhizhong 姚枝仲. 2004. Bu duichen jingzheng yu Renminbi de Yazhou zhanlue 不對稱競爭與人民幣的亞洲戰略 (Asymmetric Competition and the RMB's Strategy in Asia). World Economy and Politics, Issue 7.

Yasuyoshi Masuda (益田安良). 1998. *Ouyuan yu Riyuan—Riyuan guoji hua de weilai* 歐元與日元—日元國際化的未來 (The Euro and the Japanese Yen—Future of the Internationalization of Japanese Yen). Nippon-hyoron-sha.

Yu Tongshen 于同申. 2002. Meiyuan hua, huobi quyu hua yu fazhan zhong guojia de jinrong Anquan 美元化、貨幣區域化與發展中國家的金融安全 (The Dollarization, Currency Regionalization and Financial Security of Developing Countries). Forum on World Economy and Politics, Issue 3.

Yu Qun'e 虞群娥. 2002. Lun quyu huobi yiti hua yu Renminbi guoji hua 論區域貨幣一體化與人民幣國際化 (On the Regional Monetary Integration and RMB Internationalization). Zhejiang Social Sciences, Issue 4.

Yuan Yi 袁宜. 2002. Huobi guoji hua jincheng guilu de fenxi—Dui Renminbi guoji hua jincheng de qishi 貨幣國際化進程規律的分析-對人民幣國際化進程的啟示 (An Analysis on the Law of Currency Internationalization—The Inspriations on RMB Internationalization). Wuhan Finance Monthly, Issue 6.

Yuji Kikuchi (菊地悠二). 2000. *Riyuan de guoji shi* 日元的國際史 (International History of Japanese Yen). Yuhikaku Publishing.

Zeng Xianjiu 曾憲久, Hu Dinghe 胡定核 and Huang Daoping 黄道平. 1989. Zhongguo jinrong guoji hua tantao 中國金融國際化探討 (Research on Internationalization of Chinese Finance). International Finance Guide, Issue 3.

Zhang Bin 張斌. 2004. Dong Ya quyu huilu hezuo: Zhongguo shijiao 東亞區域匯率合作:中國視角 (The Regional Exchange Rate Cooperation in East Asia: From the Chinese Perspective). World Economy, Issue 10.

Zhang Dongming 張東明. 2006. Zhong Ri Han san guo guanxi yu jianli Dong Ya ziyou maoyi qu de ke xing xing 中日韓三國關係與建立東亞自由貿易區的可行性 (The Relations among China, Japan and South Korea and the Feasibility of Establishing the East Asian Free Trade Area). Contemporary Asia-Pacific Studies, Issue 2.

Zhang Hongmei 張洪梅, Wang Lixiang 王麗香 and Xu Yanqiu 徐豔秋. 2008. Ouyuan qu tongyi Huobi zhengce jixiao ji qi dui Zhongguo de qishi 歐元區統一貨幣政策績效及其對中國的啟示 (The Performance of Unified Monetary Policy in the Eurozone and Its Inspirations to China). Asia-Pacific Economic Review, Issue 2.

Zhang Qunfa 張群發. 2008. Meiyuan baquan he Renminbi guoji hua 美元霸權和人民幣國際化 (The US Dollar Hegemony and RMB Internationalization). Economic Survey, Issue 2.

Zhang Ying 張英. 2006. Zhongguo–ASEAN ziyou maoyi qu yu Renminbi quyu hua fazhan yanjiu 中國–ASEAN 自由貿易區與人民幣區域化發展研究 (The Studies on China-ASEAN Free Trade Area and RMB Regionalization). Economic and Social Development, August.

Zhang Yiwei 張屹巍. 1994. Cong guoji hua de Riyuan kan Renminbi de guoji hua 從國際化的日元看人民幣的國際化 (Looking at RMB Internationalization from the Perspective of the Internationalized Yen). International Finance Guide, Issue 4.

Zhang Yunling 張蘊嶺. 2006. Zhongguo tong Dong Ya de jingji yiti hua yu hezuo 中國同東亞的經濟一體化與合作 (The Economic Integration and Cooperation between China and East Asia). Contemporary Asia-Pacific Studies, Issue 1.

Zhang Zhichao 張志超. 2002. Huilu zhengce xin gongshi yu "zhongjian zhidu xiaoshi lun" 匯率政策新共識與"中間制度消失論" (The New Consensus on Exchange Rate Policy and "the Hypothesis of the Vanishing Intermediate Regime"). World Economy, Issue 12.

Zhao Chunming 趙春明 and Li Xiaoying李小瑛. 2007. Dong Ya huobi hezuo yu Renminbi hexin huobi diwei tanxi東亞貨幣合作與人民幣核心貨幣地位探析 (Research on East Asian Monetary Cooperation and the Core Monetary Position of the RMB). Contemporary Asia-Pacific Studies, Issue 2.

Zhao Haikuan 趙海寬. 2003. Lun Renminbi Keneng chengwei shijie huobi zhi yi 論人民幣可能成為世界貨幣之一 (On the Possibility of the RMB Becoming One of the World Currencies). Economic Research, Issue 3.

Zhao Qingming 趙慶明. 2005. *Renminbi ziben xiangmu ke duihuan ji guoji hua yanjiu* 人民幣資本項目可兑換及國際化研究 (Studies on the Convertibility and Internationalization of RMB Capital Account). Beijing: China Financial Publishing House.

Zhao Zhihua 趙志華. 2006. Guanyu Renminbi zai Zhong Meng bian mao kou'an liutong qingkuang de diaocha baogao 關於人民幣現金在中蒙邊貿口岸流通情況的調查報告 (An Investigation Report on RMB Circulation in the Border Trade and Port Between China and Mongolia). Huabei Finance, Issue 2.

Zheng Lingyun 鄭凌雲. 2006. Renminbi quyu hua yu bian mao ben bi jiesuan gong neng kuozhan 人民幣區域化與邊貿本幣結算功能擴展 (The RMB Regionalization and the Expansion of Its Functions of Border-Trade Settlement). International Trade, Issue 7.

Zheng Hangbin 鄭航濱. 2003. Renminbi quyu hua he haixia liang'an huobi hezuo jizhi wenti 人民幣區域化和海峽兩岸貨幣合作機制問題 (The Issues of RMB Regionalization and Cross-Strait Monetary Cooperation Mechanism). Journal of Fujian Institute of Financial Administrators, Issue 10.

Zheng Muqing 鄭木清. 1995. Lun Renminbi guoji hua de daolu 論人民幣國際化的道路 (On the Road to RMB Internationalization). Journal of Fudan University, Issue 2.

— 1995. Lun Renminbi guoji hua xiaoying 論人民幣國際化的經濟效應 (On the Economic Effects of RMB Internationalization). Studies of International Finance, Issue 7.

— 2003. Yazhou huobi hezuo jincheng: Zhongguo shijiao 亞洲貨幣合作進程:中國視角 (The Progress of Asian Monetary Cooperation: From Chinese Perspective). Asia-Pacific Economic Review, Issue 4.

Zheng Weimin 鄭偉民. 1998. *Shuailuo haishi fuxing: Quanqiu jingji zhong de Meiguo* 衰落還是復興: 全球經濟中的美國 (Decline or Revival: the United States in the Global Economy). Beijing: Social Sciences Academic Press (China).

Zheng Xiaozhou 鄭曉舟. 2007. Renminbi: Cong "bu shou huanying" dao "quan liutong" 人民幣: 從"不受歡迎"到"全流通" (RMB: From "Unpopularity" to "Full-Circulation"). Shanghai Securities News, June 29.

Zhong Wei 鐘偉. 2002. Lue lun Renminbi de guoji hua jincheng 略論人民幣的國際化進程 (On the Progress of RMB Internationalization). World Economy, Issue 3.

— 2008. Renminbi zai zhoubian guojia liutong de xianzhuang, wenti ji duice 人民幣在周邊國家流通的現狀、問題及對策 (The Status Quo, Problems and Countermeasures of RMB Circulation in Neighboring Countries). Management World, Issue 1.

Zhou Lin 周林 and Wen Xiaozheng 温小鄭, ed. 2001. *Huobi guojihua* 貨幣國際化 (Currency Internationalization). Shanghai: Shanghai University of Finance & Economics Press.

Zhou Wengui 周文貴 and Xiao Yaofei 肖鷂飛. 2003. *Guoji huobi zhidu lun* 國際貨幣制度論 (On the International Monetary System). Guangzhou: Sun Yat-sen University Press.

Zhu Fang 朱芳. 2003. Dong Ya ci quyu huobi jianli de tiaojian fenxi 東亞次區域貨幣建立的條件分析 (An Analysis of the Conditions for the Establishment of tEast Asian Sub-regional Currency). Contemporary Asia-Pacific Studies, Issue 12.

Index

Index